COGNITION AND EMOTION

COUNTERPOINTS: *Cognition, Memory, and Language*
SERIES EDITOR: Marc Marschark

Rochester Institute of Technology
National Technical Institute for the Deaf

ADVISORY BOARD

STRETCHING THE IMAGINATION
Representation and Transformation in Mental Imagery
C. Cornoldi, R. Logie, M. Brandimonte, G. Kaufmann, D. Reisberg

MODELS OF VISUOSPATIAL COGNITION
M. de Vega, M. J. Intons-Peterson, P. N. Johnson-Laird,
M. Denis, M. Marschark

WORKING MEMORY AND HUMAN COGNITION
J. T. E. Richardson, R. W. Engle, L. Hasher,
R. H. Logie, E. R. Stoltzfus, R. T. Zacks

RELATIONS OF LANGUAGE AND THOUGHT
The View from Sign Language and Deaf Children
M. Marschark, P. Siple, D. Lillo-Martin,
R. Campbell, V. Everhart

GENDER DIFFERENCES IN HUMAN COGNITION
P. J. Caplan, M. Crawford, J. S. Hyde,
J. T. E. Richardson

FIGURATIVE LANGUAGE AND THOUGHT
A. Katz, C. Cacciari, R. W. Gibbs, M. Turner

COGNITION AND EMOTION
E. Eich, J. F. Kihlstrom, G. H. Bower, J. P. Forgas, P. M. Niedenthal

COGNITION AND EMOTION

ERIC EICH
JOHN F. KIHLSTROM
GORDON H. BOWER
JOSEPH P. FORGAS
PAULA M. NIEDENTHAL

OXFORD
UNIVERSITY PRESS

2000

OXFORD
UNIVERSITY PRESS

Oxford   New York
Athens   Auckland   Bangkok   Bogotá   Buenos Aires   Calcutta
Cape Town   Chennai   Dar es Salaam   Delhi   Florence   Hong Kong   Istanbul
Karachi   Kuala Lumpur   Madrid   Melbourne   Mexico City   Mumbai
Nairobi   Paris   São Paulo   Singapore   Taipei   Tokyo   Toronto   Warsaw

and associated companies in
Berlin   Ibadan

Copyright © 2000 Oxford University Press

Published by Oxford University Press, Inc.
198 Madison Avenue, New York, New York 10016

Oxford is a registered trademark of Oxford University Press

Library of Congress Cataloging-in-Publication Data
Cognition and emotion / Eric Eich . . . [et al.].
Includes bibliographical references and index.
ISBN 0-19-511333-0; ISBN 0-19-511334-9 (pbk.)
1. Emotions and cognition.   I. Eich, Eric.
II. Counterpoints (Oxford University Press)
BF311.C5477   2000
152.4—dc21   99–034377

9 8 7 6 5 4 3 2 1

Printed in the United States of America
on acid-free paper

Dedicated to the first wave of contemporary cognition/emotion researchers—Bob Zajonc, George Mandler, Nico Frijda, Len Berkowitz, and others too many to mention—for their elegant work and enduring contributions to the area.

Preface

Since 1996, Oxford University Press has been publishing *Counterpoints*, a series of concise and affordable texts investigating issues of current concern to scientists and students in the areas of cognitive psychology, child development, linguistics, and neuroscience. Each volume consists of three or four extensive, seminar-style presentations (prepared by experts in the area) preceded by a brief introduction (written by the project editor) and followed by a broad discussion (involving all of the co-authors of the volume).

This book, the seventh in the *Counterpoints* series, is about the ways in which cognitive and emotional processes interact. Professors Gordon Bower, Joseph Forgas, John Kihlstrom, and Paula Niedenthal took primary responsibility for writing the three major chapters that form the core of this book. In addition, they provided thoughtful and revealing answers to a long list of questions—some specific, others general—that I pose in the concluding chapter. It has been a privilege to work with all of them and a pleasure to acknowledge their invaluable contributions to this book.

Recognition is also due Catharine Carlin, Robert Milks, and Philip Laughlin (at Oxford University Press) and Sherri Widen (here at UBC) for their expert editorial advice and assistance, and Sherry Eich, for applying her astute, legal mind to my often illegal prose. Last, I thank Professor Marc Marschark (*Counterpoints* series editor) not only for the invitation to serve as editor on this project but also for his sage advice and steadfast support throughout its course.

Vancouver   E. E.
March 1999

Contents

Contributors

Gordon H. Bower, Department of Psychology, Stanford University, Stanford, California

Eric Eich, Department of Psychology, University of British Columbia, Vancouver, Canada

Joseph P. Forgas, School of Psychology, University of New South Wales, Sydney, Australia

Jamin B. Halberstadt, Department of Psychology, University of Otago, Otago, New Zealand

John F. Kihlstrom, Department of Psychology, University of California, Berkeley, California

Shelagh Mulvaney, Department of Psychology, University of Arizona, Tucson, Arizona

Paula M. Niedenthal, Laboratoire de Psychologie Sociale de la Cognition, Universite Blaise-Pascal, Clermont-Ferrand, France

Jonathan W. Schooler, Learning Research and Developmental Center, University of Pittsburgh, Pittsburgh, Pennsylvania

Betsy A. Tobias, Department of Psychology, University of Arizona, Tucson, Arizona

Irene P. Tobis, Department of Psychology, University of Wisconsin, Madison, Wisconsin

COGNITION AND EMOTION

CHAPTER 1

Cognition/Emotion Interactions

Eric Eich and Jonathan W. Schooler

OVERVIEW

Recent years have witnessed a revival of research interest in the interplay between cognition and emotion—a subject that stimulated much debate and discussion among psychologists in the nineteenth century, but was shunned throughout most of the twentieth. As other writers have remarked (Izard, Kagan, & Zajonc 1984; Kitayama & Niedenthal, 1994; LeDoux, 1996; Watts, 1987), the reasons for this renaissance are several and varied. In the first place, emotion theorists have come to recognize the pivotal role that appraisal, expectations, and other cognitive constructs play in the experience of emotion and to rely on basic cognitive concepts and methods for insight in creating new models of affective space. Also, the successful application of cognitive therapies to the affective disorders has prompted clinical psychologists to work toward a clearer understanding of the connections between cognitive processes and emotional problems. Social psychologists, for their part, have shown how moods influence people's perceptions of both themselves and others. And whereas most cognitive revolutionaries of the 1960s regarded emotions with suspicion, viewing them as nagging sources of ''hot'' noise in an otherwise coolly rational and computerlike system of information processing, cognitive researchers of the 1990s regard emotions with respect, owing to their potent and predictable effects on tasks as diverse as episodic recall, word recognition, and risk assessment. These intersecting lines of interest have made cognition and emotion one of the most active and rapidly developing areas within psychological science. This same convergence makes *Cognition and Emotion* a prime candidate for inclusion in the *Counterpoints* series of texts published by Oxford University Press.

ORGANIZATION

The bulk of this book consists of three chapters written by several leading figures in the study of cognition/emotion interactions. In chapter 2, John Kihlstrom extends his well-known work on the cognitive unconscious (Kihlstrom, 1987) into the realm of emotions. Specifically, he and his colleagues—Shelagh Mulvaney, Betsy Tobias, and Irene Tobis—examine evidence from several sources (including clinical psychology, hypnosis research, and both cognitive and affective neuroscience) that emotional responses can function as implicit expressions of perception and memory. They also explore theoretical and empirical considerations that point to the provocative conclusion that emotional states themselves can be unconscious.

Chapter 3 is an ambitious attempt by Gordon Bower and Joseph Forgas to accomplish two ends: first, provide a systematic review of the burgeoning literature on emotional influences in social judgments—a literature to which Bower has long been a leading contributor; second, offer a coherent account of the relevant findings based on the Affect Infusion Model, an influential theory recently advanced by Forgas. A contribution from either Professor Bower or Professor Forgas would have benefited this book; undoubtedly, it is a real bonus to have them combine their efforts and expertise.

In chapter 4, Paula Niedenthal and her long-time collaborator, Jamin Halberstadt, take a fresh look at a problem familiar to mainstream cognitive psychologists: how do people categorize their perceptual experience, so that they "know"—confidently yet effortlessly—whether one object goes with another? The traditional solution to this problem is that people group objects together to form categories on the basis of (a) the structural or perceptual similarity of the objects, (b) their common use in facilitating a goal, or (c) their conformity to a common theory of mental representation. Although not denying the value of these strictly cognitive accounts, Niedenthal and Halberstadt develop the intriguing idea that perceptual objects may also cohere as categories because they tend to evoke the same emotional reaction in a perceiver. In addition, their chapter summarizes several recent studies designed to test the proposal of "emotional categorization."

One of the objectives of *Counterpoints* is to encourage contributors to express and exchange ideas on issues of current concern (Marschark, 1996). To this end, Professors Bower, Forgas, Kihlstrom, and Niedenthal have been asked to respond to a series of questions posed by the project editor (Eric Eich); their answers appear in chapter 5. Whereas some of their responses relate to specific points raised in earlier parts of the book, others reflect their outlook on matters of broader significance, such as where the field of cognition/emotion research is—or should be—heading.

CURRENT CONCERNS AND CONTINUING CONTROVERSIES

Taken together, the three chapters (2–4) that comprise the core of this book cover a lot of ground. For instance, consideration is given to cognitive tasks that range from the simple and quick (e.g., deciding whether a string of letters forms a word) to the complex and deliberate (e.g., deciding who is to blame for serious marital strife). Also, whereas some of the issues discussed are relatively recent in origin (e.g., whether attitudes, like memories, are expressible both explicitly and implicitly), others relate to long-standing controversies (e.g., whether moods influence "low level" perceptions as well as "higher order" cognitions).

Nonetheless, no single text can cover *all* of the issues that motivate modern research on cognition/emotion interactions: the field has become too big for that. Indeed, this book does not deal with such salient subjects as the role of affect in economic decision making or the cognitive consequences of clinical anxiety and major depression (for recent reviews of these issues, see Mellers, Schwartz, Ho, & Ritov, 1997; Watts, 1995). To fill in some of the many remaining blanks, we devote the rest of this chapter to discussion of two important topics covered only briefly in other parts of the book: mood dependent memory (MDM) and remembering emotional events.

MOOD DEPENDENT MEMORY

Are events encoded in a certain state of affect or mood more retrievable in the same state than in a different one? Stated more simply, is memory mood dependent?

In principle, the answer is plainly "yes" on two accounts. First, the cognitive literature is replete with theories that suggest that memory *should* be mood dependent; examples include such classic contributions as McGeogh's (1942) interference theory of forgetting and Miller's (1950) drive-as-stimulus hypothesis, as well as such contemporary innovations as Bower's (1981) network theory of emotions and Tulving's (1983) encoding specificity principle. Similarly, the clinical literature contains numerous conjectures implicating MDM as a causal factor in the memory deficits displayed by patients with alcoholic blackout, chronic depression, multiple personality, traumatic amnesia, and other psychiatric disorders (see Goodwin, 1974; Ludwig, 1984; Reus, Weingartner, & Post, 1979; Schacter & Kihlstrom, 1989).

In practice, however, the answer is a much more guarded "maybe." Over the past 25 years, many studies have sought to demonstrate MDM using a variety of memory materials, encoding tasks, retrieval measures, retention intervals, and mood-modification techniques (for reviews, see Bower, 1992; Eich,

1995b; Kenealy, 1997). The fact that these studies have failed about as often as they have succeeded raises a new question: even if mood dependence is not the powerful and prevalent effect many cognitivists and clinicians once thought it was, might MDM nevertheless emerge clearly and consistently under certain limited conditions? To help answer this question, attention now turns to two sets of factors that appear fundamental to the occurrence of mood dependence: one concerned with characteristics of the subjects' encoding and retrieval tasks, a second with attributes of the moods they experience while performing these tasks.

Task Factors

Intuitively, one might reasonably suppose that how strongly memory is mood dependent will depend on how the to-be-remembered or target events are encoded. To clarify, consider two hypothetical cases described by Eich, Macaulay, and Ryan (1994). In Scenario 1:

> Two individuals—one happy, one sad—are shown, say, a *rose* and are asked to identify and describe what they see. Both individuals are apt to say much the same thing and to encode the *rose* event in much the same manner. After all, and with all due respect to Gertrude Stein, a rose is a rose is a rose, regardless of whether it is seen through a happy or sad eye. The implication, then, is that the manner in which the perceivers encode the *rose* event will be largely, if not entirely, unrelated to their mood. If true, then when retrieval of the event is later assessed via nominally noncued or "spontaneous" recall, it should make little if any difference whether or not the subjects are in the same mood they had experienced earlier. In short, memory for the *rose* event will probably not appear to be mood dependent under these circumstances.
>
> Now imagine a different situation [scenario 2]. Instead of identifying and describing the rose, the subjects are asked to recall an episode, from any time in their personal past, that the object calls to mind. Rather than involving the relatively automatic or data-driven perception of an external stimulus, the task now requires the subjects to engage in internal mental processes such as reasoning, reflection, and cotemporal thought, "the sort of elaborative and associative processes that augment, bridge, or embellish ongoing perceptual experience but that are not necessarily part of the veridical representation of perceptual experience" (Johnson & Raye, 1981, p. 70). Furthermore, even though the stimulus object is itself affectively neutral, the autobiographical memories it triggers are apt to be strongly influenced by the subjects' mood. Thus, for example, whereas the happy subject may recollect receiving a dozen roses from a secret admirer, the sad subject may remember the flowers that adorned his father's coffin. In effect, then, the *rose* event becomes closely associated with or deeply colored by the subject's mood, thereby making mood a potentially potent cue for retrieving the event. Thus, when later asked to spontaneously recall the gist of the episode they had recounted earlier, the subjects should be more likely to remember

having related a vignette involving roses if they are in the same mood they had experienced earlier. In this situation, then, memory for the *rose* event should appear to be mood dependent. (pp. 213–214)

These armchair conjectures concur with the results of actual research. Many of the earliest experiments on MDM used a simple list-learning paradigm—analogous to the situation sketched in scenario 1—in which subjects memorized unrelated words while they were in a particular mood, typically either happiness or sadness, induced via hypnotic suggestions, guided imagery, mood-appropriate music, or some other means. As Bower (1992; chapter 3 here) has observed, the assumption was that the words would become associated, through temporal contiguity, to the subjects' current mood as well as to the list-context; hence, reinstatement of the same mood should enhance performance on a later test of retention. Though a few list-learning experiments found MDM, several others did not (see Blaney, 1986; Bower, 1987). Worse, attempts to replicate positive results seldom prevailed, even when undertaken by the same investigator using similar materials, tasks, and mood-modification techniques (see Bower & Mayer, 1989).

Unlike list-learning experiments, studies involving autobiographical memory—including those modeled after scenario 2—have revealed robust and reliable evidence of MDM (see Bower, 1992; Eich, 1995b). An example is experiment 2 reported by Eich et al. (1994). During the encoding session of this study, university undergraduates completed a task of *autobiographical event generation* while they were feeling either happy (H) or sad (S)—affects that had been instilled through a combination of mood-appropriate music and thought. The task required the students to recollect or generate a specific event, from any time in their personal past, that was called to mind by a probe word such as *rose*; every subject generated as many as 16 different events, each elicited by a different probe. Subjects described each event in detail and rated it along several dimensions, including its original emotional valence—that is, whether the event seemed positive, neutral, or negative when it occurred.

During the retrieval session, held two days after encoding, subjects were asked to recall—in any order, and without benefit of any observable reminders or cues—the gist of as many of their previously generated events as possible, preferably by recalling their precise corresponding probes. Subjects undertook this test of *autobiographical event recall* either in the same mood in which they had generated the events or in the alternative affective state, thus creating two conditions in which encoding and retrieval moods matched (H/H and S/S) and two in which they mismatched (H/S and S/H).

Results of the encoding session revealed that, in comparison with their sad-mood counterparts, happy subjects generated more positive events (means = 11.1 vs. 6.7), fewer negative events (3.3 vs. 6.8), and a similar number of neutral events (1.2 vs. 2.0). This pattern replicates earlier experiments (e.g., Clark & Teasdale, 1982; Snyder & White, 1982), and it provides evidence of mood *congruent* memory—the "enhanced encoding and/or retrieval of material the affective valence of which is congruent with ongoing mood" (Blaney, 1986, p. 229).

Results of the retrieval session provided evidence of mood *dependent* memory. In comparison to their mismatched-mood peers, subjects whose encoding and retrieval moods matched freely recalled a greater percentage of their previously generated positive events (means = 37% vs. 26%), negative events (37% vs. 27%), and neutral events (32% vs. 17%).

This effect does not appear to be a fluke: the same advantage appeared in two other studies using moods instilled via music and thought (Eich et al., 1994, experiments 1 and 3), as well as in three separate studies in which the subjects' affective states were altered through a change in their physical surroundings (Eich, 1995a). Moreover, similar results were obtained in a recent investigation of patients who cycled rapidly——and spontaneously—between states of mania or hypomania and depression (Eich, Macaulay, & Lam, 1997). Thus, it seems that autobiographical event generation, when combined with event free recall, constitutes a useful tool for exploring mood dependent effects under both laboratory and clinical conditions, and that these effects emerge in conjunction with either exogenous (experimentally engendered) or endogenous (naturally occurring) shifts in affective state.

Recall that this discussion of task factors began with some simple intuitions about the circumstances under which MDM would or would not be expected to occur. Though the results reviewed thus far fit these intuitions, the former are by no means "explained" by the latter. We can, however, point to two recent theoretical developments that provide a clearer and more complete understanding of why mood dependence sometimes comes, sometimes goes.

One of these developments relates to Bower's (1981; Bower & Cohen, 1982) *network model of emotions*, which has been revised to reflect recent MDM research (Bower, 1992; chapter 3 here). A key aspect of the new model is the idea, derived from Thorndike (1932), that in order for subjects to associate a target event with their current mood, contiguity alone between the mood and the event may not be sufficient. Rather, it may be necessary for subjects to perceive the event as enabling or causing their mood, for only then will a change in mood cause that event to be forgotten.

To elaborate, we alluded earlier to the conventional list-learning paradigm. According to Bower and Forgas (this volume), this paradigm is ill-suited to demonstrating mood dependence, because it

arranges only contiguity, not causal belonging, between presentation of the to-be-learned material and emotional arousal. Typically, the mood is induced minutes before presentation of the learning material, and the mood serves only as the prevailing background; hence, the temporal relations are not synchronized to persuade subjects to attribute their emotional feelings to the material they are studying. Thus, contiguity, without causal belonging, produces only weak associations at best. (p. 97)

In contrast, the new model permits strong mood dependent effects to emerge in studies of autobiographical memory, such as those reported by Eich et al. (1994). Exactly how this is accomplished is described in detail in Bower and Forgas's chapter, but as a brief illustration, suppose a person is presented with *rose* and other list items as probes for recollecting or generating specific incidents from his or her past. Theoretically, the concept of *rose* is represented in long-term memory as a node within a complex associative network that includes, among many other things, connections between *rose* and various autobiographical events: some positive in emotional tone (e.g., receiving a surprise bouquet), others negative (e.g., seeing flowers at a funeral). The theory also holds that, through causal belongingness, the bouquet event had been associated to that node in the network that corresponds to feeling happy and that the funeral event had been associated to the sadness emotion it caused. Thus, if the subject is feeling happy when probed with *rose*, he or she is more likely to generate the bouquet event than the funeral event, because the former receives activation from two separate sources (the probe and the happy emotion node), whereas the latter receives activation from only one source (*rose*). Assuming this happens, the subject will also associate the list-context to the bouquet event and to the word *rose* that evoked it. These newly formed list associations originate because the subject attributes causal belonging of the word-and-event to the experimenter's presentation of the probe *rose* within the list.

These contextual associations are called on later when the subject is asked to freely recall the probes (or the autobiographical recollections they triggered) when induced into the same mood or a different one. If the subject is happy at the time of recall testing, then the bouquet memory would benefit because it would receive the summation of activation from the happy-mood node and the list context, raising it above the threshold required for recall. However, if the subject's mood at recall were shifted to sadness, that node has no connection to the bouquet event activated during list input, so the recall of *rose* in this case would rely exclusively on the association to *rose* in the list-context node. In this manner, the revised network model provides a plausible explanation for not only the specific results obtained by Eich et al. (1994) but also the more general observation that studies involving autobiographical memory often succeed in showing MDM, whereas those using the more traditional list-learning paradigm frequently fail.

Moreover, the revised network model accommodates an important qualification: mood dependence is more apt to occur when retention is tested in the absence rather than in the presence of specific, tangible reminders or cues (see Bower, 1981, 1992; Eich, 1980, 1989). Thus, free recall is a much more sensitive measure of mood dependence than either cued recall or recognition memory. According to the network model, recognition memory for whether the word *rose* appeared in the list of probes for autobiographical event generation simply requires activation of the *rose*-to-list association, and this is no less likely to occur when there is a mismatch between encoding and retrieval moods than when there is a match.

A more complete account of the revised network model can be found in Bower and Forgas's chapter. Conveniently, their chapter also contains the second theoretical development of current concern: namely, the *affect infusion model,* or AIM, which Forgas (1995) has advanced as a comprehensive account of the role of mood states in social judgments. Affect infusion may be defined as "the process whereby affectively loaded information exerts an influence on and becomes incorporated into the judgmental process, entering into the judge's deliberations and eventually coloring the judgmental outcome" (Forgas, 1995, p. 39). For our purposes, the crucial feature of AIM is the following claim:

> Affect infusion is most likely to occur in the course of constructive processing that involves the substantial transformation rather than the mere reproduction of existing cognitive representations; such processing requires a relatively open information search strategy and a significant degree of generative elaboration of the available stimulus details. This definition seems broadly consistent with the weight of recent evidence suggesting that affect "will influence cognitive processes to the extent that the cognitive task involves the active generation of new information as opposed to the passive conservation of information given" (Fiedler, 1990, pp. 2–3). (Forgas, 1995, pp. 39–40)

Though AIM is chiefly concerned with mood *congruence*, it seems relevant to mood *dependence* as well. Compared to the rote memorization of unrelated words, the task of recollecting and recounting real-life events would seem to place a greater premium on active, substantive processing, and thereby promotes a higher degree of affect infusion. Thus, the AIM, like the revised network model, agrees with the fact that list-learning experiments often fail to find mood dependence, whereas studies involving autobiographical memory usually succeed. Also like the revised network model, the AIM can be readily reconciled with the typical finding of mood *in*dependent recognition if one assumes that recognition memory entails *direct access thinking,* Forgas's (1995) term for cognitive processing that is simpler, more automatic, and less emotionally suffused than that required for free recall.

In terms of overall explanatory power, however, the AIM *may* have an edge over the revised network model on two accounts. (We emphasize "may" for the simple reason that to our knowledge, no empirical evidence has yet been reported that clearly favors any one model over the other as a comprehensive theoretical account of mood dependent memory.) First, though several studies have sought, without success, to demonstrate mood dependent recognition, most have used simple, concrete, and easily codable stimuli (such as common words or pictures of ordinary objects) as the target items. However, the elusive effect was revealed in a recent study (Eich, Macaulay, & Lam, 1997) in which bipolar patients were tested for their ability to recognize abstract, Rorschach-like ink-blots—the sort of complex and unusual stimuli that the AIM suggests should be highly infused with affect (a point made clearer in Bower and Forgas's chapter).

Second, although the network model speaks to *explicit* measures of MDM (e.g., free recall versus recognition memory), it is silent on whether *implicit* indices of retention should show mood dependence. However, AIM suggests that implicit tests may indeed be sensitive to MDM, provided that the tests call on substantive, open-ended thinking and admit a wide range of possible re-sponses (i.e., conceptually driven tests, such as free association and category-instance generation, as opposed to data-driven tests, such as perceptual identi-fication and word-fragment completion; see Roediger, 1990; Roediger & McDermott, 1993). To date, only a handful of studies of implicit mood de-pendence have been reported, but their results are generally consistent with this reasoning (see Eich, Macaulay, Loewenstein, & Dihle, 1997; Kihlstrom, Eich, Sandbrand, & Tobias, 2000; Macaulay, Ryan, & Eich, 1993; Nissen, Ross, Wil-lingham, MacKenzie, & Schacter, 1988; Tobias, Kihlstrom, & Schacter, 1992).

Though the AIM shows promise as a way of understanding the results (both positive and negative) of prior studies of MDM, its real potential may lie in the possibilities it suggests for future MDM research. For example, suppose that happy and sad subjects read about and form impressions of named individuals, some of whom appear quite normal and some who seem rather strange. As described in the Bower and Forgas chapter, AIM predicts that atypical, unusual, or complex targets should selectively recruit longer and more substantive proc-essing strategies, and correspondingly greater affect infusion effects. Accord-ingly, strange people should be evaluated more positively by happy than by sad subjects, whereas normal individuals should be perceived similarly, a deduction verified in several studies (see Forgas, 1992).

Now suppose that the subjects are later asked to freely recall, by name, all of the people they can and that testing takes place either in the same mood they had experienced earlier or in the alternative affect. The prediction is that, relative to their mismatched mood counterparts, subjects tested under matched mood conditions will recall more of the strange people, but an equivalent number of the normal individuals. More generally, it is conceivable that mood dependence, like mood congruence, is magnified by the encoding and retrieval of atypical targets, for the reasons given by AIM. Similarly, judgments about the self, in contrast to others, may be more conducive to demonstrating MDM, as people tend to process self-relevant information more extensively and elaborately (see Forgas, 1995; Sedikides, 1995). Just how real or remote these possibilities are remains to be seen.

To close this discussion of task factors, we wish to return to the question posed earlier: even if MDM is not, as was once commonly believed, a powerful and prevalent effect, might it nevertheless emerge clearly and consistently under certain limited conditions? Though certain that the answer is "yes," we are not altogether sure why. One conjecture is that the higher the level of affect infusion achieved at encoding *and* at retrieval, the higher the likelihood of detecting mood dependence. Though admittedly simplistic, this idea accords well with current knowledge about mood dependence, and—more important—it has numerous testable implications (including those identified earlier) that seem well worth pursuing.

Mood Factors

Up to now, the focus of discussion has been on factors that determine the sensitivity of an encoding or a retrieval task to the detection of mood dependence. However, no matter how sensitive these tasks may be, their odds of demonstrating MDM are slim in the absence of an effective manipulation of mood. So what makes a mood manipulation effective?

One factor is mood strength. By definition, mood dependence demands a statistically significant loss of memory when target events are encoded in one mood and retrieved in another. It is doubtful that anything less than a substantial shift in mood, between the occasions of event encoding and event retrieval, could produce such an impairment. The same point has been made by Bower (1992; chapter 3 here), who maintains that MDM reflects a failure of information acquired in one mood to generalize to a different mood; the more dissimilar the two moods, the more likely generalization will fail. Indeed, the results of an MDM meta-analysis by Ucros (1989) revealed that the greater the difference in moods—depression versus elation, for example, as opposed to depression versus a neutral affect—the greater the mood dependent effect.

No less important than the strength of the moods is their stability over time and across tasks. In terms of demonstrating MDM, it does no good to engender a mood that evaporates as soon as the subject is given something to do, such as memorize a list of words or recall a previously studied story. Some studies probably failed to find MDM simply because they relied on moods that were potent initially but paled rapidly (see Eich & Metcalfe, 1989).

One practical means of inducing a mood—either happy or sad—that is stable as well as strong is the *continuous music technique* (CMT), alluded to earlier.

Subjects are asked to contemplate elating or depressing thoughts while they listen to various selections of sprightly or somber classical music. The music plays softly in the background all throughout testing—hence the term *continuous music technique*. (A variant of this technique has been used with success in some of the studies summarized in chapter 4.)

Periodically, subjects mark a copy of the *affect grid*: a single-item scale that assesses current levels of pleasure/displeasure and arousal/sleepiness—the two bipolar dimensions underlying the circumplex model of mood (see Russell, 1980; Russell, Weiss, & Mendelsohn, 1989). Subjects are not allowed to advance to cognitive testing until they have attained a critical level of mood: typically either *very* or *extremely pleasant* in the case of H-mood induction; *very* or *extremely unpleasant* in the case of S-mood induction. In principle, subjects can satisfy the pleasure criterion regardless of their concurrent level of arousal. In practice, however, ratings of pleasure are correlated (approximate $r = .50$) with those of arousal, meaning that H-mood subjects usually feel more active or alert than do their S-mood counterparts.

Understandably, subjects are not told in advance about the pleasure criteria, and as one might expect, the length of time it takes them to reach the critical levels of mood varies widely. Thus, the CMT does not arbitrarily limit the amount of time allocated to mood induction—the common practice in prior research on MDM, and one that virtually guarantees substantial differences in subjects' postinduction levels of mood. Rather, the CMT takes an idiographic approach to mood induction, permitting each individual to achieve a predetermined degree of pleasure or displeasure at his or her own pace. Though the CMT can be quite time consuming (taking up to an hour in some studies), it instills moods that start out strong and stay that way over time and across tasks (see Eich et al., 1994, tables 1 and 2 for supporting data).

In our most recent studies of MDM, we have asked subjects to candidly assess (postexperimentally) whether the CMT created an authentic change in their mood. Nearly 90% of the participants in these studies rate the technique as at least moderately effective (i.e., a rating of 5 or higher on a 0–10 mood genuineness scale), indicating a high degree of affective realism. Moreover, those who feel most genuinely "moved" tend to show the strongest mood dependent effects (Eich, 1995b). Thus, it seems that the odds of demonstrating MDM are improved by instilling affective states that have three important properties: strength, stability, and sincerity.

Yet a fourth influential feature relates to the fact, noted earlier, that most studies using the CMT have found a reliable correlation between ratings of pleasure and those of arousal, meaning that H-mood subjects *usually* feel more active or alert than do their S-mood counterparts. We stress "usually" because the strength of the correlation between pleasure and arousal ratings seems to have a profound impact on memory performance. To amplify, suppose that a person generates autobiographical events while in a state akin to sadness—that is, a state characterized by low pleasure combined with low arousal. Correlational evidence from several sources (see Eich et al., 1994; Eich & Metcalfe, 1989) suggests that the person will freely recall more of these events when later tested while feeling happy as a clam (high pleasure plus low arousal) as opposed to feeling happy as a lark (high pleasure plus high arousal). In short, a shift along both the pleasure and arousal dimensions of mood apparently impairs memory more than a shift along either dimension alone.

Summary

The preceding sections reviewed recent attempts to uncover key factors in the occurrence of MDM. What conclusions can be drawn from this line of research?

The broadest conclusion is that the problem of unreliability that has long beset research on mood dependence may not be as serious or stubborn as is commonly supposed. More to the point, it now appears that robust and reliable evidence of MDM can be realized under conditions in which subjects (a) are induced to experience strong, stable, and sincere moods; (b) encode the target events in a way that promotes high affect infusion; and (c) engage in similarly high affect infusion processes or strategies during event retrieval. Moreover, correlational data indicate that alterations in affective state that involve both the pleasure and arousal dimensions of mood lead to larger losses of memory than do shifts along either dimension alone.

Taken together, these observations make a start toward demystifying mood dependence, but only a start. To date, only a few factors have been examined for their role in MDM; odds are that other factors of equal or even greater weight exist, awaiting discovery. For instance, it is conceivable that mood dependent effects become stronger, not weaker, as the interval separating event encoding and retrieval grows longer (see Smith, 1988) and that such effects may emerge even when retention is assessed implicitly, or in the absence of conscious awareness (see Macaulay et al., 1993; Tobias et al., 1992). By exploring these and other possibilities in a rigorous and programmatic manner, it may be possible to reduce much of the uncertainty that still surrounds the reality of mood dependent memory.

REMEMBERING EMOTIONAL EVENTS

The impact of emotion on memory for personal events is one of the most controversial issues in all of contemporary cognition/emotion research. Though this issue has been explored in a variety of different contexts–in particular, flashbulb memory eyewitness memory, and traumatic memory–two central questions have permeated its discussion: (a) does emotion increase or decrease the strength of memory for an event, and (b) are special mechanisms required to account for the effects of emotion on memory. Although both questions have invited strong and often sharply divided opinions, recent analyses have become increasingly intricate. Claims regarding the effects of emotion on memory have evolved from relatively simple characterizations to more nuanced assessments of the distinct factors that mediate the impact of emotion. Discussions of the role of special memory mechanisms have also shifted gradually from polarized debates to a growing appreciation of the manner in which emotion and memory interact.

Effects of Emotion on Event Memory

That emotions exert powerful effects on memory has been recognized for so long, and by so many scholars, that it can safely be regarded as a truism. However, whether the influence of emotion is said to help or hinder memory has depended both on the precise characteristics of the situation and on the active paradigm. In research investigating *flashbulb memories* for salient (often shocking) news events, the hypothesis has been that emotion promotes event recollection. Conversely, in research involving *eyewitness memory*, the predominant view has been that emotion impairs recollection. And in the domain of *traumatic memory*, some have argued that the effect of emotion on recollection can go either way. These conflicting, sometimes paradoxical, claims result because emotional effects on memory differ markedly, depending on the precise conditions of encoding and retrieval.

Flashbulb memory. Emotion has often been alleged to enhance memory for major news events such as the assassination of President John Kennedy. Brown and Kulik (1977) coined the term *flashbulb memories* to characterize the vivid and accurate recollections they believed were associated with such events. Brown and Kulik's primary evidence for the accuracy of flashbulb memories was their participants' vivid and highly detailed recollections of their circumstances at the time of learning of Kennedy's assassination. One limitation of Brown and Kulik's evidence, however, is that they did not verify the accuracy of their subjects' recollections.

To circumvent this verification problem, several subsequent studies have used longitudinal designs to assess the consistency of flashbulb memories over time (consistency being a necessary if not sufficient condition for accuracy). These studies have investigated different news events, including the shooting of Ronald Reagan (Pillemer, 1984), the explosion of the space shuttle *Challenger* (Mc-Closkey, Wible, & Cohen, 1988; Neisser & Harsch, 1992), the death of Belgian King Baudoin (Finkenauer et al., 1998), and the resignation of British Prime Minister Margaret Thatcher (Conway et al., 1994).

Though the respondents' precise levels of memory performance have varied considerably across studies, the research as a whole suggests that most people provide generally consistent retrospective reports, although some produce appreciable inconsistencies. Researchers' interpretation of this pattern has depended on their focus on the accuracies or on the errors: some investigators have used the available data to argue that flashbulb memories are indeed uniquely veridical (e.g., Pillemer, 1984), yet others have interpreted the same data as evidence that so-called flashbulb memories are not especially accurate (e.g., McCloskey et al., 1988).

The main source of this discrepancy is that studies of flashbulb memories seldom make it clear to exactly what such memories should be compared. In a clever attempt at clarification, Conway and his colleagues (Conway et al., 1994; also see Conway, 1995) compared the recollections of two groups of subjects—citizens of the United Kingdom (U.K.) versus individuals who did not live in the U.K. (mostly residents of North America)—concerning the resignation of British Prime Minister Margaret Thatcher. Not surprisingly, the U.K. citizens were more emotional about the experience and perceived it as more important than their North American counterparts. Nevertheless, when tested two weeks after the incident, over 90% of subjects in both groups reported recollections of sufficient detail to be classified as flashbulb memories. However, whereas 86% of the U.K. citizens retained a flashbulb memory 11 months later, only 29% of the North American residents did. Moreover, the U.K. subjects showed markedly greater consistency in their recollections between the two testing intervals than did the others. Thus, by providing an appropriate control group, Conway et al. suggest that the quality of recollection associated with a flashbulb-type of news event is indeed more detailed and accurate than that associated with a less emotional news event.

Eyewitness memory. Though research on flashbulb memories has promoted the view that emotion enhances the accuracy of recollection, much of the original work on eyewitness memory seemed to suggest the opposite conclusion. For example, 70% of the eyewitness-memory experts surveyed by Kassin, Ellsworth, and Smith (1989) endorsed the statement that "very high levels of stress impair the accuracy of eyewitness testimony." Though such a characterization is consistent with several early reports of poor eyewitness memory for highly arousing events (e.g., Clifford & Scott; 1978; Loftus & Burns, 1982), recent research has revealed a more intricate relation between eyewitness memory and emotion. For example, several studies have shown that, although emotion impairs memory for the peripheral details of a complex event, it improves memory for central details (e.g., Christianson, 1992b; Heuer & Reisberg, 1990). Other studies have found that emotional memories can be less accurate than neutral memories when subjects are tested immediately, but more accurate when they are tested following a delay (e.g., Burke, Heurer, & Reisberg, 1992, experiment 2; Christianson, 1984; also see Kleinsmith & Kaplan, 1963, 1964). Though there have been several failures to observe this particular pattern (e.g., Burke et al., 1992, experiment 1; Christianson & Loftus, 1987), Park's (1995) recent meta-analysis suggests that the interaction between retention interval and memory for emotionally charged eyewitness events is a bona fide phenomenon. Thus, rather than simply impairing memory for eyewitness events, the effects of emotion on memory depend critically on both the centrality of the details and the interval at which retention is tested.

Traumatic memory. In no domain are the paradoxical claims regarding the effects of emotion on memory more evident than in the territory of trauma (see Bower & Sivers, 1998; Lindsay & Briere, 1997). On the one hand, victims of trauma often lament that their traumatic experiences are associated with painfully vivid recollections (see Koss, Tromp, & Tharan, 1995). On the other hand, some have claimed that trauma can cause memories to become difficult or even impossible to remember, at least temporarily. Though some research seems to support the latter, more controversial claim, much of this research has methodological problems. For example, numerous studies have given memory questionnaires to alleged victims of sexual abuse (e.g., Briere & Conte, 1993; Gold, Hughes, & Hohnecker, 1994; Loftus, Polonsky, & Fullilove, 1994). Invariably, these studies identify a substantial subset of respondents who report there was a time when they did not remember the trauma. Though consistent with the claim that traumatic experiences are apt to be forgotten, this finding must be viewed with caution because (a) there was no independent corroboration of the alleged trauma and (b) questionnaire studies rely on respondents' ability to recall periods of not remembering.

Many researchers doubt people's ability to accurately assess their prior states of forgetting. A recent case-study analyzed several individuals who reportedly forgot and subsequently remembered their traumas (Schooler, in press; Schooler, Ambadar, & Bendiksen, 1997; Schooler, Bendiksen, & Ambadar, 1997). Specifically, in several cases, individuals were found to have known about their traumatic experiences (i.e., they had told someone else about the events) at a time when they thought they had completely forgotten them. These cases highlight the difficulties of relying on retrospective reports of prior forgetting.

A more compelling demonstration of the forgetting of traumatic experiences comes from prospective studies that identify individuals on the basis of their known trauma histories (alleviating concerns about potential false memories) and that test their current recollections of abuse (alleviating concerns about retrospective assessment of forgetting). In several such studies (e.g., Widom & Morris, 1997; Williams, 1994, 1995), a substantial proportion of individuals who were known to have been abused reported no recollection of the recorded abuse incident. These studies provide reasonably strong evidence that people forget specific incidents of trauma, although they also have limitations. For example, because most of the participants in these studies were victims of repeated abuse, their failure to recall a particular incident may have been a problem of confusion rather than forgetting. Further, even if we grant that these incidents were in fact forgotten, they may not have been forgotten as a result of their emotional qualities.

In addition to this debate over the degree to which individuals can forget episodes of trauma, a related and even more contentious issue has been the accuracy of traumatic memories that were allegedly forgotten but subsequently remembered. Though typically referred to as *recovered memories*, Schooler, Ambadar, and Bendiksen (1997) have advocated the term *discovered memories*, because it maintains neutrality regarding whether the traumatic experience was truly forgotten or, indeed, whether the discovered event even occurred. In recent years, an alarming number of people have reported discovering long-forgotten memories of abuse, often in the context of intense psychotherapy. There are good reasons to believe that discovered memories can be the byproduct of therapists' overzealous search for an explanation of their clients' symptoms. It is beyond the scope of this chapter to survey the voluminous evidence for such concern, and the reader is directed to the excellent reviews on the topic written by Lindsay and Read (1994), Loftus and Ketcham (1994), Pendergrast (1996), and Schacter (1996).

Although many discovered memories may be the indirect result of therapist suggestions, others appear to correspond to actual incidents of abuse. Though much more research is needed on this issue, several investigators have successfully documented and independently corroborated cases of discovered memories (Schooler, 1999; Schooler, Ambadar, & Bendiksen, 1997; Schooler, Bendiksen, & Ambadar, 1997; Williams, 1994, 1995). For example, Schooler, Bendiksen, and Ambadar (1997) examined four cases in which discovered memories had been reported; the alleged abuse in these cases ranged from inappropriate fondling to rape. In every case, there was reasonably convincing evidence that the abuse had in fact occurred. These cases also provide some clues concerning the discovery experience. For instance, in each case, the discovery of the memory appeared to be associated with conditions that emulated the original trauma. In addition, individuals' accounts of their initial recollection of the abuse were characterized by great surprise and sudden extreme emotion, illustrating the appropriateness of referring to such experiences as memory "discoveries."

Summary. Though research on the impact of emotion on memory has spanned three rather distinct domains (flashbulb memory, eyewitness memory, and traumatic memory) and invoked all possible relations (improved recollection, impaired recollection, or no effect), several general conclusions can be drawn. First, evidence from all three domains suggests that emotion can make at least the central details of memories more vivid and memorable. At the same time, however, experiencing intense emotion during the encoding of an event does not ensure that the memory will necessarily remain accessible and accurate; indeed, emotional experiences can be misrecalled and sometimes even forgotten entirely. Finally, the conditions under which emotions aid or abate recollection are complex; an understanding of the effects of emotion on memory requires a theoretical account of the mechanisms that underlie these effects.

Mechanisms Underlying Emotional Event Memory

In addition to quarreling over how emotion influences event memory, researchers have also disputed whether the impact of emotion requires the postulation of special memory mechanisms. This issue has been central to debates about flashbulb memory, eyewitness memory, and traumatic memory. Nevertheless, we argue here (and elsewhere, see Schooler & Eich, in press) that the special mechanism issue has led us all away from the more appropriate question of how emotion-related phenomena interact with basic memory processes.

Flashbulb memory. Central to Brown and Kulik's (1977) original characterization of flashbulb memories was the claim that extremely emotional events invoke a special *now print* mechanism that produces a "permanent registration not only of the significant novelty, but of all recent brain events" (p. 76). Critics of this assertion countered that a variety of standard memory mechanisms— such as distinctiveness, rehearsal, and personal relevance—could, in principle, account for the impressive though imperfect accuracy of flashbulb-like recollections. As McCloskey et al. (1988) observed: "To the extent that we accept that ordinary memory mechanism could support reasonably good memory for experiences of learning about shocking events . . . there is no need to postulate a special flashbulb memory mechanism" (p. 180).

More contemporary research implies that flashbulb memories involve standard mechanisms that have been supplemented by the unique influences of emotion. For example, Conway et al. (1994) found that the primary differences between events that either did or did not eventually develop the canonical properties of flashbulb memories were their perceived significance and the intensity of the resulting affective reactions. Recent structural-modeling analyses (Finkenauer et al., 1998) have further highlighted the importance of affective reaction in the formation of flashbulb memories.

Though emotion apparently contributes to the detailed quality of flashbulb memories, they still share great similarity with more standard memories (Anderson & Conway, 1993; Christianson, 1989). Thus, a reasonable answer to the special mechanism question is both "yes" and "no." Emotional processes do seem to give flashbulb memories unique properties: especially strength, vividness, and detail. However, these processes appear to work in concert with, rather than apart from, more standard memory mechanisms.

Eyewitness memory. A similar reconciliation may be achievable in the case of emotion and eyewitness memory. Within this domain, researchers have argued over the extent to which the emotional intensity of actual crimes elicits processes not observed in the laboratory. For example, drawing on a study detailing the remarkably accurate memory performance of witnesses to an actual robbery and murder, Yuille and Cutshall (1986) concluded that extreme emotional events experienced in real life lead to "qualitatively different memories than innocuous laboratory events" (p. 178). Christianson and his colleagues (Christianson, 1992a; Christianson, Goodman, & Loftus, 1992) have contested this conclusion, noting that, because laboratory studies tend to show comparable albeit not identical memory performance for emotional and nonemotional episodes, the differences between lab-related and real-life emotional events may be more apparent than real.

Studies by Cahill and his associates provide evidence for both positions, suggesting that emotion may qualitatively alter memories, but it can be assessed in the lab. In one experiment (Cahill, Prins, Weber, & McGaugh, 1994), subjects were injected with either propranolol (a beta-adrenergic blocker) or a placebo before they viewed slides depicting an emotionally arousing or a neutral story. Strikingly, propranolol attenuated participants' recognition advantage for emotional elements of the story yet had no effect on their memory for nonemotional elements (the emotional story contained both arousing and neutral parts). This result implies that the normal memory advantage for the central details of emotional scenes results from the unique involvement of adrenergic hormones, which were blocked for participants receiving propranolol.

Other studies suggest a special role of the amygdala in enhancing emotional memory in the eyewitness paradigm. For instance, Cahill, Babinksy, Markowitsch, and McGaugh (1995) found no memorial advantage for emotional compared to nonemotional slides in a patient with bilateral degeneration of the amygdala complex. Moreover, using a PET imaging procedure, Cahill et al. (1996) observed that the degree of amygdala activation during the witnessing of emotional film clips predicted recall performance two weeks later ($r = .92$). They found no reliable relation between amygdala activation during the encoding and subsequent recall for neutral film clips.

The results reported by Cahill and his colleagues suggest some important truths to the claims that emotional memories involve unique processes and that laboratory-based memories are not qualitatively different from more intense real-world ones. The unique role of adrenergic hormones and the amygdala in the encoding of memories with emotional content implies the involvement of brain processes that may not be associated with nonemotional memories. At the same time, however, the success of Cahill's lab demonstrations of the unique role of emotion in eyewitness memory suggests that the memorial processes observed in the lab may not be qualitatively different from those induced in more extreme, real-life emotional situations.

Traumatic memory. As in the domains of flashbulb and eyewitness memory, the existence of special mechanisms for traumatic memory has been a topic of heated debate. A variety of special mechanisms has been postulated as invoked by trauma—specifically *repression, dissociation,* and *pure-sensory processing.* The essence of repression lies in the ego-defensive function of rejecting or keeping something out of consciousness to protect the self from intolerable stress (see Erdelyi & Goldberg, 1979). In contrast, the concept of dissociation suggests that traumatized individuals detach or dissociate themselves from ongoing experience, thereby radically altering the way in which the experience is encoded and later retrieved (see Spiegel & Cardena, 1991). Related to dissociation is the idea that traumatic memories can be recalled in a sensory form only, "without any semantic representation . . . [so that they are] experienced primarily as fragments of the sensory component of the event" (van der Kolk & Fisler, 1995, p. 513). Some have claimed that such memories are especially resistant to change (van der Kolk & van der Hart, 1991) and are elicited automatically in response to certain environmental or experiential cues (see Brewin, 1989; Brewin, Dalgleish, & Joseph, 1996).

Evidence for all three special mechanisms has been mixed. Currrently, there is little direct empirical support for repression (see Holmes, 1990; Loftus & Ketcham, 1994); nevertheless, it remains a potentially useful construct and some investigators believe repression is the best explanation for certain cases of forgetting (see Brewin, 1997; Erdelyi, 1990; Freyd, 1996; Ramachandran, 1995; Vaillant, 1992). Evidence for dissociation as a source of memory impairment is also equivocal. Though individuals with extreme dissociative tendencies are known to manifest marked impairments of memory (see Schacter & Kihlstrom, 1989), the contribution of dissociation to the specific case of forgetting and subsequent remembering of traumatic events has yet to be established empirically.

As for the pure-sensory view of traumatic memories, the most persuasive evidence to date has emerged from animal research. LeDoux (1992, 1995) suggested a potentially pivotal role of the amygdala in the formation of such memories and demonstrated that the amygdala is critically involved in the learning of fear responses by rats and other mammals. Nadel and Jacobs (1998) review additional animal studies indicating that stress may disrupt the memory consolidation functions of the hippocampus. These studies suggest that traumatic memories may foster the formation of affectively charged representations in the amygdala but at the same time impair hippocampal integration and binding processes (see Bower & Sivers, 1998; Krystal, Southwick, & Charney, 1995; Metcalfe & Jacobs, 1998).

Though special mechanisms have been favored by some students of traumatic memory, others have argued that standard mechanisms alone can do the job. For example, Shobe and Kihlstrom (1997) have commented that "nothing about the clinical evidence suggests that traumatic memories are special" (p. 74). Further, Schooler, Ambadar and Bendiksen (1997) noted a number of standard mechanisms that could lead to the discovery of seemingly forgotten recollections of abuse, including directed forgetting, encoding specificity, hypermnesia, and lack of rehearsal. In addition, Schooler and his associates argued that individuals may confuse the reinterpretation of an experience (e.g., realizing that a particular action constituted sexual abuse) with the discovery of the memory itself, thereby evoking a *forgot-it-all-along effect* that could create the illusion that a traumatic event had previously been forgotten.

Though basic memory mechanisms are apt to play important roles in the discovery of traumatic memories, they may be complemented by additional processes initiated by the special circumstances of the experience. For example, in accounting for several—albeit uncorroborated—claims that memories of sexual abuse were precipitously forgotten the morning after they had occurred, Schooler (in press) speculated about the possible involvement of forgetting processes characteristic of nocturnal experiences (e.g., those associated with the forgetting of dreams and brief awakenings). If such processes do in fact contribute to the (alleged) rapid forgetting of nocturnal abuse, they would in a sense be "special" in that they would presumably be limited to specific types of nocturnal experience. Nevertheless, they would also be quite "ordinary" in that they may be drawing on processes that occur every night (see Bonnet, 1983).

Similarly, the suggestion that trauma may reduce the ability of the hippocampus to consolidate the components of emotional memories into a single, coherent narrative does not require the *addition* of any special, new mechanisms. To the contrary, it actually points to the attenuation of standard memory processes—for example, the involvement of the hippocampus in the integration or binding of diverse perceptual experiences into discrete episodes or events (McClelland, McNaughton, & O'Reilly, 1995). Lacking cohesion and integration, such memories could be especially difficult to retrieve deliberately, so they are left at the mercy of situational retrieval cues (see Krystal et al., 1995). Such a state of affairs could resolve one of the most paradoxical aspects of traumatic memories—why they are sometimes remembered excessively but at other times not recalled at all. If traumatic recollections are primarily elicited by external or internal cues, recollections of trauma may be inescapable when such cues are present; however, when the appropriate cues are absent, so too may be the recollections.

Summary. The issue of whether memories of extreme emotional experiences rely on special mechanisms may beg the question of how emotion interacts with basic memory processes. There are good reasons to believe that such fundamental factors as event distinctiveness and rehearsal frequency contribute to the seemingly distinctive qualities of emotional memories. At the same time, however, there are reasons to think that processes more specifically associated with intense emotion, such as increased amygdaloid and decreased hippocampal activity, may be involved in at least some emotional recollections. However, if such processes are in fact involved, they seem likely to work in concert with, rather than in opposition to, more basic memory processes.

NOTES

Preparation of this chapter was aided by grants to the first author from the (American) National Institute of Mental Health (MH59636) and the (Canadian) Natural Sciences and Engineering Research Council (37335) and by the cogent comments and advice offered by Katie Shobe and Tonya Schooler.

REFERENCES

Anderson, S. J., & Conway, M. A. (1993). Investigating the structure of autobiographical memories. *Journal of Experimental Psychology: Learning, Memory, and Cognition, 19,* 1178–1196.

Blaney, P. H. (1986). Affect and memory: A review. *Psychological Bulletin, 99,* 229–246.

Bonnet, M. H. (1983). Memory for events occurring during arousal from sleep. *Psychophysiology, 20,* 81–87.

Bower, G. H. (1981). Mood and memory. *American Psychologist, 36,* 129–148.

Bower, G. H. (1987). Commentary on mood and memory. *Behavior Research and Therapy, 25,* 443–455.

Bower, G. H. (1992). How might emotions affect learning? In S.-A. Christianson (Ed.), *Handbook of emotion and memory* (pp. 3–31). Hillsdale, NJ: Erlbaum.

Bower, G. H., & Cohen, P. R. (1982). Emotional influences in memory and thinking: Data and theory. In M. S. Clark & S. T. Fiske (Eds.), *Affect and cognition* (pp. 291–331). Hillsdale, NJ: Erlbaum.

Bower, G. H., & Mayer, J. D. (1989). In search of mood-dependent retrieval. *Journal of Social Behavior and Personality, 4,* 121–156.

Bower, G. H., & Sivers, H. (1998). Cognitive impact of traumatic events. *Development and Psychopathology, 10,* 625–653.

Brewin, C. R. (1989). Cognitive change processes in psychotherapy. *Psychological Review, 96,* 379–394.

Brewin, C. R. (1997). Clinical and experimental approaches to understanding repression.

In J. D. Read & D. S. Lindsay (Eds.), *Recollections of trauma: Scientific research and clinical practice* (pp. 145–163). New York: Plenum.

Brewin, C. R., Dalgleish, T., & Joseph, S. (1996). A dual representation theory of post-traumatic stress disorder. *Psychological Review, 103*, 670–686.

Briere, J., & Conte, J. (1993). Self-reported amnesia for abuse in adults molested as children. *Journal of Traumatic Stress, 6*, 21–31.

Brown, R., & Kulik, J. (1977). Flashbulb memories. *Cognition, 5*, 73–99.

Burke, A., Heuer, F., & Reisberg, D. (1992). Remembering emotional events. *Memory & Cognition, 20*, 277–290.

Cahill, L., Babinsky, R., Markowitsch, H., & McGaugh, J. L. (1995). The amygdala and emotional memory. *Nature, 377*, 295–296.

Cahill, L., Haier, R., Fallon, J., Alkire, M., Tang, C., Keator, D., Wu, J., & McGaugh, J. L. (1996). Amygdala activity at encoding correlated with long-term, free recall of emotional information. *Proceedings of the National Academy of Sciences, 93*, 8016–8021.

Cahill, L., Prins, B., Weber, M., & McGaugh, J. L. (1994). Beta-adrenergic activation and memory for emotional events. *Nature, 371*, 702–704.

Christianson, S.-A. (1984). The relationship between induced emotional arousal and amnesia. *Scandinavian Journal of Psychology, 25*, 147–160.

Christianson, S.-A. (1989). Flashbulb memories: Special, but not so special. *Memory & Cognition 17*, 435–443.

Christianson, S.-A. (1992a). Emotional stress and eyewitness memory: A critical review. *Psychological Bulletin, 112*, 284–309.

Christianson, S.-A. (1992b). Remembering emotional events: Potential mechanisms. In S.-A. Christianson (Ed.), *The handbook of emotion and memory: Research and theory* (pp. 307–340). Hillsdale, NJ: Erlbaum.

Christianson, S.-A., Goodman, J., & Loftus, E. F. (1992). Eyewitness memory for stressful events: Methodological quandaries and ethical dilemmas. In S.-A. Christianson (Ed.), *The handbook of emotion and memory: Research and theory* (pp. 217–241). Hillsdale, NJ: Erlbaum.

Christianson, S.-A., & Loftus, E. F. (1987). Memory for traumatic events. *Applied Cognitive Psychology, 1*, 225–239.

Clark, D. M., & Teasdale, J. D. (1982). Diurnal variation in clinical depression and accessibility of memories of positive and negative experiences. *Journal of Abnormal Psychology, 91*, 87–95.

Clifford, B. R., & Scott, J. (1978). Individual and situational factors in eyewitness testimony. *Journal of Applied Psychology, 63*, 352–359.

Conway, M. A. (1995). *Flashbulb memories.* Hillsdale, NJ: Erlbaum.

Conway, M. A., Anderson, S. J., Larsen, S. F., Donnelly, C. M., McDaniel, M. A., McClelland, A. G.R., Rawles, R. E., & Logie, R. H. (1994). The formation of flashbulb memories. *Memory & Cognition, 22*, 326–343.

Eich, E. (1980). The cue-dependent nature of state-dependent retrieval. *Memory & Cognition, 8*, 157–173.

Eich, E. (1989). Theoretical issues in state dependent memory. In H. L. Roediger & F. I. M. Craik (Eds.), *Varieties of memory and consciousness: Essays in honour of Endel Tulving* (pp. 331–354). Hillsdale, NJ: Erlbaum.

Eich, E. (1995a). Mood as a mediator of place dependent memory. *Journal of Experimental Psychology: General, 124,* 293–308.

Eich, E. (1995b). Searching for mood dependent memory. *Psychological Science, 6,* 67–75.

Eich, E., Macaulay, D., & Lam, R. W. (1997). Mania, depression, and mood dependent memory. *Cognition and Emotion, 11,* 607–618.

Eich, E., Macaulay, D., Loewenstein, R. J., & Dihle, P. H. (1997). Memory, amnesia, and dissociative identity disorder. *Psychological Science, 8,* 417–422.

Eich, E., Macaulay, D., & Ryan, L. (1994). Mood dependent memory for events of the personal past. *Journal of Experimental Psychology: General, 123,* 201–215.

Eich, E., & Metcalfe, J. (1989). Mood dependent memory for internal versus external events. *Journal of Experimental Psychology: Learning, Memory, and Cognition, 15,* 443–455.

Erdelyi, M. H. (1990). Repression, reconstruction, and defense: History and integration of the psychoanalytic and experimental frameworks. In J. L. Singer (Ed.), *Repression and dissociation: Implications for personality theory, psychotherapy, and health* (pp. 1–31). Chicago: University of Chicago Press.

Erdelyi, M. H., & Goldberg, B. (1979). Let's not sweep repression under the rug: Toward a cognitive psychology of repression. In J. F. Kihlstrom & F. J. Evans (Eds.), *Functional disorders of memory* (pp. 355–402). Hillsdale, NJ: Erlbaum.

Fiedler, K. (1990). Mood-dependent selectivity in social cognition. In W. Stroebe & N. Hewstone (Eds.), *European review of social psychology* (vol. 1, pp. 1–32). Chichester, UK: Wiley.

Finkenauer, C., Luminet, O., Gisle, L., El-Ahmadi, A., van der Linden, M., & Philippot, P. (1998). Flashbulb memories and the underlying mechanisms of their formation: Toward an emotional-integrative model. *Memory & Cognition, 26,* 516–531.

Forgas, J. P. (1992). On bad mood and peculiar people: Affect and person typicality in impression formation. *Journal of Personality and Social Psychology, 62,* 863–875.

Forgas, J. P. (1995). Mood and judgment: The Affect Infusion Model (AIM). *Psychological Bulletin, 117,* 39–66.

Freyd, J. (1996). *Betrayal trauma: The logic of forgetting childhood abuse.* Cambridge, MA: Harvard University Press.

Gold, S. N., Hughes, D., & Hohnecker, L. (1994). Degrees of repression of sexual abuse memories. *American Psychologist, 49,* 441–442.

Goodwin, D. W. (1974). Alcoholic blackout and state-dependent learning. *Federation Proceedings, 33,* 1833–1835.

Heuer, F., & Reisberg, D. (1990). Vivid memories of emotional events: The accuracy of remembered minutiae. *Memory & Cognition, 18,* 496–506.

Holmes, D. (1990). The evidence for repression: An examination of sixty years of research. In J. L. Singer (Ed.), *Repression and dissociation: Implications for personality theory, psychotherapy, and health* (pp. 85–102). Chicago: University of Chicago Press.

Izard, C. E., Kagan, J., & Zajonc, R. B. (1984). Introduction. In C. E. Izard, J. Kagan, & R. B. Zajonc (Eds.), *Emotions, cognition, & behavior* (pp. 1–14). Cambridge, UK: Cambridge University Press.

Johnson, M. K., & Raye, C. L. (1981). Reality monitoring. *Psychological Review, 88,* 67–85.

Kassin, S. M., Ellsworth, P., & Smith, V. L. (1989). The "general acceptance" of psychological research on eyewitness testimony. *American Psychologist, 44,* 1089–1098.

Kenealy, P. M. (1997). Mood-state-dependent retrieval: The effects of induced mood on memory reconsidered. *Quarterly Journal of Experimental Psychology, 50A,* 290–317.

Kihlstrom, J. F. (1987). The cognitive unconscious. *Science, 237,* 1445–1452.

Kihlstrom, J. F., Eich, E., Sandbrand, D., & Tobias, B. A. (2000). Emotion and memory: Implications for self-report. In A. A. Stone, J. S. Turkkan, C. Bachrach, J. B. Jobe, H. S. Kurtzman, & V. S. Cain (Eds.), *The science of self-report: Implications for research and practice* (pp. 81–99). Mahwah, NJ: Erlbaum.

Kitayama, S., & Niedenthal, P. M. (1994). Introduction. In P. M. Niedenthal & S. Kitayama (Eds.), *The heart's eye: Emotional influences in perception and attention* (pp. 1–14). San Diego: Academic Press.

Kleinsmith, L. J., & Kaplan, S. (1963). Paired-associate learning as a function of arousal and interpolated interval. *Journal of Experimental Psychology, 65,* 190–193.

Kleinsmith, L. J., & Kaplan, S. (1964). Interaction of arousal and recall interval in nonsense syllable paired-associate learning. *Journal of Experimental Psychology, 67,* 124–126.

Koss, M. P., Tromp, S., & Tharan, M. (1995). Traumatic memories: Empirical foundations, clinical and forensic implications. *Clinical Psychology: Research and Practice, 2,* 111–132.

Krystal, J. H., Southwick, S. M., & Charney, D. (1995). Post traumatic stress disorder: Psychobiological mechanisms of traumatic remembrance. In D. L. Schacter (Ed.), *Memory distortion: How minds, brains, and societies reconstruct the past* (pp. 150–172). Cambridge, MA: Harvard University Press.

LeDoux, J. E. (1992). Emotion as memory: Anatomical systems underlying indelible neural traces. In S.-A. Christianson (Ed.), *The handbook of emotion and memory: Research and theory* (pp. 269–288). Hillsdale, NJ: Erlbaum.

LeDoux, J. E. (1995). Emotion: Clues from the brain. *Annual Review of Psychology, 46,* 209–235.

LeDoux, J. E. (1996). *The emotional brain.* New York: Simon & Schuster.

Lindsay, D. S., & Briere, J. (1997). The controversy regarding recovered memories of childhood sexual abuse: Pitfalls, bridges, and future directions. *Journal of Interpersonal Violence, 12,* 631–647.

Lindsay, D. S., & Read, J. D. (1994). Psychotherapy and memories of child sexual abuse: A cognitive perspective. *Applied Cognitive Psychology, 8,* 281–338.

Loftus, E. F., & Burns, T. E. (1982). Mental shock can produce retrograde amnesia. *Memory & Cognition, 10,* 318–323.

Loftus, E. F., & Ketcham, K. (1994). *The myth of repressed memory: False memories and allegations of sexual abuse.* New York: St. Martin's Press.

Loftus, E. F., Polonsky, S., & Fullilove, M. T. (1994). Memories of childhood sexual abuse: Remembering and repressing. *Psychology of Women Quarterly, 18,* 67–84.

Ludwig, A. M. (1984). Intoxication and sobriety: Implications for the understanding of multiple personality. *Psychiatric Clinics of North America, 7,* 161–169.

Macaulay, D., Ryan, L., & Eich, E. (1993). Mood dependence in implicit and explicit memory. In P. Graf & M. E. J. Masson (Eds.), *Implicit memory: New directions in cognition, development, and neuropsychology* (pp. 75–94). Hillsdale, NJ: Erlbaum.

Marschark, M. (1996). Foreword. In C. Cornoldi, R. H. Logie, M. A. Brandimonte, G. Kaufmann, & D. Reisberg, *Stretching the imagination: Representation and transformation in mental imagery.* New York: Oxford University Press.

McClelland, J. L., McNaughton, B. L., & O'Reilly, R. C. (1995). Why there are complimentary learning systems in the hippocampus and neocortex: Insights from the successes and failures of connectionist models of learning and memory. *Psychological Review, 3,* 419–457

McCloskey, M., Wible, C. G., & Cohen, N. J. (1988). Is there a special flashbulb-memory mechanism? *Journal of Experimental Psychology: General, 117,* 171–181.

McGeogh, J. A. (1942). *The psychology of human learning.* New York: Longmans, Green.

Mellers, B. A., Schwartz, A., Ho, K., & Ritov, I. (1997). Decision affect theory: Emotional reactions to the outcomes of risky options. *Psychological Science, 8,* 423–429.

Metcalfe, J., & Jacobs, W. J. (1998). Emotional memory: The effects of stress on "cool" and "hot" memory systems. In D. Medin (Ed.), *The psychology of learning and motivation* (vol. 38, pp. 187–222). San Diego: Academic Press.

Miller, N. E. (1950). Learnable drives and rewards. In S. S. Stevens (Ed.), *Handbook of experimental psychology* (pp. 435–472). New York: Wiley.

Nadel, L., & Jacobs, W. J. (1998). Traumatic memory is special. *Current Directions in Psychological Science, 7,* 154–157.

Neisser, U., & Harsch, N. (1992). Phantom flashbulbs: False recollections of hearing the news about *Challenger.* In E. Winograd & U. Neisser (Eds.), *Affect and accuracy in recall: Studies of "flashbulb memories"* (pp. 9–31). Cambridge, UK: Cambridge University Press.

Nissen, M. J., Ross, J. L., Willingham, D. B., MacKenzie, T. B., & Schacter, D. L. (1988). Memory and awareness in a patient with multiple personality disorder. *Brain and Cognition, 8,* 21–38.

Park, J. (1995). *The effect of arousal and retention delay on memory: A meta-analysis.* Unpublished manuscript, Yale University.

Pendergrast, M. (1996). *Victims of memory: Sex abuse accusations and shattered lives.* 2nd ed. Hinesburg, VT: Upper Access.

Pillemer, D. B. (1984). Flashbulb memories of the assassination attempt on President Reagan. *Cognition, 16,* 63–80.

Ramachandran, V. S. (1995). Anosognosia in parietal lobe syndrome. *Consciousness and Cognition, 4,* 22–51.

Reus, V. I., Weingartner, H., & Post, R. M. (1979). Clinical implications of state-dependent learning. *American Journal of Psychiatry, 136,* 927–931.

Roediger, H. L. (1990). Implicit memory: Retention without remembering. *American Psychologist, 45,* 1043–1056.

Roediger, H. L., & McDermott, K. B. (1993). Implicit memory in normal human subjects. In F. Boller & J. Grafman (Eds.), *Handbook of neuropsychology* (vol. 8, pp. 63–131). Amsterdam: Elsevier.

Russell, J. A. (1980). A circumplex model of affect. *Journal of Personality and Social Psychology, 39,* 1161–1178.

Russell, J. A., Weiss, A., & Mendelsohn, G. A. (1989). Affect grid: A single-item scale of pleasure and arousal. *Journal of Personality and Social Psychology, 57*, 493–502.

Schacter, D. L. (1996). *Searching for memory.* New York: Basic Books.

Schacter, D. L., & Kihlstrom, J. F. (1989). Functional amnesia. In F. Boller & J. Grafman (Eds.), *Handbook of neuropsychology* (vol. 3, pp. 209–230). New York: Elsevier.

Schooler, J. W. (1994). Seeking the core: The issues and evidence surrounding recovered accounts of sexual trauma. *Consciousness and Cognition, 3*, 452–469.

Schooler, J. W. (in press). Discovered memories and the "delayed discovery doctrine": A cognitive case based analysis. In S. Taub (Ed.), *Recovered memories of child sexual abuse: Psychological, legal, and social perspectives on a twentieth century controversy.* Springfield, IL: Charles C. Thomas.

Schooler, J. W., Ambadar, Z., & Bendiksen, M. A. (1997). A cognitive corroborative case study approach for investigating discovered memories of sexual abuse. In J. D. Read & D. S. Lindsay (Eds.), *Recollections of trauma: Scientific research and clinical Practice* (pp. 379–388). New York: Plenum.

Schooler, J. W., Bendiksen, M. A., & Ambadar, Z. (1997). Taking the middle line: Can we accommodate both fabricated and recovered memories of sexual abuse? In M. Conway (Ed.), *False and recovered memories* (pp. 251–292). Oxford: Oxford University Press.

Schooler, J. W., & Eich, E. (in press). Memory for emotional events. In E. Tulving & F. I.M. Craik (Eds.), *The Oxford handbook of memory.* New York: Oxford University Press.

Sedikides, C. (1995). Central and peripheral self-conceptions are differentially influenced by mood: Tests of the differential sensitivity hypothesis. *Journal of Personality and Social Psychology, 69*, 759–777.

Shobe, K. K., & Kihlstrom, J. F. (1997). Is traumatic memory special? *Current Directions in Psychological Science, 6*, 70–74.

Smith, S. M. (1988). Environmental context-dependent memory. In G. M. Davies & D. M. Thomson (Eds.), *Memory in context: Context in memory* (pp. 13–34). Chichester, UK: Wiley.

Snyder, M., & White, P. (1982). Moods and memories: Elation, depression, and the remembering of the events of one's life. *Journal of Personality, 50*, 149–167.

Spiegel, D., & Cardena, E. (1991). Disintegrated experience: The dissociative disorders revisited. *Journal of Abnormal Psychology, 100*, 366–378.

Thorndike, E. L. (1932). *The fundamentals of learning.* New York: Teachers College.

Tobias, B. A., Kihlstrom, J. F., & Schacter, D. L. (1992). Emotion and implicit memory. In S.-A. Christianson (Ed.), *Handbook of emotion and memory* (pp. 67–92). Hillsdale, NJ: Erlbaum.

Tulving, E. (1983). *Elements of episodic memory.* Oxford: Oxford University Press.

Ucros, C. G. (1989). Mood state-dependent memory: A meta-analysis. *Cognition and Emotion, 3*, 139–167.

Vaillant, G. (1992). *Ego mechanisms of defense: A guide for clinicians and researchers.* Washington, DC: American Psychiatric Press.

van der Kolk, B. A., & Fisler, R. (1995). Dissociation and the fragmentary nature of traumatic memories: Overview and exploratory study. *Journal of Traumatic Stress, 8*, 505–525.

van der Kolk, B. A., & van der Hart, O. (1991). The intrusive past: The flexibility of memory and the engraving of trauma. *American Imago, 48,* 425–454.

Watts, F. N. (1987). Editorial. *Cognition and Emotion, 1,* 1–2.

Watts, F. N. (1995). Depression and anxiety. In A. D. Baddeley, B. A. Wilson, & F. N. Watts (Eds.), *Handbook of memory disorders* (pp. 293–317). New York: Wiley.

Widom, C. S., & Morris, S. (1997). Accuracy of adult recollections of childhood victimization: Part 2. Childhood sexual abuse. *Psychological Assessment, 9,* 34–46.

Williams, L. M. (1994). Recall of childhood trauma: A prospective study of women's memories of child sexual abuse. *Journal of Consulting and Clinical Psychology, 62,* 1167–1176.

Williams, L. M. (1995). Recovered memories of abuse in women with documented child sexual victimization histories. *Journal of Traumatic Stress, 8,* 649–673.

Yuille, J. C., & Cutshall, J. L. (1986). A case study of eyewitness memory of a crime. *Journal of Applied Psychology, 71,* 291–301.

CHAPTER 2

The Emotional Unconscious

John F. Kihlstrom, Shelagh Mulvaney,
Betsy A. Tobias, and Irene P. Tobis

One of the earliest marks of the cognitive revolution in psychology was a revival of interest in consciousness, rather than behavior. The cognitive psychology that emerged immediately after World War II to replace functional behaviorism focused on the span of apprehension, primary memory, attention, and imagery. Now, as we approach the twenty-first century, cognitive psychology has begun to seriously explore *unconscious* mental life and the *psychological unconscious*: the idea that conscious experience, thought, and action is influenced by percepts, memories, and other mental states that are inaccessible to phenomenal awareness and somehow independent of voluntary control.

THE COGNITIVE UNCONSCIOUS AND BEYOND

In the modern history of cognitive psychology, one can discern four early stages in the conceptualization of the psychological unconscious (Kihlstrom, 1995b, 1999). The first of these might be called the *wastebasket view*: that the unconscious includes unattended and unrehearsed events and memories lost through decay or displacement. There is also the *file cabinet view*: that the unconscious includes passively stored memories that must be actively retrieved into short-term or working memory in order to play any role in cognitive processing. Neither view allows dynamically active unconscious percepts, thoughts, and memories. Thus, they do not really satisfy the definition of the psychological unconscious. The conscious takes a more active role in *preattentive processing*, which holds that stimulus events are subject to unconscious processes of feature detection, pattern recognition, and the like before conscious attention is directed to them. Finally, an even more active role is suggested by *automaticity*: the notion that some cognitive and motoric skills, once executed deliberately, may become automatized through extensive practice, after which we have no direct introspective access to these procedures or their operations. These ideas include unconscious processes in cognition, but they imply that the psychological unconscious is limited to mental processes and that the contents on which these processes operate are conscious.

Implicit Memory

The idea that mental *contents* might be unconscious, not just the processes that operate on them, is commonly associated with psychoanalytic theory. But as Ellenberger (1970) has shown, ideas about unconscious percepts and memories extend far beyond Breuer and Freud's (1893–1895/1957) studies of hysteria. Contemporary psychology has revived the distinction between explicit and implicit memory (Schacter, 1987). *Explicit memory* refers to the conscious recollection of some past event, as in recall and recognition. By contrast, *implicit memory* refers to any effect of a past event on a person's ongoing experience, thought, and action, regardless of whether that event can be consciously remembered.

Perhaps the most dramatic demonstration of the difference between explicit and implicit memory comes from studies of patients who have suffered bilateral damage to the medial temporal lobes (including the hippocampus) or the diencephalon (including the mammillary bodies). These patients show a gross anterograde amnesia; they generally cannot recall or recognize words that have been presented to them for study. But when asked to perform other tasks, they frequently reveal the preservation of some sort of memory.

The first investigators to document this anomaly under controlled conditions were Warrington and Weiskrantz (1968), who found relatively normal retention when the patients were tested with fragments or stems of list items. Thus, after studying a word like *elastic*, amnesics will be unable to recall or recognize it; but when asked to name a word, any word, that starts with *ela*, they are much more apt to say *elastic* than chance alone would predict. This phenomenon, known as a *priming effect*, has been demonstrated many times. When amnesic patients who cannot remember words from a study list are later given an opportunity to use those words in another sort of task, they use previously studied items more frequently than unstudied neutral items—just as neurologically intact controls do in similar tasks.

Dissociations between explicit and implicit memory can be observed in other forms of amnesia as well, including posthypnotic amnesia (Dorfman & Kihlstrom, 1994; Kihlstrom, 1980, 1985), surgical anesthesia (Cork, Couture, &

Kihlstrom, 1997; Kihlstrom, 1993b; Kihlstrom & Schacter, 1990; Merikle & Daneman, 1996), and the amnesias associated with electroconvulsive therapy (Dorfman, Kihlstrom, Cork, & Misiaszek, 1995; Squire, Shimamura, & Graf, 1985) and multiple personality disorder (Eich, Macaulay, Loewenstein, & Dihle, 1997; Kihlstrom & Schacter, 1995; Kihlstrom, Tataryn, & Hoyt, 1993). So the effect is quite commonly observed. Implicit memory is also spared in normal aging, which has deleterious effects on explicit memory (e.g., Light & Singh, 1987; Light, Singh, & Capps, 1986; for a review, see Schacter, Kihlstrom, Kaszniak, & Valdiserri, 1993).

Dissociations between explicit and implicit memory can be observed even in normal subjects under normal laboratory conditions (for a review, see Roediger & McDermott, 1993). Thus, subjects can show savings in relearning items that they can neither recall nor recognize from a previous study trial (Nelson, 1978). Priming effects are unaffected by variables such as depth of processing during encoding that profoundly affect conscious recollection (e.g., Jacoby & Dallas, 1981). The study of implicit memory in normal subjects, especially as represented by repetition priming, is now a major enterprise within cognitive psychology (for reviews, see Graf & Masson, 1993; Lewandowsky, Dunn, & Kirsner, 1989; Roediger & McDermott, 1993). At the same time, the explicit/ implicit distinction has also been extended to other domains of cognition (Kihlstrom, 1987, 1990, 1999).

Implicit Learning

Perhaps the most familiar of these extensions (and one that actually predates the explicit/implicit distinction in memory) is the phenomenon of *implicit learning*, or one's acquisition of new patterns of behavior without being aware of the patterns themselves (for reviews, see Adams, 1957; Berry & Dienes, 1993; Dienes & Berry, 1997; Kihlstrom, 1996a; Neal & Hesketh, 1997; Reber, 1993; Seger, 1994). Implicit learning has been demonstrated by Reber's (1967) work on artificial grammars, in which subjects exposed to letter strings generated according to a complex rule system can classify new instances appropriately yet cannot articulate the rules that define the category. Lewicki (1986) has reported conceptually similar experiments involving social categorization and judgment. Similarly, experiments on the control of complex systems show that subjects can learn to manipulate inputs in order to control outputs, without being able to articulate the relations between them (e.g., Berry & Broadbent, 1984). Finally, subjects apparently can acquire the ability to predict forthcoming events even while they cannot specify the underlying sequential structure they have obviously learned (e.g., Lewicki, Czyzewska, & Hoffman, 1987; Nissen & Bullemer, 1987). Razran (1961) reported that subjects could acquire interoceptive conditioned responses without being aware of either the conditioned or unconditioned stimuli (also see Papka, Ivry, & Woodruff-Pak, 1996). In all these cases, and others, subjects have apparently learned without being aware of what they have learned.

Implicit memory has been accepted, but claims for implicit learning have been highly controversial (Adams, 1957; Dulany, 1997; Shanks & St. John, 1994). Reber (1967, 1993) has defined implicit learning as abstract, automatic, and unconscious; critics have seriously questioned all three assertions. Though questions concerning automaticity and representation are interesting, in the current context only awareness is relevant. We admit that the available evidence is not completely satisfying. For example, although most subjects in artificial grammar learning cannot articulate the entire Markov process by which the grammatical strings have been generated (Reber, 1967), above-chance classification performance could result from consciously accessible knowledge of legal letters, letter positions, or bigrams. Perhaps the best positive evidence is that the subjects believe they are behaving randomly. In artificial grammar learning, the relationship between accuracy and confidence is very weak (Dienes, Altman, Kwan, & Goode, 1995), whereas in sequence learning subjects rate their accurate predictions as guesses (Willingham, Greeley, & Bardone, 1993).

Implicit Perception

A somewhat more recent extension of the explicit/implicit distinction is to perception. By analogy to implicit memory, we can define *implicit perception* in terms of the effects of a *current* event (or an event in the very recent past) on one's performance, in the absence of conscious perception of that event (Kihlstrom, 1996a; Kihlstrom, Barnhardt, & Tataryn, 1992a). Implicit perception includes *subliminal perception*, also known as *preconscious processing* or *detectionless processing*, as illustrated by priming effects involving weak, brief, or masked stimulus presentations (e.g., Greenwald, Klinger, & Liu, 1989; Marcel, 1983; Merikle & Reingold, 1990; Pierce & Jastrow, 1885). It also covers priming effects observed in experiments involving parafoveal vision (e.g., Bargh & Pietromonaco, 1982; Underwood, 1976) and dichotic listening (Eich, 1984). In each case, the priming is produced by stimuli that can be construed as degraded below the level required for conscious perception.

During the recent history of psychology, claims for subliminal perception have been very controversial (e.g., Bruner & Klein, 1960; Dixon, 1971, 1981; Eriksen, 1960; Holender, 1986; Shanks & St. John, 1994), but the effect has now been demonstrated under conditions that should satisfy all but the most incorrigible critics (Greenwald et al., 1989; Greenwald, Draine, & Abrams, 1996; Greenwald, Klinger, & Schuh, 1995). However, truly subliminal processing seems to be analytically limited to perceptual, simple semantic analyses (Greenwald, 1992; Kihlstrom, 1993a, 1996a).

However, subliminal perception does not exhaust the category of implicit perception effects because priming and similar effects can be observed under conditions not easily classified as subliminal. A neurological case in point is *blindsight* (Weiskrantz, 1986): patient D.B. can make accurate judgments about the visual properties of objects he cannot see. Another example is *neglect* resulting from temporoparietal damage (Bisiach, 1993; Rafal, 1998): in at least some cases, the patient's behavior and judgments can be influenced by stimuli presented in the neglected portion of the visual field (Marshall & Halligan, 1988). Similar effects are observed in the functional anesthesias, such as "hysterical" blindness, associated with conversion disorder (Bryant & McConkey, 1989b) and in some phenomena of hypnosis, such as suggested blindness (Bryant & McConkey, 1989a) and deafness (Spanos, Jones, & Malfara, 1982). In these cases, the stimuli in question are clearly supraliminal, and even though they are not consciously perceived, they clearly influence the subject's experience, thought, and action. For this reason, Kihlstrom et al. (1992a) preferred to use "implicit" rather than "subliminal" perception, to underscore the central role of the subject's phenomenal awareness, as opposed to stimulus properties: the subjects are perceiving yet they are unaware of what they are perceiving. Implicit perception is typically revealed by the same sorts of tasks employed in studies of implicit memory, yet in implicit memory, the events in question were consciously perceived at the time they occurred. On these grounds, then, preserved priming following general anesthesia (Cork et al., 1997) might well be classified as implicit perception rather than implicit memory.

Implicit Thought

After memory, learning, and perception, the catalog of cognition naturally turns to thought. Though William James (1890/1980) characterized unconscious thought as a contradiction in terms, evidence for *implicit thought* is mounting (Dorfman, Shames, & Kihlstrom, 1996; Kihlstrom, Shames, & Dorfman, 1996). Like implicit memory, implicit thought may be said to occur when a thought—for example, the correct solution to a problem—influences experience, thought, or action even though one is unaware of the thought itself. Implicit thoughts may consist of ideas, beliefs, or images—any cognitive content, in fact, that is neither a percept (a representation of a current event) or a memory (a representation of a past event); they appear to be closely associated with the experiences of intuition, incubation, and insight, all hallmarks of creative problem solving.

The notion of implicit thought is exemplified in the research of Bowers and his associates, who showed how the correct solution to a difficult problem can influence choice behavior, even though the subject is not consciously aware of the solution itself (Bowers, 1984; Bowers, Farvolden, & Mermigis, 1995; Bowers, Regehr, Balthazard, & Parker, 1990). Their research involved an adaptation of the Remote Associates Test (Mednick, 1962), in which subjects are presented with two word triplets, one coherent and one incoherent. In the coherent triplet, the items are all associatively related to a single word (e.g., *playing, credit, report—card*), whereas in the incoherent triplet, there is no such relation (e.g., *still, pages, music*). The subjects' task is to inspect both triplets and give the solution to the coherent triplet (the target); if they cannot do so, they indicate only which triplet is coherent. Bowers et al. (1990, experiment 1) found that subjects could discriminate between coherent and incoherent triplets at better than chance levels, even when they could not name the target. They suggested that the subjects' choices reflected information processing outside of phenomenal awareness—something like the accretion of activation spreading from semantic memory nodes representing the elements of the coherent triplet to a node representing the target. In support of this idea, Shames (1994) found that unsolved but coherent triplets primed lexical decisions concerning their respective targets.

Other experiments also show that, even though subjects do not know the correct answer, subjects' intuitions about problems, choices, and judgments are not merely random guesses. For example, Bowers et al. (1990, experiment 2) showed that subjects could discriminate picture fragments that could, when properly assembled, represent familiar objects from those that could not—even though they were unable to tell what the objects were. Durso and his colleagues were able to trace changes in cognitive structure as subjects approached the solution to a problem, even though they had not reached the solution itself (Durso, Rea, & Dayton, 1994). And Bechara and colleagues found that subjects' skin-conductance responses and choice behaviors differed when they were presented with ''good'' and ''bad'' decks of cards in a gambling game, even though they could not describe the difference (Bechara, Damasio, Damasio, & Anderson, 1994; Bechara, Damasio, Tranel, & Damasio, 1997; Bechara, Tranel, Damasio, & Damasio, 1996). These results lead to the proposition that thoughts, in the form of ideas, images, biases, and the like, can guide behavior even when we are unaware of them.

THE TRILOGY OF MIND

These four categories of phenomena—memory, learning, perception, and thought—constitute the cognitive unconscious (Kihlstrom, 1987, 1999; Rozin, 1976). But cognition is not all there is to mental life. At least since the nineteenth century, many psychologists and philosophers of mind have divided mental life into three broad faculties, including emotion and motivation as well as cognition (for a review, see Hilgard, 1980). This idea began with Christian Wolfe (1679–1754), who brought the term *psychology* into common use and who classified the mind into the *facultus cognoscitova* (knowledge) and the *facultus appetiva* (desire). Moses Mendelsohn (1729–1786) added affect (emotion) to the list. The tripartite classification of mental faculties was consolidated by the philosopher Immanuel Kant (1724–1804), who wrote in his *Critique of Judgment* that "there are three absolutely irreducible faculties of the mind, namely, knowledge, feeling, and desire" (Watson, 1888, p. 311). Kant meant that emotion and motivation exist in some sense independently of cognition and of each other. This position contrasts with the idea, still popular in psychology, that emotional and motivational states are cognitive constructions—*beliefs* about what one feels (Schachter & Singer, 1962) or wants (Lepper, Greene, & Nisbett, 1973). Kant's three independent mental faculties reappear in Hilgard's (1980) *trilogy of mind*: cognition, the mental representation of reality through perception, attention, learning, memory, and thought; emotion, the subjective experience of arousal, pleasure, and displeasure, and their expression in behavior; and motivation, the activation of behavior and its direction toward a goal. All three of these mental states affect the determination of behavior.

One usually thinks of the cognitive, emotional, and motivational processes that underlie action in terms of conscious mental states. Aware of what one thinks, feels, and desires, one acts accordingly. But here we have already concluded that cognitive states such as percepts, memories, and thoughts can affect behavior outside of awareness. If cognitive states of perception, memory, and thought can be unconscious, or implicit, can emotional states be unconscious, or implicit, as well?

THE FREUDIAN MODEL

What might implicit emotion look like? Perhaps it resembles Sigmund Freud's vision of unconscious mental life (for a detailed analysis of Freud's theory of psychoanalysis, see Macmillan, 1996). Freud (1916–1917/1963, 1933/1964) asserted that people are affected by emotional or motivational states of which they are not consciously aware. Later, when they reflect on their behavior (or perhaps after they have undergone psychoanalysis), they realize their true feelings and motives. But that insight has the character of an inference, rather than an introspection, and they were never consciously aware of their feelings or desires at the time they acted on them. So the classic Freudian defense mechanisms (A. Freud, 1936/1966; S. Freud, 1926/1959) are all designed to render a person unaware of his or her true emotions. In reaction formation, we profess love but really feel hate; in displacement, we declare hatred of one person, when we really hate another person entirely; in intellectualization and rationalization, our behavior is stripped of all of its emotional connections entirely. Freud claimed that our behavior manifests our true emotions, even if they were not represented in consciousness.

Suppes and Warren (1975) have proposed a mathematical model of the transformations involved in the Freudian defense mechanisms. They begin with a propositional representation of unconscious affect—of an actor, an action, and an object (x) of the action—as in the prototypic Freudian emotional self-disclosure:

I (actor) *love* (action) *my mother* (object *x*).

They further show that some forty-four different defense mechanisms, including all those included in the standard list, can be produced by just eight transformations applied to the actor, the action, or the object, alone or in combination— for example, the transformation of self to other, of an action into its opposite, or from object *x* to object *y*.

Thus, displacement retains the original actor and action, but changes the object from *x* to *y*: *I love my father.* In reaction formation, the actor and object remain constant, but the action is changed into its opposite: *I hate my mother.* In projection, the action and the object remain constant, but the actor is changed: *Saddam Hussein loves my mother.* Applying all three transformations, we obtain *Saddam Hussein hates my father.* This glib and vulgar Freudianism nicely illustrates the essential process by which the defense mechanisms render the actual emotional and motivational determinants of our behavior inaccessible to phenomenal awareness.

Of course, one need not embrace the whole conceptual panoply of classical (or even neofreudian) psychoanalysis: the division of the mind into id, ego, and superego; the theory of infantile sexuality; the stages of psychosexual development; repression, and so forth. And one certainly need not trace all of one's emotional life to primitive sexual and aggressive instincts. The emotions whose conscious representations pertain can be represented by the everyday concepts of folk psychology, as reflected in the affect circumplex (Russell, 1980; Watson & Tellegen, 1985), Murray's (1938) list of needs, and similar ideas. Significantly, Suppes and Warren (1975) suggest two basic ways in which the emotional unconscious can be expressed: (1) when the original emotion is represented consciously but one is unconscious of the source of that emotion, as in displacement and projection; and (2) when the emotion itself is denied conscious representation, as in reaction formation, intellectualization, and denial.

EMOTION AS AN EXPRESSION OF IMPLICIT COGNITION

In the emotional unconscious, one may be consciously aware of his or her emotional state yet unaware of its source in current or past experience. The

Roman poet and epigrammatist Martial had this concept in mind when he wrote *Epigrammata* (book 1, no. 32, freely translated by the seventeenth-century English satirical poet Thomas Brown; see Hayward, 1927):

Non amo te, Sabidi,	I do not love you Dr. Fell,
Nec possum dicere quare:	but why I cannot tell;
Hoc tantum possum dicere,	But this I know full well,
Non amo te.	I do not love you, Dr. Fell.

Compare Breuer and Freud (1893–1895/1957) in their *Studies on Hysteria*:

Hysterics suffer mainly from reminiscences. . . . [But in] the great majority of cases it is not possible to establish the point of origin by a simple interrogation of the patient, however thoroughly it may be carried out. . . . principally because he is genuinely unable to recollect it and often has no suspicion of the causal connection between the precipitating event and the pathological phenomenon. (pp. 7, 3)

For Breuer and Freud's unconscious (or repressed) memories, we can substitute implicit ones (for a fuller discussion, see Kihlstrom, 1997b). Thus, a conscious emotional state may serve as an index of implicit perception or memory. Even though one consciously experiences the emotional states themselves, these phenomena of implicit perception and memory deserve to be included in the emotional unconscious.

Emotion as an Expression of Implicit Memory

In a classic demonstration of what we now call spared implicit memory in organic amnesia, Claparede (1911/1951) pricked an unsuspecting Korsakoff's syndrome patient with a pin hidden in his hand and caused her quite a bit of distress. Claparede subsequently left the room and returned after the patient had regained her composure. During questioning, she failed to recognize Claparede and had no recollection of the unfortunate incident. Nevertheless, she refused to shake his hand. When asked why, she replied, "Sometimes people hide pins in their hands." The story illustrates the phenomenon of *source amnesia* familiar in studies of memory (see Kihlstrom, 1995a). But if the prospect of shaking hands made the patient nervous as well, her refusal suggests a dissociation between conscious awareness of an emotional state, which she probably experienced, and conscious recollection of the origins of that state in experience, which she evidently did not.

In a case of hysterical somnambulism reported by Janet (1893, 1904; see Nemiah, 1979), Madame D. suffered a breakdown after some men jokingly deposited her drunken husband on her doorstep and announced that he was dead.

Afterward, the woman had no conscious recollection of the event. But whenever she passed by her front door, she froze with terror. Moreover, she complained of dreams in which her husband was brought home dead. Here again is an example of an emotional state (terror and distress about the dreams) and emotional behavior (freezing, as well as the nightmares) but no awareness of why they occur.

A third example comes from a case of fear of running water reported by Bagby (1928). The patient had no memory of the circumstances under which this intense emotional reaction had been acquired. However, the mystery was solved when the patient was visited by an aunt who said, as an aside, "I have never told." It turned out that when the patient, as a child, had gone on a picnic with the aunt she had disobeyed instructions, strayed into a nearby creek, and become trapped under a waterfall. The child was rescued by the aunt, who promised to keep her transgression a secret. Apparently, the child lost the memory of the incident, perhaps due to a process like repression or dissociation, perhaps merely to childhood amnesia or ordinary forgetting, but the phobia remained solidly entrenched. In this case, the symptom appears to be an implicit memory for an incident lost to explicit memory.

The evidence for emotion as implicit memory is not limited to anecdote (Tobias, Kihlstrom, & Schacter, 1990). Several formal studies also demonstrate that emotional responses can persist even though one does not know how they originated. A study by Johnson, Kim, and Risse (1985) used the *mere exposure effect* on preferences (Zajonc, 1968): repeated exposure to an object tends to increase judgments of likability, even if no substantive information supports such attitudinal change. Johnson and her colleagues exposed Korsakoff patients (who are amnesic as a result of damage to diencephalic structures) and controls to unfamiliar Korean melodies. Some melodies were played only once during the study phase, whereas others were played five or ten times. Later, the subjects heard these melodies, and other Korean melodies that were entirely new, and were asked to indicate which they preferred. As one would expect from the mere exposure effect, both Korsakoff patients and controls preferred old rather than new melodies, although there was no effect of the number of exposures to the old tunes. However, compared to the controls, the patients showed greatly impaired levels of recognition. Thus, exposure affected the amnesic patients' preference judgments, an index of emotional response to the melodies, even though the patients could not remember the exposure trials.

A second study by Johnson et al. (1985) provided subjects with more substantive contact with the stimulus materials. The same amnesic and control patients who served in the melodies study were presented with pictures of two male faces, accompanied by fictional biographical information that depicted one individual positively (the "good guy") and the other negatively (the "bad guy"). When asked whom they preferred, control subjects always chose the face that had been paired with the positive information, and they were always able to say that they judged on the basis of the accompanying descriptive information. The amnesic patients also showed a strong (though not unanimous) preference for the good guy; however, they could recall only a little of the biographical material presented at the time of study. Again, information presented during the study phase altered some aspect of emotional response—liking of persons instead of melodies—even though patients could not consciously recall the description.

Unfortunately, another group of investigators failed to obtain the mere exposure effect in a mixed group of amnesic patients who were repeatedly exposed to photographs of faces (Redington, Volpe, & Gazzaniga, 1984). Perhaps the exposure effect on preferences is not always dissociable from explicit memory. However, Johnson and Multhaup (1992) essentially confirmed the findings of Johnson et al. (1985) with a new sample of amnesic patients. In the melodies experiment, amnesic patients preferred old melodies to new ones, but controls did not; controls remembered the melodies well, but amnesics did not. In the impression formation experiment, both amnesics and controls preferred the "good guy" to the "bad" one, even though the amnesics recalled very little of the biographical information presented at the time of study.

The dissociation between acquired emotional preferences and explicit memory was confirmed in an experimental case study with a patient called Boswell, who became densely amnesic following a case of herpes encephalitis (Damasio, Tranel, & Damasio, 1989). Despite a profound inability to recognize people, Boswell would go to a particularly generous staff member if he wanted something. In the experiment, Boswell had an extended series of positive, negative, and neutral encounters, respectively, with three different confederates. After questioning, Boswell was unable to recall anything about any of the people and never indicated that they were familiar in any way. Nonetheless, when asked on a forced-choice test whom he liked best, and would approach for rewards and favors, he strongly preferred the "good" confederate to the "bad" one, with the neutral confederate in between.

In addition to the disorders of memory produced by lesions to specific brain structures, there are also functional disorders of memory observed in the dissociative syndromes of psychogenic amnesia, psychogenic fugue, and multiple personality disorder. Interestingly, patients with functional amnesias often display implicit memory for events lost to conscious recollection: sometimes this implicit memory takes the form of an emotional response. For example, in a case Kaszniak and his colleagues reported, a victim of attempted homosexual rape forgot the incident but experienced severe distress when shown a TAT card picturing a person attacking another from behind (Kaszniak, Nussbaum, Berren, & Santiago, 1988). Similarly, Christianson and Nilsson (1989) observed that a woman who had suffered severe amnesia following assault and rape became extremely upset when she returned to the scene of the crime, even though she had no explicit memory of the event. Finally, in Prince's (1910) case of Miss Beauchamp, a multiple personality, one alter ego, "B-IV," experienced strong emotional reactions to people and places that had emotional meaning to personality "B-I" and vice versa; however, neither personality had explicit memory of the emotionally arousing objects for the other, and each would be puzzled by her inexplicably intense reactions to such stimuli. Similar dissociations of affect from awareness have been reported in "split brain" patients (Gazzaniga, 1985; LeDoux, Wilson, & Gazzaniga, 1977; Sperry, Gazzaniga, & Bogen, 1969).

Amnesia for the source of a consciously experienced emotion is also a familiar phenomenon in hypnosis. Whereas hypnotic suggestions are typically intended to alter some aspect of cognitive functioning, they can also have emotional and motivational effects (see Kihlstrom & Hoyt, 1988, 1990). When these suggestions are accompanied by further suggestions for amnesia, the subject can experience a profound change in mood state, without knowing why. For example, Luria (1932) suggested to hypnotized subjects that they had committed a terrible crime and then covered this paramnesia with a further suggestion for posthypnotic amnesia. On a later word-association test, the subjects showed evidence of anxiety in response to cues related to the suggested crime, even though they had forgotten the suggestion. Luria's findings were essentially replicated by Huston, Shakow, and Erickson (1934).

In a related line of hypnosis research, Levitt (1967; Levitt & Chapman, 1979) administered direct suggestions for anxiety to hypnotic subjects, followed by a suggestion for posthypnotic amnesia. Even though the subjects could not consciously remember the suggestion, they displayed elevated levels of anxiety on various test measures. Blum's (1979) research revealed similar findings; subjects received suggestions to relive a conflictual, ego-threatening experience from early childhood and then a suggestion for posthypnotic amnesia covering the experience. According to Blum, the subject then experienced free-floating anxiety not tied to any hypnotic or childhood experience.

More recently, Bower and his colleagues (Bower, 1981; Bower, Gilligan, & Monteiro, 1981; Bower, Monteiro, & Gilligan, 1978) used a variant on Luria's technique to study mood dependent memory. In these experiments, hypnotized subjects were given suggestions to relive a particularly happy or sad experience from their past and further given posthypnotic suggestions to experience those happy and sad emotional states, stripped of cognitive content about the instigating event, in response to particular cues. The suggestion was further covered by one for posthypnotic amnesia. Thus, during the experiment proper the subjects felt happy or sad without being aware that this response had been suggested to them previously or that it was distantly related to some previous experience in their lives.

The studies just described seem to demonstrate that emotional response can serve as an index of implicit memory. That is, subjects can display emotional responses attributable to some event in their past that they do not remember. However, the evidence in this regard is rather sparse, especially when compared to the vast body of literature on the perceptual and cognitive expressions of implicit memory (e.g., Roediger & McDermott, 1990; Schacter, 1987). Systematic studies need to include both amnesic patients and normal subjects to test the hypothesis that emotional response, as an expression of implicit memory, can be dissociated from conscious recollection.

Emotion as an Expression of Implicit Perception

There is considerably better evidence for emotion as an index of *implicit perception*—that is to say, when one's emotional responses are attributable to some event in the current environment that one does not consciously perceive. Once more we begin with anecdote and proceed to formal studies.

Levinson (1965) reported on a woman who came out of surgery inexplicably weepy, depressed, and disconsolate. The reasons for this state remained obscure until Levinson, on a hunch, hypnotized the patient and regressed her to the time of the surgery she then blurted out, "The surgeon says it might be malignant!" Further investigation revealed that the doctors had discovered a possible malignancy during the surgery and had discussed it while she was anesthetized (subsequent investigation proved it to be benign). Adequate anesthesia, by definition, abolishes conscious awareness and thus explicit memory of surgical events. But, as we said earlier, there is some evidence for the preservation of priming effects. Apparently, implicit perception during anesthesia can appear not just in the form of repetition priming effects but also in terms of full-blown emotional states.

More recently, Traub-Werner (1989) reported on an unusual case of simultaneous panic attacks in two agoraphobic patients. The first patient's symptoms had been well controlled by clonazepam and amitryptyline; but one day, while she was washing her face, she unexpectedly experienced anxiety, fear of falling, palpitations, and depersonalization. She hid under the bed for several minutes, until she felt better. Later that day, she received a phone call from a friend, also agoraphobic, who reported her worst panic attack in years—at precisely the same time of day. Further investigation revealed that an earthquake, registering magnitude 6 on the Richter scale, had occurred not far away at exactly the time of the two patients' panic episodes. In fact, an associated earth tremor, too weak to be consciously felt but perhaps picked up by the vestibular system, may have evoked anxiety in the first patient.

Evidence of emotion as an index of implicit perception has emerged in research on *subliminal mere exposure effects*. Recall Zajonc's (1968) discovery that mere exposure is sufficient to increase judgments of likability, an arguably affective response, and the evidence from Johnson et al. (1985) and Damasio et al. (1989) that the exposure need not be consciously remembered to affect emotion (see Moreland & Zajonc, 1977, 1979; but also see Birnbaum & Mellers, 1979a, 1979b). Interestingly, apparently the exposure need not be consciously *perceived*, either. For example, Wilson (1979) found that subjects preferred tones presented on the unattended channel during a dichotic listening procedure to tones previously unpresented. Similarly, Kunst-Wilson and Zajonc (1980) presented subjects a set of irregular polygons on a tachistoscope, with exposures so brief that the stimuli were not consciously perceived; nevertheless, rated preference was affected by prior exposure history (for an alternative interpretation, see Mandler, Nakamura, & Van Zandt, 1987).

This subliminal mere exposure effect has been replicated and extended by a number of investigators (e.g., Bonnano & Stillings, 1986; Murphy & Zajonc, 1993; Seamon, Brody, & Kauff, 1983a, 1983b; for reviews, see Bornstein, 1989, 1992). In perhaps the most dramatic extension of the Kunst-Wilson and Zajonc (1980) study, Bornstein and his colleagues found that subliminal exposures can affect not only subjects' preferences for people's faces but also their interpersonal behavior toward those people when they actually meet them later (Bornstein, Leone, & Galley, 1987). Subjects who were subliminally exposed to a picture of a confederate during the study phase were more likely to express agreement with that confederate on a judgment task. However, testing of a separate group of subjects indicated that recognition of the "old" confederate achieved only chance levels, indicating that the faces had not been consciously perceived during the study phase. In fact, a meta-analysis by Bornstein (1989) found that the magnitude of the mere exposure effect was significantly greater with subliminal than with supraliminal stimuli. Apparently, affective judgments are influenced by perceptual fluency, which in turn is enhanced by the priming effects of the subject's initial exposure to the material. When subjects consciously remember the prior exposure, they appear to correct their preference ratings accordingly; but when the initial exposure is subliminal, so that subjects do not consciously perceive (much less consciously remember) it, subjects are unable to engage in discounting, resulting in a stronger effect on preference judgments (Bornstein, 1992; Bornstein & D'Agostino, 1992, 1994; also see Klinger & Greenwald, 1994).

Other investigators have found similar sorts of effects, when subliminal or unattended stimuli have "emotional"effects on judgments and behavior. For example, Murphy and Zajonc (1993) found, like Bornstein (1989), that subliminal exposure to emotional faces produced increased liking and preference for Chinese ideographs. In their view, the familiarity produced by subliminal exposure created diffuse positive feelings like (though different in valence from) the free-floating anxiety of the clinical concept.

Of course, considerable early evidence for emotion as implicit perception was provided by investigations of perceptual defense, subception, and other aspects of the "New Look" (Bruner & Klein, 1960; also see Erdelyi, 1974; Greenwald, 1992; Kihlstrom et al., 1992a, 1992b). Bargh and Pietromonaco (1982) found that subjects who had been exposed to hostile words followed by a masking stimulus attributed significantly more negative qualities to a pictured person than subjects who had not received this masked exposure (also see Bargh, Bond, Lombardi, & Tota, 1986). Similarly, Devine (1989) found that unmasked parafoveal presentation of words related to negative stereotypes of African-Americans led to more negative evaluations of a target person whose race was unspecified.

Niedenthal and her colleagues (1990, 1992; Niedenthal, Setterlund, & Jones, 1994) have produced yet another emotional adaptation of the basic subliminal priming paradigm. In the study phase of each experiment, briefly presented primes consisting of faces expressing emotions of joy or disgust were rendered subliminal by a metacontrasting presentation of clearly supraliminal cartoon figures. In the test phase, the subjects were asked to discriminate between old, previously presented cartoons and new distractors. These were also preceded by a face prime, which again was rendered subliminal by metacontrast. On half the test trials, the affect associated with the prime was the same as it had been in the study trials; for the remainder, the prime was drawn from the opposite emotional category. Congruence between the primes generally facilitated recognition of the targets, especially when the prime was negative. A second study, in which emotionally charged faces or scenes primed emotionally neutral women's faces, obtained essentially the same effect. Moreover, the affective valence of the prime influenced the subjects' interpretations of the target's emotional state. Based on research indicating that the perception of emotionally expressive faces induces a similar emotional state in the perceiver, Niedenthal and Showers (1991) have proposed that a subliminal emotional prime elicits a corresponding emotional state in the perceiver; this state then serves as a cue for both perceptual identification and recognition memory. It is also, therefore, an expression of implicit perception.

Additional evidence that subliminal emotional primes actually elicit conscious feeling states comes from Ohman and his colleagues' research on subliminal fear conditioning (for a review, see Ohman, 1999). In one line of research (Ohman, Dimberg, & Esteves, 1989), subjects were conditioned to associate an electric shock with presentation of an angry face (an unreinforced happy face served as a control stimulus). In subsequent unreinforced test trials, the angry face was masked by a neutral face. Even though subjects could not consciously perceive the angry face, they gave conditioned electrodermal responses when it was presented, not during masked presentation of the happy face. A subsequent pilot study showed that acquisition of a conditioned fear response is possible, even when the conditioned stimulus is masked and therefore not consciously perceptible. In another line of research, Ohman and Soares (1993, 1994, 1998) substituted nonmasked pictures of snakes, spiders, flowers, and mushrooms as conditioned stimuli. In unreinforced test trials, masked pictures of snakes and spiders elicited conditioned electrodermal fear responses, but masked pictures of flowers and mushrooms did not. The researchers interpreted the fear responses to the snake and spider pictures within the framework of Seligman's (1971) preparedness theory of phobias, which claims that, because of our evolutionary history, some stimuli (such as snakes and spiders) automatically initiate rapid and long-lasting conditioned fear responses. In this case, the assumption of automaticity of the association seems valid because the fear response persists even when the fear stimulus is subliminal, and thus unattended.

To date, Greenwald and his colleagues (Greenwald et al., 1989, 1995, 1996) have conducted the most systematic exploration of preconscious emotional processing. These studies examine another emotional response—evaluative judgments of words—and are especially notable because they carefully address methodological criticisms of earlier studies purporting to demonstrate subliminal perception (e.g., Eriksen, 1960; Holender, 1986). In all the experiments of the series, subjects are asked to judge an aspect of the connotative meaning of a word: whether it is affectively positive or negative. In the earliest experiments, the target word was preceded by a prime word that was either affectively positive or negative. The prime was so effectively masked that subjects were unable to determine whether it appeared on the left or the right side of a fixation point. Nevertheless, evaluative judgments of the target were facilitated by primes drawn from the same affective category. More recently, Greenwald et al. (1996) added a further refinement, in which subjects judged the target within a very brief period of time following its presentation, further ensuring that the influence of the prime on the target judgment was not the product of conscious reflection.

On the basis of early studies showing a dissociation between preference judgments and conscious recollection (Moreland & Zajonc, 1977) and conscious perception (Kunst-Wilson & Zajonc, 1980), Zajonc (1980, 1984a, 1984b) maintained that emotional processing is independent of, and temporally prior to, cognitive processing (also see Lazarus, 1982, 1984). However, later studies documenting similar dissociations between explicit and implicit expressions of memory (e.g., Schacter, 1987) and perception (e.g., Kihlstrom et al., 1992a) shed new light on the early results. One might just as well conclude that dissociations between recall and priming show that memory *itself* is independent of, and temporally prior to, cognitive processing. It is now clear that, in the early studies and those that followed, some aspect of emotional response is serving as an implicit expression of perception or memory. But unconscious cognition is still cognition. Furthermore, an emotional system separate from cognition would still need the cognitive capacity to analyze stimuli, link them to prior knowledge, and generate emotional feelings and expressions (Leventhal, 1980, 1984). Such cognitive processes can go on outside of awareness, so that changes in evaluative judgment and other aspects of emotional response can be dissociated from explicit perception and memory; this process forms one aspect of the emotional unconscious. People can be aware of their emotional states but unaware of the percepts and memories that evoke these states.

"Feeling Memories": A Cautionary Note

Clinical folklore about posttraumatic stress disorder has revived the idea, originated by Breuer and Freud (1893–1895/1957), that unconscious memories of trauma express themselves implicitly as intrusive feelings (Bass & Davis, 1988; Blume, 1990; Frederickson, 1993; Herman, 1992; Terr, 1994; van der Kolk, McFarlane, & Weisaeth, 1996; for a detailed analysis of the parallels between Freud's theories and later clinical practices, see Bowers & Farvolden, 1996; Crews, 1995; Kihlstrom, 1996b, 1997b, 1998b). For example, Frederickson (1993) has distinguished between a conscious *recall memory* and an unconscious *feeling memory*:

> *Feeling memory* is the memory of an emotional response to a particular situation. If the situation we are being triggered to remember is a repressed memory, we will have the feelings pertaining to the event without any conscious recall of the event itself. Feeling memory is often experienced as a flood of inexplicable emotion, particularly around abuse issues. . . . A felt sense that something abusive has happened is a common form of a feeling memory. Some survivors will say, "Yes, I think I was sexually abused, but it's just a gut feeling." These clients are experiencing a feeling memory about being abused, even though at that moment they can recall nothing about their abuse. (p.92)

In some respects, the concept of a "feeling memory" finds support in the literature reviewed in this section, which indicates that emotional responses can indeed serve as expressions of implicit memory. However, there is an important difference: the experimental literature we have reviewed provides independent corroboration of the emotion-eliciting event. Implicit memory may be inferred only when such evidence is available, yet such information is rarely available in clinical practice. Nevertheless, clinical practitioners may infer a history of prior trauma and abuse from a patient's current emotional symptoms and then engage in therapeutic practices intended to recover the traumatic memories and restore them to conscious accessibility. Of course, if one cannot objectively corroborate the patient's history, such inferences are tautological and should be avoided—the techniques used to recover ostensibly lost memories are highly suggestive and may lead patients to reconstruct distorted or false memories of trauma and abuse (Kihlstrom, 1996b, 1998b; Lindsay & Read, 1994, 1995; Shobe & Kihlstrom, in press).

IMPLICIT EMOTION

But can people be unaware of their emotional states themselves? The proposition seems to contain an internal contradiction, because emotions must be felt, and feeling is by any ordinary definition a conscious experience (Clore, 1994). But environmental stimuli must be felt, too; yet cognitive psychology and cognitive neuroscience are gradually accepting that percepts can be unconscious (Greenwald et al., 1996; Kihlstrom et al., 1992a), just as they earlier agreed that memories can be unconscious (Roediger & McDermott, 1990; Schacter, 1987). If there is a cognitive unconscious, in which percepts, memories, and thoughts influence experience, thought, and action outside of phenomenal awareness, then why can there not be an emotional unconscious as well? The answer depends on how one defines emotion. If emotion is a conscious feeling state, an emotional unconscious is precluded. But if one defines emotion differently, the question could be answered through empirical evidence.

Desynchrony

In classic research on experimental neurosis in dogs, Gantt (1937, 1953) observed that separate components of a conditioned fear response could be acquired and extinguished at different rates and persist for different lengths of time, resulting in an organismic state of *schizokinesis* reflecting the "disharmony or cleavage in behavioral, somatic, and psychophysiological response systems" (Mineka, 1979, p. 987). The clear implication of Gantt's work is a multifaceted emotional response, whose facets can be separated, or dissociated, from each other.

Gantt's observations have been confirmed in more recent research on fear conditioning. For example, Mineka (1979) distinguished four quite different response systems that have been used in the study of fear conditioning in non-human animals: conditioned emotional responses, increased rate of conditioned avoidance response, passive avoidance, and conditioned heart rate. Further, she showed that these indices of fear could be dissociated from learned avoidance behavior. Animals can behave as if they are afraid, even if they do not appear to manifest fear according to standard laboratory measures (also see Mineka, 1985a, 1985b, 1992). One interpretation of such findings is that, contrary to Mowrer's (1947) two-process theory, avoidance learning is not motivated by fear. Another is that the subjective experience of fear is only one component of a broader emotional response to fear stimuli. Similar observations have been made in the case of human fears and phobias. For example, in a study of systematic desensitization of snake phobia, Lang and Lazovik (1963) found that some subjects would show substantial changes in avoidance behavior, while still expressing fear of the snake; other subjects would deny fear of the snake but show elevated cardiovascular activity and persisting avoidance behavior.

Based on observations such as these, Lang (1968, 1971, 1978, 1988; Lang, Rice, & Sternbach, 1972) proposed a *multiple-system theory of emotion*. According to this theory, every emotional response consists of several components: verbal-cognitive, corresponding to subjective feeling state (e.g., fear); overt motor, or behavioral, response (e.g., escape or avoidance); and a covert physiological response mediated by the autonomic and skeletal nervous systems (e.g., skin conductance or heart rate). Lang further proposed that these three systems are partially independent, although they also interact with each other in important ways. When all three systems act together, a person experiences intense emotional arousal. Under circumstances of attenuated emotion, however, the correlations among these systems tend to break apart, as their individual levels of activity diminish.

Moreover, Lang proposed that the different components of emotion can have different developmental histories. For example, autonomic responses to emotional stimuli may appear early in development, with the behavioral and cognitive responses emerging only later. Or, alternatively, the cognitive component of an emotional state can be acquired first, as, for example, through the social learning of fear, with the behavioral and physiological components coming later, if at all. Lang further suggested that effective psychotherapy for anxiety states and other emotional disorders should be directed at all three components: one cannot assume, for example, that flooding directed at reducing compulsive behavior will necessarily reduce subjective anxiety and physiological arousal as well.

Rachman and Hodgson (1974; Hodgson & Rachman, 1974; Rachman, 1978, 1981, 1990) adopted Lang's theme and explored the implications of *desynchrony* among emotional systems, especially between overt behavior and covert physiology, for the treatment of anxiety disorders. They proposed that different forms of treatment would have different effects on the components of fear and anxiety: for example, flooding might reduce avoidance behavior but leave autonomic arousal largely intact; on the other hand, spontaneous remission would affect autonomic arousal first, but behavioral avoidance would persist for a longer period of time. Like Lang (1968), Rachman and Hodgson believed that fear and anxiety should be assessed in terms of all three components and that treatment should be directed toward the most "abnormal" component (also see Norton, DiNardo, & Barlow, 1983). Somehow, however, the remaining components would eventually catch up. If one component persisted unchanged, in this view, the likelihood of relapse remained high.

The general idea of desynchrony is that an emotional response can be manifest at one level but not at another (Hugdahl, 1981; Turpin, 1991). Given that Lang (1968) and Rachman (1978) were writing from a tradition of behavior therapy that emphasizes objective measurement, it is perhaps natural, and certainly understandable, that both focused on desynchrony between the behavioral and physiological components of emotion. However, here we are most interested in cases that represent the emotional analog of the explicit/implicit distinction in memory: when the subjective component of an emotion (conscious feeling state) is absent, while the behavioral and physiological components persist outside of phenomenal awareness. The snake phobic denies fear but somehow never quite manages to go near the reptile house at the zoo; the agoraphobic claims to be cured and even ventures outside the house, but blood pressure and heart rate still increase dramatically. If such observations reflected merely denial, or a flight into health, they would not be too interesting. But suppose that the patients' reports accurately reflect the subjective state of affairs—that they really do not experience the emotions that used to bother them. If the behavioral and autonomic signs of emotion persist unabated, why can we not say that they are displaying unconscious emotion—or at least an unconscious emotional response?

Apparently, dissociations between subjective feelings and covert psychophysiological response are found quite commonly in the anxiety disorders (e.g., Barlow, Mavissakalian, & Schofield, 1980; Craske, Sanderson, & Barlow, 1987; Vermilyea, Boice, & Barlow, 1984; for reviews, see Barlow, 1988; Rachman, 1990). Indeed, such findings were a primary motive for Lang's proposal of the multiple-systems theory of emotion (Lang & Lazovik, 1963). Cardiology clinics frequently encounter patients who complain of behavioral and physiological symptoms associated with panic disorder yet report no subjective fear or distress, aside from concern about the presenting complaints themselves (Beitman, Mukerji, Russell, & Grafing, 1993; Kushner & Beitman, 1990). Similar patients have been seen in neurology clinics (Russell, Kushner, Beitman, & Bartels, 1991). A survey of students with a history of panic attacks found that those who reported "fearless" panic attacks were less likely to engage in avoidance behavior or to use alcohol or drugs as coping strategies.

Some evidence for desynchrony between subjective experience and covert psychophysiology is also provided in the literature on child-parent attachment. Dozier and Kobak (1992) administered an attachment interview in which subjects were asked to express their feelings about imagined scenarios involving separation from their parents. Subjects scoring high on a dimension of *deactivation/hyperactivation*, who strategically divert attention from thoughts, memories, and feelings related to attachment, showed greater skin conductance responses to scenarios involving parental separation, rejection, threats of separation, and changes in relationship with the parents.

Unfortunately, dissociations between subjective feelings and overt behavioral response appear to be much less common (e.g., Lang, Lazovik, & Reynolds, 1965). Moreover, evaluations of treatment outcome typically indicate that cognitive subjective fear persists even as behavioral and psychophysiological indices of fear diminish—precisely the opposite of the pattern of desynchrony implied by the concept of implicit emotion (Gerew, Romney, & LeBoef, 1989; Lang & Lazovik, 1963; Thomas & Rapp, 1977).

The emotional deficits (e.g., "blunted" or "inappropriate" affect) commonly associated with schizophrenia also suggest desynchrony (Dworkin, 1992). Thus, *anhedonia* refers to a deficit in the conscious experience of emotion, which may leave behavioral or physiological expressions of emotion unimpaired. Similarly, *flat affect* refers to a deficit in the behavioral expression or display of emotion, which may not extend to subjective experience or covert physiology. In fact, Kring and colleagues (Kring, Kerr, Smith, & Neale, 1993; Kring & Neale, 1996) found that schizophrenic patients expressed significantly less emotion than normal controls in response to emotional film clips; however, self-reports of emotional experience were similar for both groups, and the schizophrenics actually showed greater skin conductance reactivity. Obviously, this is not the desynchrony implied by the concept of implicit emotion.

Individual Differences in Emotional Experience and Expression

A lack of awareness of emotion may be implicated in several individual differences, the most obvious of which is repression. Though conceived by Freud as a general psychological process available to everyone, repression used as a defense may be reconstrued as an individual difference variable, as Rosenzweig did in his work on the Zeigarnik effect in memory and in his exploration of the personality correlates of hypnotizability (Rosenzweig, 1938; Rosenzweig & Mason, 1934; Rosenzweig & Sarason, 1942; Sarason & Rosenzweig, 1942). Unfortunately, early attempts to measure individual differences in repressive tendency through questionnaires, as exemplified by Byrne's (1961, 1964) Repression-Sensitization Scale (RSS; Bell & Byrne, 1978), failed because of discriminant validity: somewhat paradoxically, perhaps, repression as measured by the RSS proved to be highly correlated with anxiety and distress. However, other measurement approaches may prove more useful in explaining the differences between explicit and implicit emotion.

Repressive coping style. Weinberger and his associates have attempted to construct a measurement of repressive coping style that is free of such confounds (Weinberger, 1990; Weinberger, Schwartz, & Davidson, 1979). In Weinberger's original procedure in 1979, subjects who showed extremely low levels of trait anxiety, as shown on Taylor's Manifest Anxiety Scale (MAS; Taylor, 1953), but extremely high levels of defensiveness, as shown by the Marlowe-Crowne Social Desirability Scale (SDS; Crowne & Marlowe, 1960), are "repressors." Though repressors do report low levels of anxiety, Weinberger et al. found that they showed elevated levels of physiological response—EMG, heart rate, and galvanic skin resistance—to sexual and aggressive phrase stems. In fact, their levels of physiological reactivity were comparable to those for high-anxious, nondefensive subjects. Asendorpf and Scherer (1983) later confirmed the majority of these results. Consequently, one might want to speculate that repressors have a talent for desynchrony: they may not display high levels of stress to others, or even experience it themselves; but, at the same time, their physiology is humming anxiously. This situation may be construed as a dissociation between explicit (subjective) and implicit (behavioral or physiological) components of emotion.

Unfortunately, however, no one has followed up this early evidence of implicit emotion. Instead, research has focused on the development of new methods for assessing repression and on repression as a risk factor for medical complaints. Thus, Weinberger (1990, 1997; Weinberger & Schwartz, 1990) reformulated the concept of repressive tendency and introduced a new instrument, the Weinberger Adjustment Inventory (WAI), for measuring individual differences in repressive coping style. The WAI follows the same logic as the earlier procedure, but yields six categories instead of the original fourfold typology (produced by splitting the two dimensions of anxiety and social desirability). Subjects who are low in distress (anxiety, depression, low self-esteem, and low well-being) and at least moderately high in restraint (impulse control, suppression of aggression, consideration of others, and responsibility) are candidates for identification as repressors. However, a measure of defensiveness (denial of distress, repressive defensiveness) is added to the mix to distinguish between genuine repressors and the merely self-assured. As a means of identifying repressors, the WAI is more conservative than the older procedure employing the MAS and SDS (Mulvaney, Kihlstrom, Figueredo, & Schwartz, 1992). Still, to date no research has attempted to replicate the observations of Weinberger et al. (1979) with the new measure. And, except for the replication of Asendorpf and Scherer (1983), no one has examined repressive style in relation to implicit emotion.

Alexithymia and anhedonia. Another potentially relevant personality construct is *alexithymia* (Nemiah, Freyberger, & Sifneos, 1981; Nemiah & Sifneos, 1970; also see Apfel & Sifneos, 1979; Taylor, 1984; Taylor & Bagby, 1988; Taylor, Bagby, & Parker, 1997; Taylor & Taylor, 1997), in which people cannot easily describe their emotional states or even discriminate one state from another. Alexithymia, or restricted emotionality, seems at least superficially similar to the repressive coping style (Weinberger, 1990). Again, perhaps alexithymic individuals have "no words for feelings"—a fairly direct translation from the Greek roots—because they are not aware of their feelings in the first place (Lane, Ahern, Schwartz, & Kaszniak, 1997).

Alexithymia is a prominent feature among neurological patients with hemispheric commissurotomy (e.g., Hoppe & Bogen, 1977; TenHouten, Hoppe, Bogen, & Walter, 1985, 1986; TenHouten, Walter, Hoppe, & Bogen, 1988). Thus, the division in awareness affecting such patients includes an inability to communicate emotion arising from centers in the right hemisphere, via the language centers of the left hemisphere. In other words, the left hemisphere might not be aware of, and thus unable to communicate, emotions the right hemisphere is perfectly aware of—awareness that might be revealed if the right hemisphere possessed the same language skills as the left. In any event, the alexithymic patient's inability to discriminate between such feelings as anger and sadness suggests a rather marked deficit in explicit emotion. The question, then, is whether one can find evidence for *implicit* emotion in these patients, in terms of behavioral or physiological indices. Clinical lore, as well as an increasing body of empirical data, indicates that alexithymics are at risk for psychophysiological and somatoform disorders. Perhaps alexithymics, like repressors, have a talent for desynchrony, expressing emotion physiologically even if not subjectively.

Alexithymia should be distinguished from *anhedonia*, an inability to experience positive emotions (Chapman, Chapman, & Raulin, 1976). However, the alexithymic inability to communicate emotions to others is correlated with social anhedonia, or a preference for solitary rather than social activities (Prince & Berenbaum, 1993). However, we offer the hypothesis that physical anhedonia affects explicit (subjective) components of positive emotion, leaving implicit (behavioral and physiological) components of positive emotion intact.

Levels of emotional awareness.   Lane and his colleagues (Lane, Quinlan, Schwartz, Walker, & Zeitlin, 1990; Lane & Schwartz, 1987, 1992) have drawn on the developmental theories of Piaget and Werner (for a review, see Flavell, 1963) to propose five levels of emotional awareness determined by the organization of an individual's emotional states. According to their theory, emotional experience is progressively differentiated and integrated as the individual develops cognitively. At the lowest level, roughly corresponding to the earliest sensorimotor stage of Piagetian theory, a person is aware only of bodily sensations; at the next level, corresponding to later sensorimotor stages, a person is also aware of action tendencies. In neither case, however, is one aware of emotion as such. Awareness of emotion occurs at a level corresponding to the preoperational stage, where it is confined to awareness of single, pervasive emotions. At a level corresponding to the stage of concrete operations, a person is aware of emotion blends and simultaneous opposites. And at a level corresponding to formal operations, he or she can be aware of subtle nuances of emotion, as well as a difference between his or her own emotional reactions and those of others.

However, shifts in emotional awareness from one level to the next are not coterminous with the progress of cognitive development. Thus, it makes sense to distinguish among levels of emotional awareness in adults. Some adults, while firmly ensconced in formal operations for their cognitive abilities, may have only primitive, sensory-motor, emotional reactions—in other words, no *emotional awareness* at all. Interestingly, some of Lane's levels of emotional awareness correspond well to the three components of emotional response postulated by multiple-systems theory: physiological (bodily sensations), behavioral (action tendencies), and subjective (single emotions, blends, and nuances). Thus, one way of conceptualizing a desynchrony between explicit and implicit emotion poses an impairment at higher levels of emotional awareness that leaves lower levels intact.

Hypnotic Analgesia

A further example of desynchrony between the subjective experience of emotion and the behavioral and physiological expressions of it is provided by hypnotic analgesia (Hilgard & Hilgard, 1975). Following appropriate suggestions, many highly hypnotizable subjects report feeling no pain when exposed to normally painful stimulation. Though analgesia may be construed as a special case of sensory anesthesia, in fact pain has two components: *sensory pain*, providing information about the location and severity of irritation or injury, and *suffering*, a psychological reaction of unpleasantness that depends on the meaning of the sensory pain (Eich, Brodkin, Reeves, & Chawla, 1999; Hilgard, 1969; Melzack & Torgerson, 1971). Suffering is an explicitly emotional component not always present in the other skin senses, such as touch and temperature. Sensory pain and suffering are dissociable in terms of subjects' pain ratings (Gracely & Nabiloff, 1996; Melzack, 1975; Melzack & Torgerson, 1971) and also appear to be mediated by different brain systems: sensory pain by the somatosensory cortex, suffering by the anterior cingulate cortex (Rainville, Duncan, Price, Carrier, & Bushnell, 1997). Ordinarily, hypnotic suggestions for analgesia diminish awareness of both sensory pain and suffering (Hilgard, 1969; Knox, Morgan, & Hilgard, 1974); however, it is also possible to alter suffering while leaving sensory pain unaffected (Rainville et al., 1997).

Clinical studies conducted since the mid-nineteenth century indicate that hypnotic analgesia can be highly effective in relieving the pain of major surgery. However, the more common clinical use of analgesia is in the treatment of postoperative pain, episodic pain associated with specific medical and surgical procedures, burns, obstetrics, dentistry, and chronic pain associated with illness

(Hilgard & Hilgard, 1975; Hilgard & LeBaron, 1984). These clinical results are confirmed by more tightly controlled laboratory studies. For example, Stern and his colleagues found that hypnosis was more effective than acupuncture, placebo acupuncture, morphine, aspirin, diazepam, and placebo in counteracting both cold-pressor and ischemic pain (Stern, Brown, Ulett, & Sletten, 1977). Other laboratory studies indicated that hypnotizable subjects respond differently to analgesia suggestions than do insusceptible subjects instructed to simulate hypnosis (Hilgard, Macdonald, Morgan, & Johnson, 1978). Hypnotic analgesia is not mediated by placebo effects (McGlashan, Evans, & Orne, 1969) or by the tranquilizing effects of relaxation (Greene & Reyher, 1972). Hypnotic analgesia is not reversed by naloxone, an opiate antagonist, so it is not mediated by the release of endogenous opiates (Goldstein & Hilgard, 1975; Spiegel & Albert, 1983).

Most important, hypnotic analgesia does not appear to be mediated by a subject's engagement in *stress inoculation procedures*, such as self-distraction and reinterpretation, which alter the subject's response to, but not his or her awareness of, the pain stimulus. Miller and Bowers (1986) found that subjects administered hypnotic suggestions for analgesia did not report engaging in such strategies. Moreover, response to hypnotic analgesia suggestions was mediated by hypnotizability, whereas response to stress-inoculation instructions was not. A second essay by Miller and Bowers (1993) showed that stress inoculation strategies interfered with performance on a difficult vocabulary test, whereas hypnotic analgesia did not. Finally, Hargadon, Bowers, and Woody (1995) showed that the use of counterpain imagery, a common stress inoculation strategy, had no effect on hypnotic analgesia. These studies show that stress inoculation can reduce pain (Chaves, 1989; Meichenbaum, 1977; Spanos, 1986), but it does not mediate pain reduction in hypnotic analgesia.

Hilgard (1973, 1977) has proposed that hypnotic analgesia is mediated by an amnesia-like dissociative barrier that partially or fully blocks a subject's conscious perception and awareness of pain. Some evidence for this dissociative process comes from studies using the *hidden observer technique*, in which the analgesic subject receives a suggestion that a "hidden part" of the person may have registered, and can report, the true level of pain stimulation. In response, some subjects will report levels of pain comparable to those experienced in the absence of analgesia suggestions (Hilgard, Hilgard, Macdonald, Morgan, & Johnson, 1978; Hilgard, Morgan, & Macdonald, 1975). The hidden observer is a metaphor for the continuing cognitive representation of pain outside of conscious awareness and the means by which it may be accessed. Though hidden observer instructions may be interpreted as altering contextual demands to report pain (Spanos, 1986) or expectations about pain (Kirsch & Lynn, 1998), hypnotic subjects are much less responsive to manipulations of the testing context than are subjects instructed to simulate hypnosis (Kihlstrom, 1998a; Laurence, Perry,

& Kihlstrom, 1983). Therefore, the demand characteristics (Orne, 1962, 1979) of the experimental situation apparently are not sufficient to produce the hidden observer in analgesic subjects.

Although hypnotic analgesia alters a person's subjective awareness of pain and distress, it has little impact on physiological responses to pain stimulation (Barber & Hahn, 1962; Hilgard et al., 1974; Sears, 1932; Shor, 1962; Stern et al., 1977; Sutcliffe, 1961). This finding is ambiguous, however, because psychophysiological parameters do not show the lawful covariation with intensity of stimulation shown by self-reports of pain (Hilgard, 1969). The preservation of physiological responses to the pain stimulus does not impeach subjects' self-reports of analgesia, however, because the same dissociation is found with other analgesic agents, including aspirin, diazepam, and morphine (Stern et al., 1977). However, the basic finding of a dissociation between self-reports of analgesia and persisting physiological responses to the pain stimulus confirms desynchrony between the subjective and physiological components of pain as an emotional state. Obviously, however, further research needs to evaluate the hypothesis of desynchrony as applied to hypnotic analgesia (or, for that matter, any other analgesic). Such research should compare self-reports with psychophysiological indices but also with overt behavioral indices of pain, such as facial expression.

Implicit Attitudes

Other evidence bearing on the concept of implicit emotion comes from recent social psychological work on attitudes, stereotypes, and prejudice. In social psychology, attitudes have a central affective component: they are dispositions to favor or oppose certain objects, such as individuals, groups of people, or social policies. The dimensions of favorable-unfavorable, support-oppose, pro-anti naturally map onto affective dimensions of pleasure-pain or approach-avoidance. As Thurstone (1931) put it, "[A]ttitude is the affect for or against a psychological object" (p. 261). Like emotions, attitudes are generally thought of as conscious mental dispositions: supposedly, people are aware that they are opposed to nuclear power plants or favor a woman's right to choose. Similarly, people are generally believed to be aware of their stereotyped beliefs about social outgroups and of their prejudiced behavior toward members of such groups. And for that reason, researchers usually measure such attitudes and stereotypes by asking subjects to reflect and report on their beliefs or behavior. However, Greenwald and Banaji (1995) proposed an extension of the explicit/implicit distinction into the domain of attitudes. Briefly, they suggest that people possess positive and negative *implicit attitudes* about themselves and other people, which affect ongoing social behavior outside of conscious awareness.

Following the general form of the explicit/implicit distinction applied to memory, perception, learning, and thought in the cognitive domain, one may define an explicit attitude as the conscious awareness of one's favorable or unfavorable opinion concerning some object or issue. By contrast, an implicit attitude refers to any effect of such an opinion on a person's ongoing experience, thought, and action, whether that opinion can be consciously reported or not. From a methodological point of view, a researcher would assess explicit attitudes through tasks requiring a subject's conscious reflection on his opinions; implicit attitudes through tasks that do not require such reflection.

Greenwald and Schuh (1994) provide a particularly provocative demonstration of implicit attitudes affecting behavior in an analysis of reference citation practices among social scientists (study 1) and prejudice researchers (study 2). In these studies, the authors' names, and the names of the authors cited in their essays, were classified into three ethnic categories: Jewish, non-Jewish, or other. Authors were approximately 40% more likely to cite colleagues from their own ethnic category, a significant difference that could not be attributed to either differential assortment by ethnicity to research topic or the tendency for authors to cite their personal acquaintances. Though few of the authors in question likely would consciously admit to ethnic prejudice (social scientists in general, and prejudice researchers in particular, tending to be rather liberal), their *behavior* suggests the operation of negative attitudes toward members of a religious out-group.

Banaji and Greenwald (1995) provide a more tightly controlled demonstration of implicit attitudes in a study of the *false fame effect*. In the typical false fame procedure (Jacoby, Kelley, Brown, & Jasechko, 1989), subjects are asked to study a list consisting of the names of famous and nonfamous people. Later, they look at another list of names, including the names studied earlier and an equal number of new names and try to identify the names of famous people. Subjects, they found, are more likely to identify new rather than old nonfamous names as famous. In their adaptation, Banaji and Greenwald included both male and female names in their lists and found that subjects were more likely to identify male names as famous. This result suggests that the average subject is more likely to associate achievement with men than with women, a common gender stereotype.

Similarly, Blair and Banaji (1996) conducted a series of experiments in which subjects were asked to classify first names as male or female. Prior to the presentation of each target, the subjects were primed with a word representing a gender-stereotypical or gender-neutral activity, object, or profession. In general, Blair and Banaji found a gender-specific priming effect: judgments were faster when the gender connotations of the prime were congruent with the gender category of the name. This means that gender stereotypes influenced subjects' classification behavior.

In a study of racial stereotypes, Gaertner and McLaughlin (1983) employed a conventional lexical-decision task with positive and negative words related to stereotypes of blacks and whites and the words *black* or *white* serving as the primes. There was a priming effect when positive targets were primed by *white* rather than *black*, but no priming was found for the negative targets, regardless of the subjects' scores on a self-report measure of racial prejudice. Thus, the effect of attitudes on lexical decision making was independent of conscious prejudice.

Similarly, Dovidio, Evans, and Tyler (1986) employed a task in which subjects were presented with positive and negative trait labels and asked whether the characteristic could ever be true of black or white individuals. Although the judgments themselves did not differ according to race (even the most rabid racist will admit that there are some lazy whites and smart blacks), subjects were faster to endorse positive traits for whites and to endorse negative traits for blacks. Thus, even though conscious attitudes did not discriminate between racial groups, response latencies did.

These studies, and others like them (e.g., Devine, 1989), seem to reveal the implicit influence of sexist or racist attitudes on behavior. However, at present, interpretation of these results is incomplete. In the first place, the logic of the research maintains that stereotype-specific priming indicates that subjects actually hold the stereotype in question, that, for example, the subjects in Blair and Banaji's (1996) experiment really (if unconsciously) believe that men are athletic and arrogant whereas women are caring and dependent. However, perhaps these priming effects reflect the subjects' abstract knowledge of stereotypical beliefs held by members of society at large, though they themselves personally reject them, both consciously and unconsciously. Thus, a subject may know that people in general believe that ballet is for women and the gym is for men, without sharing that belief. Even so, this knowledge may affect a subject's performance on various experimental tasks, leading to the incorrect attribution of the stereotypical beliefs to the subject.

Moreover, most studies of implicit attitudes lack a comparative assessment of explicit attitudes. Though one might like to think that the average Gentile social psychologist is not anti-Semitic (Greenwald & Schuh, 1994), this may not be so. Implicit measures of attitudes may be useful additions to the methodological armamentarium of the social psychologist, but here their interest value rests on demonstrations of dissociations between explicit and implicit expressions of emotion. Accordingly, research should show that implicit measures reveal attitudes different from those revealed explicitly. Just as the amnesic patient shows priming while failing to remember, and the repressive subject shows autonomic arousal while denying distress, we want to see subjects displaying attitudes or prejudices they deny having and acting on stereotypes they deny holding.

Recently, Wittenbrink, Judd, and Park (1997) performed a formal comparison of explicit and implicit racial attitudes. Their subjects, all of whom were white, completed a variety of traditional questionnaire measures of self-reported racial attitudes. They also performed a lexical-decision task in which trait terms drawn from racial stereotypes of whites and blacks were primed with the words *black*, *white*, or *table*. Analysis of response latencies found, as one might anticipate from the studies already described, a race-specific priming effect: *white* speeded lexical judgments of positive traits, whereas *black* speeded judgments of negative traits. However, the magnitude of race-specific priming was correlated with scores on the questionnaire measures of racial prejudice. In this study, then, implicit attitudes about race were not dissociated from explicit ones. Such a finding does not undermine the use of implicit measures in research on attitudes and prejudice (Dovidio & Fazio, 1992), but a clear demonstration of a dissociation is critical if we are to accept implicit attitudes as evidence of an emotional unconscious whose components differ from those accessible to phenomenal awareness.

Neuroscientific Perspectives

In desynchrony, repression, alexithymia, hypnotic analgesia, and implicit attitudes, people are seemingly subjectively unaware of an emotional state that nevertheless influences behavioral and physiological outcomes. We propose a formal distinction between two expressions of emotion, explicit and implicit. Explicit emotion refers to a person's conscious awareness of an emotion, feeling, or mood state; implicit emotion, by contrast, refers to changes in experience, thought, or action that are attributable to one's emotional state, independent of his or her conscious awareness of that state. For measurement, explicit emotion tasks require the subject to reflect on, and report, his or her conscious feeling states; implicit emotion tasks do not.

Convincing evidence for emotion as implicit memory results from studies of neurological patients who acquire new emotional responses but who, because of their brain damage, cannot consciously recollect the experiences by which this learning took place. Similarly, brain-damaged patients may not subjectively experience emotional feeling states but nevertheless display overt behavioral and covert physiological responses that would be regarded as emotional. Dissociations among emotion systems would seem a natural topic for study by neuropsychologists, who are quite familiar with the concept of multiple systems in memory (Schacter & Tulving, 1994) and vision (Ungerleider & Haxby, 1994).

Unfortunately, neuropsychological evidence of multiple emotional systems, some supporting conscious feeling states and others supporting unconscious behavioral displays and physiological responses, is not readily available (for reviews, see Heilman, Bowers, & Valenstein, 1993; Kolb & Wilshaw, 1996). Perhaps the attention of most clinical and experimental neuropsychology has been focused on cognitive, rather than emotional and motivational, functions. The readers of this chapter will immediately recognize the terms *cognitive neuropsychology* and *cognitive neuroscience;* the terms *affective neuropsychology* and *emotion neuroscience* may not be as familiar to them.

The idea of dissociable emotion systems is related to the concept of the *emotional brain*, as it has evolved from Cannon (1929) and Bard (1929) to Papez (1937), MacLean (1949), and LeDoux (1996). Cannon and Bard found that decorticate animals show fear responses as long as the thalamus and hypothalamus remain intact. These observations led them to propose that the diencephalon, which contains these structures, was the seat of the emotions, which mediated skeletal and autonomic emotional responses; in contrast, the conscious experience of emotion is actually mediated by the cortex, activated by fibers ascending from the hypothalamus. In such a system, a disconnection (Geschwind, 1965) between the diencephalon and the cortex would impair the subjective experience of emotion yet leave the behavioral and physiological components intact.

Later research broadened the theory of the emotional brain to include the entire limbic system (MacLean, 1949, 1952; Papez, 1937)—a move that, according to one commentary, "had the appeal of combining behavioral phenomena having no known neurological substrates with anatomical structures having no known function" (Kolb & Wilshaw, 1996, p. 418). Papez believed that the afferent messages arriving at the thalamus were transmitted in two separate streams to the sensory cortex (the stream of thought) and to the hypothalamus (the stream of feeling). The hypothalamus, in turn, generated skeletal and autonomic responses to the stimulus and also transmitted sensory information to the cingulate cortex, which also received inputs from the sensory cortex. When inputs from the hypothalamus integrated with inputs from the sensory cortex, an emotional feeling state originated. In such a system, three different disconnections could create a desynchrony between the explicit subjective and implicit emotion: (1) between the thalamus and the sensory cortex, (2) between the hypothalamus and the cingulate cortex, and (3) between the sensory cortex and the cingulate cortex. In any of these cases, the behavioral and physiological responses to an emotional stimulus would run off unimpaired, in the absence of any corresponding subjective feeling state.

MacLean (1949, 1952, 1970, 1990) expanded the definition of the limbic system even further, including the amygdala and other structures connecting directly to the hypothalamus, and proposed that a *paleomammalian* brain mediates the visceral and emotional life of the (mammalian) organism, while the *neomammalian* brain mediates consciousness, language, and other complex cognitive functions. Thus, as Papez (1937) believed, a disconnection between the paleomammalian and neomammalian brains could impair explicit emotion while sparing implicit emotion.

Most recently, LeDoux (1995, 1996) has proposed a more specific variant on the Papez/MacLean theory in terms of both anatomy and psychology. Briefly, LeDoux claims that a particular structure in the limbic system, the amygdala, mediates a particular emotion, fear (for a similar analysis, see Damasio, 1994). Based on his studies of fear conditioning in rats and other nonhuman animals, but supported by studies of human patients who have suffered damage to the amygdala and surrounding brain tissue (e.g., Adolphs, Damasio, Tranel, & Damasio, 1996; LaBar, LeDoux, Spencer, & Phelps, 1995), LeDoux has proposed that fear stimuli are processed by the amygdala, which then generates appropriate behavioral, autonomic, and endocrine responses. Cortical arousal, feedback of somatic and visceral data, and information about the fear stimulus are then integrated in working memory to generate the subjective experience of being afraid. As in the simpler systems Papez and MacLean described, a disconnection between the amygdala and the cortex can produce a dissociation between explicit and implicit emotion: a person will respond in a fearful manner without feeling fear or anxiety. LeDoux's system is especially appealing because it also offers a mechanism by which fear can serve as an implicit expression of memory: if the eliciting stimulus is not represented in working memory, the person will experience fear without being aware of the fear stimulus.

LeDoux's (1995, 1996) analysis of the amygdala applies only to the emotion of fear. Whereas Papez and MacLean implied that all emotions were mediated by a single system (Papez's circuit or the limbic system), LeDoux postulates a number of different systems, each mediating conscious experience, motor behavior, and somatic changes, corresponding to different emotional domains. The number of such systems is not clear, but if Ekman and Friesen (1975) are right that some patterns of emotional expression have deep evolutionary roots, one can reasonably hypothesize at least seven separate systems, corresponding to the "basic emotions" of surprise, happiness, sadness, fear, anger, and disgust. Thus, the range of possible dissociations is not just between explicit and implicit expressions of emotion *in general*. At least in principle, it may also be possible to observe, in a single patient, desynchrony between explicit and implicit fear as well as synchrony between explicit and implicit anger. Of course, this prospect would daunt any prospective researcher of the emotional unconscious.

The State and the Stimulus

The logic of inferring unconscious emotions is just as daunting. Consider the analogy to implicit memory. We know that priming is evidence of implicit memory because we can trace its facilitation in lexical decision, perceptual identification, and the like to a specific, objectively observable event: the nature of the prime presented to the subject. Furthermore, we can specify objectively the relationship between the prime and the target: same versus different word, same word/same appearance versus same word/different appearance, and so on. In other words, we can identify an implicit expression of memory because we know what happened to the subject in the past—what the subject *should* be remembering.

But, by the same logic, to identify an implicit expression of emotion, we must know which emotional state the subject *should* be experiencing, or which emotional state is being represented, and expressed, outside of conscious awareness. Applying the logic of explicit and implicit memory to the problem of emotion, then, to find evidence of a dissociation between explicit and implicit emotion, demands methodological strategies.

First, one needs an adequate stimulus for emotion—that is, a set of stimuli that, under ordinary circumstances, reliably elicits particular emotions in subjects. Unfortunately, the search for such reliable elicitors has not been particularly fruitful. Apparently, just as the experience of pain depends on the subjective meaning of the pain stimulus, a person's emotional response to a situation depends greatly on his or her cognitive appraisal of that situation (e.g., Ellsworth, 1991; Lazarus, 1991; Lazarus & Smith, 1988; Ortony, Clore, & Collins, 1988, Smith & Ellsworth, 1985).

Still, some nearly universal elicitors of emotion hold promise for desynchrony research. Ekman and Friesen (1975) found, among other relations, that actual or threatened harm elicits fear, whereas loss of an object to which one was attached induces sadness. Similarly, Scherer, Wallbott, and their colleagues have found that basic pleasures elicited joy, whereas separation elicited sadness (Scherer & Walbott, 1994; Scherer, Wallbott, & Summerfield, 1986). Certainly, the relations in question are moderated to some degree by context-specific appraisals and cultural considerations, but enough cross-situational consistency pertains to offer some hope of measuring subjects' subjective, behavioral, and physiological responses to stimuli that should elicit certain emotions. If one observes diminished subjective awareness coupled with persisting behavioral and physiological responses, one would have evidence of a dissociation between explicit and implicit emotion.

Of course, documenting such a dissociation also requires reliable measures of the subjective, behavioral, and physiological responses to the emotion stimulus; and these are serious problems. Subjective feeling states can be assessed by the usual self-report measures, but one must carefully distinguish between the subjects' failure to consciously feel a particular emotion and their willingness to report what they feel to an experimenter. Implicit emotion is about awareness, not denial. The behavioral component of emotion might be indexed by gross patterns of approach/withdrawal, flight/fight, or activation/inhibition (Gray, 1987), and the physiological component by generalized levels of autonomic arousal (Schachter & Singer, 1962). Ideally, however, one would prefer implicit measures more specifically isomorphic to the lexicon of conscious emotions. For overt behavior, one possibility is facial expressions like those documented by Ekman and Friesen (1975), as well as cognate postural and gestural expression. For covert physiology, Levenson (1988, 1992) and his colleagues have been able to document specific patterns of autonomic response accompanying particular indices of emotion (Ekman, Levenson, & Friesen, 1983; Levenson, Carstensen, Friesen, & Ekman, 1991; Levenson, Ekman, & Friesen, 1990; Levenson, Ekman, Heider, & Friesen, 1988). Similarly, Davidson (1993) has suggested that particular patterns of cortical activation may also differentiate certain basic emotions.

The ideal structure of an experimental demonstration of implicit emotion is now clear. To begin, we assume that a particular emotional state is a hypothetical construct defined by the logic of converging operations (Garner, Hake, & Eriksen, 1956; also see Campbell & Fiske, 1959; Kihlstrom, 1984; Stoyva & Kamiya, 1968). These operations include specification of an eliciting stimulus and the measurement of subjective experience, overt behavior, and physiological response, as indicated in figure 2.1.

When all operations agree, we can be fairly confident that a person is in an emotional state such as fear or happiness. Agreement among the operations is sufficient to establish the presence of an emotional state. However, none of these operations is necessary for this purpose; under some circumstances two or three operations combined would suffice. For example, a subject might report feeling no fear in response to a real or imagined threat. At the same time, he or she should continue to manifest facial, postural, and gestural expressions of fear, as well as autonomic and cortical signs of fear. Under these circumstances, the diagnosis of implicit fear might well be irresistible. As researchers grow more confident about classification of emotional stimuli, and multivariate measurement of emotional responses, they can better evaluate the multiple-systems theory of emotion and search for evidence of desynchronies between emotional systems—especially the particular pattern(s) of desynchrony characteristic of a dissociation between explicit and implicit emotion.

COGNITION, EMOTION, CONSCIOUSNESS, AND THE SELF

We have presented an overview of what the emotional unconscious might look like. The research is not definitive, but we see a number of well-documented instances in which current or past events influence our emotional states outside of phenomenal awareness and another set of plausible instances when emotional responses themselves affect experience, thought, and action outside phenomenal awareness. One further question remains; what is the difference between conscious and unconscious cognitions and emotions?

Schacter (1990) proposes a cognitive module, which he calls the Conscious Awareness System (CAS), corresponding to a brain module or a system of

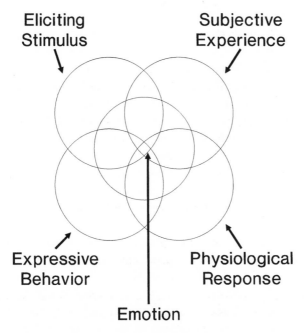

FIGURE 2.1. Emotional state defined by the convergence of eliciting stimulus, subjective experience, expressive behavior, and physiological response.

modules, that connects with other modular systems involved in perception, memory, language, emotion, and other mental functions. Damage to CAS, or more likely to the connections between it and other systems, will produce a loss of conscious awareness but not a complete loss of function. Thus, for example, if the connection between CAS and the visual system is broken, a person will not be aware of seeing but may still respond to visual events, as in the neuropsychological syndrome of blindsight. If the connection between CAS and the episodic memory system is broken, a person will be unaware of past events yet may still be influenced by the past, in the form of implicit memory, as observed in the organic amnesic syndromes. By extension, a disconnection between CAS and an emotion system would prevent one from being aware of his or her emotional states, at the same time as behavioral and physiological components of emotional response continue outside of conscious awareness. The system proposed by LeDoux (1996), though more complicated, is similar.

In psychological analysis, very close to phenomenal experience, the dissociations discussed here may be mediated by associations between various mental representations of experience and the mental representation of the self as the agent or patient of some action or as the stimulus or experiencer of some state (Kihlstrom, 1993c, 1997a). One remembers James's (1890/1980) comment:

The universal conscious fact is not "feelings and thoughts exist," but "*I* think" and "*I* feel." (p. 221; italics original)

According to James, consciousness comes when we take possession of our behaviors, thoughts, feelings, and desires—in other words, when we acknowledge them as our own, or inject ourselves into them.

Janet (1907) articulated similar ideas about the role of the self in consciousness, employing an early metaphor for spreading activation:

There are then in the [statement] "I feel," two things in presence of each other: a small, new, psychological fact, a little flame lighting up—"feel"—and an enormous mass of thoughts already constituted into a system—"I." (pp. 304-305)

The great French neurologist Claparede (1911/1951; see Kihlstrom, 1995a) discusses a classic early case of what we now call implicit memory:

If one examines the behavior of such a patient, one finds that everything happens as though the various events of life, however well associated with each other in the mind, were incapable of integration with *the me* itself. (p. 71)

This connection to the self appears to be absent in the phenomena of implicit cognition and emotion. When we perceive an event, assume that we activate fragments of preexisting knowledge; when we attend to the event, its mental representation becomes part of our working memory, along with information about our emotional reaction to the event. These activated knowledge structures then have the opportunity to contact other activated knowledge structures such as one's current processing goals, the current spatiotemporal context, and the self.[1] This self-structure, resident in working memory, routinely comes into contact with other activated pieces of knowledge about the environment in which the person exists, current and past events, and other information activated by perceptual processing, memory retrieval, and other acts of thought. This connection, which defines the self as the agent or experiencer of some ongoing event, or the stimulus or experiencer of some state, is the key to consciousness. The cognitive situation is schematically depicted in figure 2.2.

Consider what happens when a perceived or remembered event generates an emotional response. Under ordinary circumstances, the event, its surrounding context, and the emotional response all contact the self in working memory, and all are represented in consciousness (fig. 2.2A). The person knows what he or she feels, and knows why.

Now consider what happens if the subjective component of the emotional response connects to the self, but the representation of the instigating event does not (fig. 2.2B). Under these circumstances, a person will be aware of the situ-

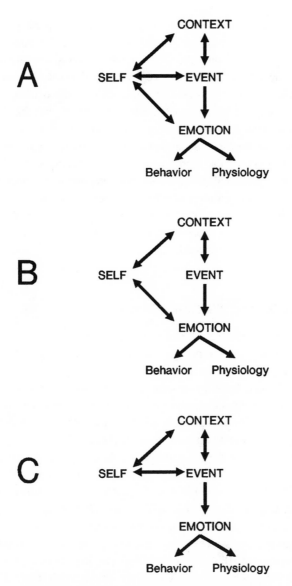

FIGURE 2.2. Mental representation of self linked to co-activated mental representations of an event, its episodic context, and emotional state (A). When the link between self and event is disrupted (B), emotional state is an expression of implicit perception or memory. When the link between self and emotion is disrupted (C), expressive behavior and physiological activity serve as implicit expressions of emotion.

ational background, his or her emotional state will be experienced consciously, and the behavioral and physiological consequences of that state will continue unimpaired. But the person will not know *why* he feels what he feels, because he is not aware of the instigating event perceived in the present or retrieved from the past. This is the usual form of a state of dissociation, reflecting an impairment of explicit perception or memory, with the emotional response reflecting spared implicit memory.

Under other circumstances, the representation of the instigating event will connect to the self, but the representation of the emotional state may not. Although the behavioral and physiological components of the emotion will manifest activity, the emotion itself will not be experienced consciously (fig. 2.2C). The result will be a state of desynchrony, reflecting an impairment of explicit emotion, whereas implicit emotion, in the form of expressive behavior and physiological changes, will be spared.

CAN EMOTIONS BE NONCONSCIOUS?

The emotional unconscious, then, has two different aspects. On the one hand, we may be unaware of the percepts, memories, and thoughts that give rise to our emotional feelings. In this case, emotion serves as an implicit expression of perception, memory, learning, or thought. On the other hand, we may be aware of what we are perceiving, remembering, and thinking but unaware of the emotions instigated by these cognitions. In this case, behavioral and physiological changes serve as implicit expressions of emotion.

But can emotions really be unconscious? A recent symposium answered this question negatively (Clore, 1994; Davidson & Ekman, 1994; LeDoux, 1994; Zajonc, 1994). There was general agreement that the cognitive and brain processes underlying emotions could operate outside of conscious awareness and conscious control. Thus, we might not be conscious of the source of our emotions; without source awareness, we might not know precisely which emotion we are experiencing. But as Clore (1994) put it, the essence of emotion is feeling, and "emotions that are felt cannot be unconscious by definition" (p. 285). And if, as Clore and Schwarz (Clore, 1992; Clore, Schwarz, & Conway, 1994; Schwarz & Clore, 1983, 1988) propose, the function of emotion is to provide information appraising the (past, current, or anticipated future) situation, the process would certainly be dysfunctional if emotions were unconscious.

On the other hand, if, as James (1884, 1890/1980) supposed, emotion is the perception of bodily (muscular and visceral) activity and perception can be unconscious, as seems the case from the literature documenting dissociations between explicit and implicit perception (Kihlstrom et al., 1992a), then emotions can be unconscious, at least in principle, and can express themselves outside awareness through overt behavioral and covert physiological responses.

Although the experimental and clinical evidence for a dissociation between explicit and implicit emotion is not yet convincing, and the methodological requirements for such a demonstration have not yet been met, the hypothesis of unconscious emotional states cannot be rejected totally. If we are willing to speak of implicit percepts, memories, and thoughts dissociated from their explicit counterparts, then we must be willing to speak of implicit emotions in the same terms. It does not matter whether unconscious emotions would be dysfunctional. What matters is whether they can happen, how they can happen, and how we would know.

NOTES

A preliminary version of this chapter was presented at the annual meeting of the Association for Applied Psychophysiology and Biofeedback (Dallas, March 1991) at the invitation of Ian Wickramasekera; a shorter version was presented at the annual EMPathy Symposium at the annual meeting of the American Psychological Association (San Francisco, August 1998) at the invitation of Charles Spielberger. The point of view represented here is based on research supported by grants from the National Institute of Mental Health (MH35856 and MH44737). We thank David Barlow, Jennifer Beer, Amy Manning Ciaschini, Jack Glaser, Michael Kim, Regina Miranda, Susan Mirch-Kretschmann, Kevin LaBar, Robert Levenson, Andres Golden Martinez, Susan Mineka, Jason Mitchell, Pradeep Mutalik, Linda O'Hara, Lillian Park, Elizabeth Phelps, John Perez, Katharine Shobe, Stephanie Tolley, and Heidi Wenk for their comments during the preparation of this essay.

1. The self, as Janet (1907) noted, is a very rich mental structure. In the social intelligence theory of personality (Cantor & Kihlstrom, 1987, 1989; Kihlstrom & Cantor, 1989, in press), the self is an organized knowledge structure that stores what one knows about oneself. This would include semantic knowledge about one's physical and personality attributes, social status, and the like. It is also tightly linked to episodic knowledge forming one's autobiographical history; autobiographical memories must represent the self, by definition (Kihlstrom & Cantor, 1984; Kihlstrom et al., 1988; Kihlstrom & Klein, 1994, 1997; Kihlstrom, Marchese, & Klein, 1997).

REFERENCES

Adams, J. K. (1957). Laboratory studies of behavior without awareness. *Psychological Bulletin, 54,* 383–405.

Adolphs, R., Damasio, H., Tranel, D., & Damasio, A. (1996). Cortical systems for the recognition of emotion in facial expressions. *Journal of Neuroscience, 16,* 7678–7687.

Apfel, R. J., & Sifneos, P. E. (1979). Alexithymia: Concept and measurement. *Psychotherapy and Psychosomatics, 32,* 180–190.

Asendorpf, J. B., & Scherer, K. R. (1983). The discrepant repressor: Differentiation between low anxiety, high anxiety, and repression of anxiety by autonomic "facial" verbal patterns of behavior. *Journal of Personality and Social Psychology, 45,* 1334–1346.

Bagby, E. (1928). *The psychology of personality.* New York: Holt.

Banaji, M. R., & Greenwald, A. G. (1995). Implicit gender stereotyping in judgments of fame. *Journal of Personality and Social Psychology, 68,* 181–198.

Barber, T. X., & Hahn, K. W. (1962). Physiological and subjective responses to pain-producing stimulation under hypnotically suggested and waking-imagined "analgesia." *Journal of Abnormal and Social Psychology, 65,* 411–415.

Bard, P. (1929). The central representation of the sympathetic system: As indicated by certain physiological observations. *Archives of Neurology and Psychiatry, 22,* 230–246.

Bargh, J. A., Bond, R. N., Lombardi, W. J., & Tota, M. E. (1986). The additive nature of chronic and temporary sources of construct accessibility. *Journal of Personality and Social Psychology, 50,* 869–878.

Bargh, J. A., & Pietromonaco, P. (1982). Automatic information processing and social perception: The influence of trait information presented outside of conscious awareness on impression formation. *Journal of Personality and Social Psychology, 43,* 437–449.

Barlow, D. H. (1988). *Anxiety and its disorders: The nature and treatment of anxiety and panic.* New York: Guilford.

Barlow, D. H., Mavissakalian, M., & Schofield, L. D. (1980). Patterns of desynchrony in agoraphobia: A preliminary report. *Behaviour Research and Therapy, 18,* 441–448.

Bass, E., & Davis, L. (1988). *The courage to heal: A guide for women survivors of child sexual abuse.* New York: Harper & Row.

Bechara, A., Damasio, A. R., Damasio, H., & Anderson, S. W. (1994). Insensitivity to future consequences following damage to human prefrontal cortex. *Cognition, 50,* 7–15.

Bechara, A., Damasio, H., Tranel, D., & Damasio, A. R. (1997). Deciding advantageously before knowing the advantageous strategy. *Science, 275,* 1293–1295.

Bechara, A., Tranel, D., Damasio, H., & Damasio, A. R. (1996). Failure to respond autonomically to anticipated future outcomes following damage to prefrontal cortex. *Cerebral Cortex, 6,* 215–225.

Beitman, B. D., Mukerji, V., Russell, J. L., & Grafing, M. (1993). Panic disorder in cardiology patients: A review of the Missouri Panic/Cardiology Project. *Journal of Psychiatric Research, 27,* 35–46.

Bell, P. A., & Byrne, D. (1978). Repression-sensitization. In H. London & J. E. Exner (Eds.), *Dimensions of personality* (pp. 449–485). New York: Wiley.

Berry, D. C., & Broadbent, D. E. (1984). On the relationship between task performance and associated verbalizable knowledge. *Quarterly Journal of Experimental Psychology, 39A,* 585–609.

Berry, D. C., & Dienes, Z. (1993). *Implicit learning: Theoretical and empirical issues.* Hove, UK: Erlbaum.

Birnbaum, M. H., & Mellers, B. A. (1979a). One-mediator model of exposure effects is still viable. *Journal of Personality and Social Psychology, 37,* 1090–1096.

Birnbaum, M. H., & Mellers, B. A. (1979b). Stimulus recognition may mediate exposure effects. *Journal of Personality and Social Psychology, 37,* 391–394.

Bisiach, E. (1993). Mental representation in unilateral neglect and related disorders. *Quarterly Journal of Experimental Psychology, 46A,* 435–462.

Blair, I. V., & Banaji, M. R. (1996). Automatic and controlled processes in stereotype priming. *Journal of Personality and Social Psychology, 70,* 1142–1163.

Blum, G. S. (1979). Hypnotic programming techniques in psychological experiments. In E. Fromm & R. E. Shor (Eds.), *Hypnosis: Developments in research and new perspectives* (pp. 457–481). New York: Aldine.

Blume, E. S. (1990). *Secret survivors: Uncovering incest and its aftereffects on women.* New York: Wiley.

Bonnano, G. A., & Stillings, N. A. (1986). Preference, familiarity, and recognition after repeated brief exposure to random geometric shapes. *American Journal of Psychology, 99,* 403–415.

Bornstein, R. F. (1989). Exposure and affect: Overview and meta-analysis of research, 1968–1987. *Psychological Bulletin, 106,* 265–289.

Bornstein, R. F. (1992). Subliminal mere exposure effects. In R. F. Bornstein & T. S. Pittman (Eds.), *Perception without awareness: Cognitive, clinical, and social perspectives* (pp. 191–210). New York: Guilford.

Bornstein, R. F., & D'Agostino, P. R. (1992). Stimulus recognition and the mere exposure effect. *Journal of Personality and Social Psychology, 63,* 545–552.

Bornstein, R. F., & D'Agostino, P. R. (1994). The attribution and discounting of perceptual fluency: Preliminary tests of a perceptual fluency/attributional model of the mere exposure effect. *Social Cognition, 12,* 103–128.

Bornstein, R. F., Leone, D. R., & Galley, D. J. (1987). The generalizability of subliminal mere exposure effects: Influence of stimuli perceived without awareness on social behavior. *Journal of Personality and Social Psychology, 53,* 1070–1079.

Bower, G. H. (1981). Mood and memory. *American Psychologist, 36,* 129–148.

Bower, G. H., Gilligan, S. G., & Monteiro, K. P. (1981). Selectivity of learning caused by affective state. *Journal of Experimental Psychology: General, 110,* 451–473.

Bower, G. H., Monteiro, K. P., & Gilligan, S. G. (1978). Emotional mood as a context for learning and recall. *Journal of Verbal Learning and Verbal Behavior, 17,* 573–585.

Bowers, K. S. (1984). On being unconsciously influenced and informed. In K. S. Bowers & D. Meichenbaum (Eds.), *The unconscious reconsidered* (pp. 227–272). New York: Wiley-Interscience.

Bowers, K. S., & Farvolden, P. (1996). Revisiting a century-old Freudian slip—From suggestion disavowed to the truth repressed. *Psychological Bulletin, 119,* 355–380.

Bowers, K. S., Farvolden, P., & Mermigis, L. (1995). Intuitive antecedents of insight. In S. M. Smith, T. M. Ward, & R. A. Finke (Eds.), *The creative cognition approach* (pp. 27–52). Cambridge, MA: MIT Press.

Bowers, K. S., Regehr, G., Balthazard, C. G., & Parker, K. (1990). Intuition in the context of discovery. *Cognitive Psychology, 22,* 72–110.

Breuer, J., & Freud, S. (1893–1895/1957). Studies on hysteria. In J. Strachey (Ed.), *The standard edition of the complete psychological works of Sigmund Freud* (vol. 2). London: Hogarth.

Bruner, J. S., & Klein, G. S. (1960). The function of perceiving: New Look retrospect. In S. Wapner & B. Kaplan (Eds.), *Perspectives in psychological theory: Essays in honor of Heinz Werner* (pp. 61–77). New York: International Universities Press.

Bryant, R. A., & McConkey, K. M. (1989a). Hypnotic blindness, awareness, and attribution. *Journal of Abnormal Psychology, 98,* 443–447.

Bryant, R. A., & McConkey, K. M. (1989b). Visual conversion disorder: A case analysis of the influence of visual information. *Journal of Abnormal Psychology, 98,* 326–329.

Byrne, D. (1961). The Repression-Sensitization Scale: Rationale, reliability and validity. *Journal of Personality, 29,* 334–349.

Byrne, D. (1964). Repression-sensitization as a dimension of personality. In B. A. Maher (Ed.), *Progress in experimental personality research* (vol. 1, pp. 87–128). New York: Academic Press.

Campbell, D. T., & Fiske, D. W. (1959). Convergent and discriminant validation by the multitrait-multimethod matrix. *Psychological Bulletin, 56,* 82–105.

Cannon, W. B. (1929). *Bodily changes in pain, hunger, fear, and rage.* New York: Appleton.

Cantor, N., & Kihlstrom, J. F. (1987). *Personality and social intelligence.* Englewood Cliffs, NJ: Prentice-Hall.

Cantor, N., & Kihlstrom, J. F. (1989). Social intelligence and cognitive assessments of personality. In R. S. Wyer & T. K. Srull (Eds.), *Advances in social cognition* (vol. 2, pp. 1–59). Hillsdale, NJ: Erlbaum.

Chapman, L. J., Chapman, J. P., & Raulin, M. L. (1976). Scales for physical and social anhedonia. *Journal of Abnormal Psychology, 85,* 374–382.

Chaves, J. F. (1989). Hypnotic control of clinical pain. In N. P. Spanos & J. F. Chaves (Eds.), *Hypnosis: The cognitive-behavioral perspective* (pp. 242–272). Buffalo, NY: Prometheus.

Christianson, S.-A., & Nilsson, L.-G. (1989). Hysterical amnesia: A case of aversively motivated isolation of memory. In T. Archer & L.-G. Nilsson (Eds.), *Aversion, avoidance, and anxiety: Perspectives on aversively motivated behavior* (pp. 289–310). Hillsdale, NJ: Erlbaum.

Claparede, E. (1911/1951). Recognition and me-ness. In D. Rapaport (Ed.), *Organization and pathology of thought: Selected sources* (pp. 58–75). New York: Columbia University Press.

Clore, G. L. (1992). Cognitive phenomenology: Feelings in the construction of judgment. In L. Martin & A. Tesser (Eds.), *The construction of social judgment* (pp. 133–164). Hillsdale, NJ: Erlbaum.

Clore, G. L. (1994). Why emotions are never unconscious. In P. Ekman & R. J. Davidson (Eds.), *The nature of emotion: Fundamental questions* (pp. 285–290). New York: Oxford University Press.

Clore, G. L., Schwarz, N., & Conway, M. (1994). Emotion and information processing. In R. S. Wyer & T. K. Srull (Eds.), *Handbook of social cognition* (vol. 2, 2nd ed., pp. 323–417). Hillsdale, NJ: Erlbaum.

Cork, R. L., Couture, L. J., & Kihlstrom, J. F. (1997). Memory and recall. In T. L.

Yaksh, C. Lynch, W. M. Zapol, M. Maze, J. F. Biebuyck, & L. J. Saidman (Eds.), *Anesthesia: Biologic foundations* (pp. 451–467). New York: Lippincott-Raven.

Craske, M. G., Sanderson, M. C., & Barlow, D. H. (1987). How do desynchronous response systems relate to the treatment of agoraphobia? *Behaviour Research and Therapy, 25,* 117–122.

Crews, F. (1995). *The memory wars: Freud's legacy in dispute.* New York: New York Review Imprints.

Crowne, C. P., & Marlowe, D. A. (1960). A new scale of social desirability independent of psychopathology. *Journal of Consulting Psychology, 24,* 349–354.

Damasio, A. R. (1994). *Decartes' error: Emotion, reason, and the human brain.* New York: Grosset/Putnam.

Damasio, A. R., Tranel, D., & Damasio, H. (1989). Amnesia caused by herpes simplex encephalitis, infarctions in basal forebrain, Alzheimer's disease and anoxia/ischemia. In F. Boller & J. Grafman (Eds.), *Handbook of neuropsychology* (vol. 3, pp. 149–166). Amsterdam: Elsevier.

Davidson, R. J. (1993). Parsing affective space: Perspectives from neuropsychology and psychophysiology. *Neuropsychology, 7,* 464–475.

Davidson, R. J., & Ekman, P. (Eds.). (1994). *The nature of emotion: Fundamental questions.* New York: Oxford University Press.

Devine, P. G. (1989). Stereotypes and prejudice: Their automatic and controlled components. *Journal of Personality and Social Psychology, 56,* 5–18.

Dienes, Z., Altman, G., Kwan, L., & Goode, A. (1995). Unconscious knowledge of artificial grammars is applied strategically. *Journal of Experimental Psychology: Learning, Memory, and Cognition, 17,* 875–887.

Dienes, Z., & Berry, D. (1997). Implicit learning: Below the subjective threshold. *Psychonomic Bulletin & Review, 4,* 3–23.

Dixon, N. F. (1971). *Subliminal perception: The nature of a controversy.* London: McGraw-Hill.

Dixon, N. F. (1981). *Preconscious processing.* New York: Wiley.

Dorfman, J., & Kihlstrom, J. F. (1994, November). *Semantic priming in posthypnotic amnesia.* Paper presented at the annual meeting of the Psychonomic Society, St. Louis.

Dorfman, J., Kihlstrom, J. F., Cork, R. C., & Misiaszek, J. (1995). Priming and recognition in ECT-induced amnesia. *Psychonomic Bulletin & Review, 2,* 244–248.

Dorfman, J., Shames, V. A., & Kihlstrom, J. F. (1996). Intuition, incubation, and insight: Implicit cognition in problem-solving. In G. Underwood (Ed.), *Implicit cognition* (pp. 257–296). Oxford: Oxford University Press.

Dovidio, J. F., Evans, N., & Tyler, R. (1986). Racial stereotypes: The contents of their cognitive representations. *Journal of Experimental Social Psychology, 22,* 22–37.

Dovidio, J. F., & Fazio, R. H. (1992). New technologies for the direct and indirect assessment of attitudes. In J. M. Tanur (Ed.), *Questions about questions* (pp. 204–236). New York: Russell Sage Foundation.

Dozier, M., & Kobak, R. R. (1992). Psychophysiology in attachment interviews: Converging evidence for deactivating strategies. *Child Development, 63,* 1473–1480.

Dulany, D. E. (1997). Consciousness in the explicit (deliberative) and implicit (evocative) senses. In J. D. Cohen & J. W. Schooler (Eds.), *Scientific approaches to consciousness* (pp. 179–212). Mahwah, NJ: Erlbaum.

Durso, F. T., Rea, C. B., & Dayton, T. (1994). Graph-theoretic confirmation of restructuring during insight. *Psychological Science, 5,* 94–98.

Dworkin, R. H. (1992). Affective deficits and social deficits in schizophrenia: What's what? *Schizophrenia Bulletin, 18,* 59–64.

Eich, E. (1984). Memory for unattended events: Remembering with and without awareness. *Memory & Cognition, 12,* 105–111.

Eich, E., Brodkin, I. A., Reeves, J. L., & Chawla, A. F. (1999). Questions concerning pain. In D. Kahneman, E. Diener, & N. Schwarz (Eds.), *Well-being: The foundations of hedonic psychology* (pp. 155–168). New York: Russell-Sage.

Eich, E., Macaulay, D., Loewenstein, R. J., & Dihle, P. H. (1997). Memory, amnesia, and dissociative identity disorder. *Psychological Science, 8,* 417–422.

Ekman, P., & Friesen, W. V. (1975). *Unmasking the face.* Englewood Cliffs, NJ: Prentice-Hall.

Ekman, P., Levenson, R. W., & Friesen, W. V. (1983). Autonomic nervous system activity distinguishes between emotions. *Science, 221,* 1208–1210.

Ellenberger, H. F. (1970). *The discovery of the unconscious.* New York: Basic Books.

Ellsworth, P. C. (1991). Some implications of cognitive appraisal theories of emotion. In K. T. Strongman (Ed.), *International review of studies on emotion* (pp. 143–161). New York: Wiley.

Erdelyi, M. H. (1974). A new look at the New Look: Perceptual defense and vigilance. *Psychological Review, 81,* 1–25.

Eriksen, C. W. (1960). Discrimination and learning without awareness: A methodological survey and evaluation. *Psychological Review, 67,* 279–300.

Flavell, J. H. (1963). *The developmental psychology of Jean Piaget.* Princeton, NJ: Van Nostrand Reinhold.

Frederickson, R. (1993). *Repressed memories: A journey to recovery from sexual abuse.* New York: Simon & Schuster.

Freud, A. (1936/1966). The ego and the mechanisms of defense (revised edition). In A. Freud (Ed.), *The writings of Anna Freud* (vol. 2). New York: International Universities Press.

Freud, S. (1916–1917/1963). Introductory lectures on psycho-analysis. In J. Strachey (Ed.), *The standard edition of the complete psychological works of Sigmund Freud* (vols. 15 & 16). London: Hogarth.

Freud, S. (1926/1959). Inhibitions, symptoms, and anxiety. In J. Strachey (Ed.), *The standard edition of the complete psychological works of Sigmund Freud* (vol. 20, pp. 87–178). London: Hogarth.

Freud, S. (1933/1964). New introductory lectures on psychoanalysis. In J. Strachey (Ed.), *The standard edition of the complete psychological works of Sigmund Freud* (vol. 22, pp. 1–184). London: Hogarth.

Gaertner, S. L., & McLaughlin, J. P. (1983). Racial stereotypes: Associations and ascriptions of positive and negative characteristics. *Social Psychology Quarterly, 46,* 23–30.

Gantt, W. H. (1937). Contributions to the physiology of the conditioned reflex. *Archives of Neurology and Psychiatry, 37,* 848–858.

Gantt, W. H. (1953). Principles of nervous breakdown: Schizokinesis and autokinesis. *Annals of the New York Academy of Sciences, 56,* 141–163.

Garner, W. R., Hake, H. W., & Eriksen, C. W. (1956). Operationism and the concept of perception. *Psychological Review, 63,* 149–159.

Gazzaniga, M. S. (1985). *The social brain: Discovering the networks of the mind.* New York: Basic Books.

Gerew, A. B., Romney, D. M., & LeBoef, A. (1989). Synchrony and desynchrony in high and low arousal subjects undergoing therapeutic exposure. *Journal of Behavior Therapy and Experimental Psychiatry, 20,* 41–48.

Geschwind, N. (1965). Disconnexion syndromes in animals and man. *Brain, 88,* 237–294.

Goldstein, A., & Hilgard, E. R. (1975). Lack of influence of the morphine antagonist naloxone on hypnotic analgesia. *Proceedings of the National Academy of Sciences, 72,* 2041–2043.

Gracely, R. H. & Nabiloff, B. D. (1996). Measurement of pain sensation. In L. Kruger (Ed.), *Pain and touch* (pp. 243–313). San Diego: Academic.

Graf, P., & Masson, M. E. J. (Eds.). (1993). *Implicit memory: New directions in cognition, development, and neuropsychology.* Hillsdale, NJ: Erlbaum.

Gray, J. A. (1987). *The psychology of fear and stress* (2nd ed.). Cambridge, UK: Cambridge University Press.

Greene, R. J., & Reyher, J. (1972). Pain tolerance in hypnotic analgesic and imagination states. *Journal of Abnormal Psychology, 79,* 29–38.

Greenwald, A. G. (1992). New Look 3: Unconscious cognition reclaimed. *American Psychologist, 47,* 766–779.

Greenwald, A. G., & Banaji, M. R. (1995). Implicit social cognition: Attitudes, self-esteem, and stereotypes. *Psychological Review, 102,* 4–27.

Greenwald, A. G., Draine, S. C., & Abrams, R. L. (1996). Three cognitive markers of unconscious semantic activation. *Science, 273,* 1699–1702.

Greenwald, A. G., Klinger, M. R., & Liu, T. J. (1989). Unconscious processing of dichoptically masked words. *Memory & Cognition, 17,* 35–47.

Greenwald, A. G., Klinger, M. R., & Schuh, E. S. (1995). Activation by marginally perceptible ("subliminal") stimuli: Dissociation of unconscious from conscious cognition. *Journal of Experimental Psychology: General, 124,* 22–42.

Greenwald, A. G., & Schuh, E. S. (1994). An ethnic bias in scientific citations. *European Journal of Social Psychology, 24,* 623–639.

Hargadon, R., Bowers, K. S., & Woody, E. Z. (1995). Does counterpain imagery mediate hypnotic analgesia? *Journal of Abnormal Psychology, 104,* 508–516.

Hayward, A. L. (1927). *Amusements, serious and comical, and other works by Tom Brown.* New York: Dodd, Mead.

Heilman, K. M., Bowers, D., & Valenstein, E. (1993). Emotional disorders associated with neurological diseases. In K. M. Heilman & E. Valenstein (Eds.), *Clinical neuropsychology* (3rd ed., pp. 461–498). New York: Oxford University Press.

Herman, J. L. (1992). *Trauma and recovery.* New York: Basic Books.

Hilgard, E. R. (1969). Pain as a puzzle for psychology and physiology. *American Psychologist, 24,* 103–113.

Hilgard, E. R. (1973). A neodissociation interpretation of pain reduction in hypnosis. *Psychological Review, 80,* 396–411.

Hilgard, E. R. (1977). *Divided consciousness: Multiple controls in human thought and action.* New York: Wiley-Interscience.

Hilgard, E. R. (1980). The trilogy of mind: Cognition, affection, and conation. *Journal of the History of the Behavioral Sciences, 16,* 107–117.

Hilgard, E. R., & Hilgard, J. R. (1975). *Hypnosis in the relief of pain.* Los Altos, CA: Kaufmann.

Hilgard, E. R., Hilgard, J. R., Macdonald, H., Morgan, A. H., & Johnson, L. S. (1978). Covert pain in hypnotic analgesia: Its reality as tested by the real-simulator design. *Journal of Abnormal Psychology, 87,* 655–663.

Hilgard, E. R., Macdonald, H., Morgan, A. H., & Johnson, L. S. (1978). The reality of hypnotic analgesia: A comparison of highly hypnotizables with simulators. *Journal of Abnormal Psychology, 87,* 239–246.

Hilgard, E. R., Morgan, A. H., Lange, A. F., Lenox, J. R., Macdonald, H., Marshall, G. D., & Sachs, L. B. (1974). Heart rate changes in pain and hypnosis. *Psychophysiology, 11,* 692–702.

Hilgard, E. R., Morgan, A. H., & Macdonald, H. (1975). Pain and dissociation in the cold-pressor test: A study of hypnotic analgesia with "hidden reports" through automatic key-pressing and automatic talking. *Journal of Abnormal Psychology, 84,* 280–289.

Hilgard, J. R., & LeBaron, S. L. (1984). *Hypnosis in the treatment of pain and anxiety in children with cancer: A clinical and quantitative investigation.* Los Altos, CA: Kaufmann.

Hodgson, R., & Rachman, S. (1974). Desynchrony in measures of fear. *Behaviour Research and Therapy, 12,* 319–326.

Holender, D. (1986). Semantic activation without conscious identification in dichotic listening, parafoveal vision, and visual masking: A survey and appraisal. *Behavior and Brain Sciences, 9,* 1–23.

Hoppe, K. D., & Bogen, J. E. (1977). Alexithymia in twelve commissurotomized patients. *Psychotherapy and Psychosomatics, 28,* 148–155.

Hugdahl, K. (1981). The three-system model of fear and emotion—A critical examination. *Behaviour Research and Therapy, 19,* 75–85.

Huston, P. E., Shakow, D. & Erickson, M. H. (1934). A study of hypnotically induced complexes by means of the Luria technique. *Journal of General Psychology, 11,* 65–97.

Jacoby, L. L., & Dallas, M. (1981). On the relationship between autobiographical memory and perceptual learning. *Journal of Experimental Psychology: General, 110,* 306–340.

Jacoby, L. L., Kelley, C. M., Brown, J., & Jasechko, J. (1989). Becoming famous overnight: Limits on the ability to avoid unconscious influences of the past. *Journal of Personality and Social Psychology, 56,* 326–338.

James, W. (1884). What is an emotion? *Mind, 9,* 188–205.

James, W. (1890/1980). *Principles of psychology.* Cambridge, MA: Harvard University Press.

Janet, P. (1893). [Continuous amnesia.] *Revue Generale des Sciences, 4,* 167–179.

Janet, P. (1904). *[Neuroses and fixed ideas.]* Paris: Alcan.

Janet, P. (1907). *The major symptoms of hysteria.* New York: Macmillan.

Johnson, M. K., Kim, J. K., & Risse, G. (1985). Do alcoholic Korsakoff's syndrome patients acquire affective reactions? *Journal of Experimental Psychology: Learning, Memory, and Cognition, 11,* 27–36.

Johnson, M. K., & Multhaup, K. S. (1992). Emotion and MEM. In S.-A. Christianson (Ed.), *The handbook of emotion and memory* (pp. 33–66). Hillsdale, NJ: Erlbaum.

Kaszniak, A. W., Nussbaum, P. D., Berren, M. R., & Santiago, J. (1988). Amnesia as a consequence of male rape: A case report. *Journal of Abnormal Psychology, 97,* 100–104.

Kihlstrom, J. F. (1980). Posthypnotic amnesia for recently learned material: Interactions with "episodic" and "semantic" memory. *Cognitive Psychology, 12,* 227–251.

Kihlstrom, J. F. (1984). Conscious, subconscious, unconscious: A cognitive perspective. In K. S. Bowers & D. Meichenbaum (Eds.), *The unconscious reconsidered* (pp. 149–211). New York: Wiley.

Kihlstrom, J. F. (1985). Posthypnotic amnesia and the dissociation of memory. In G. H. Bower (Ed.), *The psychology of learning and motivation* (vol. 19, pp. 131–178). New York: Academic Press.

Kihlstrom, J. F. (1987). The cognitive unconscious. *Science, 237,* 1445–1452.

Kihlstrom, J. F. (1990). The psychological unconscious. In L. Pervin (Ed.), *Handbook of personality* (pp. 445–464). New York: Guilford.

Kihlstrom, J. F. (1993a). The continuum of consciousness. *Consciousness and Cognition, 2,* 334–354.

Kihlstrom, J. F. (1993b). Implicit memory function during anesthesia. In P. S. Sebel, B. Bonke, & E. Winograd (Eds.), *Memory and awareness in anesthesia* (pp. 10–30). New York: Prentice-Hall.

Kihlstrom, J. F. (1993c). The psychological unconscious and the self. In T. Nagel (Ed.), *Experimental and theoretical studies of consciousness* (pp. 147–167). London: Wiley.

Kihlstrom, J. F. (1995a). Memory and consciousness: An appreciation of Claparede and his "Recognition et Moiite." *Consciousness and Cognition, 4,* 379–386.

Kihlstrom, J. F. (1995b). The rediscovery of the unconscious. In H. Morowitz & J. Singer (Eds.), *The mind, the brain, and complex adaptive systems: Santa Fe Institute studies in the sciences of complexity* (vol. 22, pp. 123–143). Reading, MA: Addison-Wesley.

Kihlstrom, J. F. (1996a). Perception without awareness of what is perceived, learning without awareness of what is learned. In M. Velmans (Ed.), *The science of consciousness: Psychological, neuropsychological, and clinical reviews* (pp. 23–46). London: Routledge.

Kihlstrom, J. F. (1996b). The trauma-memory argument and recovered memory therapy. In K. Pezdek & W. P. Banks (Eds.), *The recovered memory/false memory debate* (pp. 297–311). San Diego: Academic Press.

Kihlstrom, J. F. (1997a). Consciousness and me-ness. In J. Cohen & J. Schooler (Eds.), *Scientific approaches to the question of consciousness* (pp. 451–468). Mahwah, NJ: Erlbaum.

Kihlstrom, J. F. (1997b). Suffering from reminiscences: Exhumed memory, implicit memory, and the return of the repressed. In M. A. Conway (Ed.), *False and recovered memories* (pp. 100–117). Oxford: Oxford University Press.

Kihlstrom, J. F. (1998a). Dissociations and dissociation theory in hypnosis: A comment on Kirsch and Lynn (1998). *Psychological Bulletin, 123,* 186–191.

Kihlstrom, J. F. (1998b). Exhumed memory. In S. J. Lynn & N. P. Spanos (Eds.), *Truth in memory* (pp. 3–31). New York: Guilford.

Kihlstrom, J. F. (1999). Conscious and unconscious cognition. In R. J. Sternberg (Ed.), *The concept of cognition* (pp. 173–203). Cambridge, MA: MIT Press.

Kihlstrom, J. F., Barnhardt, T. M., & Tataryn, D. J. (1992a). Implicit perception. In R. F. Bornstein & T. S. Pittman (Eds.), *Perception without awareness: Cognitive, clinical, and social perspectives* (pp. 17–54). New York: Guilford.

Kihlstrom, J. F., Barnhardt, T. M., & Tataryn, D. J. (1992b). The psychological unconscious: Found, lost, and regained. *American Psychologist, 47,* 788–791.

Kihlstrom, J.F, & Cantor, N. (1984). Mental representations of the self. In L. Berkowitz (Ed.), *Advances in experimental social psychology* (vol. 17, pp. 1–47). New York: Academic Press.

Kihlstrom, J. F., & Cantor, N. (1989). Social intelligence and personality: There's room for growth. In R. S. Wyer & T. K. Srull (Eds.), *Advances in social cognition* (vol. 2, pp. 197–214). Hillsdale, NJ: Erlbaum.

Kihlstrom, J. F., & Cantor, N. (in press). Social intelligence. In R. J. Sternberg (Ed.), *Handbook of intelligence.* Cambridge, UK: Cambridge University Press.

Kihlstrom, J. F., Cantor, N, Albright, J. S., Chew, B. R., Klein, S. B., & Niedenthal, P. M. (1988). Information processing and the study of the self. In L. Berkowitz (Ed.), *Advances in experimental social psychology* (vol. 21, pp. 145–177). San Diego: Academic Press.

Kihlstrom, J. F, & Hoyt, I. P. (1988). Hypnosis and the psychology of delusions. In T. F. Oltmanns & B. A. Maher (Eds.), *Delusional beliefs: Interdisciplinary perspectives* (pp. 66–109). New York: Wiley.

Kihlstrom, J. F., & Hoyt, I. P. (1990). Repression, dissociation, and hypnosis. In J. L. Singer (Ed.), *Repression and dissociation: Implications for personality theory, psychopathology, and health* (pp. 181–208). Chicago: University of Chicago Press.

Kihlstrom, J. F., & Klein, S. B. (1994). The self as a knowledge structure. In R. S. Wyer & T. K. Srull (Eds.), *Handbook of social cognition* (2nd ed., pp. 153–208). Hillsdale, NJ: Erlbaum.

Kihlstrom, J. F., & Klein, S. B. (1997). Self-knowledge and self-awareness. In J. G. Snodgrass & R. L. Thompson (Eds.), *The self across psychology: Self-recognition, self-awareness, and the self-concept. Annals of the New York Academy of Sciences, 818,* 5–17.

Kihlstrom, J. F., Marchese, L. A., & Klein, S. B. (1997). Situating the self in interpersonal space. In U. Neisser & D. A. Jopling (Eds.), *The conceptual self in context: Culture, experience, self-understanding* (pp. 154–175). New York: Cambridge University Press.

Kihlstrom, J. F., & Schacter, D. L. (1990). Anaesthesia, amnesia, and the cognitive unconscious. In B. Bonke, W. Fitch, & K. Millar (Eds.), *Awareness and memory during anaesthesia* (pp. 22–44). Amsterdam: Swets & Zeitlinger.

Kihlstrom, J. F., & Schacter, D. L. (1995). Functional disorders of autobiographical memory. In A. Baddeley, B. A. Wilson, & F. Watts (Eds.), *Handbook of memory disorders* (pp. 337–364). London: Wiley.

Kihlstrom, J. F., Shames, V. A., & Dorfman, J. (1996). Intimations of memory and thought. In L. Reder (Ed.), *Implicit memory and metacognition* (pp. 1–23). Mahwah, NJ: Erlbaum.

Kihlstrom, J. F., Tataryn, D. J., & Hoyt, I. P. (1993). Dissociative disorders. In P. J. Sutker & H. E. Adams (Eds.), *Comprehensive handbook of psychopathology* (2nd ed., pp. 203–234). New York: Plenum.

Kirsch, I., & Lynn, S. J. (1998). Dissociation theories of hypnosis. *Psychological Bulletin, 123,* 100–115.

Klinger, M. R., & Greenwald, A. G. (1994). Preferences need no inferences? The cognitive basis of nonconscious mere exposure effects. In P. M. Niedenthal & S. Kitayama (Eds.), *The heart's eye: Emotional influences in perception and attention* (pp. 67–85). San Diego: Academic Press.

Knox, V. J, Morgan, A. H., & Hilgard, E. R. (1974). Pain and suffering in ischemia: The paradox of hypnotically suggested anesthesia as contradicted by reports from the "hidden observer." *Archives of General Psychiatry, 30,* 840–847.

Kolb, B., & Wilshaw, I. (1996). *Fundamentals of human neuropsychology* (4th ed.). New York: Freeman.

Kring, A. M., Kerr, S., Smith, D. A., & Neale, J. M. (1993). Flat affect in schizophrenia does not reflect diminished subjective experience of emotion. *Journal of Abnormal Psychology, 102,* 507–517.

Kring, A. M., & Neale, J. M. (1996). Do schizophrenic patients show a disjunctive relationship among expressive, experiential, and psychophysiological components of emotion? *Journal of Abnormal Psychology, 105,* 249–257.

Kunst-Wilson, W. R., & Zajonc, R. B. (1980). Affective discrimination of stimuli that cannot be recognized. *Science, 207,* 557–558.

Kushner, M. G., & Beitman, B. D. (1990). Panic attacks without fear: An overview. *Behaviour Research and Therapy, 28,* 469–479.

LaBar, K. S., LeDoux, J. E., Spencer, D. D., & Phelps, E. A. (1995). Impaired fear conditioning following unilateral temporal lobectomy in humans. *Journal of Neuroscience, 15,* 6846–6855.

Lane, R. D., Ahern, G. L., Schwartz, G. E., & Kaszniak, A. W. (1997). Is alexithymia the emotional equivalent of blindsight? *Biological Psychiatry, 42,* 834–844.

Lane, R. D., Quinlan, D. M., Schwartz, G. E., Walker, P. A., & Zeitlin, S. B. (1990). The Levels of Emotional Awareness Scale: A cognitive-developmental measure of emotion. *Journal of Personality Assessment, 55,* 124–134.

Lane, R. D., & Schwartz, G. E. (1987). Levels of emotional awareness: A cognitive-developmental theory and its application to psychopathology. *American Journal of Psychiatry, 144,* 133–143.

Lane, R. D., & Schwartz, G. E. (1992). Levels of emotional awareness: Implications for psychotherapeutic integration. *Journal of Psychotherapy Integration, 2,* 1–18.

Lang, P. J. (1968). Fear reduction and fear behavior: Problems in treating a construct. In J. M. Schlein (Ed.), *Research in psychotherapy* (vol. 3, pp. 90–103). Washington, DC: American Psychological Association.

Lang, P. J. (1971). The application of psychophysiological methods to the study of psychotherapy and behavior modification. In A. E. Bergin & S. L. Garfield (Eds.), *Handbook of psychotherapy and behavior change* (pp. 75–125). New York: Wiley.

Lang, P. J. (1978). Anxiety: Towards a psychophysiological definition. In H. S. Akiskal & W. H. Webb (Eds.), *Psychiatric diagnosis: Exploration of biological predictors* (pp. 365–389). New York: Spectrum.

Lang, P. J. (1988). What are the data of emotion? In V. Hamilton, G. H. Bower, & N. H. Frijda (Eds.), *Cognitive perspectives on emotion and motivation* (pp. 173–181). NATO ASI Series D: Behavioural and Social Sciences. Dordrecht, The Netherlands: Kluwer.

Lang, P. J., & Lazovik, A. D. (1963). Experimental desensitization of a phobia. *Journal of Abnormal and Social Psychology, 66,* 519–525.

Lang, P. J., Lazovik, A. D., & Reynolds, D. J. (1965). Desensitization, suggestibility, and pseudotherapy. *Journal of Abnormal Psychology, 70,* 395–402.

Lang, P. J., Rice, D. G., & Sternbach, R. A. (1972). The psychophysiology of emotion. In N. S. Greenfield & R. A. Sternbach (Eds.), *Handbook of psychophysiology* (pp. 623–644). New York: Holt, Rinehart, & Winston.

Laurence, J. R., Perry, C., & Kihlstrom, J. F. (1983). "Hidden observer" phenomena in hypnosis: An experimental creation? *Journal of Personality and Social Psychology, 44,* 163–169.

Lazarus, R. S. (1982). Thoughts on the relations between emotion and cognition. *American Psychologist, 37,* 1019–1024.

Lazarus, R. S. (1984). On the primacy of cognition. *American Psychologist, 39,* 124–129.

Lazarus, R. S. (1991). *Emotion and adaptation.* New York: Oxford University Press.

Lazarus, R. S., & Smith, C. A. (1988). Knowledge and appraisal in the cognition-emotion relationship. *Cognition and Emotion, 2,* 281–300.

LeDoux, J. E. (1994). Emotional processing, but not emotions, can occur unconsciously. In P. Ekman & R. J. Davidson (Eds.), *The nature of emotion: Fundamental questions* (pp. 291–292). New York: Oxford University Press.

LeDoux, J. E. (1995). Emotion: Clues from the brain. *Annual Review of Psychology, 46,* 209–235.

LeDoux, J. E. (1996). *The emotional brain.* New York: Simon & Schuster.

LeDoux, J. E., Wilson, D. H., & Gazzaniga, M. S. (1977). Manipulo-spatial aspects of cerebral lateralization: Cues to the origin of lateralization. *Neuropsychologia, 15,* 743–750.

Lepper, M. R., Greene, D., & Nisbett, R. E. (1973). Undermining children's intrinsic interest with extrinsic reward: A test of the "overjustification" hypothesis. *Journal of Personality and Social Psychology, 28,* 129–137.

Levenson, R. W. (1988). Emotion and the autonomic nervous system: A prospectus for research on autonomic specificity. In H. Wagner (Ed.), *Social psychophysiology and emotion: Theory and clinical applications* (pp. 17–42). London: Wiley.

Levenson, R. W. (1992). Autonomic nervous system differences among emotions. *Psychological Science, 3,* 23–27.

Levenson, R. W., Carstensen, L. L., Friesen, W. V., & Ekman, P. (1991). Emotion, physiology, and expression in old age. *Psychology and Aging, 6,* 28–35.

Levenson, R. W., Ekman, P., & Friesen, W. V. (1990). Voluntary facial action generates emotion-specific autonomic nervous system activity. *Psychophysiology, 27,* 363–384.

Levenson, R. W., Ekman, P., Heider, K., & Friesen, W. V. (1988). Emotion and autonomic nervous system activity in the Minangkabau of West Sumatra. *Journal of Personality and Social Psychology, 62,* 972–988.

Leventhal, H. (1980). Toward a comprehensive theory of emotion. In L. Berkowitz (Ed.), *Advances in experimental social psychology* (vol. 13, pp. 139–207). New York: Academic Press.

Leventhal, H. (1984). A perceptual-motor theory of emotion. In K. R. Scherer & P. Ekman (Eds.), *Approaches to emotion* (pp. 271–291). Hillsdale, NJ: Erlbaum.

Levinson, B. (1965). States of awareness during general anaesthesia. *British Journal of Anaesthesia, 37,* 544–546.

Levitt, E. E. (1967). *The psychology of anxiety.* Indianapolis: Bobbs-Merrill.

Levitt, E. E., & Chapman, R. H. (1979). Hypnosis as a research method. In E. Fromm & R. E. Shor (Eds.), *Hypnosis: Developments in research and new perspectives* (pp. 85–114). New York: Aldine.

Lewandowsky, S., Dunn, J. C., & Kirsner, K., Eds. (1989). *Implicit memory: Theoretical issues.* Hillsdale, NJ: Erlbaum.

Lewicki, P. (1986). *Nonconscious social information processing.* New York: Academic Press.

Lewicki, P., Czyzewska, M., & Hoffman, H. (1987). Unconscious acquisition of complex procedural knowledge. *Journal of Experimental Psychology: Learning, Memory, and Cognition, 13,* 523–530.

Light, L. L., & Singh, A. (1987). Implicit and explicit memory in young and older adults. *Journal of Experimental Psychology: Learning, Memory, and Cognition, 13,* 531–541.

Light, L. L., Singh, A., & Capps, J. L. (1986). Dissociation of memory and awareness in young and older adults. *Journal of Clinical and Experimental Neuropsychology, 8,* 62–74.

Lindsay, D. S., & Read, J. D. (1994). Psychotherapy and memories of childhood sexual abuse: A cognitive perspective. *Applied Cognitive Psychology, 8,* 281–338.

Lindsay, D. S., & Read, J. D. (1995). ''Memory work'' and recovered memories of childhood sexual abuse: Scientific evidence and public, professional, and personal issues. *Psychology, Public Policy, and the Law, 1,* 846–908.

Luria, A. R. (1932). *The nature of human conflicts.* New York: Liveright.

MacLean, P. D. (1949). Psychosomatic disease and the ''visceral brain:'' Recent developments bearing on the Papez theory of emotion. *Psychosomatic Medicine, 11,* 338–353.

MacLean, P. D. (1952). Some psychiatric implications of physiological studies of frontotemporal portion of limbic system (visceral brain). *Electroencephalography and Clinical Neurophysiology, 4,* 407–418.

MacLean, P. D. (1970). The triune brain, emotion and scientific bias. In F. O. Schmitt (Ed.), *The neurosciences: Second study program* (pp. 336–349). New York: Rockefeller University Press.

MacLean, P. D. (1990). *The triune brain in evolution: Role in paleocerebral functions.* New York: Plenum.

Macmillan, M. (1996). *Freud reevaluated: The completed arc* (rev. ed.). Cambridge, MA: MIT Press.

Mandler, G., Nakamura, Y., & Van Zandt, B. J. S. (1987). Nonspecific effects of exposure on stimuli that cannot be recognized. *Journal of Experimental Psychology: Learning, Memory, and Cognition, 13,* 646–648.

Marcel, A. (1983). Conscious and unconscious perception: Experiments on visual masking and word recognition. *Cognitive Psychology, 15,* 197–237.

Marshall, J. C., & Halligan, P. W. (1988). Blindsight and insight in visuo-spatial neglect. *Nature, 336,* 766–767.

McGlashan, T. H., Evans, F. J., & Orne, M. T. (1969). The nature of hypnotic analgesia and the placebo response to experimental pain. *Psychosomatic Medicine, 31,* 227–246.

Mednick, S. (1962). The associative basis of the creative process. *Psychological Review, 69,* 220–232.

Meichenbaum, D. (1977). *Cognitive behavior modification: An integrative approach.* New York: Plenum.

Melzack, R. (1975). The McGill Pain Questionnaire: Major properties and scoring methods. *Pain, 1,* 277–299.

Melzack, R., & Torgerson, W. S. (1971). On the language of pain. *Anesthesiology, 34,* 50–59.

Merikle, P. M., & Daneman, M. (1996). Memory for unconsciously perceived events: Evidence from anesthetized patients. *Consciousness and Cognition, 5,* 525–541.

Merikle, P. M., & Reingold, E. M. (1990). Recognition and lexical decision without detection: Unconscious perception? *Journal of Experimental Psychology: Human Perception and Performance, 16,* 574–583.

Miller, M. E., & Bowers, K. S. (1986). Hypnotic analgesia and stress inoculation in the reduction of pain. *Journal of Abnormal Psychology, 95,* 6–14.

Miller, M. E., & Bowers, K. S. (1993). Hypnotic analgesia: Dissociated experience or dissociated control? *Journal of Abnormal Psychology, 102,* 29–38.

Mineka, S. (1979). The role of fear in theories of avoidance learning, flooding, and extinction. *Psychological Bulletin, 86,* 985–1010.

Mineka, S. (1985a). Animal models of anxiety-based disorders: Their usefulness and limitations. In J. Maser & A. H. Tuma (Eds.), *Anxiety and the anxiety disorders* (pp. 199–244). Hillsdale, NJ: Erlbaum.

Mineka, S. (1985b). The frightful complexity of the origins of fears. In F. R. Brush & J. B. Overmeier (Eds.), *Affect, conditioning, and cognition: Essays on the determinants of behavior* (pp. 55–73). Hillsdale, NJ: Erlbaum.

Mineka, S. (1992). Evolutionary memories, emotional processing, and the emotional disorders. In D. Medin (Ed.), *The psychology of learning and motivation* (vol. 28, pp. 161–206). San Diego: Academic Press.

Moreland, R. W., & Zajonc, R. B. (1977). Is stimulus recognition a necessary condition for the occurrence of exposure effects? *Journal of Personality and Social Psychology, 35,* 191–199.

Moreland, R. W., & Zajonc, R. B. (1979). Exposure effects may not depend on stimulus recognition. *Journal of Personality and Social Psychology, 37,* 1085–1089.

Mowrer, O. H. (1947). On the dual nature of learning—A reinterpretation of "conditioning" and "problem-solving." *Harvard Educational Review, 17,* 102–148.

Mulvaney, S., Kihlstrom, J. F., Figueredo, A. J., & Schwartz, G. E. (1992). A continuous measure of repressive style. *EGAD Quarterly, 1,* 40–49.

Murphy, S. T., & Zajonc, R. B. (1993). Affect, cognition, and awareness: Affective priming with suboptimal and optimal stimulus. *Journal of Personality and Social Psychology, 64,* 723–739.

Murray, H. A. (1938). *Explorations in personality.* New York: Oxford University Press.

Neal, A., & Hesketh, B. (1997). Episodic knowledge and implicit learning. *Psychonomic Bulletin & Review, 4,* 24–37.

Nelson, T. O. (1978). Detecting small amounts of information in memory: Savings for nonrecognized items. *Journal of Experimental Psychology: Human Learning and Memory, 4,* 453–468.

Nemiah, J. C. (1979). Dissociative amnesia: A clinical and theoretical reconsideration. In J. F. Kihlstrom & F. J. Evans (Eds.), *Functional disorders of memory* (pp. 303–323). Hillsdale, NJ: Erlbaum.

Nemiah, J. C., Freyberger, H., & Sifneos, P. E. (1981). Alexithymia: A view of the psychosomatic process. In O. Hill (Ed.), *Modern trends in psychosomatic medicine* (vol. 3, pp. 430–439). London: Buttersworth.

Nemiah, J. C., & Sifneos, P. E. (1970). Affect and fantasy in patients with psychosomatic disorders. In O. Hill (Ed.), *Modern trends in psychosomatic medicine* (vol. 2, pp. 26–34). London: Buttersworth.

Niedenthal, P. M. (1990). Implicit perception and affective information. *Journal of Experimental Social Psychology, 26,* 505–527.

Niedenthal, P. M. (1992). Affect and social perception. In R. F. Bornstein & T. S. Pittman (Eds.), *Perception without awareness: Cognitive, clinical, and social perspectives* (pp. 211–235). New York: Guilford.

Niedenthal, P. M., Setterlund, M. B., & Jones, D. E. (1994). Emotional organization of perceptual memory. In P. M. Niedenthal & S. Kitayama (Eds.), *The heart's eye: Emotional influences in perception and attention* (pp. 87–113). San Diego: Academic Press.

Niedenthal, P. M., & Showers, C. J. (1991). The perception and processing of affective information and its influence on social judgment. In J. P. Forgas (Ed.), *Affect and social judgment* (pp. 125–143). Oxford: Pergamon.

Nissen, M. J., & Bullemer, P. (1987). Attentional requirements of learning: Evidence from performance measures. *Cognitive Psychology, 19,* 11–32.

Norton, G. R., DiNardo, P. A., & Barlow, D. H. (1983). Predicting phobics' response to therapy: A consideration of subjective, physiological, and behavioural measures. *Canadian Psychology, 24,* 50–58.

Ohman, A. (1999). Distinguishing unconscious from conscious emotional processes: Methodological considerations and theoretical implications. In T. Dalgleish & M. Power (Eds.), *Handbook of cognition and emotion* (pp. 321–352). Chichester, UK: Wiley.

Ohman, A., Dimberg, U., & Esteves, F. (1989). Preattentive activation of aversive emotions. In T. Archer & L. G. Nilsson (Eds.), *Aversion, avoidance, and anxiety* (pp. 169–193). Hillsdale, NJ: Erlbaum.

Ohman, A., & Soares, J. F. (1993). On the automaticity of phobic fear: Conditioned skin conductance responses to masked phobic stimuli. *Journal of Abnormal Psychology, 102,* 121–132.

Ohman, A., & Soares, J. F. (1994). Unconscious anxiety: Phobic responses to masked stimuli. *Journal of Abnormal Psychology, 103,* 231–240.

Ohman, A., & Soares, J. F. (1998). Emotional conditioning to masked stimuli: Expectancies for aversive outcomes following non-recognized fear-relevant stimuli. *Journal of Experimental Psychology: General, 127,* 69–82.

Orne, M. T. (1962). On the social psychology of the psychological experiment: With particular reference to demand characteristics and their implications. *American Psychologist, 17,* 776–783.

Orne, M. T. (1979). On the simulating subject as a quasi-control group in hypnosis research: What, why, and how. In E. Fromm & R. E. Shor (Eds.), *Hypnosis: Developments in research and new perspectives* (pp. 399–444). New York: Aldine.

Ortony, A., Clore, G. L., & Collins, A. (1988). *The cognitive structure of emotions.* Cambridge, UK: Cambridge University Press.

Papez, J. W. (1937). A proposed mechanism of emotion. *Archives of Neurology and Psychiatry, 79,* 217–224.

Papka, M., Ivry, R. B., & Woodruff-Pak, D. S. (1996). Eyeblink classical conditioning and awareness revisited. *Psychological Science, 8,* 404–408.

Pierce, C. S., & Jastrow, J. (1885). On small differences in sensation. *Memoirs of the National Academy of Sciences, 3,* 75–83.

Prince, J. D., & Berenbaum, H. (1993). Alexithymia and hedonic capacity. *Journal of Research in Personality, 27,* 15–22.

Prince, M. (1910). *The dissociation of a personality.* New York: Longmans-Green.

Rachman, S. (1978). Human fears: A three-system analysis. *Scandinavian Journal of Behavior Therapy, 7,* 237–235.

Rachman, S. (1981). The primacy of affect: Some theoretical implications. *Behaviour Research and Therapy, 19,* 279–290.

Rachman, S. (1990). *Fear and courage* (2nd ed.). New York: Freeman.

Rachman, S., & Hodgson, R. (1974). Synchrony and desynchrony in measures of fear. *Behaviour Research and Therapy, 12,* 311–318.

Rafal, R. (1998). Neglect. In R. Parasuraman (Ed.), *The attentive brain* (pp. 489–525). Cambridge, MA: MIT Press.

Rainville, P., Duncan, G. H., Price, D. D., Carrier, B., & Bushnell, M. C. (1997). Pain affect encoded in human anterior cingulate but not somatosensory cortex. *Science, 277,* 968–971.

Razran, G. (1961). The observable unconscious and the inferable conscious in current Soviet psychophysiology: Interoceptive conditioning, semantic conditioning, and the orienting reflex. *Psychological Review, 68,* 81–147.

Reber, A. S. (1967). Implicit learning of artificial grammars. *Journal of Verbal Learning and Verbal Behavior, 6,* 855–863.

Reber, A. S. (1993). *Implicit learning and tacit knowledge: An essay on the cognitive unconscious.* New York: Oxford University Press.

Redington, K., Volpe, B. T., & Gazzaniga, M. S. (1984). Failure of preference formation in amnesia. *Neurology, 34,* 536–538.

Roediger, H. L., & McDermott, K. B. (1993). Implicit memory in normal human subjects. In H. Spinnler & F. Boller (Eds.), *Handbook of neuropsychology* (vol. 8, pp. 63–131). Amsterdam: Elsevier.

Rosenzweig, S. (1938). The experimental study of repression. In H. A. Murray (Ed.), *Explorations in personality* (pp. 472–490). New York: Oxford University Press.

Rosenzweig, S., & Mason, G. (1934). An experimental study of memory in relation to the theory of repression. *British Journal of Psychology, 24,* 247–265.

Rosenzweig, S., & Sarason, S. (1942). An experimental study of the triadic hypothesis: Reaction to frustration, ego-defense, and hypnotizability: I. Correlational approach. *Character and Personality, 11,* 1–19.

Rozin, P. (1976). The evolution of intelligence and access to the cognitive unconscious. In E. Stellar & J. M. Sprague (Eds.), *Progress in psychobiology and physiological psychology* (vol. 6, pp. 3–480). New York: Academic Press.

Russell, J. A. (1980). A circumplex model of affect. *Journal of Personality and Social Psychology, 39,*1161–1178.

Russell, J. L., Kushner, M. G., Beitman, B. D., & Bartels, K. M. (1991). Nonfearful panic disorder in neurology patients validated by lactate challenge. *American Journal of Psychiatry, 148,* 361–364.

Sarason, S., & Rosenzweig, S. (1942). An experimental study of the triadic hypothesis: Reaction to frustration, ego defense, and hypnotizability: II. Thematic apperception approach. *Character and Personality, 11,* 150–165.

Schacter, D. L. (1987). Implicit memory: History and current status. *Journal of Experimental Psychology: Learning, Memory, and Cognition, 13,* 501–518.

Schacter, D. L. (1990). Toward a cognitive neuropsychology of awareness: Implicit knowledge and anosognosia. *Journal of Clinical and Experimental Neuropsychology, 12,* 155–178.

Schacter, D. L., Kihlstrom, J. F., Kaszniak, A. W., & Valdiserri, M. (1993). Preserved and impaired memory functions in elderly adults. In J. Cerella, J. Rybash, W. Hoyer, & M. Commons (Eds.), *Adult information processing: Limits on loss* (pp. 327–350). New York: Academic Press.

Schacter, D. L., & Tulving, E. (1994). *Memory systems 1994.* Cambridge, MA: MIT Press.

Schachter, S., & Singer, J. E. (1962). Cognitive, social, and physiological determinants of emotional state. *Psychological Review, 69,* 379–399.

Scherer, K. R., & Walbott, H. G. (1994). Evidence for universality and cultural variation of differential emotion response patterning. *Journal of Personality and Social Psychology, 66,* 310–328.

Scherer, K. R., Walbott, H. G., & Summerfield, A. B. (Eds.). (1986). *Experiencing emotion: A crosscultural study.* Cambridge, UK: Cambridge University Press.

Schwarz, N., & Clore, G. L. (1983). Mood, misattribution, and judgments of well-being: Informative and directive functions of affective states. *Journal of Personality and Social Psychology, 45,* 513–523.

Schwarz, N., & Clore, G. L. (1988). How do I feel about it? The informative function of mood. In K. Fiedler & J. P. Forgas (Eds.), *Affect, cognition, and social behavior* (pp. 44–62). Toronto: Hogrefe.

Seamon, J. J., Brody, N., & Kauff, D. M. (1983a). Affective discrimination of stimuli that are not recognized: Effects of shadowing, masking, and cerebral laterality. *Journal of Experimental Psychology. Learning, Memory, and Cognition, 9,* 544–555.

Seamon, J. J., Brody, N., & Kauff, D. M. (1983b). Affective discrimination of stimuli that are not recognized: II. Effect of delay between study and test. *Bulletin of the Psychonomic Society, 21,* 187–189.

Sears, R. R. (1932). Experimental study of hypnotic anesthesia. *Journal of Experimental Psychology, 15,* 1–22.

Seger, C. A. (1994). Implicit learning. *Psychological Bulletin, 115,* 163–196.

Seligman, M. E. P. (1971). Phobias and preparedness. *Behavior Therapy, 2,* 307–320.

Shames, V. A. (1994). *Is there such a thing as implicit problem solving?* Unpublished doctoral dissertation, University of Arizona.

Shanks, D. R., & St. John, M. F. (1994). Characteristics of dissociable human learning systems. *Behavioral and Brain Sciences, 17,* 367–448.

Shobe, K. K., & Kihlstrom, J. F. (in press). Interrogative suggestibility and "memory work." In M. I. Eisen, G. S. Goodman, & J. Quas (Eds.). *Memory and suggestibility in the forensic interview.* Mahwah, NJ: Erlbaum.

Shor, R. E. (1962). Physiological effects of painful stimulation during hypnotic analgesia under conditions designed to minimize anxiety. *International Journal of Clinical and Experimental Hypnosis, 10,* 183–202.

Smith, C. A., & Ellsworth, P. C. (1985). Patterns of cognitive appraisal in emotion. *Journal of Personality and Social Psychology, 48,* 813–838.

Spanos, N. P. (1986). Hypnotic behavior: A social-psychological interpretation of amnesia, analgesia, and "trance logic." *Behavioral and Brain Sciences, 9,* 449–502.

Spanos, N. P., Jones, B., & Malfara, A. (1982). Hypnotic deafness: Now you hear it—Now you still hear it. *Journal of Abnormal Psychology, 91,* 75–77.

Sperry, R. W., Gazzaniga, M. S., & Bogen, J. E. (1969). Inter-hemispheric relationships: The neocortical commissures; syndromes of hemisphere disconnection. In P. J. Vinken & G. W. Bruyn (Eds.), *Handbook of clinical neurology* (vol. 4, pp. 273–290). Amsterdam: North-Holland.

Spiegel, D., & Albert, L. H. (1983). Naloxone fails to reverse hypnotic alleviation of chronic pain. *Psychopharmacology, 81,* 140–143.

Squire, L. R., Shimamura, A. P., & Graf, P. (1985). Independence of recognition memory and priming effects: A neuropsychological analysis. *Journal of Experimental Psychology: Learning, Memory, and Cognition, 11,* 37–44.

Stern, J. A., Brown, M., Ulett, G. A., & Sletten, I. (1977). A comparison of hypnosis, acupuncture, morphine, valium, aspirin, and placebo in the management of experimentally induced pain. *Annals of the New York Academy of Sciences, 296,* 175–193.

Stoyva, J., & Kamiya, J. (1968). Electrophysiological studies of dreaming as the prototype of a new strategy in the study of consciousness. *Psychological Review, 75,* 192–205.

Suppes, P., & Warren, H. (1975). On the generation and classification of defence mechanisms. *International Journal of Psycho-analysis, 56,* 405–414.

Sutcliffe, J. P. (1961). "Credulous" and "skeptical" views of hypnotic phenomena: Experiments in esthesia, hallucination, and delusion. *Journal of Abnormal and Social Psychology, 62,* 189–200.

Taylor, G. J. (1984). Alexithymia: Concept, measurement, and implications for treatment. *American Journal of Psychiatry, 141,* 725–732.

Taylor, G. J., & Bagby, R. M. (1988). Measurement of alexithymia: Recommendations for clinical practice and future research. *Psychiatric Clinics of North America, 11,* 351–366.

Taylor, G. J., Bagby, R. M., & Parker, J. D.A. (1997). *Disorders of affect regulation:*

Alexithymia in medical and psychiatric illness. Cambridge, UK: Cambridge University Press.

Taylor, G. J., & Taylor, H. L. (1997). Alexithymia. In M. McCallum, & W. E. Piper (Eds.), *Psychological mindedness: A contemporary understanding* (pp. 77–104). Mahwah, NJ: Erlbaum.

Taylor, J. A. (1953). A personality scale of manifest anxiety. *Journal of Abnormal and Social Psychology, 48,* 285–290.

TenHouten, W. D., Hoppe, K. D., Bogen, J. E., & Walter, D. O. (1985). Alexithymia and the split brain: I. Lexical-level content analysis. *Psychotherapy and Psychosomatics, 43,* 202–208.

TenHouten, W. D., Hoppe, K. D., Bogen, J. E., & Walter, D. O. (1986). Alexithymia: An experimental study of cerebral commissurotomy patients and normal control subjects. *American Journal of Psychiatry, 143,* 312–316.

TenHouten, W. D., Walter, D. O., Hoppe, K. D., & Bogen, J. E. (1988). Alexithymia and the split brain: VI. Electroencephalographic correlates of alexithymia. *Psychiatric Clinics of North America, 11,* 317–329.

Terr, L. (1994). *Unchained memories: True stories of traumatic memories, lost and found.* New York: Basic Books.

Thomas, M. R., & Rapp, M. S. (1977). Physiological, behavioral and cognitive changes resulting from flooding in a monosymptomatic phobia. *Behaviour Research and Therapy, 15,* 304–306.

Thurstone, L. L. (1931). The measurement of attitudes. *Journal of Abnormal and Social Psychology, 4,* 25–29.

Tobias, B. A., Kihlstrom, J. F., & Schacter, D. L. (1990). Emotion and implicit memory. In S.-A. Christianson (Ed.), *The handbook of emotion and memory* (pp. 67–92). Hillsdale, NJ: Erlbaum.

Traub-Werner, D. (1989). Anxiety in a patient during an unconsciously experienced earth tremor. *American Journal of Psychiatry, 146,* 679–680.

Turpin, G. (1991). The psychophysiological assessment of anxiety disorders: Three-systems measurement and beyond. *Psychological Assessment, 3,* 365–375.

Underwood, G. (1976). Semantic interference from unattended printed words. *British Journal of Psychology, 67,* 327–338.

Ungerleider, L. G., & Haxby, J. (1994). What and where in the human brain. *Current Opinion in Neurobiology, 4,* 157–165.

van der Kolk, B. A., McFarlane, A. C., & Weisaeth, L. (Eds.). (1996). *Traumatic stress: The effects of overwhelming experience on mind, body, and society.* New York: Guilford.

Vermilyea, J. A., Boice, R., & Barlow, D. H. (1984). Rachman and Hodgson (1974) a decade later: How do desynchronous response systems relate to the treatment of agoraphobia? *Behaviour Research and Therapy, 22,* 615–621.

Warrington, E. K., & Weiskrantz, L. (1968). New method of testing long-term retention with special reference to amnesic patients. *Nature, 217,* 972–974.

Watson, D., & Tellegen, A. (1985). Toward a consensual structure of mood. *Psychological Bulletin, 98,* 219–235.

Watson, J. (1888). *The philosophy of Kant: As contained in extracts from his own writings.* New York: Macmillan.

Weinberger, D. A. (1990). The construct validity of the repressive coping style. In J. L. Singer (Ed.), *Repression and dissociation: Implications for personality theory, psychopathology, and health* (pp. 337–386). Chicago: University of Chicago Press.

Weinberger, D. A. (1997). Distress and self-restraint as measures of adjustment across the life span: Confirmatory factor analyses in clinical and nonclinical samples. *Psychological Assessment, 9,*132–135.

Weinberger, D. A., & Schwartz, G. E. (1990). Distress and restraint as superordinate dimensions of self-reported adjustment: A typological perspective. *Journal of Personality, 58,* 381–417.

Weinberger, D. A., Schwartz, G. E., & Davidson, R. J. (1979). Low-anxious, high-anxious, and repressive coping styles: Psychometric patterns and behavioral and physiological responses to stress. *Journal of Abnormal Psychology, 88,* 369–380.

Weiskrantz, L. (1986). *Blindsight: A case study and implications.* Oxford: Oxford University Press.

Willingham, D. B., Greeley, T., & Bardone, A. M. (1993). Dissociation in a serial response time task using a recognition measure: Comment on Perruchet and Amorin (1992). *Journal of Experimental Psychology: Learning, Memory, and Cognition, 19,* 1047–1060.

Wilson, W. R. (1979). Feeling more than we can know: Exposure effects without learning. *Journal of Personality and Social Psychology, 37,* 811–821.

Wittenbrink, B., Judd, C. M., & Park, B. (1997). Evidence for racial prejudice at the implicit level and its relationship with questionnaire measures. *Journal of Personality and Social Psychology, 72,* 262–274.

Zajonc, R. B. (1968). The attitudinal effects of mere exposure. *Journal of Personality and Social Psychology,* Monograph Supplement 9 (2, pt. 2).

Zajonc, R. B. (1980). Feeling and thinking: Preferences need no inferences. *American Psychologist, 35,* 151–175.

Zajonc, R. B. (1984a). On primacy of affect. In K. R. Scherer & P. Ekman (Eds.), *Approaches to emotion* (pp. 259–270). Hillsdale, NJ: Erlbaum.

Zajonc, R. B. (1984b). On the primacy of affect. *American Psychologist, 39,* 117–123.

Zajonc, R. B. (1994). Evidence for nonconscious emotions. In P. Ekman & R. J. Davidson (Eds.), *The nature of emotion: Fundamental questions* (pp. 293–297). New York: Oxford University Press.

CHAPTER 3

Affect, Memory, and Social Cognition

Gordon H. Bower and Joseph P. Forgas

Since time immemorial, philosophers, writers, and artists have sought to understand how and why our feelings and emotions come to influence our memories, thoughts, and judgments. Indeed, clarifying the relationship between such basic mental faculties as affect, cognition, and conation remains a perennial goal in psychology (Hilgard, 1980). Surprisingly, most psychological research in this century proceeded on the implicit assumption that affect, cognition, and conation can be studied as separate, independent features of the human mind. Of the two paradigms that have dominated our discipline so far, neither behaviorism nor cognitivism have traditionally paid much attention to the study of affect.

Early work exploring the links between affect and cognition relied either on psychoanalytic principles such as projection (Feshbach & Singer, 1957) or on conditioning theories (Clore & Byrne, 1974; Griffitt, 1970) to account for the apparent infusion of affectively valenced material into our memories, thoughts, and judgments. During the past decade or so, interest in the role of affect in cognition and behavior has increased dramatically. Contemporary theories are predominantly based on cognitive principles to explain affect infusion (Bower, 1981, 1991; Clore, Schwarz, & Conway, 1994; Fiedler, 1990,1991; Forgas, 1992b, 1995a, 1998a, 1998b, 1998c, Kruglanski, 1989). In this chapter, we discuss some of the influences of affective states on cognitive processes, especially those involved in memory and judgment.

For nearly twenty years now, an important and influential idea for explaining mood effects on memory and judgment has been the affect priming theory. According to this view, the arousal of a mood or emotion spreads activation throughout a network of associations surrounding that mood or emotion (Bower, 1981; Bower & Cohen, 1982; Bower & Forgas, 1999; Clark & Isen, 1982; Isen, 1984). As a result, material that is associatively linked to current mood is more likely to be recalled and used, leading to a marked mood congruence in constructive associations, evaluations, and judgments.

This chapter reviews and updates the affect priming theory and its revisions. In the first half of the chapter, we will outline the basic conceptual foundations of this theory and review the considerable empirical evidence indicating mood congruent effects in memory, attention, learning, associations, evaluations, preferences, and judgments.

The second half of the chapter reviews the voluminous empirical evidence now available on the theory and places it within broader contemporary theorizing about the relation of affect to cognition. We will consider some of the criticisms of the affect priming account and review some of the competing explanations for mood congruent effects. In particular, we address evidence indicating the absence or even the reversal of mood congruence. The chapter closes with a revised theory—the *affect infusion model* (AIM)—that attempts to accommodate most of the results. We review recent empirical evidence supporting this comprehensive, multiprocess theory of mood effects on cognition.

CAUSES VERSUS CONSEQUENCES OF EMOTIONS

Throughout this discussion, we will focus on the cognitive and behavioral consequences of affect, rather than their antecedent sources. Obviously, people have a perceptual-interpretive system that analyzes and evaluates environmental stimuli for their emotional significance and it "turns on" the appropriate emotion (or mixture of emotions) when the appropriate situation arises. Bower and Cohen (1982) modeled these emotion-recognition decisions using collections of production rules that specify classes of external situations that turn on particular emotions. For example, major loss of an anticipated pleasure often leads to sadness; deliberate thwarting or blocking progress toward a desired goal often elicits anger; perceived threats to one's body or self-esteem often produce anxiety; and so on. Such *emotion production rules* are also central to various appraisal theories of emotion (Blascovich & Mendes, 2000; Lazarus, 1991; Ortony, Clore, & Collins, 1988; Roseman, 1984; Smith & Ellsworth, 1985; Weiner, 1982). Our concern here is not so much with the situational antecedents of affective states, but rather with their cognitive and behavioral consequences, and in particular, the kind of thoughts and memories that come to mind when people are in different emotional states.

AFFECT, EMOTION, AND MOOD

In our discussion, we often use the terms affect, emotion and mood interchangeably, although we are aware that distinctions can be drawn between them. *Affect* is perhaps the more general term, and may be used to refer to both emotions and moods (Forgas, 1995a). An *emotion* has the properties of a reaction: it often has an identifiable cause—a stimulus or antecedent thought, it is usually a spasmodic, intense experience of short duration, and the person is typically well aware of it (i.e., emotions typically have high cognitive involvement and elaborate content). On the other hand, a *mood* tends to be more subtle, longer-lasting, less intense, more in the background, more like a frame of mind, casting a positive glow or negative shadow over experiences. Moods tend to be nonspecific (e.g., pleasant/unpleasant; energetic/lethargic; anxious/relaxed) compared to emotions, which are usually specific, are linked to clear-cut and consciously available cognitive representations about their antecedents, and are thus typically focused on an identifiable person, object, or event. In contrast, people may not be aware of their mood until their attention is drawn to it. Mood variations may be caused by subtle factors such as diurnal fluctuations in brain neurotransmitters, by sleep/waking biorhythms, by sore or tense muscles, by sunny or rainy weather, and by an accumulation of pleasant or unpleasant events (for a review, see Thayer, 1989).

Despite these differences, a sharp distinction between a mood and an emotion is difficult to draw because a frequent cause of a mood is the persisting aftereffects of a strongly aroused emotion. Thus, if a person has just experienced a series of losses or failures, he or she will experience a sad emotion. Moreover, those somber feelings may persist as a sad mood for several minutes, or even hours, especially if one periodically mentally reviews the sadness-producing events. In fact, researchers often invoke this mental review of emotional events to induce experimental subjects to achieve a particular mood by remembering and replaying in their imagination some occasion when they felt happy, sad, angry, or fearful. Such mood inductions are clearly using cognitions (memories or constructed imaginings) to elicit emotions and moods.

Just as cognitions can be used to arouse an emotion, so can they also be used to either maintain or reduce it (see Forgas, Johnson, & Ciarrochi, 1998). Morrow and Nolen-Hoeksema's (1990) experiments illustrate such effects. Nondepressed subjects who had been induced to feel temporarily sad were asked to spend 8 minutes focusing either on a series of irrelevant, distracting ideas or on themselves, their personality, and their feelings. After this brief period of cognitive activity, the mood of the distracted subjects greatly improved, whereas the self-focused, ruminating subjects became even more depressed. In a follow-up experiment (Nolen-Hoeksema & Morrow, 1993), subjects who scored as moderately depressed or nondepressed on the Beck Depression Inventory (BDI) received similar "thinking" instructions. Again, thinking about external distractors reduced the dysphoria of the moderate-BDI subjects, whereas self-focused ruminations increased their dysphoria. On the other hand, the two kinds of thinking instructions did not affect the current mood of the nondepressed (low-BDI) subjects. These results indicate that cognitive activity, depending on its nature, can either exacerbate or ameliorate people's emotions and moods.

In most of the experiments to be discussed below, subjects were induced into a pleasant (happy) or unpleasant (sad) mood, and the influence of this mood on a variety of cognitive processes was examined. Our focus here is on nonspecific mood states rather than on distinct emotions. One reason for our interest is that since moods tend to be more enduring, less specific and less conscious than specific emotions, their consequences for our thinking and judgments may be even more widespread and insidious than is the case with emotions.

We do not wish to suggest that research on the cognitive consequences of specific emotions (as distinct from moods) is not of considerable interest. However, because emotions such as anger, pride, or fear are usually highly conscious events and involve the strong activation of considerable related cognitive information about antecedents and consequences, their cognitive effects tend to be more obvious than is the case with moods. Nevertheless, a research program that induces more specific emotions (e.g., pride versus bliss; grief at loss versus guilt for harming someone) and examines their more specific consequences for social cognitions and social behaviors would be of considerable interest. Such a program, based on appraisal theories of emotions, has been emerging in recent years (Blascovich & Mendes, 2000; Leary, 2000; Ortony et al., 1988; Smith & Ellsworth, 1985; Smith & Kirby, 2000).

AFFECT AND MEMORY

Types of Investigations

In surveying research on the relation of emotion and memory, four broad categories of studies may be distinguished: (1) laboratory studies of the behavioral effects of contingent, affect-producing events (rewards and punishments); (2) memory for presented emotional materials; (3) autobiographic recall of emotional incidents; and (4) variations in memory for subjects in different prevailing emotional states. We briefly summarize the first three classes of studies before we turn to a more extensive review of the fourth type of study, which is our main concern.

Traditional learning theory consisted of many hypotheses about the influence of response-contingent rewards and punishments on learning and performance.

The so-called Law of Effect states that actions followed closely by rewards will be learned and performed more reliably, whereas actions followed closely by punishments will be suppressed and avoided in the future. Rewards and punishments are almost always events that also produce pleasant or unpleasant affective reactions, respectively, in the subject. There is simply no question that some formulation of the Law of Effect (perhaps one recognizing the relativity of the subject's "bliss-point," see Timberlake, 1980) is empirically correct. To deny it would be to deny the obvious truth that organisms strive for gains and to ameliorate pain or losses. So, in this sense, behavior is almost always strongly guided by anticipation of emotion-producing events.

Early work on classical conditioning has some implications for our understanding of the cognitive consequences of affective states. According to this view, unconditioned affective reactions elicited by an experience (such as an aversive or a pleasant environment) can become associated with previously neutral stimuli (such as a person first encountered in that environment) merely as a result of temporal or spatial contiguity (Clore & Byrne, 1974). As a result, subsequent memories, judgments, and associations about these initially neutral stimuli will become affectively distorted through such conditioned affective reactions. The potential judgmental consequences of such chance associations were first recognized in the social cognition literature by Wyer and Carlston (1979), and were later elaborated in the affect-as-information model proposed by Schwarz and Clore (1983) that will be discussed in more detail in the second half of this chapter.

In the second genre of emotion and memory studies, subjects view a film or staged series of events containing emotional scenes (e.g., a robbery and shooting; a bloody accident) mixed among neutral scenes, and their memory is tested at various delays (see chapter 1). The usual finding is that the gist of the emotional scenes is better remembered than that of the neutral scenes, probably because the former attract greater attention and are more frequently rehearsed. An issue occupying much attention in this research is what happens to memory for the peripheral details of emotional scenes. Some investigators find something like "tunnel vision"; the viewer focuses on (and later remembers) the specific emotional feature of a scene but misses peripheral details (Christianson & Loftus, 1991). This finding arises, for example, in the "weapon focus" phenomenon observed in witnesses' memory for violent crimes committed with weapons. Other investigators (e.g., Heuer & Reisberg, 1992) reach different conclusions, claiming that details that are perceptually part of the central figure or central event in an emotional scene will be better remembered than irrelevant background stimuli. Resolution of the discrepancies obviously will require agreement upon criteria for assigning stimuli in a scene to be peripheral versus central to the gist of the happening.

In the third class of studies, subjects record daily autobiographic events in a diary. The events are either self-selected or random ones initiated by a beeper they carry. Subjects rate the recorded incidents on several dimensions, often including their degree of pleasantness or unpleasantness. Subjects are later asked to recall or recognize the incidents. Nearly all such studies have found that participants' recollections are higher for highly emotional events than for non-emotional ones. This result, of better memory for more intense emotional events, holds for both positive and negative events. The result undoubtedly has multiple causes, one of which is that people are inclined spontaneously to revive and replay emotional incidents in their minds, and these extra rehearsals would improve memory.

A second potent cause is that, in most of our lives, highly emotional incidents tend to be quite rare (except at the cinema); when they do occur in real life, emotional events often involve our interactions with unusual people in unusual settings (e.g., a mugging; a job interview). Consequently, memory for these unusual incidents remains high because they are not confused with all the routine, pale experiences that otherwise fill our uneventful lives. Memories for the latter events suffer from massive interference due to their resemblance to one another.

Having briefly mentioned these three categories of emotion and memory research, we now turn to the fourth class of studies, those in which the person's mood serves as a prevailing context or background in which learning and remembering takes place.

Inducing Moods as a Context for Learning

The experiments to be reviewed nearly all involve two or more phases. College-student subjects are first induced into a feeling state, such as a happy or sad mood. This can be done in diverse ways: subjects may view a cheery or a gloomy movie, listen to mood-appropriate music, rehearse past positive or negative events, or imagine themselves experiencing a pleasant or unpleasant fantasy. They can also be given bogus feedback about their success or failure on some achievement test that should make them happy or sad. They can be asked to pose their facial muscles in a smile or frown without mentioning the corresponding feelings, yet those feelings often correspond with the facial expression.

After the mood induction, subjects are often informed that the first experiment is finished and that another experimenter would like their assistance. Then, an apparently unrelated experimenter conducts an experiment testing their memory, thinking, or evaluations. With this cover story, experimenters try to circumvent subjects' responding in the second phase to any demand characteristics conveyed during the first (mood induction) phase of the experiment. By this subterfuge, the experimenters are presumably assessing the mood's automatic influences on cognition rather than the subjects' conscious role-playing of the behavior of people feeling that mood (e.g., say, responding the way a depressed person might).

In some studies, the problem of demand characteristics is circumvented by collecting data from people in naturalistic field settings where certain emotions can be predicted (sports fans after witnessing their team win or lose an important contest; moviegoers exiting from a happy or sad movie; students receiving a good or bad grade on an important exam). Having described the usual techniques to induce moods in the laboratory, we now turn to some of the results obtained in such studies.

Mood Dependent Memory

Mood dependent memory refers to the phenomenon of a person's emotional state serving as part of the context that becomes associated with ongoing events, so that memory for those events is best obtained when that emotional context is reinstated. Thus, if people learn something in a given mood or emotional state, they can best remember it later if they return to the same or similar mood. Mood dependence is an example of the *encoding specificity principle* (Tulving, 1983), according to which memory retrieval is best when the cognitive milieu reinstates that which prevailed at the time of the original experience (see chapter 1).

Early laboratory demonstrations of mood dependence involved college students learning two unrelated word lists in an induced happy then sad mood, then later freely recalling each list in the same or the opposite mood. The results showed better free recall when subjects' mood during learning of a list matched their mood while later trying to recall that list (Bower, Monteiro, & Gilligan, 1978).

This effect occurs not only with unrelated word lists in the laboratory, but also in the recall of autobiographic memories. When asked to recollect events from the past, people should recall a selected sample of memories whose valence corresponds with their emotional state during recall. Several studies presented such a pattern. For example, when subjects were hypnotically induced to experience happy or sad moods and were asked to recall incidents from their childhood, their memories were predominantly consistent with their mood; happy subjects recalled more happy childhood episodes, and sad subjects remembered more sad events (Bower, 1981). In another experiment, recollections of emotional events recorded in a diary were also significantly biased in the direction of subjects' current mood state (Bower, 1981). As a final example, in an experiment by Snyder and White (1982), college students were induced to feel happy or sad and then were asked to recall any autobiographic episodes from the past two weeks. On average, happy subjects recalled nearly four times as many emotionally positive than negative episodes, whereas sad subjects recollected roughly twice as many negative events as positive ones. This pattern illustrates mood dependent memory, for, presumably, subjects felt appropriately happy or sad earlier when these events originally occurred.

A similar bias in recall occurs for people who exhibit sadness as a long-term affective disorder. When recalling their recent past, clinically depressed patients have a strong bias to recall mainly negative, depressing episodes. This tendency contributes to their downward spiral of negative recollections feeding into a preexisting state of dysphoria and constitutes a major obstacle to psychotherapy. In fact, several techniques employed in cognitive-behavior therapy with depressed clients aim to break this cycle of negative memories and dysphoria by having clients note and rehearse recent occasions when they acted competently and successfully and were feeling good.

The role of current mood in influencing autobiographic recall was clearly shown in a three-year study of 2,000 people by Lewinsohn and Rosenbaum (1987), who questioned their subjects about their current mood and memories of how their parents had raised them as children. They found that currently depressed people tended to recall their parents as being rejecting and unloving, which at first look suggests that an adult's depression might be caused by a deprived, abusive childhood. However, a different interpretation was suggested by the recall patterns of these same patients after their depression had remitted as a result of psychotherapy or pharmacotherapy; they now recalled their parents' behaviors and attitudes toward them in childhood as more loving and nurturant. Similarly, by examining longitudinal changes in people's recall, before the onset of a depressive episode, researchers found that the "predepressive" subjects recalled a more pleasantly loving family environment during childhood than the one they recalled during their later, depressed period. Rather than indicating a strong causal relation between a deprived, unhappy childhood and adult depression, these results suggest a retrospective bias due to people's current mood in how they remember and evaluate their parents' behavior and their predominant state of well-being during their childhood. The results are consonant with the concept of mood dependent memory.

The associative network theory.   To explain this mood dependent effect, Isen (1984; Clark & Isen, 1982) and Bower (1981) independently proposed an associative network theory. The view is summarized in figure 3.1, which depicts an emotion unit or node (say #3 is anger or sadness) situated in an associative memory structure. About six (plus or minus two) "basic" emotion nodes were presumed to be biologically wired into the brain, each with several situational triggers (detectors), each trigger becoming greatly elaborated and differentiated through cultural learning. For example, in Bower and Cohen (1982), the process of emotional elicitation was modeled by a collection of production rules that recognized situations calling for different emotions. This approach shows considerable similarity with later appraisal theories of emotions as proposed by Ortony et al. (1988),

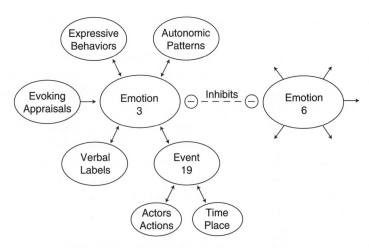

FIGURE 3.1. Sample of the connections surrounding a specific emotion node or unit. Bidirectional arrows refer to mutual exchange of activation between units. An inhibitory pathway from Emotion 3 to Emotion 6 is also shown. Source: Bower, 1981.

Roseman (1984), and Smith and Ellsworth (1985). When an emotion is aroused due to the brain recognizing an evocative situation, that emotion node spreads excitation to a variety of indicators with which it is connected.

These indicators include physiological and autonomic reactions characteristic of that emotion, facial and postural expressions, verbal labels for one's state, a collection of action tendencies, some themes associated with that emotion, and a set of memories of events that had been associated with that emotion in the past. These would ordinarily be past events that causally evoked (and "belonged to") that emotion. For example, one event recorded in your memory structure could be a description of a scene from a friend's funeral that caused you to feel sad; if you are later asked about your friend at a time when you are feeling sad, this funeral memory may receive more total activation—from the retrieval cue plus your current emotion—so that the funeral scene is more apt to come to mind and be reported than are other recollections about the friend. This kind of summation of activation, at memory-records on the intersection between a cue and a current emotion, suffices to explain mood dependent memory.

The original idea was that an aroused emotion would become associated by temporal contiguity with whatever ideas or thoughts occupied short-term memory for a while. On this account, if a subject studies a list of unrelated words (in a laboratory experiment) while feeling sad, those words would become associated with the prevailing emotion as well as with the list-context. Thus, those words should be better freely recalled later when the same emotion is induced for recall. But this contiguity account encountered some serious difficulties, as we explain.

Factors influencing mood dependent memory. Following the earlier positive demonstrations of mood dependence, several later studies questioned the size and reliability of the effect. In particular, mood dependent memory of studied word lists in the laboratory proved to be a weak, evanescent phenomenon, appearing or not across different studies in a somewhat puzzling pattern. Eventually, Eich (1995) provided an orderly explanation of the pattern of results in a review article based on his extensive research. Eich showed that mood dependence is a robust effect that best appears when the moods induced are strong, when the memory measure is free (uncued) recall rather than recognition, and when the target memories are themselves generated by the subject rather than imposed by the experimenter (Beck & McBee, 1995). For example, potent mood dependent effects emerge when the items to be learned (and later recalled) are words subjects use as cues to recollect personal episodes or events.

Most memory theories can explain the power of the first two factors. The requirement of strong moods stems from the fact that mood dependence arises from a failure of generalization of memories between two opposing states (say, happiness and sadness), and it is widely accepted that generalization is less likely to occur the greater the dissimilarity between the learning and testing conditions. Also, the absence of mood dependence in tests of recognition memory could come about because such tests require subjects to retrieve a simple association from the target item to the list context, an association that has few competitors and whose retrieval is not helped by mood matching (for details, see Bower, 1981). The less obvious fact to be explained is why mood dependence shows up best in autobiographic recall or when subjects generate their own target items, but not when the items are arbitrarily imposed upon them. One possible explanation is provided by the *causal belonging hypothesis*, to be considered below.

Other research with more complex social stimuli, and using more realistic encoding and recall contexts than is typically available in the word-list experiments, tends to reliably replicate the mood dependent effect (Fiedler, 1990, 1991, 2000; Forgas, 1991a, 1992c, 1993b; Forgas & Bower, 1987). The reason for this is probably that these studies, primarily concerned with social judgment, provide people with a much richer set of encoding and retrieval cues than is commonly available in standard memory experiments. As Bower (1981) initially suggested, affective influences should be most marked when mood can act as an effective differentiating context in learning and recall, more likely in a complex and realistic social context. The effect is more difficult to obtain in the impoverished processing environment that characterizes many word-list memory experiments. These results are also broadly consistent with Eich's (1995; Eich & Macaulay, 2000) recent delineation of the boundary conditions necessary for robust mood-priming effects to occur.

The "causal belonging" hypothesis. This hypothesis supposes that subjects will associate an emotion with a stimulus or situation only if they causally relate their emotional reaction to the stimulus or situation, if they perceive the two as "causally belonging" together. Temporal contiguity alone, without belongingness, will produce only weak or nonexistent associations (a view proposed by Thorndike, 1932). The hypothesis makes evolutionary sense: organisms should associate emotional feelings with external events or stimuli that caused those feelings to be evoked (e.g., pleasure at finding a food patch; fear at sight of a predator). In this way, organisms are enabled to react appropriately when these events recur.

To apply this hypothesis to the conditions of mood dependent memory, we note first that retrieval of autobiographic memories will show mood dependence because the emotions causally belonged originally to the events being recalled. The event-to-emotion association could be established strongly through causal belonging at the initial experience, and this strong association would be reused in the later, emotion-laden retrieval situation.

Second, presentation of unrelated laboratory materials are expected to produce only weak mood dependence because the typical memory experiment arranges only contiguity, not causal belonging, between presentation of the to-be-learned material and emotional arousal. Typically, the mood is induced minutes before presentation of the learning material, and the mood serves only as a prevailing background; hence, the temporal relations are not synchronized to persuade subjects to attribute their emotional feelings to the material they are studying. Thus, contiguity without causal belonging produces only weak associations at best.

To see how the causal belonging hypothesis helps us understand the influence of self-generated material on mood dependent memory, refer to figure 3.2. This shows a fragment of a hypothetical associative memory surrounding the concept *lake*. Suppose that in one of Eich's studies (e.g., Eich, Macaulay, & Ryan, 1994, experiment 2), the subject has been induced to feel happy and is asked to recall an incident from her life suggested by the target word *lake*. This concept has many associations including several autobiographic memories, a happy one describing a pleasantly thrilling water-skiing episode, and a sad one recounting an episode of a friend drowning in a lake. These event-memories are connected to the emotions the events caused. When feeling happy and presented with the list-cue *lake*, the subject is likely (by summation of activation) to come up with the water-skiing memory. The subject will then also associate the list-context to the water-skiing memory and to the word *lake* that evoked it. These newly formed list associations, depicted by dashed lines in figure 3.2, are formed by virtue of the subject attributing causal belonging of the word-and-memory to the experimenter's presentation of the item within the list.

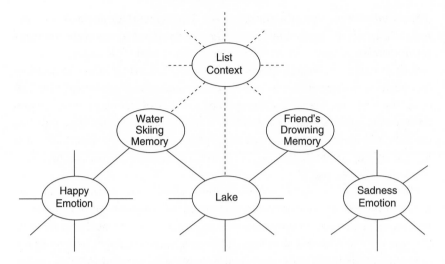

FIGURE 3.2. Fragment of a hypothetical subject's associations involving the concept of *lake*. Lines represent associations connecting emotion nodes to descriptions of two different events, one happy and one sad. The experimental context becomes associated to experiences that were aroused by cues in that setting. Source: Bower, 1992.

These contextual associations are called upon later when the subject is asked to freely recall the prompting words (or the memories prompted by them) when induced into the same mood or a different one. If the subject is happy at the time of recall testing, the water-skiing memory would be advantaged because it would receive the summation of activation from the happy-mood node and the list context, thus raising it above a recall level. On the other hand, if the subject's mood at recall shifted to sadness, that node has no connection to the water-skiing memory that was aroused during list input, so her recall of *lake* in this case would rely exclusively on the association of that item to the overloaded, list-context node in figure 3.2. Thus, mood dependent memory would follow from such a plausible associative structure.

Two features related to figure 3.2 should be noted. First, the emotion of happiness is not directly associated to the presentation of the word *lake* in the list. Rather, the emotion was associated through causal belonging to the memory of the water-skiing incident that occurred several years ago. Second, recognition memory for whether the word *lake* appeared in the list simply requires retrieval of the *lake*-to-list association; that association is not heavily overloaded at the *lake* node, so its retrieval is not aided by reinstatement of the learning mood.

Thus, the causal belonging hypothesis may account for several factors that moderate the extent of mood dependence in memory. Unfortunately, direct tests of the hypothesis are logistically difficult to arrange with human subjects, because such tests would require that subjects experience a collection of realistic (to-be-remembered) incidents in which they attribute their strong emotional reactions to arranged events. Most such experiments would be unethical and properly proscribed.

One promising approach used by Munakata and Bower (1992) provided bogus feedback, either positive or negative, that was ostensibly contingent on subjects' performance (over 2 minutes) on each of a series of distinct intellectual tasks (e.g., solving anagrams, naming novel uses for a common object, finding words in a letter matrix, etc.). After each task, subjects were told whether their performance on it was better or worse than the group average. Success or failure feedback was assigned arbitrarily to half the tasks, different for every subject. Subjects later induced to be happy recalled more of their successful than of their failed tasks; subjects induced to feel sad did just the reverse. This mood dependent effect presumably reflects the association formed (during presentation) between a given task and the pleasant or unpleasant feeling created when the experimenter' offered immediate feedback on the subject's performance on that task.

Similar effects obtained in experiments designed primarily to investigate the impact of mood on social judgments may also reflect the causal belonging hypothesis. When the information to be encoded is about people, events, or complex social situations rather than word lists, subjects are more likely to perceive a degree of causal belonging between the material and their mood than would be the case with simple and personally uninvolving stimuli. In the second half of this chapter, we shall develop a more inclusive, integrated explanation of such affect infusion effects. One objective of this theory is to specify the contextual conditions that make substantive processing, and the use of affect primed associations, more likely in cognitive tasks.

Other avenues for testing the causal belonging hypothesis of mood dependent memory would be welcome. We believe it is a plausible hypothesis to explain the somewhat conflicting pattern of results on mood dependent memory.

Mood Congruent Processing

A second central effect of emotion is called mood congruent processing, which occurs when people become selectively sensitized to take in information that agrees with their prevailing emotional state. Mood congruent processing is implied by the associative network theory depicted in figure 3.1. In an earlier essay, one of us wrote:

> When emotions are strongly aroused, concepts, words, themes, and rules of inference that are associated with that emotion will become primed and highly available for use by the emotional subject. We can thus expect the emotional person to use top-down or expectation-driven processing of his social environment. That is, his emo-

tional state will bring into readiness certain perceptual categories, certain themes, certain ways of interpreting the world that are congruent with his emotional state; these mental sets then act as interpretive filters of reality and as biases in his judgements. (Bower, 1983, p. 395)

Mood congruent learning.   One implication is that mood congruent material becomes more salient; people should attend to it more and process it more deeply with greater associative elaboration and hence should learn it better. Thus, happy people likely attend more to pleasant materials and learn more about them; sad people attend more to unpleasant stimuli in their environment and learn more about them.

An early demonstration of mood congruent learning stems from a study by Stephen Gilligan (1982), a former student of the first author. Subjects were hypnotized and put into a prevailing happy, sad, or angry mood. They then read descriptions of 36 brief incidents in which they were to imagine themselves. A third of these were happy events, such as finding a $20 bill on the sidewalk; a third were sad events, such as the death of a pet; and a third were anger-provoking events, such as having someone cut in line in front of you, causing you to miss your bus. Each event was described and imagined for 10 seconds, the three event types occurring in random order. After imagining the 36 incidents, the subjects' mood was neutralized, and a few minutes later they were unexpectedly asked to freely recall as many of the 36 incidents as they could.

The results in figure 3.3 show recall of the three types of events by the three groups of subjects who had been feeling happy, angry, or sad throughout the encoding phase of the experiment. There is a mood congruent advantage: people who were feeling happy during the initial experience learned the happy events better; angry people learned the anger-provoking events better; and sad people learned the sad events better. Because all subjects were tested for recall in a neutral mood, these recall differences reflect the three groups' differential encoding of the three types of material. An explanation of the outcome depends on the idea that when subjects are experiencing a given emotion, they can more readily come up with elaborative associations to affective events congruent with their current state. For example, the story of the death of a beloved pet can easily evoke from a sad person more autobiographic memories and more vivid images than would a story about finding a $20 bill. To complete the derivation, we need only note that a standard theory of memory suggests that retention is greatly improved when subjects construct associative elaborations around the target items (see Anderson, 1976, pp. 396–406).

Other demonstrations of mood congruent learning have been obtained in several studies that measured not only memory but also the amount of time happy and sad people take to read about the personality characteristics of a stranger (Forgas, 1992c; Forgas & Bower, 1987). In these experiments, happy subjects

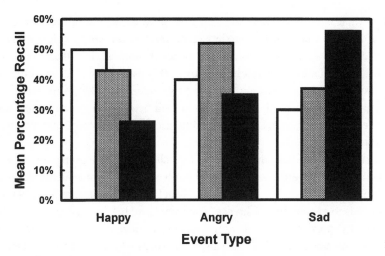

FIGURE 3.3. Happy, angry, or sad events recalled by neutral-mood subjects who studied them earlier in a happy, angry, or sad mood (white, gray, and black bars, respectively). Source: Gilligan, 1982; reprinted with permission.

spent more time reading positively valenced information about the stranger, whereas sad subjects dwelt longer on negative characteristics (see fig. 3.8 further on in this chapter). These latency differences are consistent with the affect priming theory, which predicts that subjects will take longer to encode mood congruent information into a richer and more elaborately primed associative base.

Mood congruent learning is often observed in clinically depressed patients asked to learn mixed lists of neutral words and words relevant to their disorder. Later, they will often show better memory for the depressive words. The effect is especially strong if the words are personality-trait words and subjects decide whether or not each word describes them (Watkins, Mathews, Williamson, & Fuller, 1992). Moreover, after patients have recovered from episodes of depression, they no longer show the recall advantage for emotionally negative words (Bradley & Mathews, 1983).

Whereas the results for depressed individuals consistently show mood congruent learning, the results are much more varied for people with various anxiety disorders. Though patients suffering from generalized anxiety tend to retrieve more negative autobiographic memories to neutral cues than control subjects (e.g., Burke & Mathews, 1992), they often do not show enhanced learning of negative trait words when these are presented in a list for study (Mogg, Mathews, & Weinman, 1987). Patients with more specific anxiety disorders have also produced mixed results. For example, Watts and Dalgleish (1991) reported poorer recall by spider phobics for phobia-related than for neutral words. On the other hand, McNally, Foa, and Donnell (1989) asked panic-disorder patients and normal controls to rate whether they were described by trait words that either did or did not relate to anxiety (e.g., *nervous* and *jumpy* versus *polite* and *intellectual*). Later, the panic patients recalled more anxiety than non-anxiety words, compared to the controls. Moreover, this memory bias for anxious words was exaggerated (in the panic patients only) when the subjects exercised for a few minutes before recall; exercise raised their heart rate and presumably raised their fear of a panic attack, thus providing greater activation of threat words on the study list.

In summary, whereas depressed patients show a clear learning advantage for studied negative words, anxiety patients display divergent patterns depending on their specific disorder. Mathews and MacLeod (1994) suggested a plausible hypothesis to explain the difference. They supposed that when depressed patients encounter depressing words, they use them to retrieve negative associations that elaborate on these materials, causing such words to become more memorable. In contrast, anxious patients are hypothesized to be hypervigilant to detect and defend themselves against threats and cues associated with their fears (for related results, see Ciarrochi & Forgas, 1999a). Although they are prepared to identify fear-related stimuli in their environment, they are also prepared to rapidly "escape from" those stimuli, including putting them out of mind. This view implies that threat-related words may receive less mental rehearsal during study than do non-threat words, and are thus encoded less firmly.

This selective memory advantage for disorder-related words for depressed but not anxious subjects nearly reverses in studies of selective attention. Patients with generalized anxiety disorder are biased to attend more rapidly to threat-related words or to locations in the visual field where threats have recently appeared (for a review, see Mathews & MacLeod, 1994). For example, Mac-Leod, Mathews, and Tata (1986) presented two words (a threat-related word paired with a neutral word), one above the other, on a computer screen for half a second and asked subjects to read the top word as quickly as possible. The subjects also had to look out for a small dot probe that could appear in the location of either word shortly after the pair-display was terminated. MacLeod et al. found that generalized anxiety patients detected the dot probe faster when it occurred in the location of a preceding threat word. These results reveal clinically anxious individuals' attentional bias toward threat-related words; however, the evidence of an analogous bias toward negative words for clinically depressed patients is more mixed and often negative (Gotlib, McLachlan, & Katz, 1988; Mogg et al., 1991). For example, even though depressed individuals show enhanced Stroop interference in naming the colors of depressing words (Gotlib & McCann, 1984), they do not show a negative attentional bias toward negative words in the dot-probe task (Gotlib et al., 1988).

The comparative effects of clinical anxiety and depression on attention and memory merit further research. In relation to the affect priming theory, the pattern of results is on the whole supportive in the case of depressed patients, but weak and mixed in the case of generalized anxiety patients.

Mood congruent retrieval. Just as emotional state affects the congruent encoding of material, it also influences the later retrieval of affectively congruent material from memory. Lloyd and Lishman (1975) originally demonstrated mood congruent retrieval, testing depressed and nondepressed subjects for retrieval speed for a requested pleasant or unpleasant autobiographic memory evoked by a cue word. They reported that depressed subjects retrieved unpleasant memories faster than pleasant ones, whereas nondepressed subjects did the opposite; Teasdale and Fogarty (1979), as well as Burke and Mathews (1992), obtained a similar pattern of results. From our viewpoint, however, these demonstrations confound mood dependent retrieval with mood congruent retrieval, because the autobiographic events whose memories are being retrieved presumably caused the subject to feel pleasant or unpleasant when they happened originally.

A proper demonstration of mood congruent retrieval requires that subjects-particular emotion at the time the target events are encoded, but later their positive or negative mood should differentially influence the recall of positive versus negative items. An example is provided by Teasdale and Russell (1983), who had subjects in a neutral mood study a mixed list of positive, neutral, and negative words. Subjects were then induced to feel happy or sad, and they attempted to recall the word list. Teasdale and Russell found that, although the groups recalled neutral words at similar rates, happy subjects remembered more positive than negative words, whereas sad subjects remembered more negative than positive words. The effect is claimed to be due only to mood at retrieval since no specific mood was induced during original learning of the word list.

Mood congruent retrieval is a small effect and is not always in evidence; for example, Bower et al. (1978) failed to find it. Nonetheless, the effect has been observed often enough to be considered genuine.

Mood congruence in implicit memory. Recall and recognition are examples of *explicit* memory tasks in which subjects intentionally try to retrieve prior episodes or events, such as the appearance of a familiar word in an otherwise unfamiliar list or collection of other words. Explicit memory tasks are often contrasted with *implicit* memory tasks, which do not require deliberate, conscious recollection. Implicit memory is often indexed through priming—broadly speaking, the observation that processing a stimulus once makes it easier (faster, more accurate) to do so again later. Thus, for example, priming for a previously studied item such as *admiral* might be assessed by asking subjects to name the first word they think of that begins with *adm*, to produce instances of the category "military titles," to unscramble the anagram *daliram* to form a meaningful word, to identify what they see on a screen following the fleeting appearance of the word *admiral,* or to perform some other test of implicit memory. The affect priming theory supposes that words connotatively congruent with a person's current mood should command more attention and greater processing than incongruent words. If so, congruent words should show greater priming than incongruent ones.

Though initial research by Watkins et al. (1992) and Denny and Hunt (1992) suggested that selective priming of negative words does *not* occur in depressed patients, more recent studies have strongly confirmed it. In an experiment by Ruiz-Caballero and Gonzalez (1994), subjects selected for scoring high or low on the BDI studied a mixed list of positive and negative trait words. They then performed an implicit test of stem completion in which they were asked to name any word that starts with a particular three-letter stem. Some of the stems corresponded to old items (i.e., positive or negative trait words that had been studied previously); others corresponded to new items (words that had not been memorized earlier). Afterward, the subjects freely recalled all of the studied words they could.

The results showed, first, a robust mood congruent effect in the explicit test of free recall: depressed subjects (those with high BDI scores) recalled more negative than positive words (38% versus 19%), whereas nondepressed subjects (with low BDI scores) recalled more positive than negative words (57% versus 35%). Second, priming in the implicit test of stem completion also showed mood congruence: whereas the depressed subjects produced more old negative than old positive words in response to the stems, nondepressed subjects did just the reverse.

To control for the possibility that subjects were explicitly remembering old items when completing stems, Ruiz-Caballero and Gonzalez (1994) carried out a second study identical to the first except that, in the new experiment, subjects studied the mixed list of positive and negative trait words under conditions of either intentional or incidental learning. The results were similar and also ruled out the explicit recollection argument. Although the overall level of free recall was much lower for incidental than intentional learners (no surprise there), both groups showed significant mood congruence in their performance of the explicit test. Interestingly, mood congruent priming in the implicit test of stem completion was as robust for the incidental learners as for their intentional-learning counterparts. That is, depressed incidental learners and depressed intentional learners performed similarly in completing more old negative than old positive words; furthermore, nondepressed incidental learners and nondepressed intentional learners showed the same advantage in completing more old positive than old negative words. In short, mood congruent priming in implicit memory did not seem to depend on the level of explicit memory created by incidental, versus intentional, instructions. Based on these data, the authors rejected the idea that the mood congruent effect in stem completion arose from the implicit test's "contamination" by surreptitious use of explicit memories. Instead, they concluded that their results supported the mood activation hypothesis, which supposes that depressed subjects should selectively process negative words.

Similar studies by Tobias, Kihlstrom, and Schacter (1992) found effects of induced moods on two further tests of implicit memory. Their subjects studied positive, neutral, or negative words when in a music-induced happy or sad mood, and were later tested in the same or opposite mood. Though neither of two tests of explicit memory (free or cued recall) showed reliable mood congruence, the effect was observed in both of two tests of implicit memory (word-stem and sentence-fragment completion). That is, subjects who were in a happy mood at both learning and test produced more positive than negative words from the study list in both implicit tasks; similarly, subjects who were sad during learning and testing produced more negative than positive list words in these same two tasks.

Similar results emerged from an experiment by Tobias and Kihlstrom (cited in Tobias et al., 1992) that entailed a novel form of priming. After studying a list of positive, negative, or neutral words, their subjects listened to music designed to induce a happy or sad mood. Subjects were then falsely informed that the music had contained a masked, subliminally presented list of words. They were then asked to write down whatever words "spontaneously came to mind" presumably due to the influence of the subliminal tape: subjects were provided either with no observable cues whatsoever or with the initial letter of each of the previously studied words.

Tobias et al. (1992) observed mood congruence in both of these priming tests. Subjects who had listened to happy music produced more positive than negative words from the list, whereas subjects who had listened to sad music produced more negative than positive words. According to the authors, these results demonstrate mood effects on implicit memory, because subjects were instructed not to refer to the initially presented list but rather to report whatever words came to mind spontaneously. Thus, the test circumvents intentional reference to past episodes, which is the hallmark of explicit memory tasks.

The foregoing results on mood congruence in implicit memory are closely related to the issue of whether moods directly prime the perception and processing of congruent words and pictures. Because Niedenthal and Halberstadt extensively review that topic in this volume, we will not discuss it in detail here, but instead will simply note that (a) under suitable conditions, Niedenthal and her associates find robust mood congruence in perceptual tasks involving lexical decision and word identification (see Niedenthal & Halberstadt, 2000; Niedenthal & Setterlund, 1994), and (b) recent work suggests that emotional categorization effects, based on associative principles, are far more common than previously suspected (see Greenwald et al., 2000; Showers, 2000).

Associative Effects of Moods

Earlier we noted the theory's implication that the arousal of an emotion should prime and render available all manner of associations to that emotion. Thus, words, concepts, images, themes, and rules of inference associated with an emotion should be brought into readiness and made highly available for use. Several of these effects will now be reviewed.

Word associations. One of the early demonstrations of mood congruent priming showed that people give word associations that are pleasant or unpleasant depending on their current feelings (Bower, 1981). Thus, to a stimulus word such as *life*, happy subjects will give associates such as *freedom* or *love*, whereas sad subjects might say *death* or *struggle*. The network theory explains this by noting that most words have numerous associations—some positive, some negative, many neutral in tone. When one is feeling positive or negative, those associates of *life* that lie on intersection points in the network with the emotion node will receive greater total activation, thus coming to mind as prepotent associates to be given overtly.

Mayer and his associates (Mayer, Gaschke, Braverman, & Evans, 1992; Mayer & Volanth, 1985) have observed similar associative effects in research involving naturally occurring moods. For instance, when asked to name a type of weather that starts with *s*, subjects in these studies replied with either *sunny* or *springtime* if they were happy, but with *snowy* or *stormy* if they were sad. Also, when asked to decide which is the best example of a city (Paris, Calcutta, or Omaha), happy subjects usually selected the most pleasant option (Paris, in this example), whereas sad subjects often opted for the least pleasant (Calcutta).

Interpreting ambiguous stimuli. A related effect of emotion is that it makes emotionally congruent interpretations of ambiguous stimuli more available. This interpretative bias has many forms. In an early example, subjects induced to feel happy or sad projected their feelings into judgments of the pleasantness expressed by photographs of ambiguously neutral faces (Isen, Shalker, Clark, & Karp, 1978; Schiffenbauer, 1974). However, recent experiments suggest that this effect diminishes when the faces to be judged show increasingly clear-cut emotional expressions that require less constructive processing (Forgas, 1999a). Such a diminution in the associative consequences of mood is nevertheless broadly consistent with the network model, for one is likely to recognize clear-cut emotional expressions; that is, an unambiguous stimulus can overshadow the weaker priming effects of mood on judgments. These differences reflect the different processing strategies required to deal with clear-cut rather than ambiguous stimuli, a theory that we will further develop in the second half of this chapter.

In a second example of interpretive bias, when emotional subjects daydream or devise stories about fictional characters on the Thematic Apperception Test, they often compose stories that are congruent with their current feelings (Bower, 1981): happy people concoct stories about success and romance; sad people tell tales of failure and loss; angry people invent stories about conflicts and fights. Thus, feelings prompt associated themes then revealed in the stories. These themes are associated to congruent emotions, because in the past, these same themes and related events (real or fictional) have caused the congruent emotion to be aroused, thus bonding the theme and emotion through causal belonging.

In a third example of interpretative bias, Eysenck, MacLeod, and Mathews (1987) have shown that anxious patients are apt to identify the anxiety-related word in spoken homophones (such as *pain/pane, die/dye,* and *bury/berry*) in the more anxious direction. The anxiety-related concept or word meaning is chronically more activated and available for people who frequently feel anxious. Chronic priming of disorder-related words has also been observed in depressed patients. Gotlib and McCann (1984), for example, found that depressed patients show exaggerated interference in a modified Stroop task when they name the color of depression-related words compared to control words. Similarly, Watts, McKenna, Sharrock, and Trezise (1988) found exaggerated Stroop interference on spider-related words in patients who were *beginning* treatment for specific spider phobia, an effect that vanished once their fears had remitted *following* treatment.

A final example of mood alteration in interpretations comes from experiments by McNally (1994), who studied patients with panic disorder. Such individuals are especially likely to interpret ambiguous situations in a threatening manner; for example, when asked a leading question ("You awake suddenly in the middle of the night, but all is quiet. What do you think woke you up?"), they are more likely than control subjects to identify an impending heart attack or possibly an intruder who had broken into their home.

Although such studies of neurotic patients are consonant with mood priming of interpretive rules, other explanations are plausible as well. For example, simple "habit," due to the common co-occurrence of a symptom with panic, would cause such an interpretive bias without the need to postulate that the patient is currently feeling a pervasive sense of anxiety. The frequent rehearsal of such mood congruent explanations by clinical patients, who have participated in numerous interviews and therapy sessions in which they recount their experiences, surely provides many opportunities to strengthen their mood congruent associations. A similar frequency of exposure argument may be advanced to explain the prepotency of depressing or anxiety-related words for patients suffering from depression and anxiety disorders. The crucial observation to rule out the frequent habit account is whether the disorder-specific biases are largely eliminated after the patient's emotional disorder has remitted through treatment (e.g., Watts et al., 1988).

Mood Congruent Preferences

The affect priming theory suggests that emotional people will tend to dwell on, or even prefer, mood congruent stimuli; they should find them more attractive, more worthy of attention, more interesting, more meaningful for them. Of course, these stimuli represent parts of reality that also confirm the subject's current feeling and by feedback also perpetuate those feelings. These preferences show up in several different behaviors.

What's interesting?   An early illustration of mood congruent interest arose in an experiment by Colleen Kelly (1982). She induced happy or sad feelings in college students by having them write about positive or negative experiences in their lives. Thereafter, they were asked to examine a series of slides, at their own pace, dwelling on each scene according to its intrinsic interest. The slide series contained a random mixture of pleasant scenes (weddings, victory celebrations) and unpleasant scenes (funerals, despondent faces). Kelly recorded how much time subjects spent looking at each slide, and her results revealed a mood congruent effect: in comparison with their sad-mood peers, happy subjects spent more time looking at the pleasant scenes (means = 8.5 versus 6.6 seconds) and less time viewing the unpleasant scenes (means = 7.6 versus 8.2 seconds). Subjects were often unaware of their differential viewing time—they simply said that they found the mood congruent scenes "more captivating." This difference in viewing time also led to a difference in later free recall of the pictures: happy viewers recalled more happy scenes; sad viewers recalled more sad scenes.

As we noted earlier, one of our experiments asked happy and sad subjects to look at and learn positive or negative information about other people (Forgas & Bower, 1987). The information (describing a fictional character's behaviors) was presented one sentence at a time on a computer screen, and subjects controlled the reading time, pressing a key to move from one statement to the next. Once again, we found a marked tendency for happy subjects to look longer at positive than at negative information and an equally strong bias in the opposite direction among the sad subjects. A robust mood congruent effect also emerged in a subsequent test of free recall: happy subjects remembered more of the target character's positive behaviors, and sad people remembered more of the negative actions.

Unpublished studies by Mark Snyder (personal communication, 1998) also showed mood congruent preferences. In one study, Snyder found that subjects induced to feel happy preferred fast, energetic music to slow, nostalgic tunes—exactly the opposite of the choices made by sad subjects. Many participants offered the opinion that mood congruent music evoked more elaborate associations and richer imagery than did incongruent music.

Activity preferences. Consonant with these results, temporarily sad people find it difficult to think of fun activities. Carson and Adams (1980) found that subjects induced to feel happy or sad reported an increase or decrease, respectively, in their expected enjoyment of some 300 activities listed in Lewinsohn's Pleasant Events Schedule. Mark Snyder (personal communication, 1998) extended this finding by asking temporarily happy or sad subjects to indicate how much time they intended to spend on various activities in the coming weeks. On average, happy subjects said they planned to spend more time in lighthearted, enjoyable, social activities; sad subjects said they planned to spend more time in somber, solitary, and seriously ''meaningful'' activities. (Note, however, that such emotional forecasting about the enjoyability of future events is also subject to a number of distortions and biases, as Gilbert, 2000, recently showed.)

Loss of interest in social activities is a familiar symptom of chronic depression. In a similar manner, several studies have shown that when normal people are made temporarily sad, they lose interest in socializing, finding other people somewhat less rewarding or ''attractive.'' It follows that moods may also bias people's expectations about their forthcoming interactions with others, as in the course of a negotiation.

Apropos this point, figure 3.4 shows the results of a study (Forgas, 1998c) in which happy people expected their partners to be more cooperative and reliable and as a result planned to use more cooperative and less competitive strategies in both an interpersonal and an intergroup bargaining situation. We may explain these outcomes by supposing that a person's mood alters his or her expectations of gaining social rewards or punishments from interacting with others, and the balance of these expectations biases the person's interest in socializing (or cooperating) in a mood congruent direction.

In summary, the data on preferences indicate that temporarily happy or sad people tend selectively to expose themselves to scenes, music, films, and activities in a mood congruent manner. The effect of such exposures, of course, would be to perpetuate or even exacerbate one's initial mood. This kind of exacerbation has often been noted as the ''downward spiral'' of depression, whereby a dysphoric mood leads to cognitions and activities that are likely to maintain or magnify the dysphoria. Something similar seems to happen with anxious worriers: thinking of one worry raises the level of anxiety; causing other worries to come to mind, fostering even more distress (see Roemer & Borkovec, 1993).

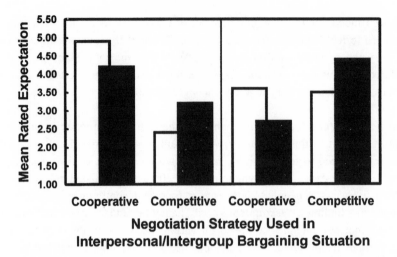

FIGURE 3.4. Rated expectation of happy and sad subjects (white and black bars, respectively) of using a cooperative or competitive strategy in negotiating an interpersonal (left panel) or intergroup (right panel) bargaining situation. Source: Forgas, 1998c.

Mood Management

The associative network model holds that these mood congruent preferences are ''natural tendencies'' primed as people experience a powerful mood or emotion. However, people clearly can often overcome their natural tendencies, just as children learn to sit still even though they are excited. Our culture teaches us to manage our moods, especially the bad ones, so that, by adulthood, most of us have learned various cognitive tricks to control our emotional expressions: examples include learning to suppress loud sobbing at the movies, to withstand the pain of the dentist's drill, to count to ten when angered, to feign interest when bored, and to fake gratitude for an unwanted gift.''Putting on a good face'' is required within polite society. People also learn how to reduce their fears and improve their moods, often by distracting themselves or by imagining counteracting scenes. Momentarily depressed people usually know that they can change their mood by watching comedies, talking to friends, pondering more pleasant times, yet such activities hold little attraction for them. Cognitive therapy for depression typically emphasizes just such mood-improving stratagems.

These mood-management strategies are relatively harmless. Of course, people may also turn to more dangerous methods for eliminating bad moods: excessive alcohol or drug abuse, for example. Indeed, Marlatt, Kosturn, and Lang (1975) found that participants in a staged wine-tasting experiment imbibed significantly more after being insulted by an experimental confederate. These results and other observations (e.g., Hull & Young, 1983) suggest that negative emotions engendered by insults, disappointment, or anger may motivate people to increase their consumption of mood-altering drugs.

People employ benign mood-repair strategies variably. In fact, to measure these coping skills, Catanzano and Mearns (1990) have developed a self-report inventory called the Negative Mood Regulation (NMR) scale, a paper-and-pencil test in which subjects estimate how much they use different mood-repair strategies in their everyday lives; it also assesses whether they believe they can alleviate their negative moods through active mood repair. Subsequent research has supported the validity of the scale, demonstrating that people who have high NMR scores experience fewer bouts of dysphoric mood (Kirsch, Mearns, & Catanzano, 1990) and cope better after negative events such as the end of a romance (Mearns, 1991). Presumably, people who score low on NMR are more vulnerable to developing depression from the accumulation of negative life events.

Smith and Petty (1995) presented evidence that mood congruent effects following a negative mood induction (a film about cancer) were predicted by individuals' NMR scores. Subjects with a low NMR score showed strong mood congruence: the more negative their mood, the more negative a subsequent fictional story they composed. On the other hand, the opposite correlation marked subjects with high NMR scores who habitually tried to repair bad moods: the more negative their mood just after the cancer film, the more positive the story they wrote. Similar results appeared in a study of autobiographical memory and in an experiment involving the free recall of previously studied newspaper headlines describing happy or sad events. Smith and Petty argued that high-NMR subjects engage in deliberate strategies to recover from a momentary negative mood, including the deliberate motivated search for pleasant ideas and happy memories to offset the effects of a negative mood induction. These results corroborate our thesis, presented in the second half of the chapter, that both the absence of mood congruence and the occurrence of mood incongruence typically occur when people have cause to engage in motivated information search, such as when they seek to overcome a bad mood.

Smith and Petty (1995) also separated their experimental subjects into subgroups with high and low self-esteem (SE; Rosenberg, 1965). People with high SE have fewer major mood swings, do not overgeneralize their failures, and are more confident of success. The authors hypothesized that such individuals would engage in more mood repair and would therefore experience fewer sad-mood congruent effects than would subjects with low SE. Consistent with this idea, low-SE subjects showed strong sad-mood congruence: the sadder the cancer film made them, the less pleasant were the stories they composed, the memories they retrieved, and the presented headlines they recalled. However, for high-SE subjects, initial negative mood had either no relation or a reversed association with the negativity of their memories and stories. Forgas (1998c) observed similar effects in a study in which subjects scoring high on measures of social desirability and Machiavellianism were much less affected by mood congruence than low-scoring subjects in interpretation of an interpersonal encounter. We thus find several personality factors that moderate the negative mood congruent effects we reviewed earlier (also see Rusting, 1998). The earlier demonstrations did not assess either SE or mood repair strategies, so the differential impact of positive and negative moods appeared as main effects, presumably despite variations in effect sizes as a result of individual personality variables.

Operative Factors in Mood Congruence: Cognitive versus Somatic Variables

We have so far used *mood* as a general term to describe the effects of various mood induction procedures, whether happy, sad, or angry in content. We understand, of course, that affective states have several constituents, including the cognitions, images, and thoughts that occupy the minds of people in particular affective states. Other components are the physiological and somatic sensations of excitement and arousal (versus lethargy and fatigue) that are also differentially linked with different affects. While our purpose here does not require us to take a stand on the relative importance of these two components of affect, we nevertheless offer our opinion that the cognitive component carries greater weight in determining mood congruence than does the somatic component (cf. Zajonc, 1980, 1984, 2000).

Several findings persuade us in this belief. Recent research by Blascovich and Mendes (2000) showed that somatic responses to emotional situations are significantly mediated by cognitive appraisals. These authors found that identical situations can produce distinctly different cardiovascular responses depending on whether individuals cognitively interpret a situation as either a challenge or a threat.

Riskind, Rholes, and Eggers (1982; also see Rholes, Riskind, & Lane, 1987) attempted to separate cognitive from physiological components of moods by using different mood inductions. They first categorized the usual Velten mood-induction statements for depression as those referring to self-devaluation (e.g., "I'm worthless; I'm a loser") and those referring to negative somatic sensations (e.g., "I'm tired, slow-moving, and lack energy"). Though subjects induced with somatic statements rated their global feelings as negatively as did subjects induced with the self-devaluative statements, only the latter subjects showed mood congruent memory (i.e., better recall of negative than of positive words). Thus, Riskind (1989) argued that the negative, self-devaluing cognitions were essential for obtaining the "mood" congruent effect and that somatic arousal is relatively unimportant. Of course, most events that cause negative feelings (e.g., failures, losses, or their imagined rehearsals) also cause self-referential negative thoughts. Mood congruence may be just another form of "cognitive priming" of the sort often studied in social perception research (e.g., Higgins, Rholes, & Jones, 1977; Wyer & Srull, 1980).

The relatively greater impact of cognitions compared to somatic sensations was demonstrated in research reported by Varner and Ellis (1998). In one experiment, subjects studied a list in which half of the words referred to feelings of depression (e.g., *lethargy*) and half related to information about writing an essay (e.g., *library*). Before studying the list, one group of subjects read self-referential statements intended to make them feel sad, a second group read pointers on how to plan and write an essay, and a third group became physically aroused by stepping up and down on a cinderblock for several minutes. On a later test of free recall, sad subjects recalled more depression-related than essay-related words, the opposite pattern emerged for the "essay" subjects, and aroused subjects recalled the two types of words equally well. Similar results occurred in a second experiment, in which subjects received one of three primings (sadness, essay, or arousal) after they had studied the list and before they were tested for free recall.

Varner and Ellis (1998) interpreted their data as showing that cognitive priming (as in the "essay" topic) suffices to produce differential processing of related words in a study list; either subjects learn them better or they are more accessible after learning. Varner and Ellis also suggested that the sadness statements probably primed negative self-concepts similarly, so that the depression-related words in the study list evoked more attention and deeper processing during encoding, making them more accessible for recall. Finally, noting that arousal (from exercise) did not affect processing of depression-related versus essay-related words, Varner and Ellis argued that the arousal component of the sadness induction contributed nothing to the sad subjects' penchant for recalling depression-related words. Their logic may be questionable, but perhaps it is true that the low "arousal" component within sadness differs from that produced by physical exercise.

Clark and her colleagues (Clark, 1982; Clark, Milberg, & Ross, 1983) have offered an alternative theory of mood dependent memory. They proposed that people associate events with the level of concurrent somatic arousal they experience and that later recall will depend on reinstatement of the same arousal level. In their view, the typical happy versus sad inductions are just disguised ways of getting people into different levels of arousal during learning or retrieval testing.

Clark et al. (1983) presented dramatic evidence consistent with this reasoning. Subjects learned two word lists for free recall—one while relaxing; the other after exercising (the step-up task)—and later attempted to recall both lists after watching either a restful (nature) or an arousing (erotic) film. As predicted, viewing the nature film enhanced subjects' recall of the list learned earlier during relaxation, whereas watching the erotic film improved recall of the list learned in the postexercise, somatically aroused state.

Clark et al.'s (1983) striking results suggest a generalized somatic context effect on memory that is independent of specific cognitions. That is, although common physiological arousal may be involved, few ideas would seem to be shared between observing sexual activity and performing the cinderblock task that would create such memory transfer.

Surprisingly, so far as we know, no one has tried to replicate Clark's results. Under Bower's supervision, Christina Van Aken (1995) attempted a replication with slight modification of the Clark et al. (1983) study as an honors thesis at Stanford University. Subjects generated two lists of 24 words (12 for each of two first letters): one list after the cinderblock exercise, one after relaxing. Ten minutes later, subjects watched either a relaxing nature video or a fear-arousing film clip (the climactic stalking episode from *The Silence of the Lambs*). Subjects then attempted to recall both lists they had generated before. Arousal was measured by heart rate that, predictably, was elevated both by exercise and, to a lesser degree, the fear-arousing film. Also, their subjective ratings of fear were raised by the scary film.

Unfortunately, Van Aken's results showed no arousal dependence whatsoever: recall percentages of the four study/recall conditions (i.e., high/high, high/low, low/high, and low/low arousal) ranged only from 67% to 70%. Thus, despite testing a sizable sample of subjects ($n = 48$) and obtaining significant heart-rate differences at testing from exposure to the different films, Van Aken failed to replicate the substance of Clark et al.'s (1983) findings. As such, the replication failure casts some doubt upon arousal dependence as a potent determinant of mood dependence. Rather, it would appear that it is the overlap or similarity of cognitions at learning and testing that may be guiding both mood congruent and mood dependent effects in memory.

MOOD EFECTS ON SOCIAL JUDGMENTS AND SOCIAL BEHAVIORS

We move now to discussing the second main topic of this chapter, namely, the manner in which people's emotions or moods influence their social judgments and behaviors. We begin this section by reviewing early studies that showed strong mood congruence across several judgment domains. We then review later studies that uncovered several factors that qualify or moderate simple mood congruent effects on social judgments. In the final section, we develop an integrative theory to account for the presence or absence of mood congruence depending on the processing strategies people employ.

Persuasive Impact of Mood Congruent Messages

The impact of social information depends in part on whether it agrees with one's current mood. This principle was first established sixty years ago by Razran (1940), who induced a good mood in subjects by providing them with a free lunch, or a bad mood by exposing them to unpleasant odors. A positive mood significantly improved subjects' willingness to accept persuasive messages—a strategy long used by politicians, used-car salesmen, and real estate brokers everywhere.

Calder and Gruder (1988) have reported other demonstrations of this effect. In one study, students were induced to feel satisfied or angry as they read a simulated newspaper review of a restaurant. The review contained a mixture of 20 positive and 20 negative statements about various aspects of the restaurant. Once their mood had been neutralized, they rated the restaurant and tried to recall the review. The results showed that subjects who had read the review when angry later rated the restaurant far more negatively than did subjects who read the review when feeling satisfied. Both groups also recalled more mood congruent rather than incongruent information from the review.

In a second study, Calder and Gruder (1988) showed that angry readers reacted more negatively to a review containing anger-provoking statements, whereas disgusted readers reacted more negatively to a review containing descriptions of disgusting attributes of the restaurant. The more intense the supposed congruent (negative) reaction during reading, the more extreme the negative rating of the restaurant, and the more frequently those congruent statements of the review were later recalled. These studies suggest that people might be preferentially disposed toward accepting and learning information that agrees with their prevailing mood.

Impression Formation

As we noted earlier, our experiment (Forgas & Bower, 1987) examined subjects' depth of processing of mood congruent information in an impression-formation task. Subjects induced to feel happy or sad (by bogus feedback about their score on a test) read descriptions of a stranger and were asked to form an impression of him. Subjects sat before a computer terminal and pressed a key to observe a series of statements one by one, each statement describing some favorable or unfavorable behavior of the stranger. We measured the time subjects took to read and think about each behavioral description. Subjects in a good mood lingered longer on positive aspects of the stranger; subjects in a sad mood lingered longer on his negative aspects. As expected, subjects in a good mood concluded with a more favorable impression of the stranger. Moreover, subjects' later memory for the descriptions of the stranger's behavior showed mood congruence: subjects in a good mood remembered more of his socially desirable behaviors; subjects in a sad mood remembered more of his undesirable behaviors.

Job Interviews

In the previous experiment, subjects formed an impression based solely on verbal descriptions of a stranger they never actually met. Baron (1987) asked his subjects to develop an impression during a face-to-face interview with a stranger. Using bogus feedback about the subjects' ability, Baron first induced them to feel mildly happy, neutral, or sad. Each participant then conducted a one-on-one interview with a person who was supposedly applying for a middle-management job, asking him a list of prearranged questions. In fact, the applicant was a confederate who gave the same predetermined answers to each interviewer— deliberately mixed and ambivalent answers.

After the interview, each subject rated the applicant on several traits. Compared to neutral interviewers, happy interviewers rated the candidate as more motivated, talented, likable, attractive, and having greater potential for the job; they also said they probably would hire him. In contrast, the momentarily depressed interviewers rated the applicant considerably less positively on all dimensions and were fairly sure they would turn him down.

Baron also tested his interviewers for their later recall of the confederate's canned answers. Recall showed mood congruence: happy interviewers recalled more of the positive remarks the applicant had made about himself; depressed interviewers recalled more of the negative remarks he had made about himself. Such studies show that, in a realistic setting, mood biases can significantly affect hiring decisions and the careers of the people and institutions involved.

Predicting Behaviors of Others

The affect priming theory implies that people in a good or bad mood generally expect others to behave well or badly, respectively. This outcome is especially likely when a person believes several conflicting but not contradictory pieces of information about someone. For example, suppose that you think that George is warm but moody, Jim is trustworthy but possessive, and Bill is understanding but unsociable. Suppose you are asked to predict the likelihood that these men will engage in behaviors characteristic of these traits. The theory implies that the adjudged "fit" or applicability of a given trait to a target person should match the judge's mood. That is, when happy, judges should expect other people to exhibit more prosocial than antisocial traits; when feeling sad, judges should expect other people's antisocial traits to dominate their prosocial traits.

Erber (1991) tested this implication and found generally confirmatory results. In one study, subjects in happy, sad, or neutral moods read about several fictional characters, each described by two conflicting but noncontradictory traits (such as the men described previously). Subjects then rated the likelihood that a given target person would exhibit specific behaviors: some were relevant to the person's positive trait (e.g., *welcomes a friend with a hug* is applicable to the trait *warm*), some to his negative trait (e.g., *gets depressed over the weather* is applicable to the trait *moody*), and some irrelevant to either of the traits ascribed to the target. Erber reported a strong mood congruent interaction. Thus, when happy, judges estimated a target's positive-trait behavior as more likely than his negative-trait behavior; when sad, judges estimated a target's negative-trait behavior as more likely than his positive-trait behavior.

In a second study, Erber (1991) confirmed the same interaction in judges' predictions after using an unusual induction for pleasant or unpleasant moods. In this instance, subjects' moods were subtly induced by having them configure their facial muscles into a "smile" (by biting lightly on a pencil, curving up the corners of their mouth) or into a "frown" (by biting tightly with the corners of the mouth down, as in anger). Smiling subjects rated applicable positive behaviors of targets as more likely than negative behaviors; frowning subjects thought applicable negative behaviors were more likely than positive behaviors. Moreover, when subjects were later asked to recall the traits ascribed to each of the four target persons, a mood congruent advantage appeared: smiling subjects remembered more positive traits than did frowning subjects, whereas frowning subjects remembered more negative traits than did smiling subjects. These results replicate those reported by Laird, Wagener, Halal, and Szegda (1982), who had subjects configure their faces into a happy, depressed, or angry countenance (without mentioning emotional expressions) as they processed and later recalled a mixture of happy, sad, and angry statements.

Prosocial Behavior

Considerable evidence indicates that happiness increases people's cooperativeness, friendliness, helping, and prosocial behaviors. The work of Lay, Waters, and Park (1989) on cooperation and compliance by 4-year-old children to parental requests provides an example. Prior research (Parpal & Maccoby, 1985) demonstrated that children's compliance to a parent's request (e.g., to clean up a messy room) greatly increased following a brief period of highly positive interaction ("responsive play") with that parent. In responsive play, the parent tries to act as the ideal childish playmate, following the child's lead in play activity, providing only positive encouragement with no questions, commands, or corrections. Lay et al. (1989) found that responsive play increased children's positive mood. Moreover, by simply inducing a happy or a sad mood (by having the child rehearse corresponding memories), Lay et al. observed that the child's compliance with parental requests increased or decreased, respectively.

These results on cooperative compliance accord with earlier results showing that positive mood promotes altruism and helping behaviors. Isen and Levin (1972) found that after receiving a cookie from a stranger, college students studying in a library were much more willing to volunteer when a second stranger asked them to serve as an experimenter's assistant. In a related field study, Isen and Levin reported that people who found a measly dime in the coin return of a public telephone were much more likely than control subjects (88% versus 4%) to help a stranger pick up a stack of papers she had "accidentally" dropped on the sidewalk in front of them. Similarly, Moore, Underwood, and Rosenhan (1973) found that, for 7- and-8-year-old children, positive moods enhanced (apparently) private contributions of money to a charity for unfortunate children, whereas negative mood decreased such contributions. This result was replicated by Rosenhan, Underwood, and Moore (1974).

In all these cases, positive affect clearly increases the positivity of one's reaction to others and one's helping behaviors. Of course, this behavior mimics others' behavior that makes us happy. This reflection is the basis for the reciprocity principle that smooths and tranquilizes the social interactions and personal interchanges of our daily lives.

Mood Effects on Evaluations

Another implication of the affect priming theory is that mood will influence one's momentary evaluation of possessions and opinions about all manner of things. A prevailing mood should prime and make more available those features of an attitude topic that agree with the mood.

Personal possessions. In an early demonstration of this bias, Isen et al. (1978) found that pedestrians in a shopping mall who received a small gift that pleased them, such as a fingernail clipper, reported on an unrelated survey given a few minutes later that their cars and television sets were working better than did people who had not received that small gift. More recently, Ciarrochi and Forgas (1999b) found that positive mood increased, and negative mood decreased, the subjective value people placed on material possessions when they contemplated selling them.

Life satisfaction. A similar effect was reported by Forgas and Moylan (1987), who interviewed nearly a thousand patrons in cinema lobbies before as well as after they viewed films that produced predominantly happy or sad feelings. In an artificial public-opinion survey, patrons took about a minute to rate, either before or after the movie, their mood and their satisfaction with several controversial political figures, the likelihood of several future prospects, satisfaction with their personal and work situation, and their opinion about the severity of penalties handed out for antisocial crimes such as drunk driving and heroin trafficking. The results showed that people who had seen a comedy such as *Back to the Future* were more satisfied with their life, more optimistic about their future, and more positive toward their politicians than were filmgoers who had just seen a profoundly saddening film such as *Terms of Endearment*. Also, people who had just seen a violent action film were more likely to recommend severe punishments for heroin trafficking and other crimes.

Health status. Moods also affect reports about physical health and medical history. A study by Salovey and Birnbaum (1989) found that people made to feel temporarily sad as they filled out a medical history reported more past illnesses, more frequent chronic symptoms and complaints, and poorer health than did subjects in a neutral mood. This bias is consistent with our prediction that sad people should selectively recall negatively valenced information, such as details from occasions when they felt sick.

Beyond that, however, mood also influenced perception or appraisal of current health status, as indicated by the number of physical complaints people reported when slightly ill. Salovey and Birnbaum (1989) found such appraisal biases in a study of Yale students: those who currently had a bad cold were first persuaded to feel happy, sad, or neutral by recalling a happy, sad, or neutral episode from their lives. They then rated the severity of their discomfort from their current illness. As expected, compared to neutral controls, temporarily sad subjects rated their cold symptoms as considerably more painful and discomforting, whereas happy subjects rated their symptoms as less painful and discomforting. This bias could be significant in medical practice since physicians' diagnoses partly depend on patients' appraisal of the severity of their symptoms (see Eich, Reeves, Jaeger, & Graff-Radford, 1985).

Salovey and Birnbaum (1989) also asked subjects to rate their vulnerability to future illnesses and their belief that alleged health-promoting behaviors would prevent those illnesses. Here, too, subjects showed mood congruent changes. For example, temporarily sad subjects believed they were destined to have many future health problems and that there was little that they could do to prevent these illnesses or alleviate their severity once they happened. Such pessimism is significant for health practices because it spawns defeatist, fatalistic attitudes toward quitting smoking, reducing alcohol consumption, losing weight, or reducing blood pressure and cholesterol levels. Such fatalistic attitudes also reduce sick patients' adherence to long-term medication or treatment plans, thus exacerbating the medical problem and their depression.

Forecasting the future.   Moods affect not only evaluation of past and present circumstances but also judgments about the enjoyability and likelihood of future events (Gilbert, 2000). In a direct assessment of these effects, Wright and Bower (1992) induced a happy or sad mood in subjects and then had them estimate the likelihood of a number of future events: half were blessings such as world peace or finding a cure for cancer; half were disasters such as a major meltdown at a nearby nuclear power plant or injury in a car accident. The results showed strong mood biases. Compared to neutral-mood controls, happy people raised their subjective probability estimates of future blessings and lowered their estimates of future disasters, whereas sad subjects did just the reverse.

Here, then, is the optimism of the happy person and the pessimism of the depressed person. One way to explain such biases is to note that people often estimate subjective probabilities by gauging the ease with which evidence supportive of the outcome comes to mind. According to the affect priming account, people who are sad will more readily think of more facts and ideas associated with a pessimistic outcome, whereas happy people will think of more pleasant facts consistent with an optimistic outcome. The differential availability of positive versus negative evidence would then tip the balance of subjective likelihood estimates in the mood congruent direction.

Social stereotypes.   Another implication of affect priming is that people's beliefs in negative or positive social stereotypes (ethnic, national, or racial) should shift negatively or positively as a result of a temporary bad or good mood. Esses, Haddock, and Zanna (1993) collected evidence relevant to this implication. They induced a happy, neutral, or sad mood in their Canadian college-student subjects using music and Velten statements. They then had the subjects freely describe typical personality traits of six ethnic groups resident in Canada: Arabic, Chinese, English Canadian, Jewish, Native Indian, and Pakistani groups. Subjects were then asked to indicate whether each trait they had listed was positive or negative (in social desirability) and what percentage of the ethnic group they believed exhibited that trait. An individual's "stereotype score" for a given group was the summed valence of the traits he had attributed to that group weighted by the percentage of that group he estimated would show that trait.

The results showed an interesting pattern. Two of the ethnic groups (Native Indian and Pakistani) had distinctly negative valence for these subjects, most of whom were English Canadians. For these two negatively valenced targets, the sad mood induction increased the negativity of the stereotypes. The effect arose largely because sad subjects rated the negative traits (e.g., "radical," "pushy") as much more undesirable than did happy or neutral subjects. The results also showed that the attitudes toward three of the target ethnic groups who were relatively neutral in valence (Arabic, Chinese, and Jewish) were not much influenced by the mood manipulation. Finally, the positive mood induction (initially mildly positive), and surprisingly, the negative mood induction, positively enhanced the stereotype rating for the subjects' own group (English Canadians).

Esses, Haddock, and Zanna (1993) interpret the former finding as a reflection of mood congruence, the latter as a form of *mood repair*. They argue that sad subjects may try to improve their mood by denigrating negative outgroups and elevating the social desirability of their own group. However, the generality of this explanation was called into question in a second experiment by Esses et al. (1993). That study replicated the enhanced positivity of one's own ethnic group by sadness for English Canadians but not for Chinese students (living in Canada at the time). A plausible conjecture is that Chinese people do not routinely upgrade their own group as a means of improving their momentary bad mood. The fact that mood effects on intergroup discrimination can be highly context dependent is also supported by Forgas and Fiedler (1996), who found that subjects induced to feel sad made significantly more discriminatory judgments about outsiders in an apparent mood repair strategy—but only when group membership was made personally relevant to them.

In sum, the affect priming theory fares only moderately well as an explanation of mood effects on stereotype expression. Inductions of sad moods produce strong negative shifts in the valence of stereotypes toward the more negative ethnic targets; however, mood congruence appears restricted to that specific condition and is not a general effect. Though the effect of sad mood apparently reflects enhanced negative valence and connotations of negative descriptors of a group, one must wonder why this effect did not appear strongly for negative traits attributed to the affectively neutral ethnic groups. Clearly, explanation of the full range of results requires more than reference to affect priming and motivated self-enhancement mechanisms. The theory presented later offers an integrative framework within which one might understnad these context-sensitive mood effects.

Attributional Biases and Mood

Explaining successes and failures. The affect priming theory predicts that people will explain their personal successes and failures in a manner that will perpetuate their prevailing mood or feelings. In particular, when happy, people should explain achievements in a self-enhancing manner; when sad, they should explain the same outcomes in a self-deprecatory manner.

Such attributional biases appeared in an experiment by Forgas, Bower, and Moylan (1990). Subjects were students in an introductory psychology class who had recently received their exam scores and rankings on an important examination. For the experiment, the students first watched one of two short films designed to make them feel happy or sad. They then rated their satisfaction with their exam performance and they judged the extent to which their exam performance was attributable to their ability and effort, the difficulty of the test, or their good or bad luck. Subjects were divided into two groups: those who had scored well on the exam and felt satisfied with their success and those who had scored poorly and felt they had failed. We found that, when in a happy mood, subjects who had done well attributed their success more to their ability and effort in studying, whereas those who had failed but were induced to feel happy attributed their failure to bad luck or an unfair test. On the other hand, when students had been induced into a sad mood, those who failed the exam blamed their failure on their lack of ability and weak efforts, whereas those sad subjects who had done well attributed their success to an easy test or to simple dumb luck. Thus, sad people blamed themselves for their failures and downplayed their successes. Happy people did just the opposite, taking credit for their successes and rejecting blame for their failures. Such attributional biases are consistent with the operation of affect priming mechanisms, and they also operate in the direction of perpetuating one's current mood.

Self-perception.   Additional evidence for the impact of moods on attributions stems from a study by Forgas, Bower, and Krantz (1984), in which happy and sad subjects rated their own behavior every 5 seconds for prosocial, neutral, or antisocial aspects by viewing themselves on videotape in a social interaction recorded the previous day. Whereas people in a happy mood judged themselves in the video as emitting plentiful positive, prosocial behaviors (appearing suave, friendly, and competent), subjects in a sad mood saw themselves as emitting many negative, antisocial behaviors (appearing as withdrawn, socially unskilled, and incompetent). These effects were all "in the eye of the beholder," for objective judges rated the videotaped subjects as displaying about the same levels of positive and negative behaviors. We can explain such results by supposing that the perceivers' mood primes into readiness mood congruent concepts, which they then use to classify as positive or negative their own ambiguous gestures, speeches, and body language they view in the videotape.

Interestingly, these mood congruent biases in interpreting ongoing social behaviors also applied to judgments of another person's behavior, with one notable exception: sad subjects identified more of their own negative behaviors than they did in the recorded interaction of another person. This selective, self-directed negativity bias has also been identified in studies of clinical depression, which suggests that mood congruent effects may be limited by politeness norms that proscribe criticizing strangers. We will discuss the role of such motivated processing strategies in limiting mood congruence later.

Self-confidence.   In related research, Kavanaugh and Bower (1985) studied how temporary moods influence people's sense of efficacy or competence in accomplishing a variety of tasks. Subjects induced to feel happy or sad rated the likelihood that they could successfully carry out diverse actions, such as attracting someone of the opposite sex, forming friendships, assertively dealing with others, and performing well in athletic and intellectual tasks. They were asked to ignore their current feelings and to judge according to their normal abilities.

Compared to control subjects in a neutral mood, happy subjects had an elevated sense of self-efficacy, confidence, and competence, whereas sad people had less assurance across all content domains. These mood influences are important because self-efficacy judgments determine which activities people will attempt and how long they will persist in the face of difficulties (Bandura, 1977). Mood congruent availability of the subjects' memories for positive and negative experiences in the questioned activity may explain these effects. Though average levels of achievement will differ greatly depending on one's history, each person has a private collection of performances (superior or inferior) evaluated according to one's standards in a given domain. A temporary happy or sad mood can then shift the availability of these two sets of memories, thus temporarily biasing estimates of one's capabilities.

Acceptance of personal feedback.   The research reviewed in the last three sections illustrates how positive or negative mood influences interpretation of behavior and explanations of achievements and failures. Mood also influences to what degree people accept or reject different feedback about themselves. Esses (1989) clearly showed such mood effects.

Esses found a personality trait (e.g., impulsiveness versus methodicalness) for which subjects rated themselves near the midpoint but professed to wishing to be more extreme. After a bogus personality test and a happy or sad mood induction, subjects were falsely informed that the personality test revealed that they were really either nearer or farther from their ideal point on this trait (viz. positive or negative feedback). Later, they rated themselves again on this trait so that Esses could calculate a change score as an index of their acceptance of the experimenter's feedback to them.

The results, illustrated in figure 3.5, indicated that while happy subjects accepted the positive feedback suggesting that they were actually nearer to their ideal (and so they changed their self-evaluation in that direction), they tended to ignore or reject the negative feedback suggesting that they were farther from their ideal point (so they barely altered their self-assessment). Sad subjects reversed this pattern: they largely accepted the negative (farther from ideal) feedback, and consequently altered their self-assessment on the relevant trait, but tended to ignore or reject the positive feedback. In sum, people accepted the personality information that agreed with their mood, and by doing so, they also changed their self-evaluations in that direction.

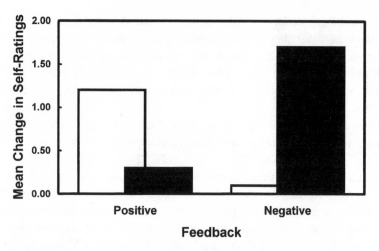

FIGURE 3.5. Change in self-ratings toward positive or negative feedback made by subjects in a happy or sad mood (white and black bars, respectively). Source: Esses, 1989; reprinted with permission.

A second study comparing depressed and nondepressed subjects arrived at similar conclusions: depressed subjects more readily embraced negative than positive feedback about their standing on the impulsive/methodical trait. Moreover, when inducted into a positive mood, the formerly depressed subjects switched, now accepting positive personality feedback more than negative feedback. We view these results as another manifestation of mood congruence in persuasion—in this case, judging the credibility of feedback about oneself. Information whose valence agrees with one's momentary mood is viewed as credible and persuasive and thus changes self-assessments.

So far, we have reviewed a range of studies supporting affect priming; in the next section we will place these results within a broader theoretical context to explain both the presence and the absence of mood congruence.

BEYOND AFFECT PRIMING

The idea that good or bad moods should color the way we see the world and ourselves is so powerful that for a long time researchers were mainly interested in demonstrating mood congruence in associations, evaluations, and social judgments (Forgas & Bower, 1988). However, this simple picture has become demonstrably more complex in recent years. As empirical evidence accumulated over the past decade or so, several intriguing findings emerged demonstrating either the complete absence of mood congruent effects or, in some cases, opposite effects—happy subjects selectively remembering sad information, or sad subjects selectively remembering happy information (Erber & Erber, 1994; Forgas, 1991a; Parrott, 1993; Parrott & Sabini, 1990; Sedikides, 1994, 1995).

Our main aim in the remainder of the chapter is to situate the affect priming theory within the broader landscape of contemporary cognition/emotion theorizing. We will argue that mood congruence is indeed a robust and reliable phenomenon, but that it occurs primarily in circumstances when people employ substantive, constructive processing strategies that allow the infusion of affect-linked information into cognitive processing. To accomplish our goal, we will consider some of the criticisms of the affect priming concept, and then examine an alterative account that explains mood congruence not in terms of an indirect influence of mood states on memory, learning, and related cognitive processes, but rather in terms of a simpler and more direct route: specifically, that one's feelings at a given moment provide immediate information about one's attitude toward a given object, person, or event. Then, we will discuss still another theory, AIM, which attempts to specify the conditions under which mood congruence is more or less likely to occur. Finally, we will survey recent empirical evidence supporting AIM.

Limitations of the Affect Priming Account

Despite the cumulative evidence supporting affect priming, some of the predicted memory effects turned out to be less robust than initially expected (Blaney, 1986; Bower & Mayer, 1985; Morris, 1989). As we noted earlier, the difficulty of obtaining reliable evidence of mood dependent memory may reflect several factors, such as the lack of sufficiently intense mood manipulations (Bower & Mayer, 1985; Eich, 1995), the lack of causal belonging between the mood induction and the experimental task (Bower, 1991), and the fact that affect priming may be difficult to obtain in conditions that are "antithetical to self-referencing" (Blaney, 1986, p. 232). In contrast to the variability of this phenomenon in standard memory tasks, studies examining social judgments typically produced far more reliable and consistent data. Why should this be so?

Compared to memory experiments involving learning of unrelated word lists, studies of social judgment provide people with a far richer, more elaborate, and more realistic set of encoding and retrieval cues. Powerful mood congruent effects have now been obtained in many such studies (for a review, see Forgas, 1995a). More surprisingly, many of these studies also found robust evidence for both mood dependent effects in memory and mood congruent effects in learning that are consistent with an affect priming account (Bower, 1991; Forgas, 1990, 1991b; 1992c; Forgas & Bower, 1987; 1988; Mayer et al., 1992; Salovey, O'Leary, Stretton, Fishkin, & Drake, 1991). On this account, mood should most often exert a selective influence on cognitive processes when incoming information is complex and ambiguous: thus, mood may more effectively function as a useful discriminating context for learning and recall. Under these conditions, typically created in studies of social judgment, affect priming seems to be a powerful mechanism of selective encoding and retrieval. Similar effects are more difficult to obtain in memory experiments that focus on a limited set of simple stimuli (e.g., unrelated words) and in which the role of mood as a discriminating context for learning and recall is likely to be constrained.

Our review of the literature indicates that a salient shortcoming of the affect priming theory is its inability to specify the boundary conditions when mood congruent effects will or will not occur. Before addressing that topic, we will review an alternative explanation for these effects.

The Affect-as-Information Model

Several theorists claim that some, but not all, of the mood congruent biases we have described can also be accounted for in terms other than the affect priming formulation. Foremost among these alternative theories is the affect-as-information (AAI) model proposed by Schwarz and Clore (1983, 1988). The model suggests that "rather than computing a judgment on the basis of recalled features of a target, individuals may . . . ask themselves: 'How do I feel about it?' [and] in doing so, they may mistake feelings due to a pre-existing state as a reaction to the target" (Schwarz, 1990, p. 529). Unlike the affect priming theory, which explains mood congruence in terms of the indirect influence of mood states on memory, learning, attention, and associative processes, AAI posits a simpler and more direct route: we use our feelings at the moment as information about our attitudes.

The AAI model shares some interesting similarities with earlier conditioning approaches to social judgments (Clore & Byrne, 1974). Both theories assume that affect can be directly linked to a novel stimulus. Earlier conditioning accounts held that this linkage between affect and novel stimuli occurred without cognitive mediation, merely as a result of temporal and spatial contiguity according to conditioning principles (Clore & Byrne, 1974). But in the AAI account, the affect-stimulus link is cognitively mediated and depends on attributional processes mediating between the affective state and the stimulus. Curiously, the historical roots of this model in associationistic theorizing are rarely recognized nowadays (but see Berkowitz, 1993, for a different view).

However, the affect-as-information model is not simply a more cognitively oriented reincarnation of the earlier conditioning theory of Clore and Byrne (1974). According to AAI, affect functions as a judgment-simplifying heuristic:

people consult their mood in order to produce a quick judgment, without trying to integrate the external features of the target, and their internal memories and associations, into a considered judgment (Clore & Parrott, 1991; Schwarz & Clore, 1988). Attributional principles have also been incorporated in the theory, as judges are assumed to "misattribute" their mood, as if it were informative about their reactions to the target.

Several studies in the literature support the AAI model, demonstrating mood congruence in evaluative judgments (Borg, 1987; Clore & Parrott, 1991; Schwarz & Bless, 1991; Schwarz & Clore, 1983, 1988; Schwarz, Strack, Kommer, & Wagner, 1987; Strack, Martin, & Stepper, 1988). The classic demonstration study was conducted by Schwarz and Clore (1983). They found, first, that when subjects in a telephone survey were asked to make rapid evaluative judgments about their happiness and life satisfaction, their evaluations showed mood congruence. That is, their evaluations were significantly more positive when they were presumably feeling good (interviewed on a pleasant, sunny day) and more negative when they were feeling bad (interviewed on a rainy, overcast day). However, when the subjects' attention was directed to the probable source of their mood (the weather) by a prior question about it, the mood effects on evaluations disappeared. In a conceptually similar study, Martin, Harlow, and Strack (1992) used manipulated facial expressions and exercise to induce mood and arousal and found a mood congruent effect on judgments about social situations. However, this effect also vanished once the source of the mood (their facial expression) was pointed out, presumably because subjects could no longer rely on the "how do I feel about it?" heuristic. The AAI model claims that when subjects are made aware of the source of their mood, they will no longer misconstrue it as an indicator of their opinion about a topic. On this account, mood congruent biases arise when unaware subjects misattribute their feelings to the attitude target.

The AAI has mainly been invoked as an alternative account of mood congruent effects in evaluation, preferences, and judgments. However, in a reformulation of the model, Clore and Parrott (1991, 1994) extended the concept of AAI to nonaffective states as well; thus, just as "affective feelings concern how much and in what way something is good or bad, . . . cognitive feelings indicate the status of one's knowledge, understanding or expectations" (Clore & Parrott, 1994, p. 102). Further, one can generalize the AAI model to explain some mood congruent phenomena of memory, if one assumes that people first consult their mood as an explicit cue to guide their subsequent search processes (Clore et al., 1994). It appears, then, that there is an obvious overlap between the range of mood congruent phenomena that affect priming and affect-as-information theories seek to explain. Let us now consider whether the AAI account has limitations as an alternative explanation of mood congruent effects.

Critical Assessment of the AAI Model

Several considerations suggest that the generality of the affect-as-information account may be limited. The AAI theory predicts that only mood states with no salient prior cause will be used to inform judgments and cognition. Once one realizes a cause for a mood other than the target of the judgment, one will discount it as information about an unrelated target. This assertion makes the theory readily falsifiable.

Unfortunately, the empirical evidence on this point is somewhat equivocal. Consistent with the AAI account, several studies by the original investigators showed that feelings, once correctly attributed, would no longer influence judgments (Clore & Parrott, 1991, 1994; Schwarz & Bless, 1991; Schwarz & Clore, 1988). However, the literature is replete with studies (several of which we summarized earlier) that found mood congruence when researchers used mood induction procedures—involving films, music, false feedback, hypnotic suggestions, or the Velten technique—that must have revealed to subjects the correct source of their moods (Clark & Waddell, 1983; Erber, 1991; Fiedler, 1990, 1991, 2000; Forgas & Bower, 1987; Forgas et al., 1984; Sedikides, 1992). Whenever moods with a salient prior cause nonetheless create a mood congruent influence on evaluations and judgments, as frequently occurs, the affect-as-information theory clearly cannot apply.

Second, the AAI account predicts mood effects only at the retrieval or judgment stage of information processing. In contrast, memory-based theories, such as affect priming, predict strong mood effects not only on retrieval but also on encoding, learning, attention deployment, and association production, as we have seen. Because encoding and associative effects have been reliably demonstrated in the literature (for reviews, see Bower, 1991; Forgas, 1991b; Forgas & Bower, 1987, 1988), the affect-as-information account appears inapplicable to such "front end" mood congruent effects.

Another shortcoming is that AAI suggests a rather simple, all-or-nothing process of affect infusion. That is, the theory implies that mood will either completely inform an evaluation (if mistakenly used as a heuristic to infer one's evaluation) or will not affect evaluations at all (if mood is attributed to another cause). Because AAI does not allow for gradual, intermediate mood effects of varying intensity on evaluations, we may need to look to other explanations—such as affect priming—to account for the kind of graded, context- and target-specific mood effects that have often been reported (e.g., Branscombe & Cohen, 1991; Fiedler, 1991; Forgas, 1992d, 1993a, 1993b; Forgas et al., 1984; Mackie & Worth, 1991; Petty, Gleicher, & Baker, 1991; Salovey & Birnbaum, 1989; Wegner, Petty, & Klein, 1994).

Most of the evidence supporting the AAI account comes from experiments in which subjects experience mild mood states, are asked to make complex judgments about vague issues (such as life satisfaction), and have insufficient processing resources available to produce a considered response (such as when asked to respond quickly in a telephone survey, as in Schwarz & Clore, 1983). Under these circumstances, subjects may indeed have no alternative but to rely on a "how do I feel about it" heuristic and to use their prevailing mood as information in formulating a response. These may be rather unusual situations, however. Under other conditions (judgment can be more considered or is more personally important and involving; adequate processing resources are available), subjects are less likely to use the affect-as-information heuristic (Forgas, 1995a).

We propose that the AAI theory offers a plausible alternative explanation for only a *limited* set of findings in the literature demonstrating mood congruence or its absence. People are most likely to resort to the affect-as-information heuristic when quick and simple processing is necessary in response to contextual requirements. In contrast, affect priming is a broad principle with implications for a range of cognitive processes, suggesting multiple avenues through which affect may infuse into cognition (for reviews, see Bower & Forgas, in press; Forgas & Bower, 1988; Singer & Salovey, 1988).

It is thus of particular importance to distinguish the circumstances in which mood congruent effects are caused by the affect priming as contrasted to the affect-as-information mechanism. The discussion so far suggests that affect priming is the dominant mechanism producing mood congruence when subjects engage in open, constructive, and substantive information-processing strategies, whereas affect-as-information more likely contributes to mood congruence when subjects use simplified, heuristic processing strategies. In most cases, these two mechanisms provide complementary rather than competing explanations of mood congruent effects. One of the objectives of the affect infusion model is to integrate these two theories within a multiprocess framework and to specify the situations when affect priming rather than affect-as-information contributes more to judgments.

However, explaining mood congruent effects is not the only task for such a comprehensive model. In some conditions, mood congruence is either absent, or its opposite, mood incongruence, occurs. What processing conditions likely produce such outcomes?

Null or Incongruent Effects of Mood

Absence of mood congruence due to direct access processing.   The absence of mood congruence has been documented when happy or sad subjects are asked to process information about highly familiar and specific issues about which they already possess extensive knowledge that can be directly accessed. For example, Srull (1983, 1984) found that evaluative judgments about con-

sumer products showed mood congruent bias only when the products were relatively unfamiliar; affect had little impact on judgments about well-known, familiar consumer products. Similarly, Salovey and Birnbaum (1989) detected strong mood congruent effects on judgments about unfamiliar, negative health events but discerned little influence of mood on judgments about highly familiar, positive health events. Thus, apparently when information is highly familiar, extensive prior information already exists, and the task is of low personal relevance, subjects may not engage in the open, constructive processing essential for affect priming effects. Instead, subjects may simply directly access their prior evaluation, in a process analogous to that for a strongly cued recognition task. As we argued previously, affect priming is unlikely in such circumstances.

A similar pattern indicating the absence of mood congruence was reported by Schwarz and his colleagues (Schwarz et al., 1987). They observed marked mood congruence when subjects made judgments concerning general issues, such as satisfaction with life, but no mood effects occurred for judgments concerning specific issues, such as satisfaction with present living quarters, about which prior evaluations could be directly accessed. Levine, Wyer, and Schwarz (1994) obtained similar results: subjects judged global aspects of self-esteem in a mood congruent manner but not domain-specific aspects, presumably because the subjects had thought previously about the latter and therefore had a ready-made opinion to retrieve. Sedikides (1995) also found that mood influenced peripheral, less salient aspects of the self-concept but not familiar, central aspects that could be directly accessed.

A common thread can be discerned in these studies: mood congruent effects tend to disappear whenever subjects do not use an open, constructive information-processing strategy. In the absence of constructive thinking, mood primed memories and associations are unlikely to influence the valence of perceptions and judgments significantly. We will refer to such a highly cued style of information processing as *direct access processing*. According to the AIM, direct access processing should be used when the target is either highly familiar or typical, when relevant past information can be directly accessed in memory, and when internal or external demand for constructive re-processing is minimal. Though this combination of circumstances is probably very common in everyday life, and many real-life cognitive tasks are presumably completed through a simple, direct access processing style, few experimental studies have set out specifically to investigate this strategy.

Absence of mood congruence due to motivated processing. The ready availability of highly cued material through direct access processing is only one reason why mood congruence may not occur. Several experiments suggest that mood congruence is unlikely whenever subjects approach a cognitive task from a highly motivated, predetermined perspective, with clear goals that guide the kind of information they look for and intend to use. We call this *motivated processing*.

Clark and Isen (1982) were among the first to recognize that controlled, motivated processing may eliminate or even reverse mood congruent effects, a theme echoed in the more recent literature. Several studies have found that affect priming effects disappear under conditions conducive to motivated processing: when subjects become cognizant of the source of priming effects, when they are motivated to maintain a good mood or improve a bad mood, and when they have a strong prior motivation to achieve a particular outcome (Berkowitz, Jo, Troccoli, & Monteith, 1994; Erber & Erber, 1994). The available evidence suggests that several factors may trigger a motivated processing style and lead to mood incongruence—the desire for mood repair, self-directed attention, self-serving motivations, group pressures, and individual differences. We examine some of these influences next.

Mood repair and mood incongruent memory. Several recent studies have reported evidence of mood incongruent effects in memory (e.g., Parrott, 1993; Parrott & Sabini, 1990). We suggest that, rather than invalidating the affect priming theory, these studies help identify the boundary conditions for affect priming effects. The AIM suggests that subjects must openly and constructively process information for affect priming to occur. In turn, mood incongruent recall should occur when subjects engage in targeted, motivated thinking, selectively seeking and finding mood incongruent material. This interpretation of mood incongruence has been confirmed in several recent studies. For example, Erber and Erber (1994) found that "when subjects were motivated to change their sad mood . . . they tended to recall mood incongruent, that is, positively valenced material" (p. 86). This is clearly a motivated mood control strategy.

A demonstration of mood incongruent recall by Sedikides (1994) also supports this explanation. In that study, subjects induced (through guided imagery) to feel happy or sad were asked to generate open-ended self-descriptions. Initial responses were predominantly mood congruent, implying the operation of affect priming mechanisms. But later self-descriptions showed a significant shift toward mood incongruence. This delayed rebound suggests that subjects progressively switched to a motivated processing strategy to repair their sad mood but only after the initial negative mood and subsequent mood congruent self-descriptions had reached a sufficiently aversive level.

Self-directed attention. Simply directing subjects' attention to their affective states often seems sufficient to induce motivated processing, leading to the reduction and even reversal of affect priming effects. Berkowitz and his associates (Berkowitz et al., 1994; Berkowitz & Troccoli, 1990) found that reactions were "affectively congruent when the subjects' attention was directed away from themselves, presumably because of the relatively automatic influence of the affective state;" in contrast, subjects "displayed an affective incongruence . . . after [they] had attended to their feelings" (Berkowitz et al., 1994, p. 2). Such results are consistent with the role of self-directed attention in triggering a motivated processing strategy. Aversive affect itself may be one important source of self-directed attention and subsequent motivated processing, as the Sedikides (1994) results suggest. Growing evidence indicates that subjects will engage in targeted information search and retrieval to alleviate dysphoria; accordingly, "people are active mood regulators who are sensitive to situational demands" (Erber & Erber, 1994, p. 86).

Self-serving motivation. An important source of motivated processing is the need to establish and maintain positive self-esteem. Tesser's (1988) self-evaluation maintenance model (SEM) suggests that the superior qualities of another person may either threaten or bolster our self-evaluation, depending on whether we adopt a comparison or reflection process. Tesser and his colleagues suggest that ego-threatening comparisons create negative affect and arousal, whereas ego-enhancing comparisons lead to positive affect. Here then is a clearly motivated cognitive strategy designed to maintain high self-esteem (Achee, Tesser, & Pilkington, 1994).

According to the AIM, people appear to use self-evaluation maintenance under conditions that should lead to motivated processing; personal relevance and closeness to a partner are critical triggering conditions. Research suggests mood incongruence in these motivated judgments. As Achee et al. (1994) conclude, it "would be difficult to understand . . . results in terms of the mood priming or mood as information hypothesis [because] information about present mood cannot be guiding behavior" (pp. 157–158).

Self-serving motivation may also influence mood effects on attribution judgments. We have already reviewed some evidence for mood congruence in causal attributions (Forgas et al., 1990); however, when subjects are motivated to improve their affect, a mood incongruent strategy of defensive attribution may be more probable (Baumgardner & Arkin, 1988). Sad subjects may then seek to blame their failures on external causes and claim that personal factors cause their successes, in an apparent reversal of the mood congruent attributional biases we found under conditions of substantive processing (Forgas et al., 1990).

Affect and interpersonal preferences. Motivated processing may be particularly common when people confront information that has personal consequences. For example, memory for and perceptions of people were repeatedly found to show mood congruence when performed in an abstract, personally uninvolving context (Forgas & Bower, 1987). In contrast, the same task is likely to be carried out using a motivated processing strategy, and show no mood congruence, when it has important personal consequences for the subject. Schachter (1959) was among the first to show that affective states such as anxiety can motivate people's interpersonal preferences: anxious subjects seemed to prefer the company of others in a similar predicament, in an apparent effort to control their fears. More recent research by Locke and Horowitz (1990) suggests that people prefer to be with others whose mood matches their own; this might be a fairly general motivated strategy in many interpersonal choices.

In recent experiments following these leads, we asked happy or sad subjects to perform a complex partner selection task that either was or was not personally relevant (choosing a partner for themselves versus for somebody else). We carefully tracked their information selection and decision strategies. The key finding was that the combination of an aversive mood and high personal relevance (expecting to meet the other person) led to a highly motivated processing strategy. Subjects in this condition selectively sought and found rewarding features in a potential partner and ignored other relevant characteristics in a typical display of targeted, motivated processing (Forgas, 1989). Under these conditions, mood congruence in information selection did not occur.

Motivated thinking also influenced the subjects' memory: rather than simply recalling mood congruent details about prospective partners, subjects now selectively remembered information that was most relevant to their motivational goal (Forgas, 1991c, experiment 1). In subsequent studies, we tracked and analyzed the subjects' step-by-step decision-making strategies by providing each unit of information on numbered cue cards (Forgas, 1991c, experiment 2) or on a computer file (Forgas, 1991c, experiment 3). Sad subjects making a personal choice selectively sought and found rewarding partners, took less time to find diagnostic information and to reach a decision, yet they studied motivationally relevant details longer and more frequently and remembered them better later. Once again, we saw no evidence for any mood congruence in these conditions.

There is some complementary evidence for the absence of mood congruence when mood repair strategies lead to motivated processing in dysphoria (Weary, Marsh, Gleicher, & Edwards, 1993). For example, instead of displaying a typical mood congruent bias, depressed subjects may selectively prefer others they perceive as potentially most useful to them (Weary, Marsh, & McCormick, 1994). These results confirm that motivated thinking, which involves highly targeted and highly cued information-processing strategies, tends to be impervious to mood congruent effects.

Group pressure.   When cognitive activity occurs in an interpersonal or group context, others' expectations and opinions may become a source of motivated thinking—a possibility rarely considered in research focusing on individual cognitive processes. In a study by Forgas (1990), people in a happy, sad, or neutral mood were asked to evaluate nine different stereotypes of people (doctors, farmers, Jews, Catholics, etc.). Isolated individuals first made these judgments: two weeks later, the same people again received a positive or a negative mood induction, discussed the issues in groups, and produced a second set of judgments.

The first judgment, made individually, showed a clear mood congruent effect: happy subjects made more positive judgments than did sad subjects. The second judgment, made after the group discussion, showed a different, asymmetrical mood effect. Good mood resulted in even more extreme positive evaluations after group discussion. However, group discussion significantly reduced the impact of negative moods; consistent with the idea that subjects adopted a more motivated processing strategy as group norms and values limiting negativity activated during the group interaction (Brown, 1965). More recent studies confirmed that motivated processing induced by greater self-relevance also tends to eliminate mood congruence in intergroup judgments (Forgas & Fiedler, 1996).

Individual differences. Short-term moods may not affect everyone the same: some individuals may habitually handle certain kinds of information in a predetermined, motivated manner rather than in an open-ended, constructive way. Despite the obvious theoretical interest of such state/trait interactions (Mayer & Salovey, 1988), few studies so far have examined individual differences in the mediation of mood effects on cognition.

A relatively early demonstration of such an effect was reported by Rhodewalt, Strube, and Wysocki (1988) found a significant mood congruent influence on perceptions of control by subjects with Type B but not Type A personality. Given that impatience, striving for control, and feelings of time pressure are typical features of the Type A personality, the disappearance of mood effects for these subjects seems to confirm their use of more motivated processing strategies.

In recent research examining mood effects on negotiation strategies, Forgas (1998a) found significant mood congruent effects on perceptions and expectations about a forthcoming encounter. However, these effects were significantly smaller for individuals who scored high on measures of need for approval and Machiavellianism. We may interpret this finding in terms of the enduring inclination of such individuals to approach information relating to a forthcoming social encounter from a predetermined, motivated perspective.

The results of these studies indicate that mood congruence is unlikely when a motivation to achieve a particular outcome dominates information processing. Under these conditions, people use targeted rather than open information search strategies that reduce the influence of affect priming. Motivated thinking seems a common yet imperfectly understood aspect of many everyday cognitive tasks (Kruglanski, 1989; Kunda, 1990; Martin, Ward, Achee, & Wyer, 1993; Neisser,

1982; Schwarz, 1990). The absence of mood congruence in these studies supports our claim that affect infusion should occur only when people employ an open, constructive processing strategy such as heuristic or substantive processing.

Having considered some of the suggested alternative explanations for mood congruent effects, as well as evidence for the absence of mood congruence in some conditions, we will now propose an integrated explanation for these results.

THE AFFECT INFUSION MODEL

We have seen that mood congruent effects arise when subjects adopt a particular kind of processing strategy; namely, open, constructive thinking. This view is increasingly shared among researchers in social cognition. Fiedler (1990), for example, concluded that affect will "influence cognitive processes to the extent that the cognitive task involves the active generation of new information as opposed to the passive conservation of information given" (pp. 2–3).

Affect Infusion

The affect infusion model, or AIM, attempts to specify the different processing conditions under which affect is liable to infuse into cognition. Affect infusion may be defined as the process whereby affective information influences and becomes incorporated into people's constructive processing, selectively influencing their learning, memory, attention, and associative processes and eventually coloring the outcome of their deliberations in an affect congruent direction (Forgas, 1995a, p. 39). Evidence reviewed here shows that affect priming likely causes mood congruent effects in cognition. However, subjects using affect-as-information in circumstances that call for simple, heuristic processing can produce similar effects. Within the AIM, these two explanations are often complementary, both capable of explaining mood congruence, although under different processing conditions. The AIM also needs to account for instances in which affect infusion does not occur—or indeed, when mood incongruent outcomes arise—because subjects either directly access a preexisting opinion or engage in targeted, motivated processing that is incompatible with affect infusion.

The Multiprocess Approach: Features and Assumptions

In order to achieve these objectives, the AIM is based on a strong assumption of process mediation; that is, the nature and extent of mood effects on cognition should depend on the particular processing strategy subjects use to handle a given task. A corollary assumption is that, other things being equal, people will try to minimize cognitive effort, adopting the easiest and simplest processing strategy that satisfies minimal contextual requirements.

Most information-processing models in cognitive psychology start out as "single process" theories in the sense that they assume robust, universal, and context-insensitive cognitive mechanisms. As empirical evidence accumulates from ever-more complex studies evaluating a model, the boundary conditions for the theory become more salient. Indeed, the original affect priming account now encompasses an increasingly broad and heterogeneous set of phenomena (Forgas & Bower, 1988). The AIM is partly a reaction to the growing diversity of findings in the literature. One of its objectives is to define and systematize current knowledge about the boundary conditions for mood congruent effects. What started as a robust, single-process theory—the affect priming theory—has now been incorporated as part of a more complex, multiprocess explanation. This trend toward multiprocess models has been particularly marked in social cognition research (Wyer & Srull, 1989). Influential dual-process theories have now been developed to explain context-sensitive cognitive processes in such areas as attitude formation, persuasive communication, stereotyping, and self-perception (see Brewer, 1988; Chaiken, 1980; Fiske & Neuberg, 1990; Fiedler, 1991; Kruglanski, 1989; Petty et al., 1991).

The AIM represents a further development of this trend. Together with earlier dual-process theories, the AIM assumes that the rule of cognitive parsimony regulates people's choices of alternative processing strategies: people are expected to be effort-minimizing information processors. The choice of more-or-less demanding processing strategies should depend on a range of contextual variables such as features of the *information* (complexity, familiarity, typicality), the *person* (affective state, cognitive capacity, motivation level, personality characteristics, personal relevance of the task), and the *situation* (demand effects, expectations). We shall next describe the four processing strategies AIM identifies and then discuss the eliciting conditions that recruit each of these processing styles.

Processing Strategies

Figure 3.6 presents a schematic outline of the four basic processing strategies identified by the AIM and the variables that trigger their use. Two of these strategies—*direct access* and *motivated processing*—involve relatively closed, directed information search processes that limit the opportunity for affect infusion. The other two strategies—*heuristic* and *substantive processing*—require more constructive, open-ended thinking that creates multiple avenues for affect infusion.

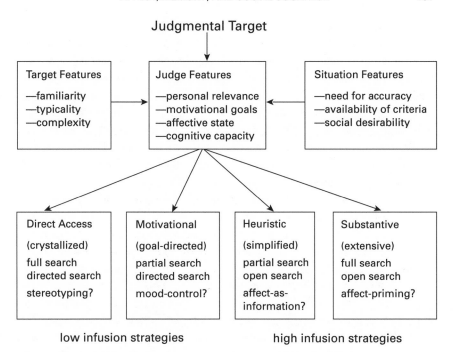

FIGURE 3.6. Outline of the multiprocess affect infusion model (AIM). Affect infusion in social judgments depends on which of four alternative processing strategies is adopted in response to target, judge, and situational features. Source: Forgas, 1995a.

The direct access strategy is the simplest method of producing an opinion or evaluation, based on the strongly cued retrieval of stored cognitive contents. Most of us have a rich repertoire of such crystallized, predetermined opinions to draw on when conditions do not warrant more extensive processing. An example would be responding to survey questions regarding one's opinion about abortion, affirmative action, political-party affiliation, and so on. One likely uses direct access when the task is familiar, when there is little or no personal involvement, and when no other motivational, cognitive, affective, or situational forces mandate more elaborate processing. By definition, the direct access strategy is a robust process that resists affect infusion, as our review of the relevant evidence showed.

The motivated processing strategy assumes that a strong, preexisting objective guides information processing; thus, little constructive or unguided processing occurs, reducing the likelihood of affect infusion. One likely uses motivated processing when one desires a specific outcome, and judges employ highly selective, motivated information search and integration strategies designed to produce a preferred outcome (Kunda, 1990). To complicate matters, the AIM also needs to explain how moods themselves often have motivational consequences and motivated processing may be employed to achieve mood maintenance as well as mood repair (Berkowitz et al., 1994; Clark & Isen, 1982; Erber & Erber, 1994). Motivated processing involves more than just a motivation to be accurate (cf. Kunda, 1990): it also suggests that a specific directional goal will often dominate and guide information search and judgments. The variables that lead to motivated processing may include enduring personality and individual characteristics that guide one's approach to a cognitive task (Forgas, 1998c; Rhodewalt et al., 1988; Smith & Petty, 1995), as well as such specific and situationally induced motives as self-enhancement, ego-defense, self-evaluation maintenance, and the like.

Highly vulnerable to affect infusion through mechanisms such as the affect-as-information heuristic, heuristic processing tends to occur when neither a crystallized response nor a strong motivational goal influences subjects's processing strategies, and they lack either personal involvement or sufficient processing resources. Therefore, they follow a heuristic strategy to compute a response with the least amount of effort, relying on limited information and using whatever shortcuts are available to them. Such heuristic processing is commonly included in dual-process theories of social cognition (Brewer, 1988; Chaiken, 1980; Petty et al., 1991). Heuristic processing is usually adopted for a relatively simple or typical task with low personal relevance, no specific motivational objectives, limited cognitive capacity, and no demand for accuracy or substantive processing. During heuristic processing, reactions may be based on irrelevant associations with environmental variables (Griffitt, 1970) or to one's prevailing mood (cf. Clore et al., 1994; Schwarz, 1990). As our earlier review suggested, affect infusion can and does occur in some situations as a result of heuristic processing, due to the operation of the affect-as-information mechanism.

Finally, substantive processing, the most extended and constructive strategy for information processing, has the greatest susceptibility to affect infusion. During substantive processing, people need to select, learn, interpret, and process information about a task and relate this information to preexisting knowledge structures using memory processes. Most single-process models imply that such vigilant information processing is the norm. In contrast, within the AIM, substantive processing is essentially a default option, adopted only when one cannot use simpler and less effortful processing strategies.

Substantive processing is more likely when a task is complex, atypical, and personally relevant, when subjects have adequate processing capacity and lack a specific motivational goal. During substantive processing, memory mechanisms such as affect priming are most likely to influence the selection, learning, interpretation, and assimilation of information into preexisting knowledge (Bower, 1991; Wyer & Srull, 1989). According to the AIM, the more extensive and prolonged the processing required to compute a judgment, the more likely that affect infusion will influence the outcome. Several recent studies showing greater mood congruence due to extended substantive processing have supported this counterintuitive prediction (Fiedler, 1991; Forgas, 1992a, 1992b, 1993a, 1993b, 1995a).

Factors Influencing Processing Choices

In this section we briefly review the role of antecedent variables associated with the task, the person, and the situation that determine a subject's selection of different processing choices mediating mood effects. Figure 3.7 presents the relationship between these variables schematically.

Task familiarity.   One generally uses the direct access strategy to process highly familiar cognitive tasks, so long as personal relevance is low and further processing is unnecessary. Because people can readily respond with highly accessible information to familiar topic questions, such as well-known products or their own living quarters, affect infusion is unlikely. On the other hand, marked mood congruent biases appear for unfamiliar tasks, when subjects are asked to evaluate little-known products or their global life satisfaction (Salovey & Birnbaum, 1989; Schwarz et al., 1987; Srull, 1983, 1984).

Task complexity and typicality.   Complex, atypical, or "problematic" tasks should require more substantive processing, enhancing the likelihood of affect infusion effects; several studies have adduced such effects (Forgas, 1992a, 1992c, 1993a, 1994b; 1995b). Examples of atypical tasks included thinking about unusual people, forming impressions about mismatched couples, or making attributions for complex conflicts. Results indicated that more complex or atypical judgments took more time and led to substantially greater mood congruence than occurred when the judgments were simpler and more typical.

Personal relevance.   Cognitive tasks with low personal relevance are more likely processed through effort-minimizing strategies such as direct access or heuristic processing. High personal relevance and specific motivation should lead to motivated processing, whereas high personal relevance without specific motivation should lead to substantive processing (see fig. 3.7). Even slight changes in personal relevance can dramatically affect how people deal with information (Brewer, 1988; Neisser, 1982). We have found that motivated processing results when an interpersonal preference task becomes personally relevant, and affect infusion effects therefore diminish (Forgas, 1989; 1991a).

Personal motivation.   As we noted before, affect infusion is unlikely when subjects have a strong goal to guide their information search and processing strategies. Positive or negative affective states can be a prominent source of

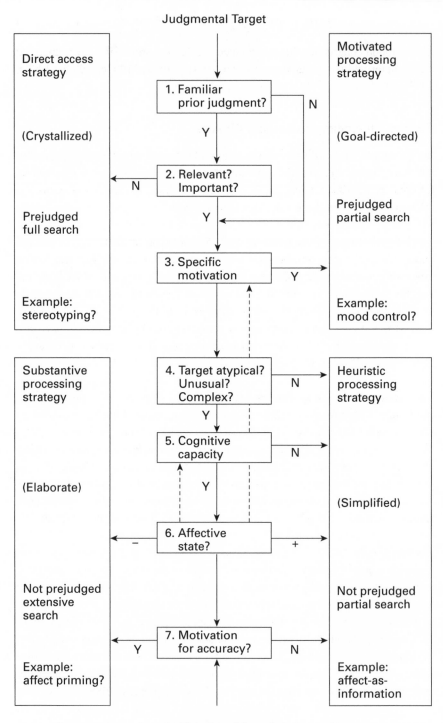

Judgmental Target

Direct access strategy

(Crystallized)

Prejudged full search

Example: stereotyping?

Motivated processing strategy

(Goal-directed)

Prejudged partial search

Example: mood control?

1. Familiar prior judgment?

N

Y

2. Relevant? Important?

N

Y

3. Specific motivation

Y

Substantive processing strategy

(Elaborate)

Not prejudged extensive search

Example: affect priming?

4. Target atypical? Unusual? Complex?

N

Y

5. Cognitive capacity

N

Y

6. Affective state?

−

+

7. Motivation for accuracy?

Y

N

Heuristic processing strategy

(Simplified)

Not prejudged partial search

Example: affect-as-information

8. Situational factors
Social desirability
Need for accuracy
Availability of criteria

motivated processing (mood maintenance or mood repair), often creating mood incongruent biases in memory and judgments (Erber & Erber, 1994). Also, certain personality traits may be an enduring source of motivated processing strategies. Recent studies suggest that mood congruence is reduced or eliminated for subjects who score high on individual difference measures such as Type A personality, self-esteem, Machiavellianism, and need for approval (Forgas, 1998c; Rhodewalt et al., 1988; Smith & Petty, 1995). High scores on these scales probably indicate a habitual tendency to approach certain cognitive tasks from a motivated perspective, which should reduce affect infusion effects. Such state/trait interactions may play an important role in triggering motivated processing and mediating mood effects on cognition (Mayer & Salovey, 1988; Rusting, 1998).

Processing capacity. When one's information-processing capacity is impaired, due to information overload or competing tasks, one is more apt to adopt simpler, heuristic processing strategies, even though one might prefer substantive processing under less stressful circumstances. Under conditions of impaired capacity, people are more prone to rely on stereotypic information (Bodenhausen, 1993) or the affect-as-information heuristic (Schwarz & Clore, 1983).

Processing consequences of mood. One of the more problematic findings to emerge in the recent cognition/emotion literature is that mood can play a dual role in influencing cognition. Affect appears to influence both what people think (informational effects) and how they think (processing effects). Positive moods generally lead to faster, simpler, more heuristic, and more superficial processing strategies linked to more open, flexible, creative, and inclusive processing solutions (Fiedler, 1991; Hertel & Fiedler, 1994; Isen, 1987; Mackie & Worth, 1991). Negative moods typically cause slower, more systematic, analytic, and vigilant processing strategies, sometimes leading to less flexible and more routine and predictable solutions (Ellis & Ashbrook, 1988; Forgas, 1994a; Forgas & Bower, 1987; Schwarz, 1990). This processing asymmetry associated with good and bad moods has been attributed to several possible causes: *capacity effects*, *functional effects*, and *motivational effects*.

Capacity effects may occur because thoughts associated with good or bad moods may intrude on one's attentional and cognitive resources, taking up scarce processing capacity (Ellis & Ashbrook, 1988; Isen, 1987; Mackie &

FIGURE 3.7. Opposite: Flowchart illustrating hierarchical relationships among various factors determining processing choices, and the multiple informational and processing effects influence of affect on judgments. Source: Forgas, 1992b.

Worth, 1991). However, although both positive and negative moods likely impair processing capacity, the evidence shows that happy and sad people tend to adopt very different processing strategies; consequently, capacity differences are unlikely sources for the asymmetric processing consequences of good and bad moods.

Explanations that appeal to functional effects hold that good and bad moods trigger different processing strategies because affective states may "exist for the sake of signaling states of the world that have to be responded to" (Frijda, 1988, p. 354). Relaxed, lazy information processing when one is in a good mood, and systematic, vigilant processing when one is in a bad mood, seem consistent with such a functional account, although conclusive evidence for such evolution-minded explanations is notoriously difficult to obtain.

Motivational effects may also account for the asymmetrical processing consequences of good or bad moods. Essentially, the idea is that bad moods motivate people to engage in controlled processing to achieve mood repair, whereas good moods motivate subjects to engage in simplified, heuristic processing to avoid cognitive effort and maintain a pleasant affective state (Clark & Isen, 1982). However, Bless (2000) proposes that positive mood promotes more internal, schema-driven processing, and Fiedler (2000) claims that negative mood facilitates externally oriented, bottom-up thinking, whereas good moods trigger a more constructive, top-down processing style.

Most of the evidence now available suggests that happy people are more likely to process information heuristically, whereas sad people will process it more substantively. Given the complex and interactive influence of affective states on specific motivations, cognitive capacity, and processing preferences (see fig. 3.7), the question arises: what happens when current mood and other variables signal conflicting processing choices? For example, how would a happy person (inclined to process heuristically) deal with a complex, atypical task requiring substantive processing?

Empirical evidence strongly suggests that the processing implications of moods are much weaker than, and secondary to, other variables such as task characteristics. Several studies (see Forgas, 1995b) have found that both happy and sad subjects process complex or atypical tasks slowly and substantively; in other words, a transient good mood will not override the processing requirements of a complex cognitive task.

Multiple influences on processing choices.   The AIM as depicted in figure 3.7 suggests a hierarchical relationship between influences on processing choices. However, the possibility of an interaction between these predictor variables must also be considered. The AIM is an integrative model and the influences on processing choices recognized within the model stem from currently available evidence. Whereas the processing consequences of strong factors such as familiarity, complexity, typicality, and specific motivation are quite clear, one can understand many processing choices only in terms of the interaction among several predictor variables. For example, it appears that the processing conse-quences of affect are usually indirect (Martin et al., 1993) and operate by influ-encing other factors, such as cognitive capacity or specific motivation (see fig. 3.7). Moreover, the processing consequences of affective states are likely weaker than, and secondary to, the processing implications of task characteristics or personal features.

According to the AIM, affect infusion may occur as a result of either heuristic processing (the affect-as-information mechanism) or substantive processing (the affect priming mechanism). Several of the predictor variables shown in figure 3.7 recruit either heuristic or substantive processing, with affect infusion pre-dicted in either case. For example, in the absence of specific motivation, high personal relevance may result in substantive processing and affect priming ef-fects, whereas low personal relevance should recruit heuristic processing (and hence affect infusion) through the affect-as-information mechanism. As the pre-diction is mood congruence in both cases, is AIM therefore unfalsifiable?

We believe the answer is "no." Though both heuristic and substantive pro-cessing should lead to mood congruence, these two processing strategies can nevertheless be distinguished empirically through analysis of information-processing variables, such as memory and processing latency data (Forgas & Bower, 1987). The next section reviews recent studies directly stimulated by the AIM, which confirm the role of processing styles in mediating mood effects. In keeping with the main interest of this chapter, we will concentrate on studies that demonstrate mood congruent effects consistent with affect priming in the course of substantive processing strategies.

EVIDENCE FOR THE AFFECT INFUSION MODEL

Most of the studies surveyed in the first half of this chapter did not specifically investigate the processing strategies subjects use while performing a particular task. In contrast, all the studies we will review here collected evidence about the processing strategies we expected to produce mood effects on cognition. Such evidence is directly relevant to an evaluation of AIM.

Encoding and Judgment Latencies

In our investigation of mood effects on person-perception judgments (Forgas & Bower, 1987), we also collected reaction-time data on two separate aspects of task performance. We used false feedback about test performance to induce happy or sad moods before asking subjects to form impressions about, and later

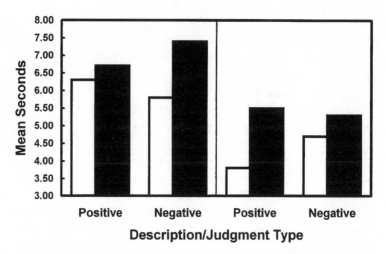

FIGURE 3.8. Time taken to read a positive or negative behavioral description (left panel) and to make a positive or negative judgment (right panel) by subjects in a happy or sad mood (white and black bars, respectively). Source: Forgas and Bower, 1987.

recall, the positive and negative features of persons they read about on a computer screen. We recorded the time each subject needed to read each item of description and to make each judgment. We noted earlier that this study found significant mood congruence in memory and judgments. As AIM suggested, subjects were slower to read mood congruent as opposed to mood incongruent information, as shown in the left panel of figure 3.8. However, as shown in the right panel, the subjects were faster to make mood congruent rather than incongruent judgments. These results were among the first to use latency data to confirm the operation of affect priming mechanisms during substantive processing (also see Bower, 1991; Forgas & Bower, 1988).

Effects of Task Typicality and Complexity

The AIM predicts that atypical, unusual, or complex cognitive tasks should selectively recruit longer and more substantive processing strategies, allowing correspondingly greater affect infusion effects. In other words, AIM implies, counterintuitively, that the longer and more extensively a subject needs to think about an atypical or complex task, the more likely affect infusion will arise.

This prediction was tested in a series of studies involving either normal versus strange people, well-matched versus odd couples, or minor versus major interpersonal conflicts; the following sections provide a snapshot of the relevant research.

Strange people: Mood effects on evaluating others. In several studies, we asked people to read and form impressions about fictional characters who were sometimes more, sometimes less prototypical. Person types such as the "radical feminist" or "the loner" are commonly shared by many subcultures and are defined by a specific pattern of nonexclusive features (Forgas, 1983). Because prototypicality is a matter of degree (Rosch & Lloyd, 1978), it seems that "the greater the prototypicality . . . the more easily would information about that person be encoded, retrieved, and elaborated" (Cantor & Mischel, 1979, p. 191), and the less likely that extended substantive processing would be required (Forgas, 1983; 1985b).

In one study (Forgas, 1992d, experiment 1), subjects feeling happy, sad, or neutral after watching a mood-appropriate film were asked to read about and form impressions of people who were either highly prototypical (all features consistent with a previously established prototype), highly atypical (half of the features are contrary to the prototype), or intermediate in prototypicality (half of the features unrelated to the prototype). Subsequent evaluations showed a clear mood congruent bias, and as predicted by the AIM, this bias was most pronounced for the least typical targets.

A subsequent study (Forgas, 1992d, experiment 2) used a different mood induction and examined mood effects on memory for typical as well as atypical targets. As expected, a significant interaction arose between mood and target prototypicality in the subjects' recall: mood had a greater impact on how much the subjects remembered about the atypical than the typical targets. The results also revealed an intriguing asymmetric effect of mood on memory: as shown in figure 3.9, recall was comparatively better for atypical targets among subjects tested in a sad mood, but for typical targets among subjects tested in a happy mood. One interpretation is that encoding and retrieving information about the atypical people was facilitated by the careful, substantive-processing strategy usually associated with dysphoria (Schwarz, 1990). In contrast, encoding and retrieving typical characters was apparently easier for subjects in a happy mood that tends to cue heuristic, schematic-processing styles (Isen, 1987).

A third study (Forgas, 1992d, experiment 3) demonstrated a link between mood effects and processing latencies. Results showed that subjects took significantly longer to encode and judge atypical than typical targets; these more extended and constructive judgments were most influenced by affect. These results are consistent with the AIM, establishing that the more elaborate and substantive processing recruited by atypical targets was indeed an essential prerequisite for greater affect priming effects on memory and judgments.

Odd couples: Mood effects on the perception of relationships. To control for the possible confounding effects of semantic priming associated with verbal descriptions of people (Wyer & Srull, 1989), follow-up experiments used

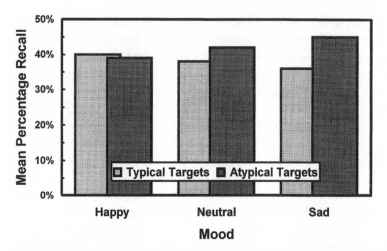

FIGURE 3.9. Details about typical and atypical target persons recalled (light and dark bars, respectively) by subjects in a happy, neutral, or sad mood. Source: Forgas, 1992d.

pictures of couples as stimuli. The couples appeared to be either matched or mismatched in physical attractiveness (Forgas, 1993b, 1995b). Superficial impressions about relationships are often based on such observable characteristics equally attractive mates tend to be more readily and more positively evaluated (Forgas & Dobosz, 1980).

Based on the AIM, we predicted, and found, significantly greater affect infusion into judgments about mismatched rather than matched couples. This effect was later confirmed when we found that an unconventional target context, such as encountering a person as part of a mixed-race dyad, would also initiate more detailed, substantive processing, which creates greater opportunity for mood-consistent associations to influence these judgments (Forgas & Moylan, 1991). In contrast, conventional targets, such as same-race couples, received less substantive processing from subjects and so displayed weaker mood effects. These findings have interesting implications for everyday social judgments and stereotyping: perceptions of atypical individuals or people encountered in an unusual context are more likely to be influenced by mood than are judgments of typical targets.

In a further development of this method (Forgas, 1995b, experiments 3 and 4), racial composition and physical attractiveness were simultaneously manipulated to create couples matched on either both, one, or neither feature. As expected, we found that the magnitude of mood effects on judgments increased directly with the degree of visible mismatch between the partners. Analysis of memory and processing-latency data revealed that greater mood effects resulted from the more extensive and prolonged processing these "odd" couples recruited.

To further confirm the role of processing strategies in the mediation of these mood congruent effects, we developed and tested a causal-path statistical model, using multiple regression procedures. The two predictor variables included in the analysis were the typicality of the target and the mood of the subject. The two mediating variables were latency of exposure to the target and time spent making a judgment; the magnitude of the mood dependent effect observed in judgment and in recall served as the dependent variables. Following Baron and Kenny (1986), the predicted mediational pattern was tested in several regression analyses. The results clearly supported the AIM, showing that processing strategy (as measured by exposure latency and judgment time) was a significant mediator of mood congruent effects on memory and judgment. Altogether, then, these studies showed that (a) people take longer to process information about unusual, atypical targets; (b) they later remember this information better; and (c) evaluative judgments about these more extensively processed targets are significantly more mood congruent.

Sad and guilty? Mood congruent effects in conflict attributions.   The research we have reviewed revealed consistent mood congruence within controlled laboratory environs. Would these counterintuitive findings also occur in more real-life situations in which people possess detailed and personal information about the target?

To find out, Forgas, Levinger, and Moylan (1994) examined the influence of mood on how people perceive and think about their own intimate relationships; Forgas (1994b) studied how they explain more or less serious interpersonal conflicts. In a preliminary exploration of this question, two experiments found that a happy or sad mood significantly influenced how people evaluated their intimate partners and close relationships. Surprisingly, these mood congruent effects were just as powerful in well-established, long-term personal relationships as in short-term, superficial liaisons. One might have expected a reduction in mood congruent effects as the longevity and familiarity of a relationship increases. In fact, because well-established relationships provide partners with particularly rich and heterogeneous experiences, mood should continue to play a critical role in selectively priming the kinds of episodes partners remember when constructing a global evaluative judgment (Forgas et al., 1994).

Later studies asked happy and sad subjects to make causal attributions for recent instances of either conflict or cooperation with their significant others (Forgas, 1994b, experiment 1). Consistent with the affect priming theory, an overall pattern of mood congruence appeared in these judgments, with more self-deprecatory attributions by sad than by happy subjects. In a second study

(Forgas, 1994b, experiment 2), subjects who had just seen a happy, sad, or neutral movie made causal attributions for simple or complex conflicts in their current intimate relationships. Sad subjects made significantly more pessimistic attributions overall, inferring more global, stable, and internal causes for their conflicts.

As the data appearing in figure 3.10 make plain, these mood effects were much greater on explanations for serious conflicts than simple ones. Once more, it seems that the extensive processing recruited by more complex tasks enhanced mood congruent effects, even when judges faced highly realistic information. Replicating earlier experiments, the last study in this series (Forgas, 1994b, experiment 3) showed that, even for these complex, real-life judgments, larger mood effects were consistently associated with longer processing times, as predicted by AIM.

These results help us understand the dynamics of everyday social judgments. Dealing with information about other people or our relationships with them is a complex, inferential cognitive task we routinely perform to make sense of our social world (Heider, 1958). The results suggest that the longer and more constructively one needs to think about such information to compute an evaluation, the more likely that affect infusion will significantly influence the outcome. In addition, the evidence indicates that mood congruence is far more likely to influence complex, atypical, or problematic information that requires extensive, substantive processing.

Mood Effects on Central versus Peripheral Aspects of the Self-Concept

In the first half of this chapter, we noted that mood congruence can distort not only self-perceptions but also people's reactions to positive or negative feedback from others (Esses, 1989; Forgas et al., 1984). In a review of mood effects on self-perception, Sedikides (1992) concluded that "self-valence is affected by mood in a congruent manner" (p. 301). Considerable clinical research also suggests that such mood-induced biases in self-perception can be an integral aspect of depression (Ottaviani & Beck, 1988). However, according to the AIM, mood effects on self-perception occur only when people must construct an opinion rather than use direct access or motivated processing to arrive at one.

The process sensitivity of affect infusion into self-perception has been confirmed in several experiments by Sedikides (1995). A guided imagery task helped to instill a happy, sad, or neutral mood in subjects, who were then asked to complete a series of self-descriptions related to their behaviors or enduring personality traits. The time they took to do so was recorded. Confirming the AIM, Sedikides (1995) found that mood effects were significantly greater on descriptions of peripheral (less salient, less elaborated, less important attributes,

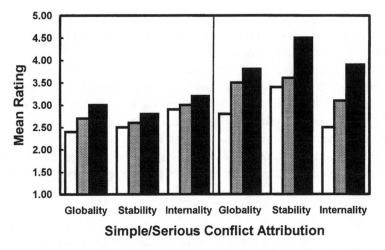

Simple/Serious Conflict Attribution

FIGURE 3.10. Ratings of the globality, stability, and internality of attributions about the causes of simple (left panel) and serious (right panel) relationship conflicts made by subjects in a happy, neutral, or sad mood (white, gray, and black bars, respectively). Source: Forgas, 1994b.

held with less certainty) rather than central aspects of the self-concept. Presumably, peripheral self-descriptions require more constructive and open processing than do central self-descriptions, which are likely to entail low-infusion strategies such as direct access or motivated processing. Also consistent with the AIM is Sedikides's (1995) comment that "high on-line elaboration magnified the mood congruence bias . . . [suggesting that] affect priming is the vehicle that carries the effects of mood on peripheral self-conceptions" (p. 40).

However, this pattern may not apply to clinically depressed individuals, who tend to show mood congruence even in central self-conceptions, possibly because of their more vulnerable, uncertain, and fluid central self-concept. From our perspective, the most important contribution of Sedikides's studies is that they were all "consistent with the AIM [predicting] the absence of mood effects in reference to central self-conceptions, but the presence of a mood congruence bias in reference to peripheral self-conceptions" (Sedikides, 1995, p. 39).

Affective Influences on Intergroup Judgments

The process sensitivity of affect infusion has been demonstrated in intergroup perceptions and judgments. Group membership can be a powerful and emotionally involving experience, and affect has long been assumed to be an important feature of prejudice and stereotyping (Stangor, Sullivan, & Ford, 1991). Interestingly, the influence of affect on intergroup relations has received relatively little attention. Some studies suggest that intergroup bias and stereotyping often arise as a result of direct-access or heuristic-processing strategies (e.g., Bodenhausen, 1993; Mackie & Worth, 1991; Stroessner & Mackie, 1992). However, other studies (e.g., Esses et al., 1993; Haddock, Zanna, & Esses, 1994) point to the role of affect priming in biasing intergroup perceptions under conditions that promote substantive processing. In an interesting investigation, Haddock et al. (1994) used music to induced their Canadian subjects to feel happy or sad and then asked them to indicate their attitudes and affective associations toward French Canadians, Pakistanis, and others. Results showed a clear mood congruent pattern and demonstrated that mood can play "a role in the favorability of intergroup attitudes, stereotypes, and emotional associates" (p. 198).

What processing strategies may have generated these effects? Fortunately, Haddock et al. (1994) collected some relevant evidence suggesting that elaborate, substantive processing was a likely prerequisite for these results. They found that, in keeping with the concept of affect priming, subjects experiencing an especially intense mood reported their images of the target groups to be clearer and made lengthier statements concerning their stereotypes and emotional associates.

More direct evidence for the process mediation of mood effects on intergroup judgments appeared in a recent series of experiments (Forgas & Fiedler, 1996). In these studies, which used a modification of the classic "minimal group" paradigm developed by Tajfel (see Tajfel & Forgas, 1981), people in happy, sad, or neutral moods allocated rewards and formed impressions about in-group and out-group members. In this task, in-group and out-group members are solely defined in terms of group category information. The mere existence of an in-group/outgroup label often appears sufficient to induce people to discriminate in favor of the group members. In terms of the AIM, we predicted that both a happy and a sad mood would increase intergroup discrimination, although under different processing circumstances. When group membership is not personally relevant and judges have little knowledge about or involvement in their groups (the traditional minimal group manipulation), a happy mood should induce a faster and more heuristic judgmental style, leading the subjects to rely more on simple categorical information about the groups and thus resulting in greater intergroup discrimination. However, when group membership is personally relevant, sad subjects should show greater intergroup bias, as they seek to increase the positive distinctiveness of their in-group as part of a self-enhancing, motivated strategy of mood repair (Clark & Isen, 1982; Forgas, 1991a; Forgas & Fiedler, 1996).

As predicted, we found that when the relevance of group membership was low, happy mood resulted in faster, heuristic processing strategies and greater intergroup bias. In contrast, when the relevance of group membership was high, sad mood enhanced intergroup discrimination as a result of more motivated processing strategies. Reaction-time data and mediational analyses confirmed that these mood effects were indeed linked to different processing styles.

Beyond Mere Thinking: Affect Priming and Interpersonal Behaviors

The studies we summarized examined how an individual's mood affects his or her ability to think, remember, and evaluate information. The influence of mood states does not necessarily end with individual cognitive activity, however. Much of everyday life consists of interactions between people; mood-induced biases in cognition likely will also influence people's actual social behaviors (Forgas, 1985a). We have seen already seen that mood influences feelings of self-efficacy, as well as how people deal with positive and negative feedback from others. In several experiments, we investigated the possibility that good or bad moods may also affect people's planned and actual interactive strategies in negotiating forthcoming encounters (Forgas, 1998c).

Negotiation, an inherently complex and unpredictable interpersonal task, involves an individual's expectations, inferences, and cognitions (Pruitt & Carnevale, 1993). Yet direct evidence for mood effects on actual interpersonal strategies is scarce. In one study, Carnevale and Isen (1986) found that subjects who had been induced to feel happy (by viewing humorous cartoons and receiving a small gift) were less inclined to adopt contentious negotiating strategies. In another study, Baron (1990) reported that subjects experiencing a good mood (as a result of a pleasant scent) set higher goals, made more concessions, and were less likely to prefer avoidance or competition in face-to-face negotiations. Both of these findings are consistent with affect priming.

Following the AIM, one would expect that as long as people adopt an open, substantive processing strategy in preparing for a face-to-face negotiation, happy subjects should make more mood congruent inferences about the task, leading them to plan and use more cooperative and integrative strategies and eventually achieve better outcomes. However, when individuals approach the task from a predetermined, motivated perspective (for example, people who have a high need for approval or who are highly Machiavellian), the AIM predicts the absence of mood congruent effects.

The negotiation task used in this research (Forgas, 1998c) involved a realistic situation: student subjects bargaining for their preferred courses to be placed in the psychology curriculum. Two consecutive negotiating sessions were held: an interpersonal negotiation, in which subjects bargained with other team members to get the highest priority for their preferred course, and an intergroup negotiation, in which two opposing teams bargained for their preferred courses. One study confirmed that happy subjects planned and actually used significantly more cooperative and integrative negotiating strategies in both kinds of tasks than did sad subjects.

Another study explored the role of individual differences in mediating mood effects on cooperative or competitive bargaining strategies. Consistent with the predictions of AIM, results (in the form of rated likelihood of engaging in a particular strategy) showed that these effects markedly decreased for subjects who approached the task from a highly motivated perspective (those scoring high on social desirability).

Thus, the results of both studies provide evidence for mood congruence in an interpersonal encounter. Positive mood beneficially influenced people's expectations, strategies, and outcomes in both bargaining encounters. The main consequence of a positive mood was a marked inclination to be more cooperative and less competitive. These effects occurred both in informal, interpersonal tasks and in more formal, intergroup negotiation tasks, suggesting cross-situational generality in the results. Conversely, negative mood resulted in less cooperative and ultimately more self-defeating bargaining strategies and outcomes. Remarkably, these affect infusion effects largely disappeared for individuals who approached these tasks from a predetermined, motivated perspective.

The practical implications of affect infusion in interactive behaviors remain incompletely delineated. When feeling good, people have a powerful tendency to adopt more cooperative and integrative strategies, and more competitive strategies when feeling bad (Baron, 1990; Berkowitz, 1993; Carnevale & Isen, 1986). These tendencies likely have important practical implications for conflict resolution, both in interpersonal and in organizational settings. Inappropriate interpersonal strategies resulting from depressed mood may also be part of the etiology of depression.

Sad and Polite? Mood Effects on Verbal Communication

The previous studies suggest that affect priming influences not only thinking and judgment but also how people plan, and perform in, interpersonal situations. A recent series of experiments investigated mood effects on *requesting*, a specific strategic behavior.

Formulating a request typically involves substantive, inferential processing as one seeks to arrange words direct enough to maximize compliance, yet polite enough to avoid offense. Affect priming can play a role in devising requests, for happy or sad subjects may have decidedly different assumptions about the difficulty their entreaties face (the "felicity conditions" of the request) and may devise their messages accordingly. We may expect happy subjects to adopt a more confident, direct requesting strategy, whereas sad subjects may prefer more cautious, polite requests because they pessimistically assess the felicity conditions for their messages.

The role of affect in the generation of strategic messages such as requests has not been explored previously. In a recently completed series of studies (Forgas, 1999b), happy or sad subjects were asked to produce requests in a variety of complex interpersonal situations. The results revealed clear evidence of affect infusion; for example, subjects feeling sad (after recalling depressing autobiographical events) preferred significantly more polite request forms when, for instance, asking for the repayment of a loan. Subsequent studies confirmed these mood effects across a broad range of requesting situations and status relationships and their link to the substantive processing styles these problematic interpersonal situations recruited. Consistent with the predictions derived from the AIM, the results also showed that mood more significantly influenced direct, unconventional requests that require more elaborate processing.

These mood effects on requesting were not confined to artificial settings. In one naturalistic requesting episode, subjects feeling happy or sad (after viewing a film) were asked to go to a neighboring office and get a file from a confederate of the experimenter, ostensibly while the next part of the experiment was being set up (Forgas, 1999c). The words they used in asking for the file were surreptitiously recorded and later analyzed for request politeness and the degree of cognitive elaboration; the subjects' recall of the words they used was also assessed. Sad subjects used more polite, indirect request forms and relied on more complex, elaborate semantic and syntactic structures than happy subjects did. Once again, mood effects were greater on less unconventional and more substantively processed request formulations, and subjects remembered them better later.

These results extend mood congruence to a new domain—the production of strategic verbal messages. Formulating a request is an intrinsically complex and demanding task; the communicator must engage in substantive processing to infer the likely costs and benefits of different request alternatives. In substantive processing, mood-primed associations may lead sad subjects to overestimate the dangers of rejection and offense and thus to use more cautious, polite forms.

Mood influences not only the production of requests but also how recipients perceive and interpret them. In a series of studies (Forgas, 1998a), an unobtrusive mood manipulation was delivered to unsuspecting students in the university library, where envelopes containing either happy or sad materials (pictures and stories) lay on unoccupied desks. Upon taking a seat, students were allowed to open the envelopes and examine their contents in detail before a confederate approached them with a request for some writing paper. The requests varied in politeness (gracious versus ill-mannered) and the degree of imposition (high versus low) they entailed. A few minutes after this unobtrusive requesting episode, a second confederate approached the subject's desk, explained that the request was part of a social psychology study, and asked (politely!) the subject to complete a brief questionnaire about the episode, measuring his or her memory for the request and perceptions of the request and the requester.

Results showed a clear mood congruence pattern: sad subjects interpreted all requests more negatively than happy subjects and were generally less likely to comply. However, these mood effects were not the same for every request. As suggested by the AIM, subjects tended to remember requests that were phrased more unconventionally, in inappropriately direct verbal forms.These messages seemed to induce more substantive processing. The degree of mood congruence was also significantly greater for these more atypical, unusual messages, whereas reactions to more conventional, typical requests were less influenced by the affective state of the recipients. In conclusion, these studies provide convergent evidence supporting the AIM and confirm the important role of affect priming in informing not only thinking and judgments but also interpersonal behaviors.

CONCLUSIONS

Philosophers, artists, and laypersons have traditionally assumed a close interdependence between affective states and the thoughts, memories, and associations that come to mind. Surprisingly, psychologists were relatively late to recognize the importance of this phenomenon, perhaps because of the artificial compartmentalization between affect, cognition, and conation—the three "faculties of mind" that have characterized our discipline since its inception (Hilgard, 1980). During the last twenty years, an impressive amount of empirical evidence has accumulated demonstrating the importance of affect infusion. Theoretical explanations of mood congruence in learning, memory, judgment, and other mental processes have also changed, from earlier psychoanalytic and conditioning explanations (Clore & Byrne, 1974; Feshbach & Singer, 1957) to the more recent cognitive accounts.

One of the more productive explanations for a range of mood congruent effects has been the affect priming theory (Bower, 1981, 1991). This account, which proposes that moods directly facilitate access to mood-related cognitions, offers a simple, parsimonious, and intuitively appealing explanation for a range of mood congruent effects, encompassing attention, perception, recollection, and decision making.

One objective of this chapter has been to review the affect priming theory. The first part of the chapter reviewed several studies, from both the memory and the social cognition literatures, attesting to the generality of mood congruence. With the rapid accumulation of the empirical evidence, however, it also became clear that mood congruence is not universal—in fact, numerous studies have failed to find any sign of mood congruence, and several have even succeeded in showing mood incongruence. Our challenge in this chapter has been to explain and integrate these failures or reversals of mood congruence with the majority of experiments that did show congruence. To this end, we reviewed the circumstances in which mood congruent effects failed to materialize. We noticed, as have others examining this literature (Fiedler, 1990, 1991), that experiments failing to find mood congruence shared certain features. Typically, subjects in those studies were asked to perform a task that was simple, well-rehearsed, and could be readily performed by accessing directly a prior solution, or they were motivated to solve the task so as to arrive at a predetermined outcome (for example, to achieve mood repair or some other self-serving result). In these conditions, there is little need—and often no opportunity—for subjects to engage in the open, constructive information processing that appears to be a prerequisite for affect infusion (Fiedler, 1991).

The proposed affect infusion model outlined in the second half of the chapter is essentially a generalization from the extensive empirical evidence now available. By assuming that affect infusion occurs only in circumstances likely to lead to constructive processing strategies, we believe that we can now account for most of the studies in the literature demonstrating mood congruence or its absence.

Our task was complicated because affect priming is not the only possible mechanism for affect infusion. The affect-as-information theory suggested by Schwarz and Clore (1983) can explain at least some of the mood congruent phenomena reported in the literature. Reconciling these two alternative explanations, sometimes regarded as incompatible, was a further objective of the AIM. We agree with Schwarz and Clore (1983) that people may indeed occasionally rely on their preexisting affective states as information when computing a judgment. However, we believe that this likely occurs only in special circumstances, namely, when the task requires constructive processing, and is of little personal relevance, or there are insufficient processing resources (either time or cognitive capacity) available to produce a carefully considered judgment. In contrast to such a heuristic processing strategy, affect priming is more probable when people engage in substantive, constructive thinking. We believe that affect priming is the most common primary mechanism leading to mood congruence in most everyday judgment tasks.

Based on these considerations, the AIM identified four distinct information-processing strategies available to individuals when performing a cognitive task: (1) a *direct access strategy*, based on the highly cued retrieval of a preexisting, crystallized opinion; (2) a *motivated processing strategy*, when information processing is limited and guided by a specific motivation, such as mood repair; (3) a *heuristic processing strategy*, when individuals seek to construct a response using whatever shortcuts and heuristics are available; and (4) a *substantive pro-*

cessing strategy, when individuals engage in the selective, constructive processing of the available information involving learning, associative, and memory processes. Such a multiprocess approach is becoming increasingly common in theories of social cognition. Dual-process and multiprocess explanations have recently been invoked to explain the disparate empirical results in such fields as persuasive communication, impression formation, stereotyping, and other social judgments (Brewer, 1988; Chaiken, 1980; Kruglanski, 1989; Petty et al., 1991). We believe that the multiprocess AIM offers a comprehensive theoretical context for delineating when and how affect priming processes most likely influence our thoughts and judgments.

The evidence reviewed toward the end of the chapter comes from studies that support specific predictions derived from the AIM. Counterintuitive results, showing that more extensive, substantive processing enhances mood congruence, provide especially strong support for the AIM (Forgas, 1992c, 1994b, 1995b). Other supportive studies are those demonstrating the disappearance of mood congruent effects whenever people approach a cognitive task from a motivated perspective (Forgas, 1991a; Forgas & Fiedler, 1996; Sedikides, 1995).

We believe that mood congruence in the way information is selected, retrieved, and interpreted occurs not only in the laboratory but also in many real-life cognitive tasks, both in private and public lives. Affect infusion has recently been identified as an important aspect of organizational decisions and personnel selection choices, consumer preferences, and clinical practice and health-related judgments (Baron, 1987; Clore & Parrott, 1991; Forgas & Moylan, 1987; Mayer et al., 1992; Salovey et al., 1991; Sedikides, 1992). The evidence now suggests that the more people engage in open, constructive processing to solve a problem, the more likely that their affective state will significantly influence the information they consider and the responses they make. Even such highly involved and complex tasks as seeking an explanation for difficult relationship conflicts exhibited these mood congruent biases (Forgas, 1994b).

We do not wish to suggest, however, that mood congruence and affect infusion are the only possible cognitive consequences of affective states. Most of the evidence we considered deals with valence effects—that is, the influence of generally good or bad moods on positive or negative thoughts and associations. In addition to valence, other features of affective states may influence our thoughts and judgments. Several emotion theorists have emphasized the functional, motivated aspects of feelings that do not require high-level cognitive processing (e.g., Berkowitz, 1993; Leary, 2000). Other theorists stress that affective states also have direct appraisal properties that provide people with immediate information about situational contingencies and probable consequences, thus obviating the need to invoke memory processes (e.g., Smith & Ellsworth, 1985). Although these effects are undoubtedly interesting, we believe that the valence of an affective state is probably its most important attribute in its impact on cognition. In any case, the four processing strategies identified by the AIM are apt to be highly relevant to our understanding of the motivational and appraisal effects of affective states.

In conclusion, we believe that affect priming continues to be the most robust and reliable mechanism of mood congruence in many settings. We also believe that evidence indicating the absence of mood congruence has been misinterpreted in the past as inconsistent with an affect priming explanation and that the AIM offers a comprehensive framework for understanding the boundary conditions for affect priming. We hope that by further clarifying the characteristics and conditions conducive to affect priming, this review will promote continued interest in this important area of research.

NOTES

Support from grant MH47575 to Gordon Bower, from the (American) National Institute of Mental Health, and to Joe Forgas from the (Australian) Research Council and the Alexander von Humboldt Foundation, Germany, is gratefully acknowledged.

REFERENCES

Achee, J., Tesser, A., & Pilkington, C. (1994). Social perception: A test of the role of arousal in Self-Evaluation Maintenance processes. *European Journal of Social Psychology, 24,* 147–160.

Anderson, J. R. (1976). *Language, memory and thought.* Hillsdale, NJ: Erlbaum.

Bandura, A. (1977). Self-efficacy: Toward a unifying theory of behavior change. *Psychological Review, 84,* 191–215.

Baron, R. (1987). Interviewers' moods and reactions to job applicants: The influence of affective states on applied social judgments. *Journal of Applied Social Psychology, 16,* 16–28.

Baron, R. (1990). Environmentally induced positive affect: Its impact on self-efficacy, task performance, negotiation, and conflict. *Journal of Applied Social Psychology, 20,* 368–384.

Baron, R. M., & Kenny, D. A. (1986). The moderator-mediator variable distinction in social psychological research: Conceptual, strategic and statistical considerations. *Journal of Personality and Social Psychology, 51,* 1173–1182.

Baumgardner, A. H., & Arkin, R. M. (1988). Affective state mediates causal attributions for success and failure. *Motivation and Emotion, 12,* 99–111.

Beck, R. C., & McBee, W. (1995). Mood-dependent memory for generated and repeated words: Replication and extension. *Cognition and Emotion, 9,* 289–307.

Berkowitz, L. (1993). Towards a general theory of anger and emotional aggression. In

T. K. Srull & R. S. Wyer (Eds.), *Advances in social cognition* (vol. 6, pp. 1–46). Hillsdale, NJ: Erlbaum.

Berkowitz, L., Jo, E., Troccoli, B. T., & Monteith, M. (1994). *Attention-activated regulation of feeling effects. Unpublished manuscript.* Department of Psychology, University of Wisconsin.

Berkowitz, L., & Troccoli, B. T. (1990). Feelings, direction of attention, and expressed evaluations of others. *Cognition and Emotion, 4,* 305–325.

Blaney, P. H. (1986). Affect and memory: A review. *Psychological Bulletin, 99,* 229–246.

Blascovich, J., & Mendes, W. B. (2000). Challenge and threat appraisals: The role of affective cues. In J. P. Forgas (Ed.), *Feeling and thinking: The role of affect in social cognition* (pp. 59–82). New York: Cambridge University Press.

Bless, H. (2000). Mood and general knowledge structures: Happy moods and their impact on information processing. In J. P. Forgas (Ed.), *Feeling and thinking: The role of affect in social cognition* (pp. 201–222). New York: Cambridge University Press.

Bodenhausen, G. V. (1993). Emotion, arousal and stereotypic judgment: A heuristic model of affect and stereotyping. In D. Mackie & D. Hamilton (Eds.), *Affect, cognition and stereotyping: Interactive processes in intergroup perception* (pp. 13–37). San Diego: Academic Press.

Borg, I. (1987). The effect of mood on different types of well-being judgments. *Archiv fur Psychologie, 139,* 181–188.

Bower, G. H. (1981). Mood and memory. *American Psychologist, 36,* 129–148.

Bower, G. H. (1983). Affect and cognition. *Philosophical Transactions of the Royal Society of London (Part B), 302,* 387–402.

Bower, G. H. (1991). Mood congruity of social judgments. In J. P. Forgas (Ed.), *Emotion and social judgments* (pp. 31–53). Oxford: Pergamon Press.

Bower, G. H., & Cohen, P. R. (1982). Emotional influences in memory and thinking: Data and theory. In M. S. Clark & S. T. Fiske (Eds.), *Affect and cognition* (pp. 291–332). Hillsdale, NJ: Erlbaum.

Bower, G. H., & Forgas, J. P. (in press). Mood and social memory. In J. P. Forgas (Ed.)., *Handbook of affect and social cognition.* Mahwah, NJ: Erlbaum.

Bower, G. H., & Mayer, J. D. (1985). Failure to replicate mood-dependent retrieval. *Bulletin of the Psychonomic Society, 23,* 39–42.

Bower, G. H., Monteiro, K. P., & Gilligan, S. G. (1978). Emotional mood as a context for learning and recall. *Journal of Verbal Learning and Verbal Behavior, 17,* 573–585.

Bradley, P. P., & Mathews, A. M. (1983). Negative self schemata in clinical depression. *British Journal of Clinical Psychology, 22,* 173–181.

Branscombe, N., & Cohen, P. (1991). Motivation and complexity levels as determinants of heuristic use in social judgment. In J. P. Forgas (Ed.), *Emotion and social judgments* (pp. 145–160). Elmsford, NY: Pergamon Press.

Brewer, M. (1988). A dual-process model of impression formation. In T. K. Srull & R. S. Wyer (Eds.), *Advances in social cognition* (vol. 1, pp. 1–36). Hillsdale, NJ: Erlbaum.

Brown, R. (1965). *Social psychology.* New York: Freeman.

Burke, M., & Mathews, A. M. (1992). Autobiographical memory and clinical anxiety. *Cognition and Emotion, 6*, 23–35.

Calder, B. J., & Gruder, C. L. (1988). *A network activation theory of attitudinal affect.* Unpublished manuscript. Kellogg School of Business, Northwestern University.

Cantor, N., & Mischel, W. (1979). Prototypes in person perception. In L. Berkowitz (Ed.), *Advances in experimental social psychology* (vol. 12, pp. 3–52). New York: Academic Press.

Carnevale, P. J. D., & Isen, A. M. (1986). The influence of positive affect and visual access on the discovery of integrative solutions in bilateral negotiation. *Organizational Behavior and Human Decision Processes, 37*, 1–13.

Carson, T. P., & Adams, H. E. (1980). Activity valence as a function of mood change. *Journal of Abnormal Psychology, 89*, 368–377.

Catanzano, S. J., & Mearns, J. (1990). Measuring generalized expectancies for negative mood regulation: Initial scale development and implications. *Journal of Personality Assessment, 54*, 546–563.

Chaiken, S. (1980). Heuristic versus systematic information processing and the use of source versus message cues in persuasion. *Journal of Personality and Social Psychology, 39*, 752–766.

Christianson, S.-A., & Loftus, E. F. (1991). Remembering emotional events: The fate of detail information. *Cognition and Emotion, 5*, 81–108.

Ciarrochi, J. V., & Forgas, J. P. (1999a). *On being anxious yet tolerant: Personality mediates mood effects on race-related judgments.* Manuscript under review.

Ciarrochi, J. V., & Forgas, J. P. (1999b). *The pleasure of possessions: Affective influences on consumer judgments.* Manuscript under review.

Clark, A. M., & Waddell, B. A. (1983). Effects of moods on thoughts about helping, attraction and information acquisition. *Social Psychology Quarterly, 46*, 31–35.

Clark, M. S. (1982). A role for arousal in the link between feeling states, judgements, and behavior. In M. S. Clark & S. J. Fiske (Eds.), *Affect and cognition* (pp. 263–290). Hillsdale, NJ: Erlbaum.

Clark, M. S., & Isen, A. M. (1982). Towards understanding the relationship between feeling states and social behavior. In A. H. Hastorf & A. M. Isen (Eds.), *Cognitive social psychology* (pp. 73–108). New York: Elsevier-North Holland.

Clark, M. S., Milberg, S., & Ross, J. (1983). Arousal cues arousal-related material in memory: Implications for understanding effects of mood on memory. *Journal of Verbal Learning and Verbal Behavior, 22*, 633–649.

Clore, G. L., & Byrne, D. (1974). The reinforcement affect model of attraction. In T. L. Huston (Ed.), *Foundations of interpersonal attraction* (pp. 143–170). New York: Academic Press.

Clore, G. L., & Parrott, G. (1991). Moods and their vicissitudes: Thoughts and feelings as information. In J. P. Forgas (Ed.), *Emotion and social judgments* (pp. 107–123). Oxford: Pergamon.

Clore, G. L., & Parrott, G. (1994). Cognitive feelings and metacognitive judgments. *European Journal of Social Psychology, 24*, 101–116.

Clore, G. L., Schwarz, N., & Conway, M. (1994). Affective causes and consequences of social information processing. In R. S. Wyer & T. K. Srull (Eds.), *Handbook of social cognition* (vol. 2, 2nd ed., pp. 323–417). Hillsdale, NJ: Erlbaum.

Denny, E. B., & Hunt, R. R. (1992). Affective balance and memory in depression: Dissociation of recall and fragment completion. *Journal of Abnormal Psychology, 101,* 575–580.

Eich, E. (1995). Searching for mood dependent memory. *Psychological Science, 6,* 67–75.

Eich, E., & Macaulay, D. (2000). Fundamental factors in mood dependent memory. In J. P. Forgas (Ed.), *Feeling and thinking: The role of affect in social cognition* (pp. 109–130). New York: Cambridge University Press.

Eich, E., Macaulay, D., & Ryan, L. (1994). Mood dependent memory for events of the personal past. *Journal of Experimental Psychology: General, 123,* 201–215.

Eich, E., Reeves, J. L., Jaeger, B., & Graff-Radford, S. B. (1985). Memory for pain: Relation between past and present pain intensity. *Pain, 23,* 375–379.

Ellis, H. C., & Ashbrook, T. W. (1988). Resource allocation model of the effects of depressed mood state on memory. In K. Fiedler & J. P. Forgas (Eds.), *Affect, cognition, and social behavior* (pp. 25–43). Toronto: Hogrefe.

Erber, R. (1991). Affective and semantic priming: Effects of mood on category accessibility and inference. *Journal of Experimental Social Psychology, 27,* 480–498.

Erber, R., & Erber, M. W. (1994). Beyond mood and social judgment: Mood incongruent recall and mood regulation. *European Journal of Social Psychology, 24,* 79–88.

Esses, V. M. (1989). Mood as a moderator of acceptance of interpersonal feedback. *Journal of Personality and Social Psychology, 57,* 769–781.

Esses, V. M., Haddock, G., & Zanna, M. P. (1993). Values, stereotypes, and emotions as determinants of intergroup attitudes. In D. M. Mackie & D. L. Hamilton (Eds.), *Affect, cognition, and stereotyping: Interactive processes in group perception* (pp. 137–166). San Diego: Academic Press.

Eysenck, M. W., MacLeod, C., & Mathews, A. M. (1987). Cognitive functioning in anxiety. *Psychological Research, 49,* 189–195.

Feshbach, S., & Singer, R. D. (1957). The effects of fear arousal and suppression of fear upon social perception. *Journal of Abnormal and Social Psychology, 55,* 283–288.

Fiedler, K. (1990). Mood-dependent selectivity in social cognition. In W. Stroebe & M. Hewstone (Eds.), *European review of social psychology* (vol. 1, pp. 1–32). Chichester, UK: Wiley.

Fiedler, K. (1991). On the task, the measures and the mood in research on affect and social cognition. In J. P. Forgas (Ed.), *Emotion and social judgments* (pp. 83–104). Oxford: Pergamon.

Fiedler, K. (2000). Toward an integrative account of affect and cognition phenomena using the BIAS computer algorithm. In J. P. Forgas (Ed.), *Feeling and thinking: The role of affect in social cognition* (pp. 223–252). New York: Cambridge University Press.

Fiske, S. T., & Neuberg, L. (1990). A continuum of impression formation, from category-based to individuating processes: Influences of information and motivation on attention and interpretation. In M. Zanna (Ed.), *Advances in experimental social psychology* (vol. 23, pp. 1–74). New York: Academic Press.

Forgas, J. P. (1983). The effects of prototypicality and cultural salience on perceptions of people. *Journal of Research in Personality, 17,* 153–173.

Forgas, J. P. (1985a). *Interpersonal behavior.* Oxford: Pergamon.

Forgas, J. P. (1985b). Person prototypes and cultural salience: The role of cognitive and cultural factors in impression formation. *British Journal of Social Psychology, 24,* 3–17.

Forgas, J. P. (1989). Mood effects on decision-making strategies. *Australian Journal of Psychology, 41,* 197–214.

Forgas, J. P. (1990). Affective influences on individual and group judgments. *European Journal of Social Psychology, 20,* 441–453.

Forgas, J. P. (1991a). Affect and cognition in close relationships. In G. Fletcher & F. Fincham (Eds.), *Cognition in close relationships* (pp. 151–174). Hillsdale, NJ: Erlbaum.

Forgas, J. P., Ed. (1991b). *Emotion and social judgments.* Oxford: Pergamon Press.

Forgas, J. P. (1991c). Mood effects on partner choice: Role of affect in social decisions. *Journal of Personality and Social Psychology, 61,* 708–720.

Forgas, J. P. (1992a). Affect and social perceptions: Research evidence and an integrative model. In W. Stroebe & M. Hewstone (Eds.), *European review of social psychology* (vol. 3, pp. 183–224). Chichester, UK: Wiley.

Forgas, J. P. (1992b). Affect in social judgments and decisions: A multi-process model. In M. Zanna (Ed.), *Advances in experimental social psychology* (vol. 25, pp. 7–275). New York: Academic Press.

Forgas, J. P. (1992c). Mood and the perception of unusual people: Affective asymmetry in memory and social judgments. *European Journal of Social Psychology, 22,* 531–547.

Forgas, J. P. (1992d). On bad mood and peculiar people: Affect and person typicality in impression formation. *Journal of Personality and Social Psychology, 62,* 863–875.

Forgas, J. P. (1993a). Affect, appraisal and action: Towards a multi-process framework. In R. S. Wyer & T. K. Srull (Eds.), *Advances in social cognition* (vol. 6, pp. 89–108). Hillsdale, NJ: Erlbaum.

Forgas, J. P. (1993b). On making sense of odd couples: Mood effects on the perception of mismatched relationships. *Personality and Social Psychology Bulletin, 19,* 59–71.

Forgas, J. P. (1994a). The role of emotion in social judgments: An introductory review and an Affect Infusion Model (AIM). *European Journal of Social Psychology, 24,* 1–24.

Forgas, J. P. (1994b). Sad and guilty? Affective influences on the explanation of conflict episodes. *Journal of Personality and Social Psychology, 66,* 56–68.

Forgas, J. P. (1995a). Mood and judgment: The Affect Infusion Model (AIM). *Psychological Bulletin, 117,* 39–66.

Forgas, J. P. (1995b). Strange couples: Mood effects on judgments and memory about prototypical and atypical targets. *Personality and Social Psychology Bulletin, 21,* 747–765.

Forgas, J. P. (1998a). Asking nicely? The effects of mood on responding to more or less polite requests. *Personality and Social Psychology Bulletin, 24,* 173–185.

Forgas, J. P. (1998b). On being happy but mistaken: Mood effects on the fundamental attribution error. *Journal of Personality and Social Psychology, 75,* 318–331.

Forgas, J. P. (1998c). On feeling good and getting your way: Mood effects on negotiator cognition and bargaining strategies. *Journal of Personality and Social Psychology, 74,* 565–577.

Forgas, J. P. (1999a). *Affective influences on the perception of more or less ambiguous facial expressions.* Unpublished manuscript, School of Psychology, University of New South Wales.

Forgas, J. P. (1999b). On feeling good and being rude: Affective influences on use and request formulations. *Journal of Personality and Social Psychology, 76,* 928–939.

Forgas, J. P. (1999c). Feeling and speaking: Mood effects on verbal communication strategies. *Personality and Social Psychology Bulletin, 25,* 850–863.

Forgas, J. P., & Bower, G. H. (1987). Mood effects on person perception judgements. *Journal of Personality and Social Psychology, 53,* 53–60.

Forgas, J. P., & Bower, G. H. (1988). Affect in social judgements. *Australian Journal of Psychology, 40,* 125–145.

Forgas, J. P., Bower, G. H., & Krantz, S. (1984). The influence of mood on perceptions of social interactions. *Journal of Experimental Social Psychology, 20,* 497–513.

Forgas, J. P., Bower, G. H., & Moylan, S. J. (1990). Praise or blame? Affective influences on attributions for achievement. *Journal of Personality and Social Psychology, 59,* 809–818.

Forgas, J. P., & Dobosz, B. (1980). Dimensions of romantic involvement: Towards a taxonomy of heterosexual relationships. *Social Psychology Quarterly, 43,* 290–300.

Forgas, J. P., & Fiedler, K. (1996). Us and them: Mood effects on intergroup discrimination. *Journal of Personality and Social Psychology, 70,* 36–52.

Forgas, J. P., Johnson, R., & Ciarrochi, J. (1998). Affect control and affect infusion: A multi-process account of mood management and personal control. In M. Kofta, G. Weary, & G. Sedek (Eds.), *Personal control in action: Cognitive and motivational mechanisms* (pp. 155–189). New York: Plenum Press.

Forgas, J. P., Levinger, G., & Moylan, S. (1994). Feeling good and feeling close: Mood effects on the perception of intimate relationships. *Personal Relationships, 2,* 165–84.

Forgas, J. P., & Moylan, S. J. (1987). After the movies: The effects of transient mood states on social judgments. *Personality and Social Psychology Bulletin, 13,* 478–489.

Forgas, J. P., & Moylan, S. J. (1991). Affective influences on stereotype judgments. *Cognition and Emotion, 5,* 379–397.

Frijda, N. (1988). The laws of emotion. *American Psychologist, 43,* 49–358.

Gilbert, D., & Wilson, T. (2000). Miswanting: Some problems in the forecasting of future affective states. In J. P. Forgas (Ed.), *Feeling and thinking: The role of affect in social cognition* (pp. 178–197). New York: Cambridge University Press.

Gilligan, S. G. (1982). *Mood intensity and learning of congruous material.* Unpublished doctoral thesis, Department of Psychology, Stanford University.

Gotlib, I. H., & McCann, C. D. (1984). Construct accessibility and depression: An examination of cognitive and affective factors. *Journal of Personality and Social Psychology, 47,* 427–439.

Gotlib, I. H., McLachlan, A. L., & Katz, A. N. (1988). Biases in visual attention in depressed and nondepressed individuals. *Cognition and Emotion, 2,* 185–200.

Greenwald, A. G., Banaji, M. R., Rudman, L. A., Farnham, A. D., Nosek, B. A., & Rosier, M. (2000). Prologue to a unified theory of affect, attitudes, stereotypes, and self-concept. In J. P. Forgas (Ed.), *Feeling and thinking: The role of affect in social cognition* (pp. 308–330). New York: Cambridge University Press.

Griffitt, W. (1970). Environmental effects on interpersonal behavior: Ambient effective temperature and attraction. *Journal of Personality and Social Psychology, 15*, 240–244.

Haddock, G., Zanna, M. P., & Esses, V. M. (1994). Mood and the expression of intergroup attitudes: The moderating role of affect intensity. *European Journal of Social Psychology, 24*, 189–206.

Heider, F. (1958). *The psychology of interpersonal relations.* New York: Wiley.

Hertel, G., & Fiedler, K. (1994). Affective and cognitive influences in a social dilemma game. *European Journal of Social Psychology, 24*, 131–146.

Heuer, F., & Reisberg, D. (1992). Emotion, arousal and memory for detail. In S.-A. Christianson (Ed.), *The handbook of emotion and memory* (pp. 151–180). Hillsdale, NJ: Erlbaum.

Higgins, E. T., Rholes, W. S., & Jones, C. (1977). Category accessibility and impression formulation. *Journal of Personality and Social Psychology, 13*, 141–154.

Hilgard, E. R. (1980). The trilogy of mind: Cognition, affection, and conation. *Journal of the History of the Behavioral Sciences, 16*, 107–117.

Hull, J. G., & Young, R. D. (1983). Self-consciousness, self-esteem, and success-failure as determinants of alcohol consumption in male social drinkers. *Journal of Personality and Social Psychology, 44*, 1097–1109.

Isen, A. M. (1984). Toward understanding the role of affect in cognition. In R. S. Wyer & T. K. Srull (Eds.), *Handbook of social cognition* (vol. 3, pp. 179–236). Hillsdale, NJ: Erlbaum.

Isen, A. M. (1987). Positive affect, cognitive processes. and social behavior. In L. Berkowitz (Ed.), *Advances in experimental social psychology* (vol. 20, pp. 203–253). New York: Academic Press.

Isen, A. M., & Levin, P. F. (1972). The effect of feeling good on helping: Cookies and kindness. *Journal of Personality and Social Psychology, 15*, 294–301.

Isen, A. M., Shalker, T. E., Clark, M., & Karp, L. (1978). Affect, accessibility of material and memory, and behavior: A cognitive loop? *Journal of Personality and Social Psychology, 36*, 1–12.

Kavanaugh, D. L., & Bower, G. H. (1985). Mood and self-efficacy: Impact of joy and sadness on perceived capabilities. *Cognitive Therapy and Research, 9*, 507–525.

Kelly, C. (1982). *Some effects of mood on attention and memory.* Unpublished doctoral thesis, Department of Psychology, Stanford University.

Kirsch, I., Mearns, J., & Catanzano, S. J. (1990). Mood-regulation expectancies as determinants of dysphoria in college students. *Journal of Counseling Psychology, 37*, 306–312.

Kruglanski, A. W. (1989). *Lay epistemics and human knowledge: Cognitive and motivational bases.* New York: Plenum.

Kunda, Z. (1990). The case for motivated reasoning. *Psychological Bulletin, 108*, 331–350.

Laird, J. D., Wagener, J. J., Halal, M., & Szegda, M. (1982). Remembering what you feel: Effects of emotion on memory. *Journal of Personality and Social Psychology, 42*, 646–657.

Lay, K. L., Waters, E., & Park, K. A. (1989). Maternal responsiveness and child compliance: The role of mood as a mediator. *Child Development, 60*, 1405–1411.

Lazarus, R. S. (1991). *Emotion and adaptation.* New York: Oxford University Press.

Leary, M. (2000). Interpersonal emotions, social cognition, and self-relevant thought. In J. P. Forgas (Ed.), *Feeling and thinking: The role of affect in social cognition* (pp. 331–356). New York: Cambridge University Press.

Levine, S. R., Wyer, R. S., & Schwarz, N. (1994). Are you what you feel? The affective and cognitive determinants of self-judgments. *European Journal of Social Psychology, 24,* 63–78.

Lewinsohn, P. M., & Rosenbaum, M. (1987). Recall of parental behavior by acute depressives, remitted depressives, and nondepressives. *Journal of Personality and Social Psychology, 52,* 611–619.

Lloyd, G. G., & Lishman, W. A. (1975). Effect of depression on the speed of recall of pleasant and unpleasant experiences. *Psychological Medicine, 5,* 173–180.

Locke, K. D., & Horowitz, L. M. (1990). Satisfaction in interpersonal interactions as a function of similarity in level of dysphoria. *Journal of Personality and Social Psychology, 58,* 823–831.

Mackie, D., & Worth, L. (1991). Feeling good, but not thinking straight: The impact of positive mood on persuasion. In J. P. Forgas (Ed.), *Emotion and social judgments* (pp. 201–220). Oxford: Pergamon.

MacLeod, C., Mathews, A. M., & Tata, T. (1986). Attentional bias in emotional disorders. *Journal of Abnormal Psychology, 95,* 15–20.

Marlatt, G. A., Kosturn, C. F., & Lang, A. R. (1975). Provocation to anger and opportunity for retaliation as determinants of alcohol consumption in social drinkers. *Journal of Abnormal Psychology, 84,* 652–659.

Martin, L. L., Harlow, T. F., & Strack, F. (1992). The role of bodily sensations in the evaluation of social events. *Personality and Social Psychology Bulletin, 18,* 412–419.

Martin, L. L., Ward, D. W., Achee, J. W., & Wyer, R. S. (1993). Mood as input: People have to interpret the motivational implications of their moods. *Journal of Personality and Social Psychology, 64,* 317–326.

Mathews, A. M., & MacLeod, C. (1994). Cognitive approaches to emotion and emotional disorders. *Annual Review of Psychology, 45,* 25–50.

Mayer, J. D., Gaschke, Y. N., Braverman, D. L., & Evans, T. W. (1992). Mood congruent judgment is a general effect. *Journal of Personality and Social Psychology, 63,* 119–132.

Mayer, J. D., & Salovey, P. (1988). Personality moderates the interaction of mood and cognition. In K. Fiedler & J. P. Forgas (Eds.), *Affect, cognition, and social behavior* (pp. 87–99). Toronto: Hogrefe.

Mayer, J. D., & Volanth, A. J. (1985). Cognitive involvement in mood response system. *Motivation and Emotion, 9,* 261–275.

McNally, R. J. (1994). Cognitive bias in panic disorders. *Current Directions in Psychological Science, 3,* 129–132.

McNally, R. J., Foa, E. B., & Donnell, C. D. (1989). Memory bias for anxiety information in patients with panic disorder. *Cognition and Emotion, 3,* 27–44.

Mearns, J. (1991). Coping with a breakup: Negative mood regulation expectancies and depression following the end of a romantic relationship. *Journal of Personality & Social Psychology, 60,* 327–334.

Mogg, K., Mathews, A. M., May, J., Grove, M., Eysenck, M., & Weinman, J. (1991).

Assessment of cognitive bias in anxiety and depression using a color perception task. *Cognition and Emotion, 5,* 221–238.

Mogg, K., Mathews, A. M., & Weinman, J. (1987). Memory bias in clinical psychology. *Journal of Abnormal Psychology, 96,* 94–98.

Moore, B. S., Underwood, B. & Rosenhan, D. L. (1973). Affect and altruism. *Developmental Psychology, 8,* 99–104.

Morris, W. N. (1989). *Mood: The frame of mind.* New York: Springer.

Morrow, J., & Nolen-Hoeksema, S. (1990). Effects of responses to depression in the remediation of depressive affect. *Journal of Personality and Social Psychology, 58,* 519–527.

Munakata, Y., & Bower, G. H. (1992). *Mood effects on recall of successes and failures.* Unpublished manuscript, Department of Psychology, Stanford University.

Neisser, U. (1982). Memory: What are the important questions? In U. Neisser (Ed.) *Memory observed* (pp. 3–19). San Francisco: Freeman.

Niedenthal, P., & Halberstadt, J. (2000). Grounding categories in emotional response. In J. P. Forgas (Ed.), *Feeling and thinking: The role of affect in social cognition* (pp. 357–386). New York: Cambridge University Press.

Niedenthal, P. M., & Setterlund, M. B. (1994). Emotion congruence in perception. *Personality and Social Psychology Bulletin, 20,* 401–410.

Nolen-Hoeksema, S., & Morrow, J. (1993). Effects of rumination and distraction on naturally occurring depressed mood. *Cognition and Emotion, 7,* 561–570.

Ortony, A., Clore, G. L., & Collins, A. (1988). *The cognitive structure of emotion.* Cambridge, UK: Cambridge University Press.

Ottaviani, R., & Beck, A. T. (1988). Cognitive theory of depression. In K. Fiedler & J. P. Forgas (Eds.), *Affect, cognition, and social behavior* (pp. 209–218). Toronto: Hogrefe.

Parpal, M., & Maccoby, E. E. (1985). Maternal responsiveness and subsequent child compliance. *Child Development, 56,* 1326–1334.

Parrott, W. G. (1993). Beyond hedonism: Motives for inhibiting good moods and for maintaining bad moods. In D. M. Wegner & J. W. Pennebaker (Eds.), *Handbook of mental control* (pp. 278–305). Englewood Cliffs, NJ: Prentice-Hall.

Parrott, W. G., & Sabini, J. (1990). Mood and memory under natural conditions: Evidence for mood incongruent recall. *Journal of Personality and Social Psychology, 59,* 321–336.

Petty, R. E., Gleicher, F., & Baker, S. (1991). Multiple roles for affect in persuasion. In J. P. Forgas (Ed.), *Emotion and social judgments* (pp. 181–200). Oxford: Pergamon.

Pruitt, D., & Carnevale, P. (1993). *Negotiation.* New York: Penguin.

Razran, G. H. S. (1940). Conditioned response changes in rating and appraising sociopolitical slogans. *Psychological Bulletin, 37,* 481–493.

Rhodewalt, F., Strube, M. J., & Wysocki, J. (1988). The Type A behavior pattern, induced mood, and the illusion of control. *European Journal of Personality, 2,* 231–237.

Rholes, W. S., Riskind, J. H., & Lane, J. (1987). Emotional mood states and memory biases: The effects of cognitive priming and mood. *Journal of Personality and Social Psychology, 52,* 91–99.

Riskind, J. H. (1989). The mediating mechanisms in mood and memory: A cognitive-priming formulation. *Journal of Social Behavior and Personality, 4,* 173–184.

Riskind, J. H., Rholes, W. S., & Eggers, J. (1982). The Velten Mood Induction Procedure: Effects on mood and memory. *Journal of Consulting and Clinical Psychology, 50,* 146–147.

Roemer, L., & Borkovec, T. D. (1993). Worry: Unwanted cognitive activity that controls unwanted somatic experience. In D. M. Wegner & J.W Pennybaker (Eds.), *Handbook of mental control* (pp. 220–238). Englewood Cliffs, NJ: Prentice Hall.

Rosch, E., & Lloyd, B. B., Eds. (1978). *Cognition and categorization.* Hillsdale, NJ: Erlbaum.

Roseman, I. J. (1984). Cognitive determinants of emotion: A structural theory. *Review of Personality and Social Psychology, 5,* 11–36.

Rosenberg, M. (1965). *Society and adolescent self-image.* Princeton, NJ: Princeton University Press.

Rosenhan, D. L., Underwood, B., & Moore, B. (1974). Affect moderates self-gratification and altruism. *Journal of Personality and Social Psychology, 30,* 546–552.

Ruiz-Caballero, J. A., & Gonzalez, P. (1994). Implicit and explicit memory bias in depressed and non-depressed subjects. *Cognition and Emotion, 8,* 555–570.

Rusting, C. L. (1998). Personality, mood, and cognitive processing of emotional information: Three conceptual frameworks. *Psychological Bulletin, 124,* 165–196.

Salovey, P., & Birnbaum, D. (1989). Influence of mood on health-related cognitions. *Journal of Personality and Social Psychology, 57,* 539–551.

Salovey, P., O'Leary, A., Stretton, M., Fishkin, S., & Drake, C. A. (1991). Influence of mood on judgments about health and illness. In J. P. Forgas (Ed.), *Emotion and social judgments* (pp. 241–262). Oxford: Pergamon.

Schachter, S. (1959). *The psychology of affiliation.* Stanford, CA: Stanford University Press.

Schiffenbauer, A. I. (1974). Effect of observer's emotional state on judgments of the emotional state of others. *Journal of Personality and Social Psychology, 30,* 31–35.

Schwarz, N. (1990). Feelings as information: Informational and motivational functions of affective states. In E. T. Higgins & R. Sorrentino (Eds.), *Handbook of motivation and cognition* (vol. 2, pp. 527–561). New York: Guilford Press.

Schwarz, N., & Bless, H. (1991). Happy and mindless, but sad and smart? The impact of affective states on analytic reasoning. In J. P. Forgas (Ed.), *Emotion and social judgments* (pp. 55–71). Oxford: Pergamon Press.

Schwarz, N., & Clore, G. L. (1983). Mood, misattribution and judgments of well-being: Informative and directive functions of affective states. *Journal of Personality and Social Psychology, 45,* 513–523.

Schwarz, N., & Clore, G. L. (1988). How do I feel about it? The informative function of affective states. In K. Fiedler & J. P. Forgas (Eds.), *Affect, cognition, and social behavior* (pp. 44–62). Toronto: Hogrefe.

Schwarz, N., Strack, F., Kommer, D., & Wagner, D. (1987). Soccer, rooms, and the quality of your life: Mood effects on judgments of satisfaction with life in general and with specific life domains. *European Journal of Social Psychology, 17,* 69–79.

Sedikides, C. (1992). Changes in the valence of self as a function of mood. *Review of Personality and Social Psychology, 14,* 271–311.

Sedikides, C. (1994). Incongruent effects of sad mood on self-conception valence: It's a matter of time. *European Journal of Social Psychology, 24,* 161–172.

Sedikides, C. (1995). Central and peripheral self-conceptions are differentially influenced by mood: Tests of the differential sensitivity hypothesis. *Journal of Personality and Social Psychology, 69,* 759–777.

Showers, C. (2000). Self-organization in emotional contexts In J. P. Forgas (Ed.), *Feeling and thinking: The role of affect in social cognition* (pp. 283–307). New York: Cambridge University Press.

Singer, J. A., & Salovey, P. (1988). Mood and memory: Evaluating the network theory of affect. *Clinical Psychology Review, 8,* 211–251.

Smith, C. A., & Ellsworth, P. C. (1985). Patterns of cognitive appraisal in emotion. *Journal of Personality and Social Psychology, 48,* 813–838.

Smith, C. A., & Kirby, L. D. (2000). Consequences require antecedents: Toward a process model of emotion elicitation. In J. P. Forgas (Ed.), *Feeling and thinking: The role of affect in social cognition* (pp. 83–108). New York: Cambridge University Press.

Smith, S. M., & Petty, R. E. (1995). Personality moderators of mood congruency effects on cognition: The role of self-esteem and negative mood regulation. *Journal of Personality and Social Psychology, 68,* 1092–1107.

Snyder, M., & White, P. (1982). Moods and memories: Elation, depression and the remembering of the events of ones life. *Journal of Personality, 50,* 149–167.

Srull, T. K. (1983). Affect and memory: The impact of affective reactions in advertising on the representation of product information in memory. In R. Bagozzi & A. Tybout (Eds.), *Advances in consumer research* (vol. 10, pp. 244–263). Ann Arbor, MI: Association for Consumer Research.

Srull, T. K. (1984). The effects of subjective affective states on memory and judgment. In T. Kinnear (Ed.), *Advances in consumer research* (vol. 11, pp. 530–533). Provo, UT: Association for Consumer Research.

Stangor, C., Sullivan, L. A., & Ford, T. E. (1991). Affective and cognitive determinants of prejudice. *Social Cognition, 9,* 359–380.

Strack, F., Martin, L. L., & Stepper, S. (1988). Inhibiting and facilitating conditions of the human smile: A non-obtrusive test of the facial feedback hypothesis. *Journal of Personality and Social Psychology, 54,* 768–777.

Stroessner, S. J., & Mackie, D. M. (1992). The impact of induced affect on the perception of variability in social groups. *Personality and Social Psychology Bulletin, 18,* 546–554.

Tajfel, S., & Forgas, J. P. (1981). Social categorisation: cognitions, values, and groups. In J. P. Forgas (Ed.), *Social cognition* (pp. 113–140). London: Academic Press.

Teasdale, J. D., & Fogarty, S. J. (1979). Differential effects on induced mood on retrieval of pleasant and unpleasant events from episodic memory. *Journal of Abnormal Psychology, 88,* 248–257.

Teasdale, J. D., & Russell, M. L. (1983). Differential effect on induced mood on the recall of positive, negative, and neutral words. *British Journal of Clinical Psychology, 22,* 163–171.

Tesser, A. (1988). Toward a self-evaluation maintenance model of social behavior. In L. Berkowitz (Ed.), *Advances in experimental social psychology* (vol. 21, pp. 181–227). New York: Academic Press.

Thayer, R. E. (1989). *The biopsychology of mood and arousal*. New York: Oxford University Press.

Thorndike, E. L. (1932). *The fundamentals of learning*. New York: Teachers College.

Timberlake, W. (1980). A molar equilibrium theory of learned performance. In G. H. Bower (Ed.), *The psychology of learning and motivation* (vol. 14, pp. 1–58). New York: Academic Press.

Tobias, B. A., Kihlstrom, J. F., Schacter, D. L. (1992). Emotion and implicit memory. In S.-A. Christianson (Ed.), *The handbook of emotion and memory* (pp. 67–92). Hillsdale, NJ: Erlbaum.

Tulving, E. (1983). *Elements of episodic memory*. Oxford: Oxford University Press.

Van Aken, C. (1995). *Mood-dependent memory: Is arousal state the underlying mechanism?* Unpublished honors thesis, Department of Psychology, Stanford University.

Varner, L. J., & Ellis, H. C. (1998). Cognitive activity and physiological arousal: Processes that mediate mood-congruent memory. *Memory & Cognition, 26*, 939–950.

Watkins, T., Mathews, A. M., Williamson, D. A., & Fuller, R. (1992). Mood congruent memory in depression: Emotional priming or elaboration. *Journal of Abnormal Psychology, 101*, 581–586.

Watts, F. N., & Dalgleish, T. (1991). Memory for phobia related words in spider phobics. *Cognition and Emotion, 5*, 313–329.

Watts, F. N., McKenna, F. P., Sharrock, R., & Trezise, L. (1988). Color naming of phobia related words. *British Journal of Psychology, 77*, 97–108.

Weary, G., Marsh, K. L., Gleicher, F., & Edwards, J. A. (1993) Social-cognitive consequences of depression. In G. Weary, F. Gleicher, & K. L. Marsh (Eds.), *Control motivation and social cognition* (pp. 121–142). New York: Springer-Verlag.

Weary, G., Marsh, K. L., & McCormick, L. (1994). Depression and social comparison motives. *European Journal of Social Psychology, 24*, 117–130.

Wegner, D. T., Petty, R. E., & Klein, D. J. (1994). Effects of mood on high elaboration attitude change: The mediating role of likelihood judgments. *European Journal of Social Psychology, 24*, 25–44.

Weiner, B. (1982). The emotional consequences of causal attributions. In M. S. Clark & S. T. Fiske (Eds.), *Affect and cognition* (pp. 185–228). Hillsdale, NJ: Erlbaum.

Wright, W. F., & Bower, G. H. (1992). Mood effects on subjective probability assessment. *Organizational Behavior and Human Decision Processes, 52*, 276–291.

Wyer, R. S., & Carlston, D. (1979). *Social cognition, inference, and attribution*. Hillsdale, NJ: Erlbaum.

Wyer, R. S., & Srull, T. K. (1980). The processing of social stimulus information: A conceptual integration. In R. Hastie, T. M. Ostrom, E. G. Ebbesen, R. S. Wyer, D. Hamilton, & D. E. Carlston (Eds.), *Person memory: The cognitive basis of social perception*. Hillsdale, NJ: Erlbaum.

Wyer, R. S., & Srull, T. K. (1989). *Memory and cognition in its social context*. Hillsdale, NJ: Erlbaum.

Zajonc, R. B. (1980). Feeling and thinking: Preferences need no inferences. *American Psychologist, 35*, 151–175.

Zajonc, R. B. (1984). On the primacy of affect. *American Psychologist, 39*, 117–123.

Zajonc, R. B. (2000). Feeling and thinking: Closing the debate over the independence of affect. In J. P. Forgas (Ed.), *Feeling and thinking: The role of affect in social cognition* (pp. 31–58). New York: Cambridge University Press.

CHAPTER 4

Emotional Response as Conceptual Coherence

Paula M. Niedenthal and Jamin B. Halberstadt

Why do certain stimuli seem to belong in groups whereas others do not? How do categories cohere? Interested theorists in cognitive science have offered several answers. Some propose that perceptual or structural similarity is the "glue" that binds objects and events. However, others have claimed that similarity is insufficient to account for the acquisition and use of categories (e.g., Goodman, 1972; Quine, 1977; but see Goldstone, 1994b; Medin, Goldstone, & Gentner, 1993) and have proposed more abstract forms of coherence. Barsalou (1983, 1985, 1987), for example, suggests that objects or events cohere because they facilitate a common goal or serve the same function, such as getting one to a high, nearly inaccessible place or holding belongings together. Murphy and Medin (1985) explain coherence as the basis of a common causal theory. Similarity, goals, and theories have all been tested as bases of conceptual coherence. Measures of coherence include the speed with which a concept is learned, the treatment of plausible members as equivalent, and perhaps the concept's relation to linguistic structure (e.g., Medin, 1989; Murphy & Medin, 1985; Rosch, 1975).

Even so, an important and qualitatively different type of conceptual coherence has been overlooked in the cognitive science literature. This chapter examines the possibility that people group things together, treat them as the same, associate them closely in memory, and generally behave as if they are using a concept when those things or events evoke the same emotional response. We call these groupings of stimuli *emotional response categories* (Niedenthal & Halberstadt, 1995; Niedenthal, Halberstadt, & Innes-Ker, 1999). An affective state or emotion, such as anger or sadness, may be a glue that binds experiences in memory and action and may motivate one's treatment of the category members as equivalents. We believe that emotion is not merely another nonemotional rule of coherence but a distinct basis of categorization.[1]

This idea was also proposed in passing by Bruner, Goodnow, and Austin (1956), who distinguished three classes of categories: *affective, functional,* and *formal.* The first class is of primary interest here. Bruner et al. (1956) asserted: "Certain forms of grouping appear to depend very heavily upon whether or not the things placed in the same class evoke a common affective response" (p. 4). More recently, Gelernter (1994) described a process similar to the current notion of emotional response categorization, which he called *affect linking.* The general emotional content of memories, he claimed, may be reduced to and represented as an "emotional code" that can link with other memories that have a similar code. As a result, "memories that underlie two adjacent thoughts in a train might be completely different in every detail except that, for whatever reason, . . . they made you feel the same way when you originally experienced them" (p. 79).

If the notion that emotional responses can form the basis of concepts has theoretical and intuitive appeal, why has it received so little empirical attention?[2] The answer to this probably lies in problems with conceptualizing emotional response categories in terms of the existing categorization literature. For example, such categories are hard to talk about—they seem to lack linguistic mapping. We do not mean to say that people do not consciously recognize emotional response categories. We also do not mean that people do not have linguistically based concepts of emotions per se, for they surely do (Fehr & Russell, 1984; Shaver, Schwartz, Kirson, & O'Connor, 1987). And, finally, we do not mean that emotional experience does not shape language, and vice versa, for it surely does (Bloom & Beckwith, 1989; Lakoff, 1987; Stein & Trabasso, 1992). We mean that people do not have concise verbal labels for the things that evoke in them the same emotional reaction. In contrast, in some approaches to concept learning, the use of a concept is indicated by one's ability to label an example of it (Lakoff, 1987; Markman, 1989). We know that a person possesses the concept "tree" when she can name a tall thing with a trunk and leaves as such.

Furthermore, most research on categorization also finds that people can easily name (non-emotionally based) category members and that there is consensus about such members and their prototypicality, at least within cultures (e.g., Mervis & Rosch, 1981; Rips, Shoben, & Smith, 1973). For example, Americans generally agree that *robin* is a prototypic member of the category *bird,* whereas *penguin* is a less prototypic member. Americans even agree about the members of goal-derived categories such as "ways to escape being killed by the Mafia" (Barsalou, 1983). In contrast, people probably have neither explicit nor consensual knowledge about the members of emotional response categories. Bruner et al. (1956) said that "categories marked by an affective defining response are not amenable to ready description in terms of the properties of the objects comprising them'' (p. 4). And emotion category members are likely as idiosyncratic as people's learning histories. Of course, some consensually meaningful labels—such as *elegant mathematical solutions, like grandma's house,* and *mean dogs*—implicate emotional response more or less awkwardly as conceptual glue. But not everyone liked his grandmother, or even knew her; most people neither encounter nor respond emotionally to elegant mathematical solutions; some people have been bitten by dogs, but others have been rescued by them. Thus, the traditional linguistic approach to concepts, which includes the notions of verbal labels and consensual explicit knowledge about category instances, casts doubt on the very existence of emotional response categories.

Among the many ways to address these objections, one might say that response categories are in fact ontologically primary and their representation partially separate from language-based categorization. Bruner et al. (1956), for example, suggested that emotional associations to stimuli may have been forged in a prelinguistic developmental stage and that emotional response categories may therefore ''resist conscious verbal insight by virtue of having been established before the full development of language'' (p. 4). Alternatively, affective experience may be incompatible with the language used to describe it. For example, Gelernter (1994) has proposed that emotional response categorization is a hallmark of ''low focus'' (nonanalytic) cognition, which may not be compatible with the kind of processing required to form a linguistic designation for the concept. By its very nature, ''affective linking'' may be cognitively impenetrable.

On the other hand, emotional response categories are probably more constrained than they seem on first impression. Niedenthal and Halberstadt (1995) have argued that, although many object-emotion associations are learned (e.g., the connection between happiness at being nurtured by one's grandmother and the smell of her furniture polish), there are probably biological constraints on the possible stimuli that can be associated with certain emotional states. For example, in a study by Ohman and Dimberg (1978; also see Dimberg & Ohman, 1983), participants' electrodermal responses were conditioned to pictures of faces that displayed expressions of anger, happiness, or neutral emotion, with electric shock as the unconditioned stimulus. Responses to conditioned angry faces were quite resistant to extinction, whereas responses to the happy and neutral faces extinguished very rapidly.

Ohman and Dimberg's results, as well as others (e.g., Lanzetta & Orr, 1980; Orr & Lanzetta, 1980; and see Mineka, 1992, for a review of related research on animals), have been used to argue that individuals are prepared to learn certain associations (Seligman, 1970), such as the response to a shock and an angry face. The adaptive value of stimuli may determine how easily they can be associated with different emotional reactions. Because an association between a happy face and the aversive experience of shock is not adaptive (and, in fact, has a clear disadvantage), happy faces, as a rule, will never be part of an anger response category and will not be equivalent to other things that produce anger. Thus, although emotional response categories may seem hopelessly idiosyncratic, the categories probably have some adaptive, prewired structure. That is, the development of emotional response categories proceeds in an adaptive and somewhat predictable way, except perhaps in the (interesting) cases of phobia and pathology (Lang, 1984; Plutchik, 1980).

WHAT ARE THE EMOTIONAL RESPONSE CATEGORIES?

Which common emotional responses can link diverse objects and events? For typical, non-emotionally based categories, researchers can generate plausible (normative) groupings through introspection and can make good guesses about which categories will make sense to participants in experimental research and which ones are used in daily life.

Matters are not so simple in the study of emotional response categories. which, as we said, do not necessarily correspond to people's semantic knowledge about their emotions. Whereas asking people what they would take from a fire is a good way to learn about the category "things to take from one's home during a fire" (Barsalou, 1983), asking people to enumerate the things that make them feel sad, particularly when they are not experiencing sadness, will probably be a futile stab at establishing the "things that make one sad." Many of the exemplars are likely to be objects and events that, in theory, could or should make one sad but may not be associated with sad feelings for any one individual. Furthermore, the very question "what makes one sad?" assumes, controversially, that we equate objects and events on the basis of a discrete emotion, rather than according to their value as a dimension of emotional experience. In fact, dimensional theories about how to parse the affect space abound in the emotion literature. First, we will explore the structure of emotional response and then examine emotional response categories.

Dimensional Approaches

One possible parsing of affective space is unidimensional. For example, perhaps all emotional states vary only in valence—that is, positivity versus negativity. If so, there would essentially be two superordinate emotion categories: things that evoke positive feelings and things that evoke negative feelings. Within these two could be many subordinate categories, such as "people who make me feel good," "foods that make me feel bad," and so forth. This valence view stems from the empirical observation that a single positive/negative dimension explains the greatest variance in apprehension of meaning (e.g., Osgood & Suci, 1955), in perception of objects (e.g., Abelson & Sermat, 1962), and in self-reports of the subjective experience of emotion (e.g., Mayer & Gaschke, 1988).

The valence view appears in many models of emotion structure and processing, such as Clark and Isen's (1982) network theory of affect, which holds that positive affect in particular serves as a primary basis for organizing cognitive material. Following the contextualist approach in cognitive psychology (e.g., Bransford, McCarrell, Franks, & Nitsch, 1977), Isen has suggested that positive affect, even mild states of pleasure caused by everyday events, can reorganize material in memory (Isen, 1984, 1987; Isen, Daubman, & Gorgoglione, 1987). Central to Isen's account is the idea that (a) positive affect cues positive material in memory, and (b) this material is very extensive. Therefore, by cognitive necessity, positive affect induces more integrative thought that groups material in larger, more inclusive, units. In support of these priming and organization hypotheses, Isen and her associates have demonstrated that people expand the boundaries of both positive and neutral object categories when they are feeling good (e.g., Isen & Daubman, 1984). For example, people include more items in positive social categories and produce more unusual associates to neutral words in an association task (Isen, Johnson, Mertz, & Robinson, 1985; Isen, Niedenthal, & Cantor, 1992). In our terms, Isen's findings suggest that people experiencing positive feelings create inclusive "positive response categories" in that they preferentially group positive associations of stimuli. The more general view that positive and negative information form separate categories in memory has motivated extensive research on the relation between emotion and memory (see Blaney, 1986; Singer & Salovey, 1988).

Though sometimes ignored in cognitive models of affect, arousal typically emerges as an important second dimension of emotional experience. For example, Russell (1979, 1980), using diverse data-modeling techniques (including multidimensional scaling of emotion terms and principle components analysis of self-ratings of affective states), found support for a bipolar model of affect. Specifically, Russell asserts that emotions and the terms that denote them can form a circle describing their values on the dimensions of pleasure/displeasure and high/low arousal. The relative importance of the arousal dimension seems to vary with the person, situation, and task. Feldman (1995a, 1995b), for instance, reports significant individual differences in the weighting of valence and arousal in affective space and finds that people may weigh the two dimensions more evenly in their judgments about the semantic structure of emotions than in judgments about emotions themselves. Furthermore, high or low arousal appears to facilitate the processing of material associated with a similar level of arousal. Clark, Milberg, and Ross (1983), for example, taught subjects two word lists—one under high arousal and one under low arousal—and then asked them to recall the lists later under either high or low arousal. Results indicated that congruent arousal at learning and test facilitated recall (also see Clark, Milberg, & Erber, 1984). The researchers contended that arousal is coded along with valence and suggest it may even account for some of the facilitative effects of positive affect (for a dissenting opinion, see Bower & Forgas, chapter 3, this volume).

Davidson (1992, 1993) also parses the affective space in two dimensions but, relying on data from neuropsychology and psychophysiology, argues that approach and withdrawal are the defining responses. He suggests that these responses correspond to two primary situations, approach and avoidance, that reoccur in our evolutionary history and that separate neural systems (left and right frontal regions, respectively) appear to support the responses. Davidson's superordinate emotion categories, then, would consist of "things associated with approach" and "things associated with avoidance." Subordinate categories may include "situations that we approach," "people we avoid," and so forth.

Specific Emotions

An alternative view, which we currently favor on both empirical and theoretical grounds (Niedenthal et al., 1999), is that affective space is organized according to some number of specific or basic emotions. In theory, such emotions might develop in response to a set of problems posed during evolution (e.g., Ekman, 1982; MacLean, 1993; Plutchik, 1984; Tooby & Cosmidis, 1990). MacLean (1993), for example, offers six types of behaviors—searching, aggressive, protective, dejected, gratulant (triumphant), and caressive—that have evolved in response to primary problems. These specific behaviors are associated with the (presumably motivating) basic emotions of desire, anger, fear, sadness, joy, and affection. Similarly, Plutchik (1984) counts eight adaptive behaviors—withdrawing, attacking, mating, crying for help, pair bonding, vomiting, examining, and stopping/freezing—associated with fear, anger, joy, sadness, acceptance, disgust, expectancy, and surprise.

Though emotion theorists disagree about which emotions are basic, many theories of emotion consistently include happiness, sadness, anger, disgust, and fear (e.g., Ekman, 1984; Izard, 1977; Johnson-Laird & Oatley, 1992; Plutchik, 1980; Tomkins, 1962, 1963). These five emotions emerge early in human development (Sroufe, 1979), appear to be communicated through universally recognized facial gestures (Ekman, 1994; Ekman & Friesen, 1971; Izard, 1994; but also see Russell, 1994), and seem to organize language (e.g., Shaver et al., 1987). The notion of basic emotions has also been supported by data indicating distinct patterns of autonomic nervous system activity (Levenson, 1992; Levenson, Ekman, & Friesen, 1990), although these data remain controversial (Davidson, 1993).[3]

Finally, recent research has demonstrated categorical perception of facial expressions. In categorical perception, individuals are better able to distinguish between physically different stimuli when they are members of different categories. For example, using a digital blending or "morphing" technology, a study by Etcoff and Magee (1992) constructed facial expression continua between pairs of faces that expressed different basic emotions (e.g. happy/sad). The procedure resulted in eight continua, each of which contained eleven faces of uniform physical difference. The subjects' task was to discriminate pairs of faces from along these continua. Results revealed categorical perception of all expressions except for surprise.

It should be noted that although the concept of specific emotions is appealing to many emotion theorists who do not endorse a strict dimensional account of emotional experience, the idea of biologically basic emotions is not appealing to some (e.g., Ortony & Turner, 1990). However, one can posit the existence of discrete, non-decomposable emotional states without assuming that such states have a biological basis. In this "discrete emotions" view, emotional states are seen as being differentiated, defined, and labeled through experience, represented as schemas or organized units of information in memory (perhaps corresponding to clusters of mid-level emotion terms in the individual's native language), and bound by culture (e.g., Oatley & Johnson-Laird, 1996). The discrete-emotions account is consistent with many of the results, cited earlier, that are taken to support a basic-emotions theory. However, proponents of this account question the meaning of findings that bear on the universality and developmental primacy of some facial expressions of emotion (e.g., Fridlund, 1991; Russell, 1994). For present purposes, the distinctions between the basic- and discrete-emotions views are not at issue. Instead, our concern is whether categories of emotionally equivalent things are likely to be grounded in specific emotional states or to correspond to a dimensional model of the subjective experience of emotion. One way of evaluating the competing views of emotional structure for a theory of emotional response categorization is to judge the success of the process models that rely on them.

A specific model of emotion has been instantiated in Bower's (1981) associative network/spreading activation model of emotion (also see Bower, 1992; Bower & Forgas, chapter 3, this volume). This model represents discrete emotions as specific units of information linked by semantic pointers to other units that represent causally and associatively related information. Such information might include past events that have evoked the emotion, verbal labels for the emotion, statements and descriptions about the emotion, and the behaviors, expressive activity, and other physiological events that constitute the emotion. Bower proposed that some links are innate (e.g., links to representations of facial expressions of emotion), whereas others are created through learning at the individual or cultural level (e.g., links to verbal labels for the emotion). In this approach, the experience of an emotion entails the activation of the appropriate emotion unit in memory. Activation then spreads from the central unit to the related information, thereby potentiating the use of those concepts in ongoing information processing.

Bower's model appears to combine in the same network both representations of emotional feelings and declarative knowledge about the emotions. However, as we have suggested elsewhere, semantic emotion knowledge is likely only partially and imperfectly informed by people's emotional experiences (Niedenthal, Setterlund, & Jones, 1994). And although representations of emotion and emotion knowledge may be interactive, they are not likely isomorphic; if they were, emotion regulation would probably be a more simple exercise than it actually is. LeDoux (1994) has claimed that emotional learning and declarative knowledge about emotions are processed separately and are supported by separate memory systems. Furthermore, he suggests that the former system operates largely outside of conscious awareness.

COGNITIVE ORGANIZATION ACCORDING TO SPECIFIC EMOTIONS

In our own work, we have used accepted cognitive tasks for assessing automatic processes to evaluate the claim that cognitive material is organized according to specific emotions, as suggested by Bower's (1981) original model. If emotions are indeed organized into specific emotion categories in memory, then according to this model, information that is specifically related to an experienced emotion should be processed more efficiently than other information. Therefore, the general procedure in our studies was to induce specific emotional states in experimental participants, and then measure the speed with which the subjects encoded words that were or were not related to their specific emotion, in addition to words that were or were not related to their state only by virtue of emotional valence.

The manipulation of emotional states in the laboratory presents some fascinating and unique research challenges. First, the procedure used to induce a given state must avoid both experimental demand and direct semantic or visual priming. For example, both the Velten (1968) procedure (in which participants read and internalize the emotion suggested by a series of self-referential statements) and guided imagery (in which participants imagine a prior or potential emotional situation) guide priming, because the emotional words and images involved in these manipulations activate emotion knowledge. One need not assume that emotional state per se is responsible for any observed effects. Other manipulations that avoid these confounds may be imprecise, producing more than one emotion or a blend of emotions in the participant. Contrived failure feedback, for example, although sometimes used as a manipulation of sadness, may also induce anger, guilt, anxiety, or some combination of these emotions. To study emotion categories, one must know which emotion subjects are experiencing. We discuss the manipulation of emotional states in some detail before describing the studies relevant to the organization of emotional memory.

Manipulation of Emotional States

To conduct the research reported in this chapter, we have relied on music and films, nondirective, but powerful, manipulations of emotion. Music, at least, has no semantic and visual confounds (e.g., Gerrards-Hesse, Spies, & Hesse, 1994; McHugo, Smith, & Lanzetta, 1982; Philippot, 1993). Furthermore, both music and films appear to induce specific emotions (Gerrards-Hesse et al., 1994; Philippot, 1993). In this section, we describe our procedures in more detail recording our extensive pilot testing as an introduction to our research.

Music induction. This method is based on a procedure described by Eich and Metcalfe (1989). Subjects hear selections of either happy or sad classical music for 8–10 minutes, followed by recorded instructions about the experimental task; the music continues throughout the entire experimental session. The procedure thus maintains emotional state but does not rely on either visual cues or verbal means of inducing emotion (e.g., Niedenthal, Halberstadt, & Innes-Ker, 1999). Happy condition music includes allegros from *Eine Kleine Nachtmusik*, Divertimento no. 136, and *Ein Musikalischer Spass*, all by Mozart, and portions of Concerto for Harpsichord and Strings in C Major by Vivaldi. Sad musical selections include Adagio for Strings by Barber, Adagietto by Mahler, and the adagio from Piano Concerto no. 2 in C Minor by Rachmaninov. Fearful music has included *Threnody to the Victims of Hiroshima* and *Polymorphy*, both by Pederecki.[4] In some experiments, subjects in control or neutral-mood conditions have listened to *Common Tones in Simple Time* by John Adams or to selected movements of Brahms' First or Third Symphonies.

During emotion induction, subjects sit in comfortable chairs in quiet, private cubicles with muted lighting and listen to the music over high-quality stereo headphones. Careful cover stories mask the real reason for the music (see Halberstadt & Niedenthal, 1997; Halberstadt, Niedenthal, & Kushner, 1995; Niedenthal, Halberstadt, & Setterlund, 1997; Niedenthal & Setterlund, 1994). For example, in the experiments described in the next section, subjects were told that the purpose of the research was to examine the interaction of auditory and visual perception, to address questions such as "how does listening to music while you are driving influence your ability to perceive other objects in the environment."

The efficacy of the musical induction of happiness and sadness appears in data reported by Niedenthal and Setterlund (1994). Approximately 300 subjects received the continuous music induction of those emotions and then completed the Brief Mood Introspection Scale (BMIS; Mayer & Gaschke, 1988), which lists 16 emotion adjectives and directs subjects to indicate how much of each they are experiencing at that moment. Discriminant analysis indicated that the musical selections exerted specific effects, eliciting happiness and sadness, not just generally good and bad feelings. Sad-condition subjects rated their feelings as significantly more *sad, gloomy, drowsy,* and *tired* than did happy subjects, whereas happy-condition subjects rated their feelings as significantly more *happy, content, peppy, lively,* and *active* than did sad subjects. In addition, and significantly, subjects in the two conditions rated *calm, loving, caring, grouchy, nervous,* and *jittery* similarly.

Recent evidence further shows that the music does not invariably lead subjects to label their feelings. If subjects bring to mind explicit labels for their feelings during music induction, effects of the induction on the processing of emotional information could reflect the subject-generated labels, not their emotional feelings. In a study reported in Niedenthal et al. (1997), subjects (n = 47) listened to happy or sad music and then listed 15 words they had thought about during the induction period. The word lists were later analyzed for their references to specific emotional states. Of the more than 700 items produced, the only emotional labels mentioned by participants in the happy music condition were *delight* (1), *joy* (1), *sadness* (1), and some form of *happiness* (6) (frequencies in parentheses). Emotional labels mentioned by participants in the sad music condition included *passion* (1), *sadness* (6), *anger* (1), and some form of *happiness* (2). These findings indicate very little explicit labeling of emotional states. Only one-quarter of the participants in the pilot study mentioned a word that named the feeling the music cued. In three-quarters of the cases, these feeling words were listed at the very bottom of the 15-item list, indicating that these words were not very accessible.

Film induction.   In this procedure subjects view one set of three or four film clips, each lasting about 15 minutes, on individual VCR monitors located in comfortable, private cubicles. Happiness, sadness, fear, and control (neutral mood) inductions have been developed. The happy set includes clips from *Benny and Joon, Butch Cassidy and the Sundance Kid,* and *Hoosiers*; sad clips are from *Harry and Tonto, Terms of Endearment,* and *Sophie's Choice*; fear clips come from *Cape Fear, The Shining, Fatal Attraction,* and *Silence of the Lambs*; and control films include portions of documentaries about golf and lions. In a pilot experiment, subjects completed the BMIS after viewing either the happy, sad, or neutral clips. Happiness and sadness scores were computed for each subject by averaging their ratings of the items *happy, active, lively, peppy,* and *content,* and of *sad, gloomy, tired,* and *drowsy,* respectively (based on Niedenthal & Setterlund, 1994). The mean happiness scores of happy (14.8), neutral

(11.3), and sad (8.9) groups matched predicted directions, as did the happy (8.1), neutral (10.3), and sad (11.3) groups' mean sadness scores.

In another pilot study, subjects saw the happy, sad, or fear clips and then completed a modified version of the BMIS, which included the terms *fearful* and *anxious*, in addition to the 16 standard emotion terms. These two items were summed with responses to the items *nervous* and *jittery* to create an index of fearfulness. Happy films made subjects feel more happy than sad, and more happy than fearful; sad films made subjects feel more sad than either happy or fearful; fear films made subjects feel more fearful than either sad or happy. Also, subjects in each condition reported feeling more of the congruent emotion in all relevant comparisons.

Combined music/film induction.   Music is a subtle and surprisingly effective specific manipulation. The selections we use contain no visual or semantic content that would cause an emotional priming confound. Furthermore, because music can be played in the background over headphones, it is ideal for even lengthy or attention-demanding tasks. Yet individuals respond differently to music; typically 5–10% of a sample will indicate that they did not respond to the induction or that they felt the opposite of the intended emotional state.

On the other hand, films—which take advantage of processes of emotional contagion—may be a more acute and powerful emotion induction. The films we used are famous for their emotional content; when viewing them, subjects actually appear to be outwardly experiencing the emotion intended for their condition, even if they sometimes report only marginally more extreme states than music-induced subjects (Halberstadt & Niedenthal, 1997). However, the films cannot be presented concurrently with most experimental tasks, and the emotional states will wear off after a sufficiently long and involved cognitive task, no matter how effective the films are.

To overcome these disadvantages, we have developed a combined music/film induction that capitalizes on the advantages of both methodologies. In the general technique, subjects first view the appropriate films for their experimental condition. Immediately following the last clip, a message on the video monitor instructs them to don a pair of headphones and to begin an experimental task. Emotion-inducing music (or sometimes silence in control conditions) plays through the headphones for the duration of the task. Thus, after the films create an intense emotional state, the music maintains or gradually dissipates the emotion over the course of the experiment the result is more extreme group differences than we have seen with either manipulation alone.

Lexical Decision Studies

Armed with these methods of eliciting specific emotional states, we began our exploration of emotional response categories by testing the hypothesis that emotional information is organized according to specific emotions (Niedenthal & Halberstadt, 1995; Niedenthal et al., 1999).

In the first two studies, happiness and sadness were induced by the continuous music technique. Then, subjects performed a lexical decision task in which they indicated whether letter strings presented on a computer screen were words or nonwords by pressing appropriately labeled buttons on a response box. The words in the task were related to *happy* (e.g., *delight, joy*) or *sad* (e.g., *despair, regret*); some were positive (but happiness-unrelated; e.g., *wisdom, grace*), some negative (but sadness-unrelated; e.g., *blame, decay*), some neutral (e.g., *habit, cluster*). A single letter in each of 48 neutral English words was changed to create pronounceable nonwords.

Based on the basic emotions model we have endorsed, we expected happy subjects to make lexical decisions about happiness-related words more quickly than sad subjects, and sad subjects to respond to sadness-related words more quickly than happy subjects. At the same time, we expected that happiness and sadness would *not* mediate responses to positive and negative words in the same way. A valance organization model, on the other hand, predicts that happy subjects will respond more quickly to both happiness-related and positive words, and sad subjects more quickly to both sadness-related and negative words (e.g., Clark et al., 1983; Gerrig & Bower, 1982; Powell & Hernsley, 1984).

Both experiments supported the predictions of the categorical emotions model. Happy subjects did indeed make lexical decisions about happiness-related words faster than did sad subjects, and sad subjects responded to sadness-related words faster than did happy subjects. We did not observe this interaction in either the happy or the sad subjects' responses to positive and negative words. To pursue the matter further, we combined the data from the two experiments to perform regression analyses using self-reports of experienced emotion (rather than emotion induction condition) to predict lexical decision speed. These analyses indicated that, across subjects, happiness and sadness facilitated lexical decisions about happiness- and sadness-related words, respectively, but did not predict response latencies to positive and negative words.

Thus, the first two studies provided initial support for a categorical model of emotion; a particular emotional state (either happiness or sadness) facilitated the processing of words that are related to that particular state but not those related only on the more general basis of shared valence (i.e., positive or negative). However, one shortcoming of the experiments is that the words categorically related to the emotional states of the participants also referred to emotional states per se (as can be seen in the examples). The words related to the feelings of the participants by valence, but not category—positive and negative words— did not refer to emotional experience at all. Therefore, the induced emotions may have primed words of similar valence and associated with the concept of emotion but not words that merely shared valence. A comparison of the processing efficiency of stimuli associated with the emotion experienced by the perceiver (e.g., sadness) with the processing of stimuli associated with a different emotion that shares the same valence (e.g., anger) might provide even stronger evidence for the categorical emotions model.

To this end, we carried out two more lexical decision experiments using words from four specific emotion categories: happiness, sadness, love, and anger (Niedenthal et al., 1997). In addition, we matched each emotion word with an affectively neutral control word of equivalent frequency, length, concreteness, and first letter; examples appear in table 4.1. We calculated response facilitation by subtracting the response latencies to the emotion words from latencies to matched neutral control words.

Contrary to expectation, the results of the first experiment revealed equal levels of facilitation for words related to happiness and love across emotion conditions. With the negative word categories, results were as predicted: a state of sadness, but not one of happiness, facilitated lexical decisions about words related to sadness; however, sadness did not facilitate lexical decisions about words related to anger. All subjects, regardless of emotion condition, showed inhibition in their responses to words related to anger. Finally, analyses of absolute response latencies revealed that happy subjects responded to happiness-associated words more quickly than did sad subjects, and sad subjects responded to sadness-associated words more quickly than did happy subjects. The interaction was statistically marginal but clearly replicated the pattern of data observed in the initial studies.

In a second experiment, we added a neutral-mood condition and increased both the number of subjects and the number of words in each category, in order to boost power. We obtained stronger support for the emotion congruence prediction: happy subjects showed greater facilitation for happiness-related words than did sad or control subjects, and sad subjects showed facilitation for sadness-related words, whereas happy and control subjects did not.[5] Analyses of absolute response latencies replicated the previous study's emotion congruent interaction, which, with the increased power, was statistically reliable.

Word Naming Study

As a package, the four lexical decision experiments provide quite compelling support for the hypothesis that emotional states mediate word perception. Furthermore, this mediation apparently conforms to a categorical rather than a dimensional model of emotion. The results are also consistent with another effect of category learning: increased perceptual sensitivity and discrimination. The idea that concepts influence perception is usually associated with Whorf but has also received more recent empirical support from Goldstone (1994a). Furthermore, the intriguing idea that emotions influence perceptual processes is intui-

TABLE 4.1. Emotion words [and matched controls].

Happy words	Love words
Cheer [codes]	Affection [afterward]
Pleasure [platform]	Caring [census]
Delight [depends]	Desire [detail]
Joy [sum]	Passion [plastic]

Sad words	Anger words
Defeat [device]	Anger [agent]
Despair [degrees]	Rage [rent]
Sorrow [sector]	Dislike [diagram]
Gloom [globe]	Fury [folk]

tive, as evidenced by the way we talk about emotional experience. We say, for example, that people who are happy "see the world through rose-colored glasses," that people who are sad "see only the dark side of life," and that angry people "see red." These expressions convey not only our conviction that discrete emotions mediate perception but also our opinion that emotions determine the content of perception—happy people see happy things and angry people see angry things. We believe that emotional people more readily see stimuli consistent with their emotional state.

However, although lexical decision is a good overall measure of word perception, it is not sufficient to demonstrate emotion congruent perception. It is generally agreed that lexical decision assesses both stimulus encoding and postaccess decision processes; the effects we observed could occur in either stage. In either case, emotion congruent lexical decisions would be considered quite low-level, but it would be premature to conclude that the effects occur at a truly perceptual level. The word naming task is considered a "purer" indicator of word perception because it does not require a subject to make a postaccess decision regarding the lexical status of an item (e.g., Balota & Chumbley, 1985; Lorch, Balota, & Stamm, 1986; Seidenberg, Waters, Sanders, & Langer, 1984; for reviews, see Neely, 1991; Papp, McDonald, Schvaneveldt, & Noel, 1987).

Thus, in a fifth experiment, we presented the emotional words and matched controls used in the previous study (Niedenthal et al., 1997, experiment 3) to subjects who had been induced to feel happy, sad, or neutral with the continuous music technique. Subjects said each word aloud as it appeared on the computer screen, as quickly and accurately as possible.[6] Results were highly consistent with the lexical decision experiments: happy subjects showed significantly greater facilitation in naming happiness-related words than did neutral or sad subjects, and sad subjects showed greater facilitation in naming sadness-related words than did neutral or happy subjects.[7] Analyses of absolute word naming latencies also produced results that paralleled those found for lexical decisions.

Summary

What do these experiments tell us about how emotional material is organized in memory? Whether one adopts a spreading activation model such as Bower's or the contextualist model of Isen, the data suggest that emotional states and their effects are quite specific: emotions facilitate the processing of cognitive material that is coded with the same specific emotional response information. Similar valence alone is not sufficient for an emotional state to facilitate stimulus processing—a conclusion supported by other recent research on memory, lexical access, and text processing (see Gernsbacher, Goldsmith, & Robertson, 1992; Halberstadt et al., 1995; Hansen & Shantz, 1995; Laird, Cuniff, Sheehan, Shulman, & Strum, 1989; Laird, Wagener, Halal, & Szegda, 1982; Niedenthal et al., 1994).

The experiments are also consistent with the present conceptualization of emotional response categories, which supposes that, in the same way that nonemotional category names prime category members, emotional responses should prime material associated with that response. We saw evidence of this effect in the form of facilitated lexical decisions and word naming. However, the lexical decision and naming responses do not involve categorization judgments; therefore, although the effects are obviously important in their own right, they provide only indirect evidence for emotional response categorization. The experience of emotion associated with the tendency to group stimuli on the basis of their emotional response similarity needs to be demonstrated. We explore this general hypothesis in the next section and then propose some possible mechanisms.

EMOTION, SIMILARITY, AND CATEGORIZATION

To test the idea that, when emotional, people group things together on the basis of common emotional response, we relied on a standard triad task in which subjects see three concepts: a target and two comparison concepts. The subject is asked to indicate whether the target is more similar to the first or second of the two comparison concepts. In four studies, subjects who were experiencing either experimentally induced or naturally occurring states of happiness, sadness, fear, or neutrality were asked to indicate whether the target concepts (e.g., *kiss*) were more similar to things associated with a similar emotional response (e.g., *fortune*) or to emotionally neutral concepts that shared a (relatively remote) taxonomic or associative relationship (e.g., *handshake*). The emotional response that linked a comparison concept to the target was sometimes the emotion that the subject was experiencing (e.g., happiness) and other times a different emotion (e.g., sadness). Table 4.2 presents examples of triads in which the target concept shared a happiness, sadness, or fear relation to one comparison concept and a (nonemotional) taxonomic or associative relation to the other.[8]

At least two predictions about how individuals would choose to group targets with comparison concepts made theoretical sense. Our earlier research on emotion congruence in word perception, and past research from other laboratories, suggests that emotions can prime emotion congruent thoughts. Access to emotion congruent thoughts may enhance detection of emotional similarity for emotion congruent triads. If so, happy subjects would link things things on the basis of their relation to happiness (but not sadness) and sad subjects would link things on the basis of their relation to sadness (but not happiness).

However, it is not clear that the priming effects are relevant to predictions about the triad task. Because priming involves the passive spread of activation, one would expect to see priming effects in tasks that assess automatic processing—lexical decision and word naming, for example. However, when controlled processes (such as those involved in learning, helping, decision making, or categorization) are assessed, other motivated processes (such as mood maintenance, mood relief, or a motivation to control bias) may intervene and emotion congruence may not be observed (e.g., Bodenhausen, Kramer, & Susser, 1994; Clark & Isen, 1982; Forgas, 1994; for reviews, see Blaney, 1986; Isen, 1984; Schwarz & Clore, 1988; Singer & Salovey, 1988). Because categorization responses are not automatic, we may not confidently predict the enhancement of perceived similarity between emotion congruent concepts. Furthermore, greater efficiency of processing does not guarantee greater use of the information in categorization or judgment (Halberstadt & Niedenthal, 1997).

The key idea behind our studies was that, when people are emotional, they focus on the emotional nature or meaning of information more than they normally do. We know that emotional information, probably because of its nature, and neutral information are processed differently (e.g., Bruner & Postman, 1947; Kitayama, 1990, 1991; Kitayama & Howard, 1994). There is clearly something special about emotional information, and individuals who are experiencing emotion may process complex information in terms of its emotional significance. Why? Our general bias to attend to emotional information makes evolutionary sense because emotional responses to stimulus events and situations inform the perceiver about the present potential hedonic consequences (e.g., Hansen & Hansen, 1994; Pratto, 1994). Furthermore, emotional states seem to motivate one to seek emotionally relevant information in the environment (Schwarz & Clore, 1988). In fact, some motivational/functionalist theories define emotion by the process of attentional orientation. According to Frijda (1988), ''emotions exist

TABLE 4.2. Example triads presented in the order {X: A,B} where X is the target and A and B are comparison concepts; A is always the taxonomic associate and B is always the emotional associate.

Triad Type	Examples
Happy triads	Joke: speech, sunbeam
	Puppy: beetle, parade
	Water-ski: elevator, celebration
	Kiss: handshake, fortune
Sad trials	Cancer: pulse, divorce
	Ambulance: wheel barrow, poverty
	Bankruptcy: teller, tomb
	Tears: breath, disease
Fear triads	Nightmare: thought, punishment
	Noose: garden hose, rabies
	Vulture: parakeet, insanity
	Shark: minnow, bomb

for the sake of signaling states of the world that have to be responded to, or that no longer need response and action'' (p. 354). If emotions are cues that important events are occurring in one's internal or external environment, then emotional state should direct attention to the emotional aspects of the stimuli. Because people in emotional states might be particularly focused on the emotional meaning of information, they might link emotionally similar stimuli (sad with sad, happy with happy, and so forth), despite any specific relation to their own emotional state. This then is a *general emotions prediction*.

It should be mentioned here that emotion congruent priming (predicted for the word recognition tasks) and general selective attention to emotional meaning are not in conflict with each other. Priming due to the passive spread of activation is a well-documented effect in cognitive psychology (see Neely, 1991). Certain tasks, such as lexical decision and word naming, are particularly appropriate for measuring the passive spread of activation because it is assumed to be an automatic process. Social psychologists also measure priming with tasks in which exposure to potential priming stimuli occurs in one task, and spread of activation is measured in a second. Often the second task involves the presentation of an ambiguous stimulus and the measurement of the use of the primed concept in the interpretation of that ambiguous stimulus (e.g., Bargh & Pietromonaco, 1982; Devine, 1989).

Selective attention, on the other hand, is a critical mechanism in several influential models of categorization and category learning (e.g., Kruschke, 1992; Medin & Schaffer, 1978; Nosofsky, 1986, 1992). In such models, selective attention to a dimension that characterizes stimuli (e.g., color, size)—due, for instance, to prior training or sensitization—is assumed to be spread over the entire dimension, not just part of it. That is, if attention is directed toward color, this means that all colors are attended to more than other possible stimulus features, such as size. The result of attention to a particular dimension (which may represent discrete categories such as color categories) is to increase the discriminability of stimuli in terms of that dimension, and to decrease discriminability on other, relatively unattended dimensions. Consequently, stimuli with similar values on the attended-to aspect appear more similar overall, while stimuli with discrepant values appear relatively dissimilar. Tasks involving judgments of similarity and categorization are sensitive to this mechanism.

In our first study, subjects were randomly assigned to happy, sad, or control (neutral mood) conditions; the combined music/film induction was used to manipulate emotional states. After viewing the films for their condition, subjects received instructions for the similarity task, and then appropriate music began over stereo headphones and continued for the remainder of the session. For all 45 trials in the task, a target word appeared at the top of the computer monitor. One second later, two comparison concepts appeared in a left-to-right display below the target. Subjects pressed a key on the left side of the keyboard if the target matched the concept displayed on the left, and they pressed a key on the right if they thought it matched the concept displayed on the right. Each subject viewed a random ordering of triads and the spatial (left/right) locations of the comparison concepts. We interspersed 9 happy and 9 sad triads, such as those listed in table 4.2, among 27 affectively unbiased triads. The experiment thus conformed to a 3×2 mixed design; one factor (happy, sad, or neutral emotional state) varied between subjects, and the other factor (happy versus sad triad) varied within subjects.

The dependent measure was the percentage of happy and sad triads in which subjects matched the emotional associate with the target concept. As can be seen in figure 4.1, the results provided clear evidence of a general emotions effect: compared to subjects in the control (neutral mood) condition, both happy and sad subjects were much more likely to link both happy and sad items on the basis of emotional similarity.

To generalize beyond the manipulation procedures used in the first experiment, the second study attempted to replicate this effect with naturally occurring emotion (see Mayer, McCormick, & Strong, 1995). Subjects responded to the same triads as those used in the first study; then their current emotional states were assessed. Subjects' level of happiness was estimated by summing their responses to the items *happy, content, peppy, lively,* and *active* on the BMIS, and sadness was estimated by summing their responses to the items *sad, gloomy, drowsy,* and *tired* (Niedenthal & Setterlund, 1994). These two scores were negatively correlated ($r = -.44$). Median splits were performed separately on the two emotion scores to gather data that could be easily compared to data from the previous study. Subtracting the sadness score from the happiness score was

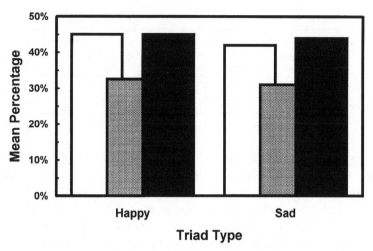

FIGURE 4.1. Percentage of happy and sad triads—varied *within* subjects—in which the emotional associate was chosen as the concept to which the target was more similar by subjects in a happy, neutral, or sad emotional state (white, gray, and black bars, respectively). Source: Niedenthal, Halberstadt, & Innes-Ker, 1999.

not appropriate, for that would subtract a different kind of "emotionality" from the happiness score.

Table 4.3 shows the average use of emotional similarity for people who reported high and low levels of happiness and sadness. The level of naturally occurring sadness was associated with the use of emotional similarity; people who reported high levels of sadness tended to link targets and comparison targets according to their happy and sad emotional similarity more so than those who reported low levels of sadness. However, the association did not appear for high and low levels of self-reported happiness. Thus, this correlational study replicated only half of the results of the initial experiment.

Why was happiness not related to greater use of emotional similarity in this experiment? Examination of the happiness and sadness scores revealed that both were normally distributed and had equivalent variances. On average, however, subjects reported being much more happy than sad. Because emotional state was not manipulated in this study, it is possible that dividing subjects on the basis of their sadness scores, compared to their happiness scores, was a more valid sorting of "emotional" versus "nonemotional" respondents; subjects in the "high" and "low" happiness groups were all rather happy, and significantly more happy than sad.

One problem with the initial studies is that we studied only happiness and sadness and also stimuli that could be related to these two emotions. Happiness and sadness are special in that they are often considered to be "opposite" emo-

TABLE 4.3. Mean percentage of emotional similarity responses.

Emotion level	Happiness		Sadness	
	Low	High	Low	High
Happy triads	39	37	35	41
Sad triads	43	40	39	44

tions. When people are sad, they are encouraged to smile, "lighten up," or be happy. Dimensional analyses of self-reports confirm that these emotions are negatively correlated (e.g., Plutchik, 1980). Thus, the general emotions effect detected in the first two studies may have occurred as a result of the relation between happy and sad information; this dimensional relation may have been particularly salient when both happiness-related and sadness-related information appeared in the task and may have encouraged the use of both as bases for categorization among happy and sad subjects.

To address the possibility that our stimulus set was itself responsible for the emergence of a general emotions effect, we performed a third study in which we manipulated emotional state as in the first study but also varied the stimulus set between subjects, so that subjects who were happy, sad, or neutral saw either happy or sad triads embedded among more neutral distractor triads. In this way we neutralized the relation between happy and sad information that the experimental stimuli might have compelled. Otherwise, the experimental procedure was identical to that for the initial study in this series.

The key results are depicted in figure 4.2. An interaction between emotion condition and stimulus set appeared. When subjects saw happy triads embedded among neutral triads, a pattern of results identical to that observed in the first experiment emerged: happy and sad subjects relied on emotional (specifically, happy) response categorization much more than control subjects did. However, when the stimulus set contained only sad triads, there was no effect of emotion condition on the use of emotional (specifically, sad) similarity.

Close examination of figure 4.2 suggests that this effect did not occur because control subjects used emotional similarity *more* in the sad than in the happy stimulus set conditions, rather than that emotional subjects used emotional similarity less. Data analyses confirmed that control subjects used significantly more emotional similarity in responding to the sad stimulus set than to the happy stimulus set; in contrast, happy and sad subjects relied on emotion-based categorization to the same degree in both sets.

What is the explanation for this unexpected result? The manipulation check showed that, at the end of the study, subjects in the two sad conditions were equally sad (regardless of which set of triads they saw), that subjects in the two happy conditions were equally happy, and that, most important, subjects in the

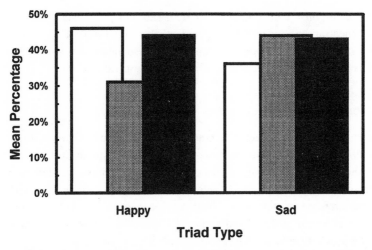

FIGURE 4.2. Percentage of happy and sad triads—varied *between* subjects—in which the emotional associate was chosen as the concept to which the target was more similar by subjects in a happy, neutral, or sad emotional state (white, gray, and black bars, respectively). Source: Niedenthal, Halberstadt, & Innes-Ker, 1999.

two control conditions were feeling equally neutral. Thus, it does not appear that the stimulus sets differentially affected the emotional states of the subjects.

The greater emotional response categorization of the control subjects in the sad triads condition could mean that the sad triads, when not mixed with happy triads (as in the first study), drew more attention and that a sadness "rule" for categorization emerged from the salience of the sad concepts. This explanation is consistent with other results suggesting that negative information commands greater attention, and perhaps deeper processing, than positive or neutral information (e.g., Pratto & John, 1991).

Did the use of both happy and sad concepts account for the general emotions effect observed in the previous studies? The results of the happy condition indicate that sad triads are not necessary for the use of happy-based similarity by both happy and, more significantly, sad subjects. That is, we still observed a general emotions effect: both happy and sad subjects used similarity to happiness much more than control subjects did, even when the relation of happy information to sadness was not salient.

Nevertheless, to provide a better test of the generality of the emotional categorization effect, we repeated the first experiment reported in this section. In this fourth study, subjects were in manipulated states of sadness, fear, or neutral emotion as they responded to triads in which concepts could be grouped together due to their shared relation to the emotions of fear and sadness. The results replicated the pattern of the first experiment; that is, fearful subjects displayed emotional response categorization for both sad and fear triads more than did control (neutral emotion) subjects (Niedenthal et al., 1999). Thus, fear, in addition to happiness and sadness, seems to be associated with a reorganization of the conceptual space according to emotional equivalence.

Emotional Response Categories or Emotionality?

We have suggested that people in emotional states form categories around specific emotional states. However, the data from the four studies just reported may reflect the fact that people in emotional states preferentially use single category of "emotion-associated things," whether the category members are related to the same emotion or not. Such a category is inconsistent with our reasoning about the structure of emotional response categories and with our conclusions from the previous lexical decision and word naming studies.

To address this problem, we conducted a final study in which participants judged whether a target word (e.g., *ambulance*) was more similar to a non-emotional associate (*wheelbarrow*) or to an emotional associate of an opposite valence (*sunbeam*). The stimuli were the original happy and sad triads used in the previous studies. However, for half of the critical emotional triads, we replaced the original emotional associates with emotional associates of randomly selected triads of opposite valence, with the constraint that the new associate and the target did not belong to an obviously neutral category (general-emotion triads); the other half of the triads remained unchanged (specific-emotion triads). Thus, the general- and specific-emotion triads were different in each set.

Results indicated that, for the specific-emotion triads, reliance on emotional similarity varied as in the previous experiments. People in an emotional state, particularly sadness, were more likely to choose the emotional associate as being more similar to the target. For the general-emotion triads, however, the (opposite valence) emotional associate was chosen far less often as more similar to the target, a trend unmediated by the emotional state of the subject. These follow-up data, therefore, do not suggest that emotionality itself is the basis for categorization when individuals are experiencing emotion, but rather that the common association to a specific emotional state is enhanced during emotional states.

Summary

The five studies reported in this section provide direct evidence for emotional response categorization, but the results suggest that the phenomenon is more complicated than we first suspected. First, it appears that emotional response categorization is enhanced when people become emotional and that emotions change the preferred basis for sorting conceptual stimuli. We observed this phenomenon in the first four studies. In addition, those studies indicated that people focus on all emotional similarities, not just those congruent with their current mood. That is, sad people are just as likely to link objects associated with fear, and happy people are just as likely to link objects associated with sadness, as they are to group sad and fearful things, respectively. Our first and fourth study demonstrated these effects and the second study extended them for naturally occurring sadness. However, the stimuli themselves appear to have effects. Things that might be categorized according to emotional meaning are themselves emotional and might affect even an unemotional person's categorization rule. Moreover, the influence on emotional state of negative emotional stimuli might be particularly powerful. This type of effect was evident in the third study, in which subjects who were exposed only to sad triads (mixed with some distractor stimuli) tended to use emotional similarity to the same elevated degree, whether they had received an experimental induction of emotion or not. Finally, the fifth study showed that the enhanced use of emotional similarity by individuals in emotional states does not mean that they perceive all emotional things as similar. Subjects in the last study tended to group sad things with other sad things and happy things with other happy things. However, they did not tend to group happy things with sad things merely because both concepts were emotional.

EMOTION AND ATTENTION IN CATEGORIZATION

Now that we have some evidence that people in emotional states will create and use emotional response categories, we can ask how this happens. In discussing the categorization experiments, we implicated a selective attention mechanism, suggesting that emotions draw attention to stimuli that elicit, or previously elicited, emotional responses. In fact, selective attention is the critical mechanism in many influential theories of similarity and categorization (Nosofsky, 1986, 1992; Smith & Zarate, 1992). In general, researchers assume that attention to a dimension increases one's discriminative ability along that dimension, and decreases discriminative ability on other, relatively unattended dimensions, resulting in a "clustering" effect. Stimuli with similar values on the attended dimension appear more similar, and stimuli with relatively discrepant values more dissimilar. We have assumed that an emotional response to an object or event is a valid stimulus dimension that can be weighted more or less heavily in similarity judgment. Attention to this emotion dimension, then, should increase the similarity of stimuli eliciting that emotion, clustering them into emotional response categories (Halberstadt & Niedenthal, 1997; also see Isen, 1987).

Significant research supports our claims about emotion-driven selective attention. Many studies have assessed the degree to which attention is automatically oriented to emotional material as a function of emotional traits such as anxiety and phobia (see Derryberry & Tucker, 1994). The Stroop task has been a popular tool in this research, because attention to word meaning in this case actually impedes optimal performance of the task (typically to identify the ink color in which the words are printed). The interference of word meanings in color naming, despite one's intention to ignore them, presumably reflects automatic attention to meaning. For example, Pratto and John (1991) employed the Stroop task to demonstrate that negative stimuli categorically interfere with word naming. Other researchers have found that the perceiver's own emotional state mediates this general effect in surprisingly specific ways. Hope, Rapee, Heimberg, and Dombeck (1990), for example, reported that social phobics are distracted in the Stroop task by words specifically related to their fear (e.g., *rejection*), and similar results have been found with other clinical populations (e.g., Mogg, Mathews, & Weinman, 1989; Watts, McKenna, Sharrock, & Trezise, 1986).

Other researchers have found related effects, using logic similar to that of the Stroop paradigm. Mathews and MacLeod (1986), for example, found that anxious (but not control) individuals had more difficulty shadowing information when threat words were presented in the unattended auditory channel, although they were unaware of the threat words. MacLeod, Mathews, and Tata (1986) asked subjects to monitor the computer screen for a small dot that sometimes followed the appearance of either threat or neutral words. Anxious, but not nonanxious or depressed, individuals detected the probe faster when it replaced a threat word (also see Broadbent & Broadbent, 1988). Conversely, Roskos-Ewoldsen and Fazio (1992) found that subjects detected a target more slowly when another object, about which they had a strong attitude, appeared somewhere else in the stimulus array. These findings are important because they further establish the strength and specificity of the relationship between affect and emotion-related stimuli and because the tasks required neutral responses to neutral stimuli, obviating the possibility of response bias (Dalgleish & Watts, 1990).

Thus, it appears that emotional stimuli attract attention, particularly when a person is in an emotional state. Furthermore, a bias to attend to emotional information makes evolutionary sense, because affective responses to objects inform the perceiver about the object's potential hedonic consequences (e.g., Hansen & Hansen, 1994; Pratto, 1994). However, a distinction sometimes lost in discussions of attention is that allocating or orienting attention to a dimension is not the same as *weighting* or *using* that dimension in judgment. Dalgleish and Watts (1990) note that even if participants orient their attention to a particular stimulus (as indicated by longer looking time, distraction from a primary task, etc.), this alone does not provide information about whether or how the stimulus was processed. Indeed, perceptual vigilance involves enhanced detection of negative or threatening information for the paradoxical purpose of avoiding it. We want to know, not whether people orient their toward attention emotional dimensions, but whether those dimensions are actually used or weighted in judgment.

To address this question, we conducted two experiments to quantify directly the weight that people in emotional states give to emotional and nonemotional dimensions of stimuli. The experiments used INDSCAL (Carroll & Chang, 1970), an individual-difference multidimensional scaling (MDS) approach, to model the similarity judgments of people subjected to our emotion manipulations. An MDS reveals psychological dimensions in large sets of similarity data by representing those data as distances in space. In a series of iterations, the model adjusts the points in the space (representing the judged stimuli) until the interstimulus distances correspond to rated similarities. Furthermore, INDSCAL includes subject-specific attention parameters that represent the weight that each perceiver places on each dimension (Arabie, Carroll, & DeSarbo, 1987). Thus, the model actually produces both a group space, based on all participants' ratings, and a set of personal spaces, distortions of the group space based on each individual's dimension weights.

The INDSCAL approach has several advantages. First, the group space itself verifies that the experimental participants perceive the emotional dimensions built into the stimuli. Second, INDSCAL isolates the psychological dimensions of the stimuli and thus allow a more fine-grained analysis of where attention is directed. In other words, unlike prior research that measured changes in attention to emotional *stimuli*, the INDSCAL method quantifies the attention allocated to emotional and nonemotional *dimensions* of these stimuli. The distortion of the subject space by dimension weights captures the clustering of emotional stimuli by emotional state, which we propose accounts for emotional response categorization. More important, however, the dimension weights reflect not only the orientation of attention to a dimension but also dimension use, or the degree to which similarity judgments were actually based on differences along a particular dimension. Finally, the task used to derive the weights, similarity judgment (unlike impression formation), does not require participants to use emotional information at all. Therefore, dimension use can be attributed to the nature of the stimuli and their interactions with the individual's emotional state, rather than to characteristics of the task. We predicted that participants experiencing either happiness or sadness would use (or give greater weight to) the emotional dimensions of stimuli more, and nonemotional dimensions less, than would people experiencing a neutral mood. This pattern would emerge from either a general emotion or an emotion congruence effect; INDSCAL cannot determine whether certain (perhaps emotion congruent) areas of a dimension are differentially weighted.

In this experiment, the stimuli were high-resolution photographs of the faces of male and female actors expressing happiness and sadness. We chose faces because emotional expressions have been shown to produce corresponding emotions in the perceiver through processes of mimicry and contagion (e.g., Hatfield, Cacioppo, & Rapson, 1993; Laird et al., 1994). We created seven male and seven female faces that expressed emotions ranging from very happy to very sad by digitally blending or morphing a photograph of each actor expressing extreme happiness with a photograph of the same actor expressing extreme sadness. Thus, within each gender, the faces represented a happy/sad continuum of emotional expression, and this ordering was confirmed by an inspection of the group space produced by INDSCAL.

In two separate studies using our music and film manipulations, participants first received a happy, sad, or control (neutral mood) induction and then judged the similarity between every possible pair of the 14 faces (not including self-similarities), presented in a different random order for each participant. These similarity ratings were submitted to INDSCAL analysis, from which a three-dimensional group solution emerged. By examining a plot of the faces, we determined that two dimensions were our a priori dimensions of emotional expression and gender, whereas the third was tentatively interpreted as ''head orientation'' (although the exact interpretation is not critical). Each participant's weights for each dimension were then submitted to a 3 (dimension) × 3 (emotional state) analysis of variance (ANOVA), with the first factor as a repeated measure.

The results, which appear in figure 4.3, were consistent across the two studies. First, a main effect of dimension emerged: emotional expression was the most heavily weighted dimension overall, followed by gender, and then head orientation. Thus, regardless of participants' emotional state, the stimuli were judged largely according to their values on the emotional expression dimension, a trend consistent with other research on the importance of evaluative or valenced information in judgment. More important, and as predicted, dimension use also interacted with emotional state, such that happy and sad subjects weighted emotional expressions more heavily, and the other two dimensions less heavily, than did control subjects. The dimension-weight data thus provide the first direct evidence that both happy and sad subjects did not just orient their attention toward emotion-associated information but actually used this information more, and nonemotional information less, than did their neutral-mood peers. Together, these shifts in dimension use should polarize the emotional faces into groups based on the emotion they elicit, thus composing what we are calling emotional response categories.

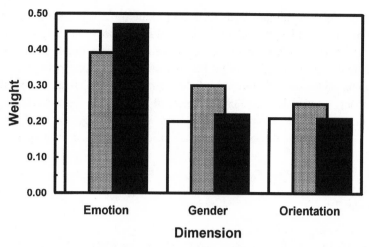

FIGURE 4.3. Weights for emotion, gender, and orientation dimensions derived from individual-difference multidimensional scaling of similarity ratings made by subjects in a happy, neutral, or sad emotional state (white, gray, and black bars, respectively). Source: Halberstadt and Niedenthal, 1997.

CONCLUSIONS

In this chapter we reviewed three research programs that relate to our initial hypothesis: emotions, like perceptual similarity, functional equivalence, and theories, serve as a kind of conceptual coherence, or an organizing theme for objects and events in the world. We began by suggesting that emotions organize cognitive material into specific emotion categories. Results of four lexical-decision experiments and one word-naming study demonstrated that emotional states are associated with facilitated processing of material that is specifically associated with the experienced emotional state, but not that of material associated only by emotional valence (see Gerrig & Bower, 1982). Our second line of research, which examined groupings of similar concepts, showed that when in emotional states, people tend to categorize according to a common emotional association in an orderly fashion: they group things associated with happiness and they group things associated with sadness. Finally, the last research program pursued the idea that the mediating mechanism in the emotional categorization results is selective attention. Multidimensional scaling analyses revealed that, in making similarity judgments, individuals who are experiencing distinct emotional states (happiness or sadness) emphasize emotional as compared to non-emotional dimensions of stimuli.

We believe that the findings we have presented, along with those reported in the other chapters of this book, support the conclusion that emotions are mental processes that are important in their own right for a full account of mental functioning. It is likely that the role of emotional response in categorization has been obscured by the need for researchers to label categories, and to ask experimental participants for insight into the question of what makes two things the same, and different from a third (Niedenthal & Halberstadt, 1995). But as researchers employ less explicit indicators of category use, emotional response categories will likely figure more prominently in resulting models of categorization, just as they have in recent models of other cognitive phenomena.

NOTES

1. One could object and say that two things might be similar in that they evoke similar emotions and that, therefore, emotional response equivalence is a type of similarity. But this is just semantic quibbling. We suggest that two things are treated as the same sort of thing because they evoke the same emotion, not because they are similar in that they evoke the same emotion.

2. Indeed, the idea seems so right that when the first author told one of her graduate school professors about it, he responded, "Really? How can this be a new problem?"

3. Though the conclusion that these data support the existence of basic emotions (as well as the data themselves) has been criticized (e.g., Davidson, 1993), we question whether the demonstration of autonomic nervous system differentiation should be a burden on the theory of basic emotions. This system may be far too general to make such distinctions, and physiological differentiation is likely to be an extremely complicated issue involving more than autonomic nervous system processes.

4. To date, fear-related music has only been used in conjunction with the fear films in the combined music-film induction.

5. All subjects showed facilitation to *love* words and (marginal) inhibition to *anger* words.

6. Unlike the lexical decision experiments, the emotional music used to induce emotional states did not continue as background during the word naming task because pilot testing indicated that the music interfered with performance.

7. In this study, all subjects showed facilitation to both *love* and *anger* words, and emotional state did not mediate the effect. See Niedenthal, Halberstadt, and Innes-Ker (1999) for an explanation of these effects.

8. In pilot testing, subjects rated the concepts that constituted the happy and sad triads on a 3 (very happy) to −3 (very sad) Likert-type scale. Results revealed that happy triad targets and their emotional associates were strongly and equivalently associated with happiness (means = 2.1 and 2.0, respectively), while their nonemotional associates were rated as neither sad nor happy (mean = 0.4). Analogously, for the sad triads, the means for the target, emotional associate, and nonemotional associate were −2.1, −2.2, and 0.6, respectively. Thus, for happy and sad triads alike, emotion-related concepts were rated comparably (on a happiness/sadness scale) to the target concepts, whereas the nonemotional concepts received neutral ratings. Fear-related data are forthcoming.

REFERENCES

Abelson, R. P., & Sermat, V. (1962). Multidimensional scaling of facial expressions. *Journal of Experimental Psychology, 63,* 546–554.

Arabie, P., Carroll, J. D., & DeSarbo, W. S. (1987). *Three-way scaling and clustering.* Sage University Paper Series on Quantitative Applications in the Social Sciences, Number 07-065. Beverly Hills: Sage Publications.

Balota, D. A. & Chumbley, J. I. (1985). The locus of word frequency effects in the pronunciation task: Lexical access and/or production? *Journal of Memory and Language, 24,* 89–106.

Bargh, J. A., & Pietromonaco, P. (1982). Information processing and social perception: The influence of trait information presented outside of conscious awareness on impression formation. *Journal of Personality and Social Psychology, 43,* 437–449.

Barsalou, L. W. (1983). Ad hoc categories. *Memory & Cognition, 11,* 211–227.

Barsalou, L. W. (1985). Ideals, central tendency, and frequency of instantiation as determinants of graded structure in categories. *Journal of Experimental Psychology Learning, Memory, and Cognition, 11,* 629–654.

Barsalou, L. W. (1987). The instability of graded structure in concepts. In U. Neisser (Ed.), *Concepts and conceptual development: Ecological and intellectual factors in categorization* (pp. 101–140). New York: Cambridge University Press.

Blaney, P. H. (1986). Affect and memory: A review. *Psychological Bulletin, 99,* 229–246.

Bloom, L., & Beckwith, R. (1989). Talking with feeling: Integrating affective and linguistic expression in early language development. *Cognition and Emotion, 3,* 313–342.

Bower, G. H. (1981). Mood and memory. *American Psychologist, 36,* 129–148.

Bransford, J. D., McCarrell, N. S., Franks, J. J., & Nitsch, K. E. (1977). Toward unexplaining memory. In R. E. Shaw & J. D. Bransford (Eds.), *Perceiving, acting, and knowing* (pp. 431–466). Hillsdale, NJ: Erlbaum.

Broadbent, D. E., & Broadbent, M. (1988). Anxiety and attentional bias: State and trait. *Cognition and Emotion, 2,* 165–183.

Bruner, J. S., Goodnow, J. J., & Austin, G. A. (1956). *A study of thinking.* New York: Wiley.

Bruner, J. S., & Postman, L. (1947). Emotional selectivity in perception and reaction. *Journal of Personality, 16,* 69–77.

Carroll, J. D., & Chang, J. J. (1970). *A "quasi-non-metric" version of INDSCAL, a procedure for individual differences in multidimensional scaling.* Paper presented at meetings of the Psychonomic Society, Stanford, California.

Clark, M. S. & Isen, A. M. (1982). Towards understanding the relationship between feeling states and social behavior. In A. H. Hastorf & A. M. Isen (Eds.), *Cognitive social psychology* (pp. 73–108). New York: Elsevier-North Holland.

Clark, M. S., Milberg, S., & Erber, R. (1984). Effects of arousal on judgments of others' emotions. *Journal of Personality and Social Psychology, 66,* 551–560.

Clark, M. S., Milberg, S., & Ross, J. (1983). Arousal cues arousal-related material in memory: Implications for understanding effects of mood on memory. *Journal of Verbal Learning and Verbal Behavior, 22,* 633–649.

Dalgleish, T., & Watts, F. N. (1990). Biases of attention and memory disorders of anxiety and depression. *Clinical Psychology Review, 10,* 589–604.

Davidson, R. J. (1992). Emotion and affective style: Hemispheric substrates. *Psychological Science, 3,* 39–43.

Davidson, R. J. (1993). Parsing affective space: Perspectives from neuropsychology and psychophysiology. *Neuropsychology, 7,* 464–475.

Derryberry, D., & Tucker, D. M. (1994). Motivating the focus of attention. In P. M. Niedenthal & S. Kitayama (Eds.), *The heart's eye: Emotional influences in perception and attention* (pp. 167–196). San Diego: Academic Press.

Devine, P. G. (1989). Stereotyping and prejudice: Their automatic and controlled components. *Journal of Personality and Social Psychology, 56,* 5–18.

Dimberg, U., & Ohman, A. (1983). The effects of directional facial cues on electrodermal conditioning to facial stimuli. *Psychophysiology, 20,* 160–167.

Eich, E., & Metcalfe, J. (1989). Mood dependent memory for internal versus external events. *Journal of Experimental Psychology: Learning, Memory, and Cognition, 15,* 443–455.

Ekman, P. (1982). Emotion in the human face. 2nd ed. Cambridge, UK: Cambridge University Press.

Ekman, P. (1984). Expression and the nature of emotion. In K. Scherer & P. Ekman (Eds.), *Approaches to emotion* (pp. 319–343). Hillsdale, NJ: Erlbaum.

Ekman, P. (1994). Strong evidence for universals in facial expressions: A reply to Russell's mistaken critique. *Psychological Bulletin, 115,* 268–287.

Ekman, P., & Friesen, W. V. (1971). Constants across culture in the face and emotion. *Journal of Personality and Social Psychology, 17,* 124–129.

Etcoff, N. L., & Magee, J. J. (1992). Categorical perception of facial expressions. *Cognition, 44,* 227–240.

Fehr, B., & Russell, J. A. (1984). The concept of emotion viewed from a prototype perspective. *Journal of Experimental Psychology: General, 113,* 464–486.

Feldman, L. A. (1995a). Valence focus and arousal focus: Individual differences in the structure of affective experience. *Journal of Personality and Social Psychology, 16,* 153–166.

Feldman, L. A. (1995b). Variations in the circumplex structure of mood. *Personality and Social Psychology Bulletin, 21,* 806–817.

Frijda, N. H. (1988). The laws of emotion. *American Psychologist, 43,* 349–358.

Fridlund, A. J. (1991). Evolution and facial action in reflex, social motive, and paralanguage. *Biological Psychology, 32,* 3–100.

Gelernter, D. (1994). *The muse in the machine: Computerizing the poetry of human thought.* New York: Free Press.

Gernsbacher, M. A., Goldsmith, H. H., & Robertson, R. R. (1992). Do readers mentally represent characters' emotional states? *Cognition and Emotion, 6,* 89–111.

Gerrards-Hesse, A., Spies, K., & Hesse. F. W. (1994). Experimental inductions of emotional states and their effectiveness: A review. *British Journal of Psychology, 85,* 55–78.

Gerrig, R. J., & Bower, G. H. (1982). Emotional influences on word recognition. *Bulletin of the Psychonomic Society, 19,* 197–200.

Goldstone, R. L. (1994a). The role of similarity in categorization: Providing a groundwork. *Cognition, 52,* 125–157.

Goldstone, R. L. (1994b). Influences of categorization on perceptual discrimination. *Journal of Experimental Psychology: General, 123,* 178–200.

Goodman, N. (1972). Seven strictures on similarity. In N. Goodman (Ed.), *Problems and projects* (pp. 437–447). New York: Bobbs-Merrill.

Halberstadt, J. B., & Niedenthal, P. M. (1997). Emotional state and the use of stimulus dimensions in judgment. *Journal of Personality and Social Psychology, 72,* 1018–1034.

Halberstadt, J. B., Niedenthal, P. M., & Kushner, J. (1995). Resolution of lexical ambiguity by emotional state. *Psychological Science, 6,* 278–282.

Hansen, C. H., & Hansen, R. D. (1994). Automatic emotion: Attention and facial efference. In P. M. Niedenthal & S. Kitayama (Eds), *The heart's eye: Emotional influences in perception and attention* (pp. 217–243). San Diego: Academic Press.

Hansen, C. H., & Shantz C. A. (1995). Emotion-specific priming: Congruence effects on affect and recognition across negative emotions. *Personality and Social Psychology Bulletin, 21,* 548–557.

Hatfield, E., Cacioppo, J. T., & Rapson, R. L. (1993). Emotional contagion. *Current Directions in Psychological Science, 2,* 96–99.

Hope, D. A., Rapee, R. M., Heimberg, R. G., & Dombeck, M. J. (1990). Representations of the self in social phobia: Vulnerability to social threat. *Cognitive Therapy and Research, 14,* 177–189.

Isen, A. M. (1984). Toward understanding the role of affect in cognition. In R. S. Wyer & T. K. Srull (Eds.), *Handbook of social cognition* (vol. 3, pp. 179–236). Hillsdale, NJ: Erlbaum.

Isen, A. M. (1987). Positive affect, cognitive processes, and social behavior. In L. Berkowitz (Ed.), *Advances in experimental social psychology* (vol. 20, pp. 203–253). New York: Academic Press.

Isen, A. M., & Daubman, K. A. (1984). The influence of affect on categorization. *Journal of Personality and Social Psychology, 47,* 1206–1217.

Isen, A. M., Daubman, K. A., & Gorgoglione, J. M. (1987). The influence of positive affect on cognitive organization: Implications for education. In R. E. Snow & M. J. Farr (Eds.), *Aptitude, learning, and instruction: Cognitive and affective process analysis* (pp. 143–164). Mahwah, NJ: Erlbaum.

Isen, A. M., Johnson, M. M., Mertz, E., & Robinson, G. F. (1985). The influence of positive affect on the unusualness of word associations. *Journal of Personality and Social Psychology, 48,* 1413–1426.

Isen, A. M., Niedenthal, P. M., & Cantor, N. (1992). An influence of positive affect on social categorization. *Motivation and Emotion, 16,* 65–78.

Izard, C. E. (1977). *Human emotions.* New York: Plenum Press.

Izard, C. E. (1994). Innate and universal facial expressions: Evidence from developmental and cross-cultural research. *Psychological Bulletin, 115,* 288–299.

Johnson-Laird, P. N., & Oatley, K. (1992). Basic emotions, rationality, and folk theory. *Cognition and Emotion, 6,* 201–223.

Kitayama, S. (1990). Interaction between affect and cognition in word perception. *Journal of Personality and Social Psychology, 58,* 209–217.

Kitayama, S. (1991). Impairment of perception by positive and negative affect. *Cognition and Emotion, 5,* 255–274.

Kitayama, S., & Howard, S. (1994). Affective regulation of perception and comprehension: Amplification and semantic priming. In P.M. Niedenthal & S. Kitayama (Eds.), *The heart's eye: Emotional influences in perception and attention* (pp. 41–65). San Diego: Academic Press.

Kruschke, J. K. (1992). ALCOVE: An exemplar-based connectionist model of category learning. *Psychological Review, 99,* 22–44.

Laird, D. L., Alibozak, T., Davainis, D., Deignan, K., Fontanella, K., Hong, J., Levy, B., & Pacheco, C. (1994). Individual differences in the effects of spontaneous mimicry on emotional contagion. *Motivation and Emotion, 18,* 231–247.

Laird, J. D., Cuniff, M., Sheehan, K., Shulman, D., & Strum, G. (1989). Emotion specific effects of facial expression on memory for life events. *Journal of Social Behavior and Personality, 4,* 87–98.

Laird, J. D., Wagener, J. J., Halal, M., & Szegda, M. (1982). Remembering what you feel: Effects of emotion on memory. *Journal of Personality and Social Psychology, 42,* 646–657.

Lakoff, G. (1987). *Women, fire, and dangerous things.* Chicago: University of Chicago Press.

Lang, P. J. (1984). Cognition in emotion: Concept and action. In C. E. Izard, J. Kagan, & R. B. Zajonc (Eds.), *Emotions, cognition, and behavior* (pp. 192–226). Cambridge, UK: Cambridge University Press.

Lanzetta, J. T., & Orr, S. P. (1980). Influences of facial expressions on the classical conditioning of fear. *Journal of Personality and Social Psychology, 39,* 1081–1087.

LeDoux, J. E. (1994). Emotion, memory and the brain. *Scientific American, 270,* 32–39.

Levenson, R. W. (1992). Autonomic nervous system differences among emotions. *Psychological Science, 3,* 23–27.

Levenson, R. W., Ekman, P., & Friesen, W. V. (1990). Voluntary facial action generates emotion-specific autonomic nervous system activity. *Psychophysiology, 27,* 363–384.

Lorch, R. F., Balota, D. A., & Stamm, E. G. (1986). Locus of inhibition effects in the priming of lexical decisions: Pre- or postlexical? *Memory and Cognition, 14,* 95–103.

MacLean, P. D. (1993). On the evolution of three mentalities. In J. B. Ashbrook (Ed.), *Brain, culture, and the human spirit: Essays from an emergent evolutionary perspective* (pp. 15–44). Lanham, MD: University Press of America.

MacLeod, C., Mathews, A. M., & Tata, P. (1986). Attentional bias in emotional disorders. *Journal of Abnormal Psychology, 95,* 15–20.

Markman, E. (1989). *Categorization and naming in children.* Cambridge, MA: MIT Press.

Mathews, A. M., & MacLeod, C. (1986). Discrimination of threat cues without awareness in anxiety states. *Journal of Abnormal Psychology, 95,* 131–138.

Mayer, J. D., & Gaschke, Y. N. (1988). The experience and meta-experience of mood. *Journal of Personality and Social Psychology, 55,* 102–111.

Mayer, J. D., McCormick, L. J., & Strong, S. E. (1995). Mood-congruent memory and natural mood: New evidence. *Personality and Social Psychology Bulletin, 21,* 736–746.

McHugo, G. J., Smith, C. A., & Lanzetta, J. T. (1982). The structure of self-reports of emotional responses to film segments. *Motivation and Emotion, 6,* 365–385.

Medin, D. L. (1989). Concepts and conceptual structure. *American Psychologist, 44,* 1469–1481.

Medin, D. L., Goldstone, R. L., & Gentner, D. (1993). Respects for similarity. *Psychological Review, 100,* 254–278.

Medin, D. L., & Schaffer, M. M. (1978). Context theory of classification learning. *Psychological Review, 85,* 207–238.

Mervis, C. B., & Rosch, E. (1981). Categorization of natural objects. *Annual Review of Psychology, 32,* 89–115.

Mineka, S. (1992). Evolutionary memories, emotional processing, and the emotional disorders. In D. L. Medin (Ed.), *The psychology of learning and motivation* (vol. 28, pp. 161–206). New York: Academic Press.

Mogg, K., Mathews, A., & Weinman, J. (1989). Selective processing of threat cues in anxiety states: A replication. *Behavior Research and Therapy, 27,* 317–323.

Murphy, G. L., & Medin, D. L. (1985). The role of theories in conceptual coherence. *Psychological Review, 92,* 289–316.

Neely, J. H. (1991). Semantic priming effects in visual word recognition: A selective review of current findings and research. In D. Besner & G. Humphreys (Eds.), *Basic processes in reading: Visual word recognition* (pp. 264–336). Hillsdale, NJ: Erlbaum.

Niedenthal, P. M., & Halberstadt, J. B. (1995). The acquisition and structure of emotional response categories. In D. L. Medin (Ed.), *The psychology of learning and motivation* (vol. 33, pp. 23–64). New York: Academic Press.

Niedenthal, P. M., Halberstadt, J. B., & Innes-Ker, A. H. (1999) Emotional response categorization. *Psychological Review, 106,* 337–361.

Niedenthal, P. M., Halberstadt, J. B., & Setterlund, M. B. (1997). Being happy and seeing "happy": Emotional state mediates visual word recognition. *Cognition and Emotion, 11,* 403–432.

Niedenthal, P. M., & Setterlund, M. B. (1994). Emotion congruence in perception. *Personality and Social Psychology Bulletin, 20,* 401–410.

Niedenthal, P. M., Setterlund, M. B., & Jones, D. E. (1994). Emotional organization of perceptual memory. In P. M. Niedenthal & S. Kitayama, (Eds), *The heart's eye: Emotional influences in perception and attention* (pp. 87–113). San Diego: Academic Press.

Nosofsky, R. M. (1986). Attention, similarity, and the identification-categorization relationship. *Journal of Experimental Psychology: General, 115,* 39–57.

Nosofsky, R. M. (1992). Exemplar-based approach to relating categorization, identification, and recognition. In F. G. Ashby (Ed.), *Multidimensional models of perception and cognition* (pp. 363–393). Hillsdale, NJ: Erlbaum.

Oatley, K., & Johnson-Laird, P. N. (1996). The communicative theory of emotions: Empirical tests, mental models, and implications for social interaction. In L. L. Martin & A. Tesser (Eds.), *Striving and feeling: Interactions among goals, affect, and self-regulation* (pp. 363–393). Mahwah, NJ: Erlbaum.

Ohman, A., & Dimberg, U. (1978). Facial expressions as conditioned stimuli for electrodermal responses: A case of "preparedness?" *Journal of Personality and Social Psychology, 36,* 1251–1258.

Orr, S. P., & Lanzetta, J. T. (1980). Facial expressions of emotion as conditioned stimuli for human autonomic conditioning. *Journal of Personality and Social Psychology, 38,* 278–282.

Ortony, A., & Turner, T. J. (1990). What's basic about basic emotions? *Psychological Review, 97,* 315–331.

Osgood, C. E., & Suci, G. J. (1955). Factor analysis of meaning. *Journal of Experimental Psychology, 50,* 325–338.

Papp, K. A., McDonald, J. E., Schvaneveldt, R. W., & Noel, R. W. (1987). Frequency and pronounceability in visually presented naming and lexical decision tasks. In M. Coltheart (Ed.), *Attention and performance XII* (pp. 221–244). Hillsdale, NJ: Erlbaum.

Philippot, P. (1993). Inducing and assessing differentiated emotion-feeling states in the laboratory. *Cognition and Emotion, 7,* 171–193.

Plutchik, R. (1980). *Emotion: A psychoevolutionary synthesis.* New York: Harper and Row.

Plutchik, R. (1984). A psychoevolutionary theory of emotions. *Social Science Information, 21,* 529–553.

Powell, M., & Hernsley, D. R. (1984). Depression: A breakdown of perceptual defense? *British Journal of Psychiatry, 145,* 358–362.

Pratto, F. (1994). Consciousness and automatic evaluation. In P. M. Niedenthal & S. Kitayama (Eds.), *The heart's eye: Emotional influences in perception and attention* (pp. 115–143). San Diego: Academic Press.

Pratto, F., & John, O. P. (1991). Automatic vigilance: The attention-grabbing power of negative information. *Journal of Personality and Social Psychology, 61,* 380–391.

Quine, W. V. O. (1977). Natural kinds. In S. P. Schwartz (Ed.), *Naming necessity, and natural kinds* (pp. 155–175). Ithaca, NY: Cornell University Press.

Rips, L. J., Shoben, E. J., & Smith, E. E. (1973). Semantic distance and the-verification of semantic relations. *Journal of Verbal Learning and Verbal Behavior, 12,* 1–20.

Rosch, E. (1975). Cognitive representations of semantic categories. *Journal of Experimental Psychology: Human Perception and Performance, 1,* 303–322.

Roskos-Ewoldsen, D. R., & Fazio, R. H. (1992). On the orienting value of attitudes: Attitude accessibility as a determinant of an object's attraction of visual attention. *Journal of Personality and Social Psychology, 63,* 198–211.

Russell, J. A. (1979). Affective space is bipolar. *Journal of Personality and Social Psychology, 37,* 345–356.

Russell, J. A. (1980). A circumplex model of affect. *Journal of Personality and Social Psychology, 39,* 1161–1178.

Russell, J. A. (1994). Is there universal recognition of emotion from facial expressions? A review of the cross-cultural studies. *Psychological Bulletin, 115,* 102–141.

Schwarz, N., & Clore, G. L. (1988). How do I feel about it? The informative function of affective states. In K. Fiedler & J. Forgas (Eds.), *Affect, cognition, and social behavior. New evidence and integrative attempts* (pp. 44–62). Toronto: Hogrefe.

Shaver, P. Schwartz, J., Kirson, D., & O'Connor, G. (1987). Emotion knowledge: Further exploration of a prototype approach. *Journal of Personality and Social Psychology, 52,* 1061–1086.

Seidenberg, M. S., Waters, G. S., Sanders, M., & Langer, P. (1984). Pre- and postlexical loci of contextual effects on word recognition. *Memory & Cognition, 12,* 315–328.

Seligman, M. E. P. (1970). On the generality of the laws of learning. *Psychological Review, 77,* 406–418.

Singer, J. A., & Salovey, P. (1988). Mood and memory: Evaluating the network theory of affect. *Clinical Psychology Review, 8,* 211–251.

Smith, E. R., & Zarate, M. A. (1992). Exemplar-based model of social judgment. *Psychological Review, 99,* 3–21.

Sroufe, L. A. (1979). The coherence of individual development: Early care, attachment, and subsequent developmental issues. *American Psychologist, 34,* 834–841.

Stein, N. L., & Trabasso, T. (1992). The organization of emotional experience: Creating links among thinking, language, and intentional action. *Cognition and Emotion, 6,* 225–244.

Tomkins, S. S. (1962). *Affect, imagery, consciousness,* Volume 1: *The positive affects.* New York: Springer Verlag.

Tomkins, S. S. (1963). *Affect, imagery, consciousness,* Volume 2: *The negative affects.* New York: Springer Verlag.

Tooby, J., & Cosmidis, L. (1990). The past explains the present: Emotional adaptations and the structure of ancestral environments. *Ethology and Sociobiology, 11,* 375–424.

Velten, E. A. (1968). A laboratory task for induction of mood states. *Behavior Research and Therapy, 6,* 473–482.

Watts, F. N., McKenna, F. P., Sharrock, R., & Trezise, L. (1986). Colour naming of phobia-related words. *British Journal of Psychology, 77,* 97–108.

CHAPTER 5

Q and A

Eric Eich

As the Introduction noted, one of the main aims of *Counterpoints* is to provide contributors with a venue in which they can compare their personal points of view and voice their opinions on issues of wider interest. To that end, this chapter shares the answers that Professors Bower, Forgas, Kihlstrom, and Niedenthal gave to a series of questions I raised after they had read each other's work. In addition to clarifying several specific issues that arose in the core chapters, their replies candidly assess the general state of cognition/ emotion research—its successes, its shortcomings, and its prospects for the future.

Before turning to the first question, a couple of comments are in order. First, apart from adding bibliographic references, I made no major editorial changes to the contributors' answers—for the simple reason that none seemed necessary or useful, either to me or my co-authors (among whom all replies were circulated). Further, all questions were raised, and answers received, via electronic mail—the only viable option, given that when this book was being written, its five authors were living in four countries on three continents. As it happened, e-mail proved more than merely practical; it seemed to prompt answers that were not only scientifically informed but refreshingly informal as well. Though e-mail may not be as "hot" a medium (in the McLuhan sense of the term) as, say, radio, it is certainly "warm," an altogether fitting attribute for a book about the interplay between emotion and cognition.

GENERAL QUESTIONS

1. Looking back over the past 20 years or so of research on cognition/emotion interactions, what do you see as the major accomplishments (theoretical or empirical) of this period? What concepts or findings published by others have most influenced your own work?

Gordon Bower

There have been several empirical and theoretical accomplishments in the past two decades. Some major contributions that I have found impressive are the following:

1. Eric Eich's (1995) resolution of when mood dependent memory is observed in laboratory studies and when it isn't, and why. That line of research required courage to undertake (given its prior odds of success) and great care in critically analyzing procedural variables that made a difference to the outcome of such experiments. Mood dependence should now be viewed as a robust finding that can take its proper place in the archives of our field, thanks largely to Eric's labors.

2. Research by Jerry Clore, Norbert Schwarz, Joe Forgas, Klaus Fiedler, and their associates delineating limits and boundary conditions for demonstrations of mood congruence in personal judgments and memory (e.g., Clore & Parrott, 1994; Fiedler, 1990; Forgas, 1995; Schwarz & Clore, 1988). As discussed in our chapter, classifying and systematizing these side conditions has been a central focus of Joe's affect infusion model.

3. Henry Ellis's demonstrations of various cognitive deficits caused by induced elation and depression have been very important. Ellis and his associates (e.g., Ellis, Ottaway, Varner, Becker, & Moore, 1997; Ellis, Seibert, & Herbert, 1990; Seibert & Ellis, 1991) have found that moods—even positive ones—interfere with central cognitive tasks (memorizing complex materials, detecting contradictions in texts, etc.), and they do so by evoking task-irrelevant thoughts. While that idea has been around for ages in the research on performance anxiety (e.g., Mandler & Sarason, 1952), Ellis was the first to demonstrate robust effects for positive mood inductions and to measure irrelevant thoughts with an on-line thought listing procedure. Ellis has also helped elucidate the boundary conditions for producing mood congruence effects in memory.

4. Paula Niedenthal and colleagues have succeeded in showing mood congruent effects in low-level perceptual tasks such as lexical decision and word naming (see Niedenthal & Halberstadt, this volume; Niedenthal, Halberstadt, & Set-

terlund, 1997; Niedenthal & Setterlund, 1994). Jerry Clore and I had searched for these perceptual effects long ago without much success (see Bower, 1987; Gerrig & Bower, 1982). Paula appears to have produced the effect by using more restricted, emotion-specific sets of words and stronger mood inductions.

5. On the theoretical side, useful advances have occurred in the way psychologists now characterize emotions and the stimulus conditions that elicit them. Beginning with the emotional attribution work of Bernie Weiner (1982) and Ira Roseman (1984), the field has been materially advanced by the careful semantic analyses of emotional terms by Andrew Ortony, Jerry Clore, and Allen Collins (1988), the hierarchical classification scheme proposed by Phillip Shaver and his associates (Shaver, Schwartz, Kirson, & O'Connor, 1987), and the dimensional analyses of emotional feelings proposed by Phoebe Ellsworth and Craig Smith (1988). Moreover, the eliciting conditions for various emotions have been well described by Nico Frijda (1988), by Nancy Stein and Judy Levine (1989), and by Keith Oatley and Phil Johnson-Laird (1987). These researchers have greatly advanced our description of the emotional domain.

Additionally, Richard Lazarus (1991), Bob Levenson (1992), and Albert Bandura (1997) have continued providing demonstrations of the importance of individuals' coping skills in modulating their emotional reactions to external situations. Of relevance to clinicians, Bandura (1991, 1994) has continued his analyses of conditions that help people learn how to cope with otherwise threatening and debilitating emotional situations.

Joseph Forgas

I think the past twenty years have seen a steady development in our understanding of how affective states and cognition interact. I would say that the major research achievements during this time were threefold. First, the discovery, documentation, and initial theoretical explanation of basic affect priming phenomena. Second, the empirical demonstration of the boundary conditions for mood congruence in memory and judgments, and early research demonstrating the information-processing consequences of affective states. And third, the emergence of more comprehensive integrative theories of cognition and emotion, and the rapid extension of cognition/emotion research to a variety of applied areas (clinical, social, developmental, organizational, etc.).

The first several years of this period (up to 1985) were marked by an intense initial interest in mood congruence phenomena. The associative network model proposed by Gordon Bower (1981) provided perhaps the first truly integrative theoretical treatment of these findings. The next period could be described as one of growing complexity, and even confusion. There was growing recognition that mood congruence in cognition is not as robust or reliable a phenomenon as first assumed, and it also turned out that mood dependence in memory is itself subject to boundary conditions. Competing theoretical explanations for affect congruence and affect incongruence in cognition were proposed. Finally, the information-processing consequences of affective states started to be systematically explored for the first time. This period probably lasted from 1985 until about 1992. The third period, still continuing today, was marked by the emergence of integrative theoretical models seeking to account for mood congruence and incongruence within a comprehensive framework, and the extension of cognition/emotion research to a large number of applied areas. I think Gordon's network theory was the single most influential development in this regard.

John Kihlstrom

I think that the major accomplishment of this period is that we have begun to talk about emotion at all. And not only that, but emotion researchers have now begun to band together into a kind of interdisciplinary affective science, or affective neuroscience, expressly modeled on cognitive science and cognitive neuroscience.

The history of the cognition/emotion interface is quite interesting (see Le-Doux, 1996). I think it's fair to say that research on emotion and memory revived the whole field of emotion. Before that, there really wasn't that much outside the clinical literature on anxiety, depression, and other affective disorders. Cannon's critique had pretty much dispensed with the James-Lange theory. There was some interest in the limbic system, but most of it was hand waving. Schachter and Singer (1962) changed all of that by showing that the physiological basis of emotion was undifferentiated autonomic arousal, and that the factors that differentiated the emotions were the attributions that people made about their emotions. That led to the view that emotions were products of cognitive construction—that they were, in essence, "beliefs" about one's emotions. This cognitive-constructivist view was further developed by George Mandler (1975, 1980), Richard Lazarus (1991; Lazarus & Smith, 1988), Phoebe Ellsworth and Craig Smith (1988; Smith & Ellsworth, 1985), Gerald Clore and Andrew Ortony (Ortony, Clore, & Collins, 1988), Keith Oatley and Philip Johnson-Laird (1987), and others. At the same time, Aaron Beck (1967, 1976), Martin Seligman (1971), and others, including Lyn Abramson, Lauren Alloy, and Susan Mineka (Alloy & Abramson, 1988; Mineka & Tomarken, 1989), introduced cognitive theories of clinical depression, which were followed quickly by cognitive theories of clinical anxiety.

So by the mid-1970s there was a kind of cognitive hegemony over the study of emotion. Almost two centuries earlier, in the *Critique of Pure Reason*, Immanuel Kant had argued that emotion was an irreducible mental faculty, along with cognition and conation. But now, psychologists had reversed all that: far from being seen as a separate mental faculty, with its own structure and rules of operation, emotion was viewed as a cognitive construction (something similar happened to motivation, too, though that's another story). This turn of events had two consequences, in my view.

The first was to legitimize the study of the emotional effects on cognition. This had been a favorite topic of the psychoanalysts, of course, and Bruner and Postman (1949) had revived the issue as part of the New Look. But now it became possible to talk about such matters as mood congruent and mood dependent memory. Gordon Bower's (1981) *American Psychologist* article was extremely important in stimulating work on this topic. Later, Joe Forgas and others (Forgas, 1995; Forgas & Bower, 1987; Forgas & Moylan, 1991) expanded research on emotional effects on cognition to judgment and decision making, and Paula Niedenthal and Shinobu Kitayama (1994) revived the New Look program in the domain of perception. All of this work, in turn, increased the contact between cognitive and social personality psychology, and between the laboratory and the clinic.

The second consequence was to induce a reaction to the hegemony of the cognitive. Social psychology has always been ambivalent about the proposition, which I take to be axiomatic, that social behavior is cognitively mediated, and emotional constructs, at least in the form of attitudes, have always been central to the understanding of social behavior. So what happened, and it happened pretty quickly, was that some social psychologists began to argue that there were at least some aspects of emotion that were independent of cognitive involvement. Robert Zajonc's (1980) article was seminal in this regard, and his ensuing debate with Richard Lazarus (1982, 1984), mostly played out in the pages of the *American Psychologist*, is emblematic of the whole controversy. Richard Solomon's (1977) opponent-process theory of acquired motivation strongly suggested that some aspects of emotional experience were nonassociative. The work of Ekman and Friesen (1971, 1975) on facial expressions of emotion also contributed to the reaction, because they claimed that certain aspects of emotional experience and expression (the basic emotions) were part of our evolutionary heritage, prewired, automatic, and thus in some sense noncognitive. The anticognitive reaction was also fueled by research by Gary Marshall and Philip Zimbardo (1979), and by Christina Maslach (1979), which cast strong doubt on Schachter and Singer's original findings and theory. In the early 1980s, John Cotton (1980; Cotton, Baron, & Borkovec, 1980) and Rainer Reisenzein (1983) had published devastating reviews of the whole Schachterian program.

So now we have to be prepared to live with the proposition that at least some aspects of emotional experience and expression may not involve cognition at all—at least not in any important way. We no longer take it for granted that emotion is a cognitive construction. Fortunately, work on the cognition/emotion interface doesn't require that emotion be a product of cognition. All we need is a way for the cognitive and emotional systems to connect, so that each can influence the other. And it's pretty clear that they do connect, so that emotional states can influence perception, memory, and thought, and cognitive processes can influence emotional states.

Finding out where, and how, and to what extent cognition and emotion connect is an enduring problem for psychology. Some theorists have had interesting things to say about this issue. Howard Leventhal (1984), for example, has been very influential on my own thinking: his perception-motor theory of emotion carefully works its way between the Scylla of cognitive constructivism and the Charybdis of affective independence and deserves a lot more attention than it has gotten. And Peter Lang's (1984) multiple systems view of emotion, coupled with Jack Rachman's (1990) notion of desynchrony, on which my own speculations about the emotional unconscious are based, also provide a means for understanding the cognitive and noncognitive contributions to emotion.

Paula Niedenthal

Here in France I am teaching a course in cognition and emotion, a course that I have not taught for about 10 years. So, it has been interesting to examine the contributions to this area in the last 10 years. There seem to me to be three conceptual advances, but I have to admit that I think that they are rather modest advances.

First, it seems to have taken a long time to get past the debate between Zajonc (1980) and Lazarus (1982) on the primacy of affect versus cognition, but it has been achieved. The realization that there are reciprocal influences, and that we need to be much more careful in our definitions of the two processes, or the parts of the two processes of interest, has allowed researchers to go beyond this question and to study both the emotional consequences of various cognitive processes and structures (as in self-discrepancy theory, self-complexity theory, work on counterfactual thinking and emotion, models of adult attachment, etc.) and to examine the influences of emotion in perception, categorization, impression formation and judgment, without getting hung up on which comes first, affect or cognition.

Getting away from which comes first has gone hand in hand (in my mind) with the refinement of, if not the concepts, perhaps at least the differential manipulation of and measurement of affect, evaluations, moods, emotions, and emotional traits. I have no doubt that this issue has not been of equal concern to even the authors of this volume. However, for years I worried about the fact that models of cognition/emotion interactions, as well as models of emotion per se, were based primarily on studies of pain, which should not stand alone as a prototypical emotion; or phobias, which should not be considered to be the same as the state of fear; or depression, which probably should not be considered the same as sadness. Furthermore, very often researchers who intended to manipulate emotions in the laboratory manipulated processes in addition to emotion (e.g., self-evaluation). Often they have not been precise about which emotion they were inducing, or else they induced a mood and called it an emotion or vice versa. I believe that researchers in this area are finally worried about the differences among the concepts I mentioned and seem to be a little more concerned about what generalizations that can be drawn from a given set of studies, given the population studied or the manipulation techniques employed.

Relatedly, there is finally some concern about whether emotional state is required for conclusions about observed changes in cognitive processes at all. Not too long ago the Velten technique was used to induce emotions. Or else subjects were told to imagine an emotion-inducing experience from their past. Or else they were instructed to read a sad or exhilarating story. Then, as the dependent measure, changes in the accessibility of memories or the learning of words was assessed. Because there was no reason to reject the alternative hypothesis that the priming of verbal material by verbal material accounted for the observed effect, in fact there was often no need to invoke the notion of emotional feelings to explain the observed results.

Third, I would say that a sufficient number of researchers have broken away from a concern with the influences of emotion on the content of mental activity and focused on changes in the processes themselves. The possibility, which originates perhaps most clearly in the work of Alice Isen, that emotions influence not only the content of information processing but also the structure of information processing itself, has certainly become important in this area. Thus, a fair number of researchers, particularly those who study persuasion, stereotyping, and decision making, have suggested that certain emotions or certain moods are associated with more or less systematic processing, or more or less bottom-up encoding of information.

2. To what extent, and in what specific ways, has research on cognition/emotion interactions (a) contributed to a better understanding of basic cognitive processes, and (b) changed the way we think about the nature and function of emotions (or "affects" or "moods")?

Paula Niedenthal

In response to (a), I must say that this was the intention of the work that Jamin Halberstadt and I presented in our chapter for this volume. We specifically tried to link work on emotion to the literature on basic processes of categorization and to argue that a full account of categorization requires attention to the idea that emotions serve to organize categories of objects and event in memory.

In their reviews of the manuscript that reports the theory and data in their entirety (Niedenthal, Halberstadt, & Innes-Ker, 1999) categorization researchers were initially very skeptical that emotion belonged anywhere in their models and that the representation and processing of emotion was neither specific nor unique. Existing models of category learning and use could account for the whole story. They seemed to be satisfied with the final story, however. And people who study abstract concepts and decision making are starting to tell me that they are thinking seriously about emotion.

It is hard to imagine that the cognitive community as a whole would be much influenced by the work on emotion and cognition, however. Many cognitive psychologists think that emotion is too vague a concept to work with, and they mostly see emotional states as annoying potential sources of error. I must say that the researchers of cognition/emotion interactions also contribute to this problem. Those of us who have been trained in social and clinical psychology have not always followed carefully enough the research on the basic cognitive processes that we invoke in our models, or presume to be measuring, and thus often do not report work that the cognitive psychologists would ever consider pertinent to them. It seems to me, for example, that many researchers confuse emotion congruence effects themselves with the network model of emotion. There is the effect and there is the model. The effect is predicted by the model for certain responses. The presence of the effect does not actually always provide support for the model because the prediction is made by many accounts. But, more critically, the *absence* of emotion congruence often cannot be interpreted as a failure to support the model. Any time a task is used in which automatic spread of activation is not measured, all bets are off. Take an impression formation task, which measures many cognitive processes, not only priming. If emotion congruent priming does occur, this may or may not be revealed in the impression that is formed. But if emotion congruence is not observed, this fact says absolutely nothing about the possibility that emotions prime emotion-related material in memory. And yet the reasoning in the literature is all over the place. Why should cognitive psychologists care if we can't discuss the emotion network model separately from an emotion congruence effect?

Furthermore, I think we often leave emotion seeming to be an example, and potentially not an interesting one, of another category of cognitive process. Cognitive psychologists do sometimes call emotions just another feature (e.g., of a category), just another cognitive context, just another type of cognitive load, or just another retrieval cue. I am not sure that enough of the work in emotion and cognition has forced cognitive psychologists to take seriously the possibility that emotion processes are fundamental and special.

With regard to (b), I do think that research on emotion/cognition interactions has contributed to how theorists think about the function of emotion. In order to account for changes in processing style during positive and negative moods, several writers (e.g., Schwarz & Bless, 1991) have proposed that positive moods signal that the environment is safe, which triggers the use of heuristic, or top-down, processes. That is, since the environment is safe, there is no reason to scrutinize the environment very carefully. If, on the other hand, negative moods signal the presence of danger or cause for concern, this would perhaps account for the findings that negative moods of some kinds enhance the use of systematic or bottom-up processing. Thus, as emotions theorists have often argued, emotions and moods can in part be thought of as signals about the state of the current environment and the necessity for action.

Barbara Fredrickson (1998) has recently posed the question: what good are positive emotions? In developing her answer, she invokes the work of Alice Isen and others (e.g., Isen, Niedenthal, & Cantor, 1992) on the relation between positive emotions and information processing. The possibility that positive emotions in particular enhance creativity through the priming of distantly associated ideas and through the sometimes novel reorganization of material in memory seems one of many adaptive functions of positive emotions. In general, such emotions are less urgent and longer lasting, and so perhaps exert interesting effects later in the time course of experience than do many negative emotions.

Gordon Bower

Concerning the first part of your question, from my perspective as a cognitive psychologist, there's been precious little influence of emotion research upon theorizing in cognitive psychology, certainly not in publications in the standard cognitive journals. The main cognitive theorists simply have other interests that engage their attention. Emotion receives mention in most cognitive textbooks only briefly as an example of a "context" effect rather like that produced by situational (room) cues. Emotion is also sometimes mentioned in reference to memory enhancement for emotional material, as in "flashbulb" memories. Possibly cognitive researchers have been turned off by replication failures of some of the earlier mood dependent effects on memory, as well as by unresolved controversies about whether emotion helps or hinders memory.

Concerning the second part of your question, my impression is that the change in thinking for people working in the emotion field has been substantial (see my reply to question 1). Regrettably, this sophistication regarding conceptions of emotions has not yet spread beyond our narrow confines into the outer reaches of academic psychology.

Joseph Forgas

I think cognition/emotion research has had a major impact on our understanding of basic cognitive processes. For the first time, affective reactions could be seen as an important and independent source of functional information in realistic information-processing tasks, rather than merely as a source of noise and disturbance in idealized "affect-less" cognition. There have been several accompanying developments that hastened the reincorporation of affect into cognition, such as (a) the growing popularity of functionalist, evolutionary theories of affect, and (b) neuroanatomical evidence indicating the close involvement of affective reactions as a source of adaptive information in complex cognitive processing. Research during the past 20 years also helped to fundamentally change how we think about the nature and functions of emotions. By employing cognitive, information-processing theories, the careful and precise analysis of the role of affective reactions in thinking and behavior became possible for the first time. Rather than seeing affect as a source of irrational, dangerous, and disruptive impulses, as was often the case in much psychological theorizing previously, affect has now been reintegrated into mainstream psychological research.

John Kihlstrom

For cognitive psychology, I think that the most important legacy of cognition/ emotion research has been to bring the study of cognitive processes into closer contact with "the real world." While earlier cognitive psychology (and its predecessor, the study of human learning) tended to be somewhat dry and abstract, with stimulus materials selected either arbitrarily or with an eye toward internal methodological considerations (e.g., holding imagery value or number of syllables constant in a word list), once you start studying emotion you almost inevitably move into the area of personal, social, and cultural meaning. The cognition/emotion interface took us farther from Ebbinghaus and closer to Bartlett, who, you'll remember, proposed that the first thing people remember about an event is their attitude toward it. And the consequence of that was to give cognitive psychology a fuller, richer understanding of how the mind operates.

For the psychology of emotion, I think that the most important legacy of cognition/emotion research has been to raise questions about the independence of affect from cognition. In a very real sense, the "affective revolution" began in 1980, with the appearance of both Gordon Bower's analysis of the mood effects on memory and Bob Zajonc's declaration that "preferences need no inferences." I think that Zajonc overstated his case: in my view, he erred both in identifying "cognition" with the conscious and the deliberate (when in fact some cognitive processes are unconscious and automatic) and in identifying emotion with preferences (when in fact emotions go beyond mere preferences, and preferences can be formed on purely cognitive grounds). But he did issue an important challenge to cognitive psychology, and it may well be that there are certain aspects of our emotional lives in which cognition plays a relatively trivial role.

And if that's the case, cognitive psychology can't provide a complete account of mental life. Nor, by extension, can cognitive science or cognitive neuroscience do so, for the simple reason that, evidently, there's more to mental life than cognition. And it's the dawning awareness that there might be more to mental life than cognition that has led to the development of affective neuroscience. If cognitive science could do it all, then we wouldn't need affective neuroscience. Before we're finished, we'll probably see the development of a conative neuroscience as well, studying motivation independent of both cognition and emotion. And then the question will be whether these interdisciplinary fields really should be proceeding independently of each other. I think that the answer will be negative: they shouldn't proceed independently, and they *can't* proceed independently, because ultimately cognition, emotion, and motivation are inextricably linked.

And when it's all said and done, we'll need a framework for putting the cognitive, affective, and conative neurosciences back together. That framework, of course, is the old discipline of psychology. I've been a member of two different cognitive science programs, but I've always believed that cognitive science didn't do anything that a properly defined psychology couldn't have done on its own, and there are things that psychology can do that cognitive science can't. Cognitive science arose chiefly because psychology, which should have been studying how the mind worked, was mired in functional behaviorism instead. And it's told us a lot about cognition, and there are some things that cognitive science can do which psychology can't—like build machines with their own intelligence. But it's not clear that cognitive science can tell us what we need to know about emotion and motivation, and how cognitive, emotion, and motivation interact to produce behavior in an interpersonal context. Maybe only psychology can do that. And if so, that discovery is one of the byproducts of cognition/emotion research.

3. Generally speaking, are you satisfied with or disappointed by the rate at which the field has progressed?

Joseph Forgas

I would have to say that I am fundamentally satisfied with the achievements of cognition/emotion research during the past two decades. There has been a steady progression of interesting empirical findings, an exemplary development of ever-more sensitive and inclusive theories, and the discovery of important and reliable effects that have widespread practical implications. Many of the most fruitful ideas started out from information-processing cognitive psychology and were concerned with memory effects (e.g., Gordon Bower's work). Inevitably, the kind of robust and universal predictions initially made needed to be qualified and modified as the theories were tested in ever-more complex and realistic circumstances. I know that Gordon was kind of disappointed that his affect priming predictions also proved to be context dependent. Perhaps because of my different background, coming to this from social psychology, I always expected context dependence and was in a way more interested in the puzzle of when and why the effect occurs, and when and why it does not.

Paula Niedenthal

One might ask if this is a field—I am not sure it is. Am I too cynical for this book? I find that often people who are studying cognition/emotion interactions are not the same people as those who are working on emotion or affect, and that communication between the two groups is rather weak. Thus, sometimes developments in emotion research are not incorporated in the interactions work. This seems to me perhaps one reason why the interaction work of some researchers is quite atheoretical. In interactions work, there is often little concern with how emotions are conceptualized, how to manipulate emotions thus conceptualized, or the possible differences among emotions. Furthermore, emotion or mood is often used as an independent variable. That is fun, but the underlying models and, therefore, the predictions, are weak and very vague.

Partly as a consequence of a failure to conceptualize emotion and related constructs, some empirical findings have had a larger impact on theory building than perhaps they should have. As an example, in investigations of the influence of emotion on memory, the typical finding is that happiness enhances access to happy memories. Although the parallel prediction is made for sadness, this effect is not always detected. Rather than asking whether this asymmetry occurs for statistical or experimental reasons, some theorists have gone ahead and interpreted it, arguing that positive and negative emotional states have different effects on memory and coming up with possible reasons why. However, when you look at the results of experiments focusing on the effects of positive and negative emotions on memory, sometimes there actually is a similar effect of the negative mood, but it just does not quite reach an accepted level of significance.

More often, however, the conceptualization of negative mood and the related stimuli is just not well developed, or at least not developed as well as it is for positive mood. That is, there is usually only one positive state induced in the laboratory—happiness—and the effects of this state are examined only on one type of information—happy information. The manipulation of happy mood and the selection or coding of happy material is usually realized experimentally in a reasonable way. With negative states, however, things are more complicated.

Sometimes sadness is induced, sometimes anger, and sometimes a negative state that cannot be categorized as sad or angry. Then the stimuli are used as the dependent variable, or the coding of subject-generated material, are negative in general, and are not clearly associated with the induced state (at least as far as the reader can tell). Sometimes, both the negative state and the related material are just vaguely negative. This means that the effects of positive states are given a much stronger test than are the effects of negative states. Before developing models in which positive and negative emotions have different influences (i.e., one yields mood congruence and the other one doesn't), the states need to be defined and manipulated according the definition. Then stimuli, or systems for coding subject-generated output, have to be equally well matched to the induced states. In my opinion, the tendency to generate theories based on a small number of empirical findings that could be the consequence of the failure to adopt a clear theory or definition is all too common in this area.

There are also effects that have been demonstrated once or twice, or for which there are competing accounts that have never been eliminated, never mind addressed empirically. They sound good and so take on a reality all their own. I think the problem is that people want to have their own models or effects, and not necessarily the best ones. And so there is not enough competitive model testing in this area. The result is a bunch of models that are not even designed to account for the same data. Since they cannot speak directly to each other, there is no way to evaluate different models.

Gordon Bower

I'm pleased about progress in some areas, but disappointed in others. The pleasing aspect is the extension of mood congruence findings into far-reaching domains of social and personality psychology.

The truly disappointing feature for me is the near total lack of more precise computational (or computer simulation) models of the emotional system—of how emotions are triggered, interact with past habits and one another, and produce varieties of performances. Ken Colby's (1976) early simulation work on PARRY still stands as the primary major effort in this respect. Paul Cohen and I made a further stab at the goal (Bower & Cohen, 1982), but Paul earned his PhD and went off into computer science and I hadn't the skills to pursue the matter. Few people seem to have noticed or followed up on the Bower-Cohen chapter. Nico Frijda (1987) and his associates developed circumscribed computer models that recognized several types of emotional situations, but they did little with them. Colby's UCLA student Bill Faught (1978) also wrote interesting computer simulation programs for emotional interactions, but most of this work is still unknown to emotion researchers and the theories have never been critically examined and tested by detailed experimental work (but see Colby, Gould, & Aronson, 1989).

The absence of actual computational models exacts a considerable cost on this field, which is renown for its "fuzziness," partly because the central constructs (emotions) can't be observed and counted directly like responses in a Skinner box. The popular verbal theories of emotion often stumble into apparent conflicts with one another, which provoke debates that quickly degenerate into quagmires of semantic vagueness replete with the slipperiness of everyday language terms—debating whether a given result is due to affect or cognition, whether one comes before the other, whether mood congruence is only semantic or cognitive priming, whether it reflects an automatic or interpretive influence, whether it reflects conscious or unconscious factors, and so on. Not enough researchers recognize the costs exacted on scientific progress by such vague verbal theories. The problem was long ago recognized in mathematical models of learning—Bill Estes (1987) and Doug Hintzman (1991) wrote dire warnings—but that lesson seems not have been taken to heart by emotion theorists (admittedly, including the present author).

Consequently, a number of fundamental issues have still not been resolved and in our present circumstances appear to be unresolvable. Examples are questions such as these:

What exactly is an emotion as distinct from a thought or cognition?

Can one feel an emotion without a corresponding thought?

Can one "be having" an emotion without feeling it, without awareness of it?

How many emotions are there? How are we to decide?

Are some emotions primary and others derivative? How are we to decide that?

How do people's emotional experiences and expressions vary with their cultural or familial upbringing that's taught them how (or how not) to talk and think about their emotions?

Do people really remember emotional feelings directly or only covert memories that restimulate those emotions in the present?

Why exactly do emotional thoughts reverberate longer than unemotional ones, and why are they harder to suppress?

How are we to understand phenomena surrounding "dissociation" from emotional feelings, about "numbing" of emotions? How are we to understand alexithymia?

Can people feel several emotions at one time? Or do they just rapidly shift their attention among different causal antecedents (e.g., when witnessing a beating, feeling distressed when attending to the victim and angry when attending to the bully)?

Can we have blended emotions?

Which emotions amplify or inhibit which other emotions?

And that's just a small list. Does anyone see any real prospects for genuine answers to such questions in the coming decade? I am fairly skeptical. Consider just one example: we had formerly believed that the research of Paul Ekman (1989, 1992) on universal facial expressions of emotions could be used to resolve questions regarding innate primary emotions and their universality. But Jim Russell (1994) has provided a trenchant methodological critique of that earlier cross-cultural work, raising doubts about Ekman's interpretation and conclusions. Although Ekman (1994) has tried to counterargue Russell's critique, the issue is far from resolved and still posted on the research agenda.

Another disappointment to me is that laboratory emotion researchers have yet to fully exorcise the demon called "experimenter demand." It is an albatross, a bugaboo that, no matter how often it has been discounted in previous work, nevertheless continually arises to haunt our every step along the research path. Practically every mood induction used in the laboratory has the potential for introducing either experimenter demand (e.g., for the subject to "play the role" of a depressed person) or some variety of unwanted cognitions (e.g., an experimenter-contrived failure causes the subject to believe he is more similar to, and thus more attracted to, others who fail). Such unintended factors can confound the interpretation of the mood effects.

A small methodological advance on this problem capitalizes on "natural occurring" emotions by questioning unsuspecting people just after they've experienced an emotional event—sports fans just after their team wins or loses a match, cinema-goers after a comedy or tragedy, and so on. But these methods carry their own problems, including the fact that contact with the respondent is necessarily brief and one-shot, and that the emotions are evoked emphatically and are not quite "real" (e.g., viewers know that the movie stalker is not about to kill them).

As a curmudgeon in this field, I may perhaps be permitted a perogative to issue the standard lament, that some of my critics seem not to have familiarized themselves sufficiently with my former writings on cognition and emotion. I would estimate that about 90% of the criticism of my cognition/emotion theorizing has taken aim solely at my early *American Psychologist* article (Bower, 1981). But they fail to note that I was delivering an award speech at an American Psychological Association (APA) convention, during which time pressures require speakers to simplify rather than exhaustively cover all aspects of the topic and elaborate its complexities.

A more extensive treatment was provided in the Bower and Cohen (1982) chapter, which I mentioned earlier. That chapter anticipated and tried to respond to several deficiencies and potential criticisms of the simple theory advanced in my APA speech—indeed, several that were later discovered by our critics. To illustrate, the network theory in the APA speech has often been criticized for not making a distinction between "hot" versus "cold" uses of emotion, between talking about versus feeling emotions. Yet exactly that distinction (between words, concepts, and bodily referents) was discussed and modeled in the Bower and Cohen chapter. The distinction is completely parallel to the manner in which associative networks have dealt with distinctions between action terms (walk, grasp, press space-bar, turn 90-degrees left), their corresponding concepts, and a command to execute that action by the control system (e.g., the model of typing developed by Norman and Rumelhart, 1975; the internal knowledge base of any of the robot systems that execute external actions). Obviously, one needs a goal-based control system that can activate different productions depending on its temporary "goal"—whether that be talking cooly about the concept of fear or noticing conditions and then activating the emotion itself (feeling fear now). The APA speech has been similarly criticized for not dealing with antecedents of emotions, although time limitations confined my speech to dealing only with some consequences of emotional arousal. Antecedents were discussed in the Bower and Cohen chapter, and in a chapter published in the later *Handbook of Emotion and Memory* (Bower, 1992).

John Kihlstrom

I'll confine my comments to the memory literature, which Eric Eich and I recently reviewed for a conference sponsored by the NIH Office of Behavioral and Social Science Research (Kihlstrom, Eich, Sandbrand, & Tobias, 2000). Here we have the oldest, most-studied aspect of the emotion cognition interface. We know a great deal about it, but there is still a great deal that we don't know.

One area where we have made genuine progress has to do with mood dependent memory, which has experienced a genuine reversal of fortune. It can be predicted on theoretical grounds, having to do with Tulving and Thomson's (1973) principle of encoding specificity, that mood should have state-dependent effects on memory, just as many centrally acting drugs do. Gordon Bower and his colleagues (Bower, 1981; Bower, Monteiro, & Gilligan, 1978) initially demonstrated the effect, in studies that really got research on the cognition/emotion interface going, and which, in my judgment, sparked the "affective revolution" in psychology. But later, Bower (1987; Bower & Mayer, 1989) expressed doubts about the phenomenon, and it fell into a kind of disrepute. But now, Eric Eich and his colleagues (Eich, 1995; Eich, Macaulay, & Ryan, 1994) have demonstrated the phenomenon convincingly. It's a relatively weak effect, but all such effects on human memory are relatively weak, regardless of whether they involve emotional states, drug states, or environmental context. The progress is that we can now believe in the effect again. But there are other effects that haven't shown that kind of progress.

The oldest reported effect of emotion on memory is the affective valence effect: material associated with a positive emotional valence is remembered better than material associated with a negative valence. More than 50 years ago, David Rapaport (1942) reviewed this literature in the context of Freud's theory of repression, and Matlin and Stang (1979), following Boucher and Osgood (1969), called it the "Pollyanna Principle." The claim makes a great deal of sense, intuitively, and especially if you are something of a Freudian, but it's still controversial. In particular, Banaji and Hardin (1994) showed that when you control for the intensity of affect represented by the stimulus, the affective valence effect disappears. Put another way, on average, positive items seem to be more arousing than negative ones, and it's this intensity of arousal, not its direction, that determines memory. We need more research to determine whether there is an affective valence effect on memory, independent of affective intensity.

A second area that deserves more research is the effect of emotion on the allocation of cognitive resources. Henry Ellis and his colleagues (Ellis & Ashbrook, 1989; Ellis, Thomas, & Rodriguez, 1984) have argued that depression increases a person's information-processing load, and thus impairs performance on effortful memory tasks, but not automatic ones. I think the empirical point is now pretty well established, but as I noted in a commentary on Ellis'work (Kihlstrom, 1989), the mechanisms underlying the effect remain open to question. For example, does depression, as an emotional mood state, drain cognitive resources directly, or is it the person's thoughts about being depressed that do the draining? Or is the impairment in effortful cognitive processing just a by-product of low levels of motivation, and not really a resource allocation effect at all? Is the effect specific to depression, or do other emotional states also drain resources?

A third area has to do with mood congruent effects on memory. These are pretty well established, but again I think we need to know more details—for example, comparing the effects of mood congruence on encoding with its effects on retrieval. But it has also been proposed that there are mood incongruent effects on memory—for example, that being happy makes sad events stand out in memory (see Keuler & Safer, 1998; Parrott & Sabini, 1990). Mood incongruence might seem to contradict mood congruence, but in fact there is a precedent. Long ago, Reid Hastie (1981) resolved the controversy over Bartlettian schematic effects on memory by showing that memory favors both schema congruent and schema incongruent material—the first mediated by cues generated at the time of retrieval, the second by elaboration at the time of encoding. By analogy, mood congruence might occur because mood itself functions as a retrieval cue, while mood incongruence might occur because of a kind of contrast between the emotional valence of the event and the valence of the person's background mood. But all this is hypothesis, and I think we need a more determined effort to see whether mood incongruent memory actually occurs.

4. How do you see the area of cognition and emotion developing over, say, the next 10 or 20 years? What problems are most important to pursue?

John Kihlstrom

In addition to resolving the leftover problems of emotion and memory just discussed, and problems of emotion and thought (as represented by Gordon Bower and Joe Forgas, and by Paula Niedenthal and Jamin Halberstadt, in their contributions to this volume), I'd like to see more work done on the perceptual side. Niedenthal and Kitayama (1994) have done a great service by reviving, in their book, the whole question of whether, how, and to what extent emotion can influence "lower" cognitive processes such as perception, as well as "higher" cognitive processes such as memory and thought. But I think that they'd be the first to say that they've only broken the surface here, and there's lots more to be done.

Joseph Forgas

I think cognition/emotion research is likely to be influenced by two major factors during the next 10 years. The first is the very rapid advances being made in neuropsychology and neuroanatomy, which should help us better understand the interaction between affective and cognitive functions. The second area that I think will be interesting is the more precise exploration of how affective states and different information-processing strategies interact. I think much of the existing research up to now was concerned with unidirectional relationships—the exploration of how affect influences cognition, and how cognition influences affect (appraisal theories). There is now strong evidence that positive and negative affective states produce very different information-processing strategies, although there is not yet clear agreement as to the mechanisms responsible for this. I think the stage is just about set for theories that will start looking at emotion and cognition in a genuinely interactive, dynamic way. For example, it is possible that continuous and gradual shifts in information-processing style (leading to either mood congruence or incongruence) are a key element in how people control and manage everyday mood fluctuations. So we do know that different affective states produce different processing strategies, and we also know that different processing strategies produce different levels of affect infusion and mood congruence. If we put these two ideas together, we may be on the way toward developing genuinely interactive, dynamic cognition/emotion theories. I think such an interactive cognition/emotion system has obvious evolutionary, adaptive characteristics that we are only just beginning to appreciate.

Gordon Bower

Joe's answer is just fine except I would add that I think the issue of unconscious emotions, which John Kihlstrom and his associates pursued earlier in this book, will come increasingly to the forefront.

Paula Niedenthal

I think that this area will be and has to be informed by, as well as be prepared to inform, advances in the cognitive sciences and neurosciences. We do not have to develop biological models—we can leave that for the neuroscientists—but I think our models have to be informed by their data, just as their progress should be informed by our theories and empirical research. Similarly, computer scientists and other cognitive scientists may lead us down some roads that are dead ends because much of the complexity of emotion cannot be accounted for with their methods (at least for now). But they will engage in the simulation and modeling of large quantities of data that our models and methods cannot handle. In addition, whatever insights that dynamical systems models reveal about emotion is likely to be seriously interesting and important for us to consider. Since emotions have time courses and may be considered self-organizing systems, it is clear that such approaches will be useful.

Cognition/emotion research is plagued by the problem that it is not clear what is the emotion, what is its antecedent, and what are the cognitive consequences. This is a problem that will have to be addressed in future research using these approaches.

A related difficulty is that sometimes stimuli used to measure the cognitive process of interest also temporarily or even permanently affect emotional state. I recently completed some experiments on emotion and the perception of facial expression of emotion with a doctoral student, Ase Innes-Ker. Our finding were influenced by the fact that the face stimuli altered the momentary emotional states of the subjects, something I should have anticipated, given my own past work on emotion and perception (e.g., Niedenthal, 1992). But our theories were not really ready to handle the interactions between emotional state and momentary emotional reaction in a way that could provide us with confident predictions.

5. *In terms of clinical issues, it seems that much current research on cognition/ emotion interactions is only tangentially related to the sorts of problems that clinicians deal with on a daily basis. As basic-research scientists, do we—should we—have a responsibility to do work that is more directly relevant to clinical concerns? Or should we continue to follow the lines of investigation that are suggested by our latest results? In either case, as basic researchers, what can we offer to clinicians—and their clients—who have to confront real-life, hot-button issues, like exhuming "repressed" memories?*

Joseph Forgas

Personally, I don't think that there is anything wrong with pursuing theoretically driven research programs even if these projects have no immediate relevance to practical concerns, such as clinical problems. In any case, whatever we can contribute to understanding the links between affect and cognition will inevitably have some implications for clinical work on mood disorders as well. I think there has already been a pretty impressive record of cross-fertilization of ideas between laboratory-based experimental work—for example, on mood dependence in memory—and clinical research.

Gordon Bower

I think the relevance of our kind of cognition/emotion laboratory research to clinical problems is recognized by some clinical researchers, such as Andrew Mathews, Colin MacLeod, John Teasdale, Richard McNally, Edna Foa, Susan Mineka, David Barlow, Fraser Watts, Chris Brewin, Tim Dalgleish, and Ian Gotlib, to mention just a few (see Barlow, 1997; Brewin, 1997; Brewin, Dalgleish, & Joseph, 1996; Foa & Hearst-Ikeda, 1996; Gotlib & MacLeod, 1997; Kuyken & Dalgleish, 1995; MacLeod, 1996; Mathews & MacLeod, 1994; McNally, 1994; Mineka & Nugent, 1995; Teasdale & Barnard, 1993; Watts, 1995). Some of that work is reviewed in the chapter that Joe Forgas and I wrote for this book. Their research often runs parallel to the laboratory findings, but has the added complication that different "neurotic" populations have considerably different milieu exposures, probably different initial temperaments and upbringing, differential practice using the vocabulary of their disorder, differential elaboration of their conceptual networks, and so on. Moreover, comorbidity between depression and anxiety disorders is a major complication for interpreting results as due to one or the other emotional complex, as are complications introduced by associated drug abuse or medications.

We may sincerely hope that our laboratory research on emotional control would stimulate discovery of novel therapeutic methods for treating mood disorders. However, the history of innovations in psychotherapy suggests other-wise: ingenious clinicians devise one or another novel application of a known principle (e.g., extinction by evoking competing responses; contingency con-tracts) whose success is then evaluated and received with acclaim if it proves to be somewhat successful in the clinic. For example, techniques of the now-popular cognitive behavior therapy arose from the clinical methods tried out by Albert Ellis (1962) and Tim Beck (1967, 1976) with practically no direct influ-ence from laboratory research. I predict that our future will replicate the past in this regard.

Regarding Eric's question about the nature of "exhumed memories," emo-tion researchers have made several contributions to those discussions (e.g., Bower & Sivers, 1998; Christianson, 1992; de Rivera, 1998; Kihlstrom, 1996; Lindsay & Read, 1994; Schooler & Eich, in press). But the main issues to be sorted out regard the clinical "facts" of the matter and what mechanisms we have in cognitive theories of memory to explain how memories unavailable at one time may become available later, and why this may be especially likely to happen with negatively charged memories (see Bower, 1990).

Paula Niedenthal

I think we have to be clear what we are basic researchers *of*. As I implied previously, I do not think that people should be quick to generalize from studies of manipulated emotions to clinical issues (e.g., affective disorders) just as we should not draw simple conclusions from work on phobia, depression, or chronic anxiety when trying to model the influences of state emotion on cognition. However, the two areas should proceed in an interacting way because each has something to say to the other.

John Kihlstrom

This is another area that it's really important to pursue. As I noted earlier, the cognitive/emotion interface helped connect cognitive psychology to the real world, and the laboratory to the clinic. But I think that, for the most part, the transfer between laboratory and clinic has been unidirectional. That is to say, there has been a lot of transfer from the lab to the clinic, as any reading of the literature on cognitive-behavioral therapy will show. But now I think it's time for laboratory psychologists to take up, more fully and more deliberately, prob-lems that are raised first and foremost in the clinic.

For example, what is the clinical significance of mood congruent memory? The effect is clearly present in the laboratory, but how important is it, really, in real life—including real life in the clinic? Some researchers and theorists have cautioned that mood congruence may distort autobiographical memory—

for example, biasing depressed patients to remember unpleasant rather than pleasant experiences or, perhaps, to reconstruct events in a negative manner. On the other hand, Brewin and his associates (Brewin, Andrews, & Gotlib, 1993) have concluded that the evidence for this proposition is inconsistent and unconvincing. If they're right, then we need to obtain better evidence on this matter one way or the other. The issue is an important one to resolve, and resolve fairly quickly, because of the effect it can have on clinical practice.

Another critical issue is whether traumatic stress can have special effects on memory. In general, the finding from the laboratory is that emotional valence enhances memory, presumably by making events more salient and distinctive. But at least since the time of Janet and Freud, there have also been claims that emotional trauma can impair memory through a process of dissociation or repression. More recently, the Janet/Freud proposal has been revived by proponents of the trauma-memory argument and recovered-memory therapy. These theorists, such as Bessel van der Kolk (1994; Van der Kolk & van der Hart, 1991), essentially reject the laboratory evidence as irrelevant to clinical practice and rely on clinical studies to claim that traumatic memories fail to be integrated into the normal stream of consciousness and express themselves instead through fragmentary images, inexplicable feelings, involuntary behaviors, and somatic changes.

Katharine Shobe and I recently reviewed a number of the most prominent of these claims and found them to be both internally inconsistent and inadequately supported by the evidence (Shobe & Kihlstrom, 1997). Even the clinical evidence cited in support of them isn't very good. Yet the controversy continues and it has spilled over into the courts, where individuals who claim to have recovered memories of sexual and physical abuse have brought charges against the alleged perpetrators. And so judges and juries increasingly have to sort through the laboratory and clinical evidence and deal with presentations by opposing "experts." It's important to get this issue resolved one way or the other. And the only way to do this, in my view, is to get clinicians to collaborate with experimental psychologists to produce methodologically adequate clinical studies.

QUESTIONS FOR GORDON BOWER AND JOSEPH FORGAS

6. Your chapter begins with a review of the history and current status of Gordon's network theory of emotions, and then moves on to a detailed account of Joe's affect infusion model (AIM). Do you see your respective views as being complementary? To the extent that they're different, can they be reconciled?

Gordon Bower and Joseph Forgas

From our perspective, we see no difficulty at all in reconciling the network theory and the affect infusion model. Indeed, the AIM was developed in direct response to growing evidence in the literature at the time that there are important boundary conditions that regulate mood congruence in cognition. Whereas one of us (Bower) moved toward emphasizing things like causal belonging, the other (Forgas) thought that the critical requirement for the affect priming theory to work is that people must engage in genuinely constructive, generative processing strategies where affectively primed information has a good chance to be incidentally used. Forgas moved in this direction because (a) he was always sensitive to the highly constructive nature of social cognitive tasks, where mood congruence was more reliably obtained, and (b) people like Fiedler (1991) explicitly drew attention to a processing dichotomy, contrasting constructive versus nonconstructive processing. In a sense, all that the AIM does is to emphasize and systematize the contextual circumstances within which substantive, constructive processing is most likely, and when affect priming effects should be most reliably obtained. In short, we see the AIM (Forgas, 1995) as being completely consistent with and complementary to the affect priming principle, as instantiated in the original network theory of emotions (Bower, 1981).

7. My impression is that neither the updated network model nor the AIM would expect reliable mood effects to emerge in the performance of automatic, data-driven, fast-paced tasks like lexical decision or word naming. Yet this is just what Paula and her colleagues have found in a series of recent studies (several of which are reviewed in her chapter). What do you make of this, and are you inclined to revise your theories accordingly?

Joseph Forgas

I don't see Paula's results as necessarily being inconsistent with the fundamental implications of priming theories—and thus, the affect infusion model. Indeed, what is really surprising is that others have not found such effects more reliably. The way I see it, lexical decision and word naming, even though fast-paced and data-driven tasks, nevertheless do involve an element of constructive processing, in the sense of "going beyond the information given" to produce a response. They are also constructive in the sense that performance on similar kinds of tasks has been previously shown to be sensitive to various context effects and even semantic priming effects. The fact that a task is fast and almost automatic does not mean that it cannot at the same time be constructive; that is, I would not define "constructive" as necessarily meaning only high-level, inferential thinking. To take another example, in a study done with Gordon (Forgas, Bower,

& Krantz, 1984), we found significant mood priming effects on rapid on-line judgments of observed behaviors. This task is in some ways similar to Paula's— fast, automatic, and apparently stimulus-driven—yet at the same time, responses are essentially constructive.

Nevertheless, I can understand that you may feel that I am pushing the notion of "constructive" too far here. Perhaps there is a need to distinguish between high-level, inferential construction (as in a social judgment) and the kind of construction involved in front-end cognition as demonstrated by Paula's work. To my mind, the similarities (i.e., needing to go beyond the information given to produce a response) are just as important as the differences.

Gordon Bower

The network theory of spreading activation has always expected a "top-down" influence of strong emotion on perceptual processing of strongly associated words (see Bower, 1981). Its prediction here arises for the same reason that semantic priming arose in John Morton's (1969) old logogen theory (for an update, see Bower, 1996). The emotion spreads a little activation onto those strongly associated words in advance of the input stimulus arriving, thus making them more readily available (to cross threshold) given minimal stimulus input. This theory expects all manner of word priming measures to reveal emotional congruence effects: perceptual identification, reading speed, word-fragment and picture-fragment completion, word associations, lexical decisions, resolving the meaning of ambiguous homophones (e.g., *die* vs. *dye*; *pain* vs. *pane*), and so on.

Postman and Brown (1952) had earlier demonstrated allied effects in the tachistoscopic identification of success versus failure words after subjects had received a success versus failure manipulation. The problem is that the first several attempts we made to verify the prediction failed. Richard Gerrig and I found no mood congruent enhancement in perceptual identification of pleasant versus unpleasant words following the induction of happiness or anger (Gerrig & Bower, 1982). I knew, too, of a similar pattern of partial successes and failures of mood congruence across several experiments on perceptual identification found (though not published) by Professor Michelle Millis of San Jose State University in the mid-1980s. Later, I found no mood congruence when subjects judged whether or not two words agreed in their pleasantness or unpleasantness. David Clark and his colleagues (Clark, Teasdale, Broadbent, & Martin, 1983) found no mood congruence in lexical decisions regarding pleasant and unpleasant words. Ian Gotlib and McCann (1984) found no emotional congruence in Stroop interference (color naming) following the induction of sad moods in normal subjects, confirming earlier unpublished, negative findings that Jerry Clore and I had obtained in 1981. So the problem became one of explaining why the emotional congruence effect did not arise as predicted. It was in that unrelentingly negative environment that I reluctantly (and tentatively) suggested that perhaps emotional effects did not operate on well-practiced, automatic perceptual processes such as word perception.

In their chapter in this volume, Paula Niedenthal and Jamin Halberstadt have materially advanced the analysis by noting that perhaps emotion congruence in perception is a genuine phenomenon, but the words have to be selected with far more specificity to the exact emotion induced beforehand. They noted that the earlier failures had used mainly pools of undifferentiated positive and negative words. Accordingly, their experiments used specifically happy and sad words as stimulus materials following happy and sad mood inductions, and indeed found significant mood congruence in word identification and in lexical decision. Thus, a sad mood induction enhanced perceptual processing of a word like *depressed* but not more remote (unpleasant) associates such as *doom* or *debacle*.

While these recent results are most welcome, I am still left to wonder why there weren't at least some small effects in the several earlier experiments (mentioned above) that averaged over pools of affective words which, of course, included synonyms for the induced happy, angry, or sad moods. The new results could be accommodated in the network theory by supposing that activation from the mood spreads appreciably (enough to be noticed in these behavior measures) only for words very highly associated to the specific emotion. But that is indeed a lame explanation of the variety of results.

QUESTION FOR GORDON BOWER

8. Intuitively, it seems that once a particular mood has taken effect, it tends to linger for quite a while and to change much less quickly that any of the specific ideas, images, or recollections that it may trigger by virtue of prior association. Can (or does) the network model accommodate this observation?

Yes, I agree: real arousal of an intense emotion usually produces an aftereffect that lasts for many minutes. The reason is obvious and has been known for at least 75 years: strong emotional reactions are accompanied by neuroendocrinal discharges (e.g., adrenaline, norepinephrine) that circulate in the blood stream and provide a persisting discharge and tonus within the sympathetic nervous system (see Bower, 1992). These endocrine changes probably also lead to short-term changes in the supply of various biogenic amines in the brain (dopamine, epinephrine). These cholinergic biochemicals continue to have a biological impact for many minutes, at least until they are metabolized out of the bloodstream.

This biological observation can be rendered into our psychological model by a correspondent assumption: once an emotion node is turned on (e.g., by re-membering or recognizing a fearful scene), it has a long life due to a very slow decay rate compared to the "cognitive, ideational" nodes that provide cognitive representations of the ideas, images, and propositions that fill the working memory of the mental system. Such emotion nodes are embedded in a cognitive architecture which must assume that activation on nonemotional concepts and propositions in working memory is quenched or decays rapidly (150 ms?), as soon as the flow of ideational thought moves on to another associated idea or proposition. The result of this slower decay rate is that the emotional subject is capable of fleetingly thinking over a collection of many emotionally congruent ideas and memories all during the course of a single episode of emotional arousal. That, at least, is a first rough sketch of how I would try to model the distinction in duration between thoughts and emotional arousal.

QUESTION FOR JOSEPH FORGAS

9. Though AIM is chiefly concerned with mood congruent effects, it seems relevant to mood dependent effects as well. As an example, suppose that happy and sad subjects are asked to read about and form impressions of fictitious individuals who seems rather ordinary or quite odd. From your earlier work, one would expect stronger mood congruence in the subjects' judgments of the odd as opposed to the ordinary targets, because the former are more amenable to high affect infusion than are the latter. Now suppose that the subjects are later asked to freely recall as many of the targets as possible, and that testing takes place in either the original or the alternative mood. My hunch is that a change in mood state would have a greater adverse impact on the recall of the odd targets. More generally, it may be that mood dependent effects are most likely to emerge in a robust and reliable manner when both the encoding and the retrieval task are conducive to high affect infusion; high infusion at either encoding or retrieval alone won't work. What do you think?

I think this is a really interesting issue. It is correct to suggest that the AIM was initially developed to account for the observed presence or absence of mood congruence in social judgmental tasks, so mood dependence was of less importance initially.

However, the logic of the model clearly predicts that all affect priming effects—both mood congruence and mood dependence—should be more reliably obtained whenever more constructive processing is required to deal with a task. So it follows that mood dependent effects should also be enhanced whenever both the encoding and the retrieval tasks are conducive to constructive processing, as Eric suggests. In fact, we have found some evidence indicating just such a pattern in several of our studies, even though we have never attempted to independently manipulate the kind of processing used at the encoding and at the retrieval stage. An ideal experiment to test this hypothesis would be one where the level of substantive processing used is separately manipulated at encoding and retrieval; we could then predict that overall mood dependence in recall should be an additive function of the degree of constructive processing at both stages. As far as I know, this has not been done before. However, we did have some indications that more constructive processing of more complex or problematic targets at the encoding stage does in fact result in superior recall (e.g., Forgas, 1992, 1995, 1998).

QUESTIONS FOR PAULA NIEDENTHAL

10. Referring back to question 7, which was posed to Gordon and Joe, why do you think that you've had success in demonstrating emotional effects on perceptual kinds of tasks, while others haven't?

I think the main reason is the very reason that motivated the research in the first place. We believed (and believe) that the spread of activation from an emotion node is likely to be detectable only for closely related information. The number of, say, positive words is enormous, and we did not think that any reasonable model would predict that a state of happiness would detectably prime all positive words, or that any negative state would detectably prime all negative words. I have talked to a number of psycholinguists who say they would be very suspicious of findings that a state of sadness detectably facilitated recognition of all negative words. Perhaps more sensitive paradigms could show this, but not our present lexical decision and word naming tasks.

Of course, I am not the only one to find emotion congruence in these low-level tasks. The British group has also observed these effects (e.g., Mathews & MacLeod, 1986; Mogg, Mathews, & Weinman, 1989). However, at least two conditions are always met: the emotions and stimuli are closely matched, and the emotional states are strong (and pure).

But there is still a potential problem, which I mentioned in response to another question. Several years ago (Niedenthal, 1992), I reviewed models (e.g., Solley & Murphy, 1960) in which the idea was clearly put forth that the percept can change the emotional state of the perceiver, which in turn can affect operations on the percept in real time. This is where we have to go in understanding emotion and perception, especially when looking at emotional faces and other social stimuli. There will be changes in or interactions with ambient state caused by the stimuli of interest.

11. Your first set of studies showed strikingly specific effects of emotional state on word perception: happy subjects responded faster than sad subjects to happy words (either in making lexical decisions or in naming the words aloud), and conversely, sad subjects responded faster than happy subjects to sad words (again in both the lexical decision and word naming tasks). In contrast, your second set of studies showed an equally striking but general effect of emotional state on categorization: subjects who are feeling either happy or sad put together both happy and sad items on the basis of their perceived emotional similarity to a much greater extent than do subjects who are experiencing a neutral mood. Would you care to elaborate on why these different patterns might have emerged?

In the first place, the word perception tasks (especially word naming) used in the previous work are supposed to assess automatic processes (priming in this case). In contrast, the categorization tasks measure probably several processes, some of which are attentional processes (but not necessarily automatic ones). If emotions automatically prime related material, we should expect to see this in word perception tasks—and we did in five studies (involving either lexical decision or word naming). Emotions are also thought to be associated with attention to emotionally evocative elements in the world (according to most emotion theorists). This is not only a brief or automatic effect but a functional consequence of being in an emotional state. The attention to emotionally evocative stimuli and the emotional interpretations or features of external and internal stimuli (and nowhere is the argument that this attention is directed to emotionally congruent information) led us to predict a general attention to emotional features or meanings and thus a general emotion categorization effect.

Furthermore, we were influenced in this prediction by our many categorization colleagues. In their models (e.g., Nosofsky, 1992; Smith & Zarate, 1992), sensitization to a "dimension" yields uniform attention to the entire "dimension" (in quotes because this is based on multidimensional scaling language, not to be confused with the notion of a dimensional vs. categorical account of emotional experience). Thus, if someone's attention is drawn to two colors during categorization training, it is the dimension of color, and not just the particular colors involved in training, that will be used in a subsequent categorization task.

Of course, both processes can operate. We have recently completed experiments in which subjects in happy and sad states performed the triad categorization task, described in our chapter, either under substantial time pressure or under no time pressure. The expectation was that there is a time course to these two effects, and that emotion congruence in categorization can be observed under conditions of time pressure due to the facilitated encoding of emotion congruent material. Emotion congruent categorization is the tendency by individuals in happy states to group together happy things, but not sad things, and for sad subjects to group together sad things, but not happy things, more than do control subjects.

Under conditions of no time pressure, we replicated the typical result of enhanced emotional response categorization by subjects in induced emotional states. In addition, we found that time-pressured subjects in both emotion conditions also grouped together happy concepts more than did control subjects. However, for the sad concepts, emotion congruence emerged. Under time pressure, sad individuals grouped together sad concepts more than did happy or control subjects (which did not differ between themselves). Although we are pursuing these findings further, we suspect that the difference in the findings for happy and sad triads has to do with the speed with which positive versus negative information is encoded, regardless of emotional state. As the word-recognition results reported in chapter 4 showed, words with a positive meaning are processed very quickly. Perhaps because of this basic feature of positive information, emotion congruence in the categorization of items related to happiness cannot be easily detected; the triad task is not as sensitive to encoding speed as are other tasks. On the other hand, it appeared that sad concepts were more likely to be grouped together by sad subjects. Because sad information is processed more slowly (as our word recognition work also showed), it isn't surprising that we had a greater chance to detect the influence of the automatic spread of activation in the triad task.

In any event, the first study in this new line of research suggests that tasks which assess the automatic spread of activation, and tasks which assess selective attention to features of experimenter-provided stimuli, tap into processes that are influenced in different ways by emotional states.

12. Though you clearly favor a categorical as opposed to a dimensional conceptualization of emotions, is this preference critical for understanding your current data and for planning your future research on emotional coherence?

I think that when appropriate methods are used, categorical and dimensional accounts of the subjective experience of emotion will both be supported (and they are). I also think they are not opposed to each other but reflect different methods, measures, and statistical techniques and are sensitive to different processes.

However, with available methods and tasks, at least those we use, I suspect that often the categorical organization of cognitive material can be detected more reliably. My research is guided by the model because I am convinced by the data suggesting that there are categorical emotions. However, with regard to conceptual coherence, I think the question of whether emotional response categories are grounded in the basic emotions is an empirical question. In the end, perhaps there will be either situations or people for whom the valence grouping is preferred. I am thinking here of Lisa Feldman Barrett's (Feldman, 1995a, 1995b) work showing that some people represent their emotions internally in terms of categories while others really favor a valence representation. This may or may not be true for emotional response categories, but Lisa and I are addressing this question in collaborative research.

QUESTIONS FOR JOHN KIHLSTROM

13. In your chapter, you cite several studies using the mere exposure effect to alter affective judgments for particular stimuli and interpret their results as evidence of implicit emotion. But there's also evidence that mere exposure strongly influences judgments that are not ostensibly emotional in nature (e.g., stimulus brightness or perceived exposure duration). Does this concern you in any way?

First, that's not exactly what we say. We cite the mere exposure studies as evidence for emotion as an expression of implicit memory or implicit perception. In the mere exposure studies, I am assuming that the feeling state of "liking something" is consciously accessible, even if the current or past events giving rise to that feeling state are not.

Still, your point is well taken, and a lot of my argument relies on the assumption that the mere exposure effects on liking are emotional in nature. In one of the studies you're referring to, George Mandler and his colleagues (Mandler, Nakamura, & Van Zandt, 1987) questioned that assumption. They found that mere exposure enhanced judgments of lightness and darkness as well as of liking. Their point was that there was nothing inherently emotional about the effects of mere exposure, but that exposure produced a priming effect that facilitated performance on any stimulus-relevant task. This argument doesn't bother me too much, because I don't share Zajonc's view that the effects of exposure on emotion are direct, unmediated by "higher level" cognitive processes. And that's the view that Mandler et al. were attacking. Rather, I tend to think that exposure effects are attributional in nature: priming produces an experience of fluency, or availability, that is then interpreted in terms of liking (or whatever). This is in line with the general view, which I think Mandler shares to some degree, that emotional states can occur as a product of cognitive activity. But once you've made the judgment that you like a nonsense polygon, or a

Turkish word, or whatever, that judgment, and the feelings arising from it, probably tends to stick. In the "subliminal" case, it's still an emotional response (albeit one based on an attributional judgment) whose source is an event perceived outside of awareness—emotion as implicit perception. Frankly, I think that Mandler et al. scored some points with their study, which may be one reason why there's been so little response to it. One exception has been Seamon, McKenna, and Binder (1998), who attempted to confirm the findings of Mandler and his colleagues. Apparently at the suggestion of Bob Zajonc, Mandler et al. (1987) had also tried to show that priming could enhance judgments of disliking as well as of liking—that would have really clinched the attributional case. That didn't quite work: the priming effect on disliking was in the right direction, but not significant. Seamon et al. (1998) essentially repeated the Mandler et al. (1987) study and got priming effects on both liking and disliking judgments, but not on judgments of brightness and darkness. Their finding qualifies the attributional story somewhat, but the more important point was that it took 7 years, from 1980 to 1987, for anyone to put Zajonc's mere exposure hypothesis to a critical test, and another 11 years, from 1987 to 1998, for anyone to follow up on the results of that test. One of our purposes in writing this chapter is to get more people working on this problem so we can find out what's what.

14. Phil Merikle and his associates (Merikle, 1992; Merikle & Daneman, 1998; Merikle & Joordens, 1997) have argued that the most convincing evidence for unconscious (subliminal) perception comes from studies showing qualitative—not just quantitative—differences in task performance when a stimulus is presented above as opposed to below the subjective threshold of awareness. By extension, is there any evidence that unconscious emotions are qualitatively distinct from their conscious counterparts?

This is a reasonable position to take, though I sometimes think (though not in Merikle's case) that the requirement of a qualitative difference is an act of desperation by researchers and theorists who are made nervous by talk of consciousness, awareness, and other mentalistic constructs. Often, I think, it's a holdover from behaviorism, a reflection of what the philosopher Owen Flanagan (1991) has called "positivistic reserve." And it can lead us into trouble if we make a fetish of it.

Consider a lesson from the history of implicit memory. The distinction between explicit and implicit memory, as it was originally formulated, was essentially phenomenal: implicit memory was reflected in the effect of a past event on experience, thought, or action in the absence of conscious recollection of that event. But cognitive psychologists don't like self-reports of awareness—even though, if you think about it, virtually all of cognitive psychology is based on people's self-reports of what they perceive, think, and remember. And so they proposed additional criteria for implicit memory, such as independence of level of processing. If explicit memory is affected by level of processing, but implicit memory is not, that's a qualitative difference that makes some people feel more comfortable about using the language of consciousness. But it turns out that implicit memory *is* affected by level of processing, although the effect is weaker than the corresponding effect on explicit memory (Brown & Mitchell, 1994; Challis & Brodbeck, 1992). And even that quantitative dissociation is questionable, because levels-of-processing studies of implicit memory have been almost exclusively confined to repetition priming, which may require only shallow, perceptual processing at the time of encoding. Semantic priming counts as implicit memory, too, and it would be surprising if semantic priming were independent of levels of processing, because it would seem to require semantic processing at the time of encoding.

The same lesson could be drawn from the history of automaticity. In the beginning some theorists had the notion that some perceptual and cognitive processes were executed involuntarily, without any conscious intention on the part of the person. But I suspect that this sole criterion for automaticity, which seems to rely on self-reports of what subjects intended to do, made them nervous. As a result, theorists piled on other criteria—for example, that automatic processes consume no attentional capacity. But again, it turns out that automatic processes do consume attentional capacity (e.g., Logan, 1997; Pashler, 1998). This shouldn't have surprised anyone, because the criteria were unreasonable to begin with. After all, even thermostats consume resources—especially after they've automatically turned on your furnace or air conditioner.

As they might have said in *Ghostbusters*, "I ain't afraid of no unconscious mind," and I'm not embarrassed to use terms like *conscious* and *unconscious*, or *voluntary* and *involuntary*, as if they meant something. It may turn out that the only qualitative difference between explicit and implicit emotion, like explicit and implicit memory, is phenomenological: the former is accessible to conscious awareness, the latter is not.

Still, if consciousness is functional and not just an afterthought, as some cognitive scientists seem to want to argue, then being unaware of something ought to have consequences for experience, thought, and action that are different from those that attend being conscious of it. For example, conscious awareness may be a logical prerequisite for conscious control. So it might be that unconscious (I prefer the term *implicit*, to continue the analogy to cognition) emotions are less subject to self-regulation. Alternatively, it may be that implicit emotion is limited to relatively primitive feeling states, what Ekman (1992) calls "basic emotions," whereas more complex emotional states, like the counterfactual emotions (regret, frustration), require so much prior cognitive analysis that they can't be elicited outside of awareness.

15. Is your hypothesis of unconscious emotional states falsifiable?

Oh, absolutely, and in precisely the same terms as the hypothesis of unconscious perceptual or memorial states is falsifiable. We know precisely how to recognize implicit memory when we see it: a change in experience, thought, or action that is attributable to a past event, in the absence of conscious recollection of that event. Once we've overcome our initial nervousness about the fact that the essential distinction between the explicit and the implicit is phenomenological— which is something I just think we have to get used to, despite our tendencies toward positivistic reserve—then we can go ahead and take whatever further methodological steps are necessary. In the case of implicit memory, that further step was to expand our definition of memory from verbal self-reports of recall and recognition to other verbal reports, such as reports of perceptual identification, or judgments of lexicality or pleasantness, or even to physiological indices like changes in skin conductance, which don't require conscious recollection on the part of the subject. We recognized these as valid, if implicit, indicators of memory because they were reliably tied to prior stimulus events.

The same thing goes for implicit emotion. We need to expand our definition of an emotional response from verbal statements like "I like it" or "it's disgusting" to other things, like facial expressions or other overt behaviors, or covert psychophysiological responses such as changes in skin conductance or heart rate. If these kinds of behaviors are reliably related to the presentation of emotional stimuli, and if they're correlated with phenomenological self-reports of emotion under ordinary circumstances, then they're candidates for implicit expressions of emotion. Then the task is to determine whether these implicit expressions of emotion can be dissociated from explicit expressions in various ways. So, for example, are there brain-damaged patients who don't feel emotions? If so, do they still respond behaviorally or physiologically in a way that we recognize as emotional? That's the hypothesis, and it's easy to see how it can be disconfirmed.

If, if, . . . there's always an "if." In order to test the hypothesis about implicit emotion, we have to have reliable and valid behavioral and physiological indices of specific emotional states—or, failing that, indices of positive or negative emotional arousal, or at least indices of general emotional arousal. In the chapter, we suggest that facial expressions of the sort studied by Ekman and his colleagues (Ekman, 1989; Ekman & Friesen, 1975) might work on the behavioral side; on the physiological side, studies by Levenson and his colleagues (Levenson, 1992; Levenson, Ekman, & Friesen, 1990) have suggested that, despite what we have been told since Cannon and Bard, and since Schachter and Singer, there might be autonomic indices of emotions after all. The more specific we can get, the better we can test the hypothesis.

I should say in conclusion that there will be some people who will seize on a chapter with a title like "The Emotional Unconscious" to say that Freud had it right all along, and that our conscious experience, thought, and action is, after all, determined by unconscious emotional states. This actually happened when I wrote my piece on "The Cognitive Unconscious" (Kihlstrom, 1987). But that's not a legitimate conclusion. The emotional unconscious revealed by laboratory research is not the psychodynamic unconscious of Freud: it's not seething with repressed sex and aggression. The only way this research can be claimed by psychoanalysis is to abandon whatever it was that is uniquely Freudian in the Freudian theory of unconscious mental life. It's a situation reminiscent of Vietnam—destroying a village in order to save it.

Far from coming from Freud, the inspiration for our chapter came from behavioral theory—from the very positivistic reserve that Owen Flanagan described. In an important article that came out after we completed our chapter, Richard Zinbarg (1998) has argued, I think correctly, that Lang's (1984) three-systems model and Rachman's (1990) notion of desynchrony were products of behavior therapists who, having read their Watson and Skinner, were extremely suspicious of self-reports and who wanted to avoid "mentalistic" references to conscious states of fear and anxiety whenever possible. And so they proposed measuring emotion "objectively," in terms of behavioral and physiological changes. And they found that behavioral and physiological changes were dissociable, to some extent, from self-reported emotional states. Thus, the radical attempt to produce a strictly behavioral and physiological analysis of emotion ends up providing the rationale for a program of research on dissociations between conscious and unconscious emotional life. It's an ironic situation, and in some respects the irony is delicious.

REFERENCES

Alloy, L. B., & Abramson, L. Y. (1988). Depressive realism: Four theoretical perspectives. In L. B. Alloy (Ed.), *Cognitive processes in depression* (pp. 223–265). New York: Guilford.

Banaji, M. R., & Hardin, C. (1994). Affect and memory in retrospective reports. In N. Schwarz & S. Sudman (Eds.), *Autobiographical memory and the validity of retrospective reports* (pp. 71–86). New York: Springer-Verlag.

Bandura, A. (1991). Self-efficacy conception of anxiety. In R. Schwarzer & R. A. Wicklund (Eds.), *Anxiety and self-focused attention* (pp. 89–110). New York: Harwood Academic Publishers.

Bandura, A. (1994). Social cognitive theory and exercise of control over HIV infection. In R. J. DiClemente & J. L. Peterson (Eds.), *Preventing AIDS: Theories and methods of behavioral interventions* (pp. 25–59). New York: Plenum.

Bandura, A. (1997). *Self-efficacy: The exercise of control.* New York: Freeman.

Barlow, D. H. (1997). Cognitive-behavioral therapy for panic disorder: Current status. *Journal of Clinical Psychiatry, 58,* 32–37.

Beck, A. T. (1967). *Depression: Clinical, experimental, and theoretical aspects.* New York: Harper & Row.

Beck, A. T. (1976). *Cognitive therapy and the emotional disorders.* New York: International Universities Press.

Boucher, J., & Osgood, C. E. (1969). The Pollyanna hypothesis. *Journal of Verbal Learning and Verbal Behavior, 8,* 1–8.

Bower, G. H. (1981). Mood and memory. *American Psychologist, 36,* 129–148.

Bower, G. H. (1987). Commentary on mood and memory. *Behavior Research and Therapy, 25,* 443–455.

Bower, G. H. (1990). Awareness, the unconscious, and repression: An experimental psychologist's perspective. In J. L. Singer (Ed.), *Repression and dissociation: Implications for personality theory, psychopathology, and health* (pp. 209–231). Chicago: University of Chicago Press.

Bower, G. H. (1992). How might emotions affect learning? In S.-A. Christianson (Ed.), *Handbook of emotion and memory* (pp. 3–31). Hillsdale, NJ: Erlbaum.

Bower, G. H. (1996). Reactivating a reactivation theory of implicit memory. *Consciousness and Cognition, 5,* 27–72.

Bower, G. H., & Cohen, P. R. (1982). Emotional influences in memory and thinking: Data and theory. In M. S. Clark & S. T. Fiske (Eds.), *Affect and cognition* (pp. 291–332). Hillsdale, NJ: Erlbaum.

Bower, G. H., & Mayer, J. D. (1989). In search of mood-dependent retrieval. *Journal of Social Behavior and Personality, 4,* 121–156.

Bower, G. H., Monteiro, K. P., & Gilligan, S. G. (1978). Emotional mood as a context for learning and recall. *Journal of Verbal Learning and Verbal Behavior, 17,* 573–578.

Bower, G. H., & Sivers, H. (1998). Cognitive impact of traumatic events. *Development and Psychopathology, 10,* 625–653.

Brewin, C. R. (1997). Clinical and experimental approaches to understanding repression. In J. D. Read & D. S. Lindsay (Eds.), *Recollections of trauma: Scientific research and clinical practice* (pp. 145–163). New York: Plenum.

Brewin, C. R., Andrews, B., & Gotlib, I. H. (1993). Psychopathology and early experience: A reappraisal of retrospective reports. *Psychological Bulletin, 113,* 82–98.

Brewin, C. R., & Dalgleish, T., & Joseph, S. (1996). A dual representation theory of posttraumatic stress disorder. *Psychological Review, 103,* 670–686.

Brown, A. S., & Mitchell, D. B. (1994). A reevaluation of semantic versus nonsemantic processing in implicit memory. *Memory & Cognition, 22,* 533–541.

Bruner, J. S., & Postman, L. (1949). Perception, cognition, and personality. *Journal of Personality, 18,* 14–31.

Challis, B. H., & Brodbeck, D. R. (1992). Level of processing affects priming in word fragment completion. *Journal of Experimental Psychology: Learning, Memory, and Cognition, 18,* 595–607.

Christianson, S.-A. (1992a). Remembering emotional events: Potential mechanisms. In

S.-A. Christianson (Ed.), *The handbook of emotion and memory: Research and theory* (pp. 307–340). Hillsdale, NJ: Erlbaum.

Clark, D. M., Teasdale, J. D., Broadbent, D. E., & Martin, M. (1983). Effect of mood on lexical decisions. *Bulletin of the Psychonomic Society, 21,* 175–178.

Clore, G. L., & Parrott, G. (1994). Cognitive feelings and metacognitive judgments. *European Journal of Social Psychology, 24,* 101–116.

Colby, K. M. (1976). Clinical implications of a simulation model of paranoid processes. *Archives of General Psychiatry, 33,* 854–857.

Colby, K. M., Gould, R. L., & Aronson, G. (1989). Some pros and cons of computer-assisted psychotherapy. *Journal of Nervous and Mental Disease, 177,* 105–108.

Cotton, J. L. (1980). Verbal reports on mental processes: Ignoring data for the sake of theory? *Personality and Social Psychology Bulletin, 6,* 278–281.

Cotton, J. L., Baron, R. S., & Borkovec, T. D. (1980). Caffeine ingestion, misattribution therapy, and speech anxiety. *Journal of Research on Personality, 14,* 196–206.

de Rivera, J. (1998). Some emotional dynamics underlying the genesis of false memory syndrome. In W. F. Flack & J. D. Laird (Eds.), *Emotions in psychopathology: Theory and research* (pp. 417–426). New York: Oxford University Press.

Eich, E. (1995). Searching for mood dependent memory. *Psychological Science, 6,* 67–75.

Eich, E., Macaulay, D., & Ryan, L. (1994). Mood dependent memory for events of the personal past. *Journal of Experimental Psychology: General, 123,* 201–215.

Ekman, P. (1989). The argument and evidence about universals in facial expressions of emotion. In H. Wagner & A. Manstead (Eds.), *Handbook of social psychophysiology* (pp. 143–164). Chichester, UK: Wiley.

Ekman, P. (1992). An argument for basic emotions. *Cognition and Emotion, 6,* 169–200.

Ekman, P. (1994). Strong evidence for universals in facial expressions: A reply to Russell's mistaken critique. *Psychological Bulletin, 115,* 268–287.

Ekman, P., & Friesen, W. V. (1971). Constants across culture in the face and emotion. *Journal of Personality and Social Psychology, 17,* 124–129.

Ekman, P., & Friesen, W. V. (1975). *Unmasking the face.* Englewood Cliffs, NJ: Prentice-Hall.

Ellis, A. (1962). *Reason and emotion in psychotherapy.* New York: Lyle Stuart.

Ellis, H. C., & Ashbrook, P. W. (1989). The "state" of mood and memory research: A selective review. *Journal of Social Behavior and Personality, 4,* 1–21.

Ellis, H. C., Ottaway, S. A., Varner, L. J., Becker, A. S., & Moore, B. A. (1997). Emotion, motivation, and text comprehension: The detection of contradictions in passages. *Journal of Experimental Psychology: General, 126,* 131–146.

Ellis, H. C., Seibert, P. S., & Herbert, B. J. (1990). Mood state effects on thought listing. *Bulletin of the Psychonomic Society, 28,* 147–150.

Ellis, H. C., Thomas, R. L., & Rodriguez, I. A. (1984). Emotional mood states and memory: Elaborative encoding, semantic processing, and cognitive effort. *Journal of Experimental Psychology: Learning, Memory, and Cognition, 10,* 470–482.

Ellsworth, P. C., & Smith, C. A. (1988). From appraisal to emotion: Differences among unpleasant feelings. *Motivation and Emotion, 12,* 271–302.

Estes, W. K. (1987). One hundred years of memory theory. In D. S. Gorfein & R. R.

Hoffman (Eds.), *Memory and learning: The Ebbinghaus Centennial Conference* (pp. 11–33). Hillsdale, NJ: Erlbaum.

Faught, W. S. (1978). *Motivation and intentionality in a computer simulation model of paranoia.* Basel, Switzerland: Birkhaeuser-Verlag.

Feldman, L. A. (1995a). Valence focus and arousal focus: Individual differences in the structure of affective experience. *Journal of Personality and Social Psychology, 16,* 153–166.

Feldman, L. A. (1995b). Variations in the circumplex structure of mood. *Personality and Social Psychology Bulletin, 21,* 806–817.

Fiedler, K. (1990). Mood-dependent selectivity in social cognition. In W. Stroebe & M. Hewstone (Eds.), *European review of social psychology* (vol. 1, pp. 1–32). Chichester, UK: Wiley.

Fiedler, K. (1991). On the task, the measures and the mood in research on affect and social cognition. In J. P. Forgas (Ed.), *Emotion and social judgments* (pp. 83–104). Oxford: Pergamon.

Flanagan, O. (1991). *The science of mind.* 2nd. ed. Cambridge, MA: MIT Press.

Foa, E. B., & Hearst-Ikeda, D. (1996). Emotional dissociation in response to trauma: An information-processing approach. In L. K. Michelson & W. J. Ray (Eds.), *Handbook of dissociation: Theoretical, empirical, and clinical perspectives* (pp. 207–224). New York: Plenum.

Forgas, J. P. (1992). On bad mood and peculiar people: Affect and person typicality in impression formation. *Journal of Personality and Social Psychology, 62,* 863–875.

Forgas, J. P. (1995). Mood and judgment: The Affect Infusion Model (AIM). *Psychological Bulletin, 117,* 39–66.

Forgas, J. P. (1995). Strange couples: Mood effects on judgments and memory about prototypical and atypical targets. *Personality and Social Psychology Bulletin, 21,* 747–765.

Forgas, J. P. (1998). Asking nicely? The effects of mood on responding to more or less polite requests. *Personality and Social Psychology Bulletin, 24,* 173–185.

Forgas, J. P., & Bower, G. H. (1987). Mood effects on person perception judgments. *Journal of Personality and Social Psychology, 53,* 53–60.

Forgas, J. P., Bower, G. H., & Krantz, S. (1984). The influence of mood on perceptions of social interactions. *Journal of Experimental Social Psychology, 20,* 497–513.

Forgas, J. P., & Moylan, S. J. (1991). Affective influences on stereotype judgements. *Cognition and Emotion, 5,* 379–397.

Fredrickson, B. L. (1998). What good are positive emotions? *Review of General Psychology, 2,* 300–319.

Frijda, N. H. (1987), Can computers feel? Theory and design of an emotional system. *Cognition and Emotion, 1,* 235–257.

Frijda, N. H. (1988). The laws of emotion. *American Psychologist, 43,* 49–358.

Gerrig, R. J., & Bower, G. H. (1982). Emotional influences on word recognition. *Bulletin of the Psychonomic Society, 19,* 197–200.

Gotlib, I. H., & MacLeod, C. (1997). Information processing in anxiety and depression: A cognitive-developmental perspective. In J. A. Burack & J. T. Enns (Eds.), *Attention, development, and psychopathology* (pp. 350–378). New York: Guilford.

Gotlib, I. H., & McCann, C. D. (1984). Construct accessibility and depression: An examination of cognitive and affective factors. *Journal of Personality and Social Psychology, 47,* 427–439.

Hastie, R. (1981). Schematic principles in human memory. In E. T. Higgins, C. P. Herman, & M. P. Zanna (Eds.), *Social cognition: The Ontario Symposium* (vol. 1, pp. 39–88). Hillsdale, NJ: Erlbaum.

Hintzman, D. L. (1991). Why are formal models useful in psychology? In W. E. Hockley & S. Lewandowsky (Eds.), *Relating theory and data: Essays on human memory in honor of Bennet B. Murdock* (pp. 39–56). Hillsdale, NJ: Erlbaum

Keuler, D. J., & Safer, M. A. (1998). Memory bias in the assessment and recall of pre-exam anxiety: How anxious was I? *Applied Cognitive Psychology, 12,* S127–S137.

Kihlstrom, J. F. (1987). The cognitive unconscious. *Science, 237,* 1445–1452.

Kihlstrom, J. F. (1989). On what does mood-dependent memory depend? *Journal of Social Behavior and Personality, 4,* 23–32.

Kihlstrom, J. F. (1996). The trauma-memory argument and recovered memory therapy. In K. Pezdeck & W.P Banks (Eds.), *The recovered memory/false memory debate* (pp. 297–311). San Diego: Academic Press.

Kihlstrom, J. F., Eich, E., Sandbrand, D., & Tobias, B. A. (2000). Emotion and memory: Implications for self-report. In A. A. Stone, J. S. Turkkan, C. Bachrach, J. B. Jobe, H. S. Kurtzman, & V. S. Cain (Eds.), *The science of self-report: Implications for research and practice* (pp. 81–99). Mahwah, NJ: Erlbaum.

Kuyken, W., & Dalgleish, T. (1995). Autobiographical memory and depression. *British Journal of Clinical Psychology, 34,* 89–92.

Lang, P. J. (1984). Cognition in emotion: Concept and action. In C. E. Izard, J. Kagan, & R. B. Zajonc (Eds.), *Emotions, cognition, and behavior* (pp. 192–226). Cambridge, UK: Cambridge University Press.

Lazarus, R. S. (1982). Thoughts on the relations between emotion and cognition. *American Psychologist, 37,* 1019–1024.

Lazarus, R. S. (1984). On the primacy of cognition. *American Psychologist, 39,* 124–129.

Lazarus, R. S. (1991). *Emotion and adaptation.* New York: Oxford University Press.

Lazarus, R. S., Smith, C. A. (1988). Knowledge and appraisal in the cognition-emotion relationship. *Cognition and Emotion, 2,* 281–300.

LeDoux, J. E. (1996). *The emotional brain.* New York: Simon & Schuster.

Levenson, R. W. (1992). Autonomic nervous system differences among emotions. *Psychological Science, 3,* 23–27.

Levenson, R. W., Ekman, P., & Friesen, W. V. (1990). Voluntary facial action generates emotion-specific autonomic nervous system activity. *Psychophysiology, 27,* 363–384.

Leventhal, H. (1984). A perceptual-motor theory of emotion. In K. R. Scherer & P. Ekman (Eds.), *Approaches to emotion* (pp. 271–291). Hillsdale, NJ: Erlbaum.

Lindsay, D. S., & Read, J. D. (1994). Psychotherapy and memories of child sexual abuse: A cognitive perspective. *Applied Cognitive Psychology, 8,* 281–338.

Logan, G. D. (1997). The automaticity of academic life: Unconscious application of an implicit theory. In R. S. Wyer (Ed.), *Advances in social cognition* (vol. 10, pp. 157–179). Mahwah, NJ: Erlbaum.

MacLeod, C. (1996). Anxiety and cognitive processes. In I. G. Sarason, G. R. Pierce, & B. R. Sarason (Eds.), *Cognitive interference: Theories, methods, and findings* (pp. 47–76). Mahwah, NJ: Erlbaum.

Mandler, G. (1975). *Mind and emotion.* New York: Wiley.

Mandler, G. (1980). The generation of emotion: A psychological theory. In R. Plutchik & H. Kellerman (Eds.), *Emotion: Theory, research, and experience* (vol. 1, pp. 219–243). New York: Academic Press.

Mandler, G., Nakamura, Y., & Van Zandt, B. J.S. (1987). Nonspecific effects of exposure on stimuli that cannot be recognized. *Journal of Experimental Psychology: Learning, Memory, and Cognition, 13,* 646–648.

Mandler, G., & Sarason, S. B. (1952). A study of anxiety and learning. *Journal of Abnormal and Social Psychology, 47,* 166–173.

Marshall, G. D., & Zimbardo, P. G. (1979). Affective consequences of inadequately explained physiological arousal. *Journal of Personality and Social Psychology, 37,* 970–988.

Maslach, C. (1979). Negative emotional biasing of unexplained arousal. *Journal of Personality and Social Psychology, 37,* 953–969.

Mathews, A. M., & MacLeod, C. (1986). Discrimination of threat cues without awareness in anxiety states. *Journal of Abnormal Psychology, 95,* 131–138.

Mathews, A. M., & MacLeod, C. (1994). Cognitive approaches to emotion and emotional disorders. *Annual Review of Psychology, 45,* 25–50.

Matlin, M., & Stang, D. (1979). *The Pollyanna principle: Selectivity in language, memory, and thought.* Cambridge, MA: Schenkman.

McNally, R. J. (1994). Cognitive bias in panic disorders. *Current Directions in Psychological Science, 3,* 129–132.

Merikle, P. M. (1992). Perception without awareness: Critical issues. *American Psychologist, 47,* 792–795.

Merikle, P. M., & Daneman, M. (1998). Psychological investigations of unconscious perception. *Journal of Consciousness Studies, 5,* 5–18.

Merikle, P. M., & Joordens, S. (1997). Measuring unconscious influences. In J. D. Cohen & J. W. Schooler (Eds.), *Scientific approaches to consciousness* (pp. 109–123). Mahwah, NJ: Erlbaum.

Mineka, S., & Nugent, K. (1995). Mood-congruent memory biases in anxiety and depression. In D. L. Schacter (Ed.), *Memory distortion: How minds, brains, and societies reconstruct the past* (pp. 173–193). Cambridge, MA: Harvard University Press.

Mineka, S., & Tomarken, A. J. (1989). The role of cognitive biases in the origins and maintenance of fear and anxiety disorders. In T. Archer & L.-G. Nilsson (Eds.), *Aversion, avoidance, and anxiety: Perspectives on aversively motivated behavior* (pp. 195–221). Hillsdale, NJ: Erlbaum.

Mogg, K., Mathews, A., & Weinman, J. (1989). Selective processing of threat cues in anxiety states: A replication. *Behavior Research and Therapy, 27,* 317–323.

Morton, J. (1969). Interaction of information in word recognition. *Psychological Review, 76,* 165–178.

Niedenthal, P. M. (1992). Affect and social perception: On the psychological validity of rose-colored glasses. In R. F. Bornstein & T. S. Pittman (Eds.), *Perception without awareness* (pp. 211–235). New York: Guilford Press.

Niedenthal, P. M., Halberstadt, J. B., & Innes-Ker, A. H. (1999). Emotional response categorization. *Psychological Review, 106,* 337–361.

Niedenthal, P. M., Halberstadt, J. B., & Setterlund, M. B. (1997). Being happy and seeing "happy": Emotional state mediates visual word recognition. *Cognition and Emotion, 11,* 403–432.

Niedenthal, P. M., & Kitayama, S., Eds. (1994). *The heart's eye: Emotional influences in perception and attention.* San Diego: Academic Press.

Niedenthal, P. M., & Setterlund, M. B. (1994). Emotion congruence in perception. *Personality and Social Psychology Bulletin, 20,* 401–410.

Norman, D. A., & Rumelhart, D. E. (1975). *Explorations in cognition.* San Francisco: Freeman.

Nosofsky, R. M. (1992). Exemplar-based approach to relating categorization, identification, and recognition. In F. G. Ashby (Ed.), *Multidimensional models of perception and cognition* (pp. 363–393). Hillsdale, NJ: Erlbaum.

Oatley, K., & Johnson-Laird, P. N. (1987). Towards a cognitive theory of emotions. *Cognition and Emotion, 1,* 29–50.

Ortony, A., Clore, G. L., & Collins, A. (1988). *The cognitive structure of emotion.* Cambridge, UK: Cambridge University Press.

Parrott, W. G., & Sabini, J. (1990). Mood and memory under natural conditions: Evidence for mood incongruent recall. *Journal of Personality and Social Psychology, 59,* 321–336.

Pashler, H. (1998). *The psychology of attention.* Cambridge, MA: MIT Press.

Postman, L., & Brown, D. (1952). The perceptual consequences of success and failure. *Journal of Abnormal and Social Psychology, 47,* 213–221.

Rachman, S. (1990). *Fear and courage.* 2nd ed. New York: Freeman.

Rapaport, D. (1942). *Emotions and memory.* Baltimore: Williams and Wilkins.

Reisenzein, R. (1983). The Schachter theory of emotion: Two decades later. *Psychological Bulletin, 94,* 239–264.

Roseman, I. J. (1984). Cognitive determinants of emotion: A structural theory. *Review of Personality and Social Psychology, 5,* 11–36.

Russell, J. A. (1994). Is there universal recognition of emotion from facial expression? A review of methods and studies. *Psychological Bulletin, 115,* 102–141.

Schachter, S., & Singer, J. E. (1962). Cognitive, social, and physiological determinants of emotional state. *Psychological Review, 69,* 379–399.

Schooler, J. W., & Eich, E. (in press). Memory for emotional events. In E. Tulving & F. I.M. Craik (Eds.), *The Oxford handbook of memory.* New York: Oxford University Press.

Schwarz, N., & Bless, H. (1991). Happy and mindless, but sad and smart? The impact of affective states on analytic reasoning. In J. P. Forgas (Ed.), *Emotion and social judgments* (pp. 55–71). Oxford: Pergamon Press.

Schwarz, N., & Clore, G. L. (1988). How do I feel about it? The informative function of affective states. In K. Fiedler & J. P. Forgas (Eds.), *Affect, cognition, and social behavior* (pp. 44–62). Toronto: Hogrefe.

Seamon, J. G., McKenna, P. A., & Binder, N. (1998). The mere exposure effect is differentially sensitive to different judgment tasks. *Consciousness and Cognition, 7,* 85–102.

Seibert, P. S., & Ellis, H. C. (1991). Irrelevant thoughts, emotional mood states, and cognitive task performance. *Memory & Cognition, 19,* 507–513.

Seligman, M. E.P. (1971). Phobias and preparedness. *Behavior Therapy, 2,* 307–320.

Shaver, P. Schwartz, J., Kirson, D., & O'Connor, G. (1987). Emotion knowledge: Further exploration of a prototype approach. *Journal of Personality and Social Psychology, 52,* 1061–1086.

Shobe, K. K., & Kihlstrom, J. F. (1997). Is traumatic memory special? *Current Directions in Psychological Science, 6,* 70–74.

Smith, C. A., & Ellsworth, P. C. (1985). Patterns of cognitive appraisal in emotion. *Journal of Personality and Social Psychology, 48,* 813–838.

Smith, E. R., & Zarate, M. A. (1992). Exemplar-based model of social judgment. *Psychological Review, 99,* 3–21.

Solley, C. M., & Murphy, G. (1960). *Development of the perceptual world.* New York: Basic Books.

Solomon, R. C. (1977). *The passions.* New York: Anchor.

Stein, N. L., & Levine, L. J. (1989). The causal organization of emotional knowledge. *Cognition and Emotion, 3,* 343–378.

Teasdale, J. D., & Barnard, P. J. (1993). *Affect, cognition, and change.* Hove, UK: Erlbaum.

Tulving, E., & Thomson, D. M. (1973). Encoding specificity and retrieval processes in episodic memory. *Psychological Review, 80,* 352–373.

van der Kolk, B. A. (1994). The body keeps the score: Memory and the evolving psychobiology of PTSD. *Harvard Review of Psychiatry, 1,* 253–265.

van der Kolk, B. A., & van der Hart, O. (1991). The intrusive past: The flexibility of memory and the engraving of trauma. *American Imago, 48,* 425–454.

Watts, F. N. (1995). Depression and anxiety. In A. D. Baddeley, B. A. Wilson, & F. N. Watts (Eds.), *Handbook of memory disorders* (pp. 293–317). New York: Wiley.

Weiner, B. (1982). The emotional consequences of causal attributions. In M. S. Clark & S. T. Fiske (Eds.), *Affect and cognition* (pp. 185–228). Hillsdale, NJ: Erlbaum.

Zajonc, R. B. (1980). Feeling and thinking: Preferences need no inferences. *American Psychologist, 35,* 151–175.

Zinbarg, R. E. (1998). Concordance and synchrony in measures of anxiety and panic reconsidered: A hierarchical model of anxiety and panic. *Behavior Therapy, 29,* 301–323.

Author Index

245

Subject Index